S0-CUK-298

COMPUTER
SCIENCES

COMPUTER SCIENCES

Second Edition
Volume 4
Electronic Universe

K. Lee Lerner
Editor-in-Chief

Brenda Wilmoth Lerner
Managing Editor

MACMILLAN REFERENCE USA
A part of Gale, Cengage Learning

PARIS JUNIOR COLLEGE
PARIS, TX 75460

QA
76
.C572

PARIS JUNIOR COLLEGE

Computer sciences.

39902000959207

GALE
CENGAGE Learning·

Detroit • New York • San Francisco • New Haven, Conn • Waterville, Maine • London

GALE
CENGAGE Learning®

Computer Sciences
2nd Edition

Editor-in-Chief: K. Lee Lerner

Managing Editor: Brenda Wilmoth Lerner

Product Manager: Douglas A. Dentino

Project Editor: Kimberley A. McGrath

Rights Acquisition and Management: Margaret
    Chamberlain-Gaston

Composition: Evi Abou-El-Seoud

Manufacturing: Wendy Blurton; Dorothy Maki

Imaging: John Watkins

Product Design: Kristine Julien

© 2013 Gale, Cengage Learning

ALL RIGHTS RESERVED. No part of this work covered by the copyright herein may
be reproduced, transmitted, stored, or used in any form or by any means graphic,
electronic, or mechanical, including but not limited to photocopying, recording,
scanning, digitizing, taping, Web distribution, information networks, or information
storage and retrieval systems, except as permitted under Section 107 or 108 of the 1976
United States Copyright Act, without the prior written permission of the publisher.

For product information and technology assistance, contact us at
Gale Customer Support, 1-800-877-4253.
For permission to use material from this text or product,
submit all requests online at **www.cengage.com/permissions.**
Further permissions questions can be emailed to
permissionrequest@cengage.com

Cover photographs courtesy of the following: Technician working on server rack;
© Yurchyks/ShutterStock.com. Screens with program web code; © Taiga/ShutterStock.com.
Three business people working at meeting; © Dmitriy Shironosov/ShutterStock.com.
Hands holding a tablet or a Pad; © Luis Louro/ShutterStock.com. Computer classroom;
© sixninepixels/ShutterStock.com. Wireless computer mouse; © AlexGul/ShutterStock.com.

While every effort has been made to ensure the reliability of the information presented
in this publication, Gale, a part of Cengage Learning, does not guarantee the accuracy of the
data contained herein. Gale accepts no payment for listing; and inclusion in the publication
of any organization, agency, institution, publication, service, or individual does not imply
endorsement of the editors or publisher. Errors brought to the attention of the publisher and
verified to the satisfaction of the publisher will be corrected in future editions.

LIBRARY OF CONGRESS CATALOGING-IN-PUBLICATION DATA

Computer sciences / K. Lee Lerner, editor-in-Chief, Brenda Wilmoth Lerner,
managing editor. -- Second edition.
    v. cm
Summary: "Computer Sciences, 2nd Edition reviews the history of the discipline and
concepts, as well as profiles contributors in the field. The impact of computers on the
economy and society is explored, with examples in literature, film, and science provided
to illustrate and support trends. These illustrated volumes also include sidebars,
bibliographies, a timeline, charts, and a glossary. This title is organized in four separate
topical volumes, although articles in each volume will be in an A-Z arrangement; the
set's comprehensive cumulative index is found in each volume"-- Provided by publisher.
    Includes bibliographical references and index.
    Contents: v. 1. Foundations : ideas and people
    ISBN-13: 978-0-02-866220-6 (set : hardback)
    ISBN-10: 0-02-866220-2 (set : hardback)
    ISBN-13: 978-0-02-866221-3 (v. 1 : hardback)
    ISBN-10: 0-02-866221-0 (v. 1 : hardback)
[etc.]
    1. Computer science. I. Lerner, K. Lee. II. Lerner, Brenda Wilmoth.
QA76.C572 2013
004--dc23
                                                                    2012037340

Gale
27500 Drake Rd.
Farmington Hills, MI, 48331-3535

ISBN-13: 978-0-02-866220-6 (set)   ISBN-10: 0-02-866220-2 (set)
ISBN-13: 978-0-02-866221-3 (vol. 1)   ISBN-10: 0-02-866221-0 (vol. 1)
ISBN-13: 978-0-02-866222-0 (vol. 2)   ISBN-10: 0-02-866222-9 (vol. 2)
ISBN-13: 978-0-02-866223-7 (vol. 3)   ISBN-10: 0-02-866223-7 (vol. 3)
ISBN-13: 978-0-02-866224-4 (vol. 4)   ISBN-10: 0-02-866224-5 (vol. 4)

This title is also available as an e-book.
ISBN-13: 978-0-02-866225-1 ISBN-10: 0-02-866225-3
Contact your Gale, a part of Cengage Learning, sales representative for ordering information.

Printed in China
1 2 3 4 5 6 7 17 16 15 14 13

Table of Contents

· ·

Table of Contents

Table of Contents

Volume 4: Electronic Universe

Preface

Computer Sciences, 2nd Edition is devoted to providing younger students and general readers with a foundation upon which to build an understanding of modern computer science. Because applications of technology now invigorate almost all fields of study, topics in Computer Sciences are carefully selected to present insightful information related to topics in the news. Both updated and new entries, for example, help explain both technical and ethical dimensions of issues related to social media and online privacy. Special entries on digital photography and digital filmmaking highlight applications of computer science that enhance how we view and understand our world.

The articles in Computer Sciences are meant to be understandable by anyone with a curiosity about basic computer science. When topics move into highly technical research and development areas, every effort has been taken to explain concepts clearly and simply, without sacrifice of fundamental accuracy. Accordingly, entries in Computer Sciences include treatments of topics designed to excite less-experienced students while simultaneously providing a solid reference for students preparing for more specialized studies. The editors have taken special care to provide treatment of topics that foster essential critical thinking skills that will enable students and readers to tackle emerging issues.

We live in an increasingly digital world where an understanding of basic computer science principles and applications is essential. The Internet, for example, is now a global network connecting, with more than a billion computers used by billions of people. Personal information, medical records, opinions, industrial secrets, military communications, financial transactions, messages between conspirators, orders for goods and services, and many other types of communications travel over the Internet. Computer Sciences enables students and readers to understand how the digital world works.

Equally as important, however, for citizens of the digital age, Computer Sciences enables students and readers to understand how increases in computing capacity relate to the capacity to wage cyberwarfare; how viruses transform from annoyances to instruments of covert operations and computer crime; and how breakthroughs in technology enable online activism that contributes to social and political change.

Contributors and Advisors

In addition to engineers specializing in computer science, Computer Sciences contributors include scientists, journalists, artists, teachers, and writers who explain the practical applications of computer science.

In this and the previous edition of Computer Sciences, a number of experts have written and advised on topics related to their expertise. We would like to express our sincere appreciation to:

Tom Abel: Penn State University, University Park, PA.

Martyn Amos: University of Liverpool, United Kingdom.

Richard Archer: Pittsburgh, PA.

Pamela Willwerth Aue: Royal Oak, MI.

William Atkins: Independent research consultant, Normal, IL.

Nancy J. Becker: St. John's University, New York.

Mark Bedau: Reed College, Portland, OR.

John Micheal Bell: LMG research associate. Harvard DCE Graduate Professional Program in Journalism. Harvard University, Cambridge MA.

Mercy Bell: LMG research associate. Nashville, TN.

Pierfrancesco Bellini: University of Florence, Italy.

Gary H. Bernstein: University of Notre Dame, Noire Dame, IN.

Anne Bissonnette: Kent State University Museum, Kent, OH.

Kevin W. Bowyer: University of Notre Dame, Notre Dame, IN.

Stefan Brass: University of Giessen, Germany.

Barbara Britton: Windsor Puttie Library, Windsor, Ontario, Canada.

Kimberly Mann Bruch: San Diego Supercomputer Center, University of California, San Diego.

Ivan Bruno: University of Florence, Italy.

Dennis R. Buckmaster: Pennsylvania State University, University Park, PA.

Dan Burk: University of Minnesota, Minneapolis, MN.

Guoray Cai: Pennsylvania State University, University Park, PA.

Shirley Campbell: University of Pittsburgh, Pittsburgh, PA.

Sara V. Castillo: Independent media consultant. Dubai, United Arab Emirates.

Siddharth Chandra: University of Pittsburgh, Pittsburgh, PA.

J. Alex Chediak: University of California, Berkeley, CA.

Kara K. Choquette: Xerox Corporation.

John Cosgrove: Cosgrove Communications, Pittsburgh, PA.

Cheryl L. Cramer: Digimarc Corporation, Tualatin, OR.

Anthony Debons: University of Pittsburgh, Pittsburgh, PA.

Salvatore Domenick Desiano: NASA Ames Research Center (QSS Group, Inc.).

Ken Doerbecker: Perfection Services, Inc.; WeirNet LLC; and FreeAir Networks, Inc.

Judi Effis: KPMG, LLP, Pittsburgh, PA.

Karen E. Esch: Karen Esch Associates, Pittsburgh, PA.

Ming Fan: University of Notre Dame, Notre Dame, IN.

Jim Fike: Ohio University, Athens, OH.

Ida M. Flynn: University of Pittsburgh, Pittsburgh, PA.

Roger R. Flynn: University of Pittsburgh, Pittsburgh, PA.

H. Bruce Franklin: Rutgers University, Newark, NJ.

Thomas J. Froehlich: Kent State University, Kent, OH.

Chuck Gaidica: WDW-TV, Detroit, MI.

G. Christopher Hall: PricewaterhouseCoopers.

Gary Hanson: Kent State University, Kent, OH.

Shaquilla T. Harrigan, Production intern at LernerMedia Global, Summer 2012. Harvard College (Class of 2016), Cambridge, MA.

Karen Hartman: James Monroe Center Library, Mary Washington College, Fredericksburg, VA.

Melissa J. Harvey: Carnegie Mellon University, Pittsburgh, PA.

Albert D. Helfnck: Embry-Riddle Aeronautical University, Daytona Beach, PL.

Angelia Herrin: Harvard Business Publishing, Cambridge, MA.

Stephen Hughes: University of Pittsburgh, Pittsburgh, PA.

Joseph Patterson Hyder: Hyder Law Group, Jacksonville, FL.

Bruce Jacob: University of Maryland, College Park, MD.

Radhika Jain: Georgia State University, Atlanta, GA.

Wesley Jamison: University of Pittsburgh at Greensburg.

Sid Karin: San Diego Supercomputer Center, University of California, San Diego.

Declan P. Kelly: Philips Research, The Netherlands.

Betty Kirke: New York, NY.

Mikko Kovalainen: University of Jyväskylä, Finland.

Paul R. Kraus: Pittsburgh, PA.

Prashant Krishnamurthy: University of Pittsburgh, Pittsburgh, PA.

Marina Krol: Mount Sinai School of Medicine, New York, NY.

Susan Landau: Sun Microsystems Inc., Mountain View, CA.

Nicholas C. Laudato: University of Pittsburgh, Pittsburgh, Pennsylvania.

George Lawton: Eutopian Enterprises.

Cynthia Tumilry Lazzaro: Pinnacle Training Corp., Stonebam, MA.

Joseph J. Lazzaro: Massachusetts Commission for the Blind, Boston, MA.

John Leaney: University of Technology, Sydney, Australia.

Robert Lembersky: Ann Taylor, Inc., New York, NY.

Adrienne Wilmoth Lerner: Hyder Law Group, Jacksonville, FL.

Terri L. Lenox: Westminster College, New Wilmington, PA.

Joyce H-S Li: University of Pittsburgh, Pittsburgh, PA.

Michael R. Macedonia: USA STPJCOM, Orlando,.

Dirk E. Mahling: University of Pittsburgh, Pittsburgh, PA.

Cynthia J. Martincic: St. Vincent College, Latrobe, PA.

Michael J. McCarthy: Carnegie Mellon University, Pittsburgh, PA.

Ann McIver McHoes: Carlow College, Pittsburgh PA.

Genevieve McHoes: University of Maryland, College Park, MD.

John McHugh: CERTTM Coordination Center, Software Engineering Institute, Carnegie Mellon Pittsburgh, PA.

Donald M. McIver: Northrop Grumman Corporation, Baltimore, MD.

Maurice McIver: Integrated Databases, Inc., Honolulu, HI.

William J. McIver, Jr.: University at Albany, State University of New York.

Trevor T. Moores: University of Nevada, Las Vegas.

Christopher Morgan: Association for Computing Machinery, Nero York, NY.

Bertha Kugelman Morimoto: University of Pittsburgh, Pittsburgh, PA.

Tracy Mullen: NEC Research Inc., Princeton, NJ.

Paul Munro: University of Pittsburgh, Pittsburgh, PA.

Stephen Murray: University of Technology, Sydney, Australia.

Carey Nachenberg: Symantec Corporation.

John Nau: Frank R. Rusch.

Paolo Nesi: University of Florence, Italy.

Kai A. Olsen: Molde College and University of Bergen, Norway.

Evan Austin Ott: University of Texas, Austin, TX.

Ipek Ozkaya: Carnegie Mellon University, Pittsburgh, PA.

Bob Patterson: Perfection Services, Inc.

Robert R. Perkoski: University of Pittsburgh, Pittsburgh, PA.

Thomas A. Pollack: Duquesne University, Pittsburgh, PA.

Guylaine M. Pollock: IEEE Computer Society; Sandia National Laboratories, Albuquerque, NM.

Wolfgang Porod: University of Notre Dame, Notre Dame, IN.

Anwer H. Puthawala: Park Avenue Associates in Radiology, P.C., Binghamton, NY.

Mary McIver Puthawala: Binghamton, NY.

Sudha Ram: University of Arizona, Tucson, AZ.

Edie M. Rasmussen: University of Pittsburgh, Pittsburgh, PA.

Robert D. Regan: Consultant, Pittsburgh, PA.

Allen Renear: University of Illinois, Urbana-Champaign.

Sarah K. Rich: Pennsylvania State University, University Park, PA.

Mike Robinson: Sageforce Ltd., Kingston on Thames, Surrey, United Kingdom.

Elke A. Rudensteiner: Worcester Polytechnic Institute, Worcester, MA.

Frank R. Rusch: University of Illinois at Urbana-Champaign.

William Sherman: National Center for Supercomputing Applications, University of Illinois at Urbana-Champaign.

Marc Silverman: University of Pittsburgh, Pittsburgh, PA.

Munindar P. Singh: North Carolina State University, Raleigh, NC.

Cindy Smith: PricewaterhouseCoopers, Pittsburgh, PA.

Barry Smyth: Smart Media Institute, University College, Dublin, Ireland.

Amanda Spink: Pennsylvania State University, University Park, PA.

Michael B. Spring: University of Pittsburgh, Pittsburgh, PA.

Savitha Srinivasan: IBM Almaden Research Center, San Jose, CA.

Maria Stenzel: Photojournalist. *National Geographic*, Washington, D.C.

Igor Tarnopolsky: Westchester County Department of Laboratories and Research, Valhalla, NY.

George A. Tarnow: Georgetown University, Washington, DC.

Lucy A. Tedd: University of Wales, Aberystwyth, Wales, United Kingdom.

Umesh Thakkar: National Center for Supercomputing Applications, University of Illinois at Urbana-Champaign.

Richard A- Thompson: University of Pittsburgh, Pittsburgh, PA.

James E. Tomayko: Carnegie Mellon University, Pittsburgh, PA.

Christinger Tomer: University of Pittsburgh, Pittsburgh, PA.

Upkar Varshney: Georgia State University, Atlanta, GA.

Jonathan Vos Post: Magic Dragon Multimedia, http://magicdragon.com.

Tom Wall: Duke University, Durham, N.

Brett A. Warneke: University of California, Berkeley, CA.

Patricia S. Wehman: University of Pittsburgh, Pittsburgh, PA.

Isaac Weiss: University of Maryland, College Park, MD.

Martin B. Weiss: University of Pittsburgh, Pittsburgh, PA.

Jeffrey C. Wingard: Leesburg, VA.

Victor L. Winter: University of Nebraska, Omaha.

Charles R. Woratschek: Robert Morris University, Moon Township, PA.

Peter Y. Wu: University of Pittsburgh, Pittsburgh, PA.

William J. Yurcik: Illinois State University, Normal, IL.

Gregg R. Zegarelli: Zegarelli Law Group, P.C.

Acknowledgments

The editors offer special thanks to: Angelia Herrin and Maria Stenzel for bringing their expertise in modern practice of journalism and photojournalism to, respectively, the *Computer Sciences*. Herrin, a former Knight Fellow in Journalism at Stanford University reporter for Knight-Ridder newspapers, served as Washington, D.C., editor of *USA Today*. Herrin is now an editor at Harvard Business School

Publishing. Stenzel, a frequent and long-time contributor to *National Geographic* served as a Knight Fellow in Science Journalism at MIT.

Writing on tight deadlines from Dubai in the United Arab Emirates, Sara V. Castillo contributed the article on digital filmmaking.

Evan Ott at the University of Texas offered invaluable assistance in advising and updating topics related to on emerging applications of computer science.

The editors thank Shaquilla T. Harrigan, our summer 2012 production intern at LernerMedia Global. Ms. Harrigan, a member of the class of 2016 at Harvard College in Cambridge, Massachusetts, assisted in photo selection and captioning.

This book would not have been possible without the efforts of project manager Kim McGrath. Her perspectives, patience, and penchant for asking good questions across a broad spectrum of topics added significantly to the quality of all aspects of *Computer Sciences*.

K. Lee Lerner and Brenda Wilmoth Lerner, editors
Cambridge, MA

December, 2012

How To Use This Book

. . . .

Computer Sciences, 2ⁿᵈ Edition provides an overview of the history and current status of the computer science industry, as well as its economic and cultural impact. This is a broad scope, and for ease of use, entries have been grouped into four subject-based volumes.

Volume 1: Foundations: Ideas and People This volume discusses the foundation of computer science, including computing history and important innovators. Ranging from Charles Babbage, binary numbers, and slide rule to Steve Jobs, World Wide Web, and windows interfaces, the entries in this volume provide a solid background on the development of the field of computer sciences.

Volume 2: Software and Hardware Articles in this volume cover topics from system analysis and design (the cornerstone of building a system) to operating systems, compilers, and parallel processing (which discuss some of the technical aspects of computing). Here, too, users will find valuable information on the growing field of telecommunications, including cellular and wireless technologies.

Volume 3: Social Applications From ATM machines to social media and weather forecasting, the use of computers impacts our everyday lives. For example, computer technology has greatly influence the study of biology, molecular biology, physics, and mathematics, not to mention the large role it plays in air traffic management and aircraft flight control, navigation and geographic information systems. Businesses—large and small—have significantly benefited from applications that track product growth, costs, and the way products are managed. Other articles in this volume include economic modeling, hacking, and home system software.

Volume 4: Electronic Universe Volume 4 delves into our vastly interconnected, networked society. The Internet is explored in detail, including its history, applications, and backbone. Molecular computing and artificial life are discussed as are mobile computing and encryption technology. The reader will find articles on censorship (national and international), online privacy, digital filmmaking, E-commerce, and search engines. Ethical matters pertaining to the electronic universe are also addressed.

All entries include a bibliography to assist in conducting additional research. Where appropriate, technical terms are defined in the margins of the entries, and photos and charts are used to illustrate most entries.

Entries are arranged in alphabetical order within each volume, with biographies listed by their last names. All four volumes include a comprehensive table of contents and cumulative index that can further assist the reader in locating the information they need. Other features found in every volume are:

- **Preface** — An essay by editors K. Lee Lerner and Brenda Wilmoth Lerner discussing the importance of computer sciences as it relates to critical thinking and living in the digital age.

- **For Your Reference** — This section defines scientific units of measurement and supplies conversion charts to customary units of measurement. It also provides examples from various base numbering systems and their equivalents, as well as the relative sizes of objects.

- **Timeline: Significant Events in the History of Computing** — This chronology lists major events and milestones in the field of computer sciences.

■ **Timeline: The History of Programming, Markup, and Scripting Languages** — This chronology is focused on achievements and milestones as related to computer programming and languages.

■ **Glossary** — The glossary defines over 580 technical terms used throughout the set.

■ **Directory of Computer Sciences Organizations** — This directory provides contact information for over 50 computer sciences-related organizations.

For Your Reference

This section provides information that may be of assistance in understanding the entries that make up this book: definitions for SI terms and symbols, and; conversion tables for SI measurements to other measurement systems. Also included are examples from various base numbering systems and their equivalents, as well as the relative sizes of objects.

SI BASE AND SUPPLEMENTARY UNIT NAMES AND SYMBOLS

Physical Quality	Name	Symbol
Length	meter	m
Mass	kilogram	kg
Time	second	s
Electric current	ampere	A
Thermodynamic temperature	kelvin	K
Amount of substance	mole	mol
Luminous intensity	candela	cd
Plane angle	radian	rad
Solid angle	steradian	sr

Temperature

Scientists commonly use the Celsius system. Although not recommended for scientific and technical use, earth scientists also use the familiar Fahrenheit temperature scale (°F). 1°F = 1.8°C or K. The triple point of H_2O, where gas, liquid, and solid water coexist, is 32°F.

- To change from Fahrenheit (F) to Celsius (C):
  °C = (°F-32)/(1.8)
- To change from Celsius (C) to Fahrenheit (F):
  °F = (°C x 1.8) + 32
- To change from Celsius (C) to Kelvin (K):
  K = °C + 273.15
- To change from Fahrenheit (F) to Kelvin (K):
  K = (°F-32)/(1.8) + 273.15

UNITS DERIVED FROM SI, WITH SPECIAL NAMES AND SYMBOLS

Derived Quantity	Name of SI Unit	Symbol for SI Unit	Expression in Terms of SI Base Units
Frequency	hertz	Hz	s^{-1}
Force	newton	N	$m \cdot kg \cdot s^{-2}$
Pressure, stress	pascal	Pa	$m^{-1} \cdot kg \cdot s^{-2}$
Energy, work, heat	joule	J	$m^2 \cdot kg \cdot s^{-2}$
Power, radiant flux	watt	W	$m^2 \cdot kg \cdot s^{-3}$
Electric charge	coulomb	C	$s \cdot A$
Electric potential, electromotive force	volt	V	$m^2 \cdot kg \cdot s^{-3} \cdot A^{-1}$
Electric resistance	ohm	Ω	$m^2 \cdot kg \cdot s^{-3} \cdot A^{-2}$
Celsius temperature	degree Celsius	°C	K
Luminous flux	lumen	lm	Cd
Illuminance	lux	lx	$m^{-2} \cdot cd$

UNITS USED WITH SI, WITH NAME, SYMBOL, AND VALUES IN SI UNITS

The following units, not part of the SI, will continue to be used in appropriate contexts (e.g., angtsrom):

Physical Quantity	Name of Unit	Symbol for Unit	Value in SI Units
Time	minute	min	60 s
	hour	h	3,600 s
	day	d	86,400 s
Plane angle	degree	°	(π/180) rad
	minute	'	(π/10,800) rad
	second	"	(π/648,000) rad
Length	angstrom	Å	10^{-10} m
Volume	liter	l, L	$1 \text{ dm}^3 = 10^{-3} \text{ m}^3$
Mass	ton	t	$1 \text{ Mg} = 10^3$ kg
	unified atomic mass unit	u	$\approx 1.66054 \times 10^{-27}$ kg
Pressure	bar	bar	$10^5 \text{ Pa} = 10^5 \text{ N m}^{-2}$
Energy	electronvolt	eV (= e X V)	$\approx 1.60218 \times 10^{-19}$ J

CONVERSIONS FOR STANDARD, DERIVED, AND CUSTOMARY MEASUREMENTS

Length

1 angstrom (Å)	0.1 nanometer (exactly) 0.000000004 inch
1 centimeter (cm)	0.3937 inches
1 foot (ft)	0.3048 meter (exactly)
1 inch (in)	2.54 centimeters (exactly)
1 kilometer (km)	0.621 mile
1 meter (m)	39.37 inches 1.094 yards
1 mile (mi)	5,280 feet (exactly) 1.609 kilometers
1 astronomical unit (AU)	1.495979×10^{13} cm
1 parsec (pc)	206,264.806 AU 3.085678×10^{18} cm 3.261633 light-years
1 light-year	9.460530×10^{17} cm

Area

1 acre	43,560 square feet (exactly) 0.405 hectare
1 hectare	2.471 acres
1 square centimeter (cm^2)	0.155 square inch
1 square foot (ft^2)	929.030 square centimeters
1 square inch (in^2)	6.4516 square centimeters (exactly)
1 square kilometer (km^2)	247.104 acres 0.386 square mile
1 square meter (m^2)	1.196 square yards 10.764 square feet
1 square mile (mi^2)	258.999 hectares

MEASUREMENTS AND ABBREVIATIONS

Volume

1 barrel (bbl)*, liquid	31 to 42 gallons
1 cubic centimeter (cm^3)	0.061 cubic inch
1 cubic foot (ft^3)	7.481 gallons 28.316 cubic decimeters
1 cubic inch (in^3)	0.554 fluid ounce
1 dram, fluid (or liquid)	$1/_8$ fluid ounce (exactly) 0.226 cubic inch 3.697 milliliters
1 gallon (gal) (U.S.)	231 cubic inches (exactly) 3.785 liters 128 U.S. fluid ounces (exactly)
1 gallon (gal) (British Imperial)	277.42 cubic inches 1.201 U.S. gallons 4.546 liters
1 liter	1 cubic decimeter (exactly) 1.057 liquid quarts 0.908 dry quart 61.025 cubic inches
1 ounce, fluid (or liquid)	1.805 cubic inches 29.573 milliliters
1 ounce, fluid (fl oz) (British)	0.961 U.S. fluid ounce 1.734 cubic inches 28.412 milliliters
1 quart (qt), dry (U.S.)	67.201 cubic inches 1.101 liters
1 quart (qt), liquid (U.S.)	57.75 cubic inches (exactly) 0.946 liter

Units of mass

1 carat (ct)	200 milligrams (exactly) 3.086 grains
1 grain	64.79891 milligrams (exactly)
1 gram (g)	15.432 grains 0.035 ounce
1 kilogram (kg)	2.205 pounds
1 microgram (μg)	0.000001 gram (exactly)
1 milligram (mg)	0.015 grain
1 ounce (oz)	437.5 grains (exactly) 28.350 grams
1 pound (lb)	7,000 grains (exactly) 453.59237 grams (exactly)
1 ton, gross or long	2,240 pounds (exactly) 1.12 net tons (exactly) 1.016 metric tons
1 ton, metric (t)	2,204.623 pounds 0.984 gross ton 1.102 net tons
1 ton, net or short	2,000 pounds (exactly) 0.893 gross ton 0.907 metric ton

Pressure

1 kilogram/square centimeter (kg/cm^2)	0.96784 atmosphere (atm) 14.2233 pounds/square inch (lb/in^2) 0.98067 bar
1 bar	0.98692 atmosphere (atm) 1.02 kilograms/square centimeter (kg/cm^2)

---

* There are a variety of "barrels" established by law or usage. For example, U.S. federal taxes on fermented liquors are based on a barrel of 31 gallons (141 liters); many state laws fix the "barrel for liquids" as $31^1/_2$ gallons (119.2 liters); one state fixes a 36-gallon (160.5 liters) barrel for cistern measurment; federal law recognizes a 40-gallon (178 liters) barrel for "proof spirts"; by custom, 42 gallons (159 liters) comprise a barrel of crude oil or petroleum products for statistical purposes, and this equivalent is recognized "for liquids" by four states.

Base 2 (Binary)	Decimal (Base 10) Equivalent	Approximations to Powers of Ten
2^0	1	
2^1	2	
2^2	4	
2^3	8	
2^4	16	
2^5	32	
2^6	64	
2^7	128	10^2; 100; one hundred; 1 followed by 2 zeros
2^8	256	
2^9	512	
2^{10}	1,024	10^3; 1,000; one thousand; 1 followed by 3 zeros
2^{11}	2,048	
2^{12}	4,096	
2^{13}	8,192	
2^{14}	16,384	
2^{15}	32,768	
2^{16}	65,536	
2^{17}	131,072	
2^{18}	262,144	
2^{19}	524,288	
2^{20}	1,048,576	10^6; 1,000,000; one million; 1 followed by 6 zeros
2^{21}	2,097,152	
2^{22}	4,194,304	
2^{23}	8,388,608	
2^{24}	16,777,216	
2^{25}	33,554,432	
2^{26}	67,108,864	
2^{27}	134,217,728	
2^{28}	268,435,456	
2^{29}	536,870,912	
2^{30}	1,073,741,824	10^9; 1,000,000,000; one billion; 1 followed by 9 zeros
2^{31}	2,147,483,648	
2^{32}	4,294,967,296	
2^{33}	8,589,934,592	
2^{34}	17,179,869,184	
2^{35}	34,359,738,368	
2^{36}	68,719,476,736	
2^{37}	137,438,953,472	
2^{38}	274,877,906,944	
2^{39}	549,755,813,888	
2^{40}	1,099,511,627,776	10^{12}; 1,000,000,000,000; one trillion; 1 followed by 12 zeros
2^{50}	1,125,899,906,842,624	10^{15}; 1,000,000,000,000,000; one quadrillion; 1 followed by 15 zeros
2^{100}	1,267,650,600,228,229,401,496,703,205,376	10^{30}; 1 followed by 30 zeros
2^{-1}	1/2	
2^{-2}	1/4	
2^{-3}	1/8	
2^{-4}	1/16	
2^{-5}	1/32	
2^{-6}	1/64	
2^{-7}	1/128	1/100; 10^{-2}; 0.01; 1 hundredth
2^{-8}	1/256	
2^{-9}	1/512	
2^{-10}	1/1,024	1/1000; 10^{-3}; 0.001; 1 thousandth

For Your Reference

Base 16 (Hexadecimal)	Binary (Base 2) Equivalent	Decimal (Base 10) Equivalent	Approximations to Powers of Ten
16^0	2^0	1	
16^1	2^4	16	
16^2	2^8	256	2×10^2; 2 hundred
16^3	2^{12}	4,096	4×10^3; 4 thousand
16^4	2^{16}	65,536	65×10^3; 65 thousand
16^5	2^{20}	1,048,576	1×10^6; 1 million
16^6	2^{24}	16,777,216	
16^7	2^{28}	268,435,456	
16^8	2^{32}	4,294,967,296	4×10^9; 4 billion
16^9	2^{36}	68,719,476,736	68×10^9; 68 billion
16^{10}	2^{40}	1,099,511,627,776	1×10^{12}; 1 trillion
16^{-1}	2^{-4}	1/16	
16^{-2}	2^{-8}	1/256	
16^{-3}	2^{-12}	1/4,096	$1/4 \times 10^{-3}$; 1/4-thousandth
16^{-4}	2^{-16}	1/65,536	
16^{-5}	2^{-20}	1/1,048,576	10^{-6}; 1 millionth
16^{-8}	2^{-32}	1/4,294,967,296	$1/4 \times 10^{-9}$; 1/4-billionth
16^{-10}	2^{-40}	1/1,099,511,627,776	10^{-12}; 1 trillionth

Base 10 (Decimal)	Equivalent	Verbal Equivalent
10^0	1	
10^1	10	
10^2	100	1 hundred
10^3	1,000	1 thousand
10^4	10,000	
10^5	100,000	
10^6	1,000,000	1 million
10^7	10,000,000	
10^8	100,000,000	
10^9	1,000,000,000	1 billion
10^{10}	10,000,000,000	
10^{11}	100,000,000,000	
10^{12}	1,000,000,000,000	1 trillion
10^{15}	1,000,000,000,000,000	1 quadrillion
10^{-1}	1/10	1 tenth
10^{-2}	1/100	1 hundredth
10^{-3}	1/1,000	1 thousandth
10^{-6}	1/1,000,000	1 millionth
10^{-9}	1/1,000,000,000	1 billionth
10^{-12}	1/1,000,000,000,000	1 trillionth
10^{-15}	1/1,000,000,000,000,000	1 quadrillionth

Sizes of and Distance to Objects	Equivalent	Additional Information
Diameter of Electron (classical)	5.6×10^{-13} centimeters	5.6×10^{-13} centimeters; roughly 10^{-12} centimeters
Mass of Electron	9.109×10^{-28} grams	roughly 10^{-27} grams (1 gram = 0.0353 ounce)
Diameter of Proton	10^{-15} meters	10^{-13} centimeters
Mass of Proton	1.67×10^{-24} grams	roughly 10^{-24} grams (about 1,836 times the mass of electron)
Diameter of Neutron	10^{-15} meters	10^{-13} centimeters
Mass of Neutron	1.673×10^{-24} grams	roughly 10^{-24} grams (about 1,838 times the mass of electron)
Diameter of Atomic Nucleus	10^{-14} meters	$\sim 10^{-12}$ centimeters (10,000 times smaller than an atom)
Atomic Mass (Atomic Mass Unit)	1.66×10^{-27} kilograms	one atomic mass unit (amu) is equal to 1.66×10^{-24} grams
Diameter of Atom (Electron Cloud)	ranges from 1×10^{-10} to 5×10^{-10} meters	$\sim 10^{-10}$ meters; $\sim 10^{-8}$ centimeters; $\sim 3.94 \times 10^{-9}$ inches (roughly 4 billionth of an inch across or 1/250 millionth of an inch across)
Diameter of (standard) Pencil	6 millimeters (0.236 inches)	roughly 10^{-2} meters
Height (average) of Man and Woman	man: 1.75 meters (5 feet, 8 inches) woman: 1.63 meters (5 feet, 4 inches)	human height roughly 2×10^{0} meters; 1/804.66 miles; 10^{-3} miles
Height of Mount Everest	8,850 meters (29,035 feet)	~ 5.5 miles; roughly 10^{4} meters
Radius (mean equatorial) of Earth	6,378.1 kilometers (3,960.8 miles)	$\sim 6,400$ kilometers (4,000 miles); roughly 6.4×10^{6} meters
Diameter (polar) of Earth	12,713.6 kilometers (7,895.1 miles)	$\sim 12,800$ kilometers (8,000 miles); roughly 1.28×10^{7} meters (Earth's diameter is twice the Earth's radius)
Circumference (based on mean equatorial radius) of Earth	40,075 kilometers (24,887 miles)	$\sim 40,000$ kilometers (25,000 miles) (about 8 times the width of the United States) (Circumference = $2 \times \pi \times$ Earth's radius)
Distance from Earth to Sun	149,600,000 kilometers (92,900,000 miles)	$\sim 93,000,000$ miles; ~ 8.3 light-minutes; roughly 10^{11} meters; roughly 10^{8} miles
Distance to Great Nebula in Andromeda Galaxy	2.7×10^{19} kilometers (1.7×10^{19} miles)	~ 2.9 million light-years; roughly 10^{22} meters; roughly 10^{19} miles

Timeline: Significant Events in the History of Computing

· ·

The history of computer sciences has been filled with many creative inventions and intriguing people. Here are some of the milestones and achievements in the field.

c. 300-500 BCE	The counting board, known as the ancient abacus, is used. (Babylonia)
1200 CE	The modern abacus is used. (China)
1500	Leonardo da Vinci drafts a design for a calculator. (Italy)
1614	John Napier suggests the use of logarithms. (Scotland)
1617	John Napier produces calculating rods, called "Napier's Bones." (Scotland)
	Henry Briggs formulates the common logarithm, Base 10. (England)
1620	Edmund Gunter devises the "Line of Numbers," the precursor to slide rule. (England)
1623	Wilhelm Schickard conceives a design of a mechanical calculator. (Germany)
1632	William Oughtred originates the slide rule. (England)
1642	Blaise Pascal makes a mechanical calculator which can add and subtract. (France)
1666	Sir Samuel Morland develops a multiplying calculator. (England)
1673	Gottfried von Leibniz proposes a general purpose calculating machine. (Germany)
1777	Charles Stanhope, 3rd Earl of Stanhope, Lord Mahon, invents a logic machine. (England)
1804	Joseph-Marie Jacquard mechanizes weaving with Jacquard's Loom, featuring punched cards. (France)
1820	Charles Xavier Thomas (Tomas de Colmar) creates a calculating machine, a prototype for the first commercially successful calculator. (France)
1822	Charles Babbage designs the Difference Engine. (England)
1834	Charles Babbage proposes the Analytical Engine. (England)
1838	Samuel Morse formulates the Morse Code. (United States)
1842	L. F. Menabrea publishes a description of Charles Babbage's Analytical Engine. (Published, Italy)
1843	Ada Byron King, Countess of Lovelace, writes a program for Babbage's Analytical Engine. (England)
1854	George Boole envisions the Laws of Thought. (Ireland)

1870	William Stanley Jevons produces a logic machine. (England)
1873	William Thomson, Lord Kelvin, devises the analog tide predictor. (Scotland)
	Christopher Sholes, Carlos Glidden, and Samuel W. Soule invent the Sholes and Glidden Typewriter; produced by E. Remington & Sons. (United States)
1875	Frank Stephen Baldwin constructs a pin wheel calculator. (United States)
1876	Alexander Graham Bell develops the telephone. (United States)
	Bell's rival, Elisha Gray, also produces the telephone. (United States)
1878	Swedish inventor Willgodt T. Odhner makes a pin wheel calculator. (Russia)
1884	Dorr Eugene Felt creates the key-driven calculator, the Comptometer. (United States)
1884	Paul Gotlieb Nipkow produces the Nipkow Disk, a mechanical television device. (Germany)
1886	Herman Hollerith develops his punched card machine, called the Tabulating Machine. (United States)
1892	William Seward Burroughs invents his Adding and Listing (printing) Machine. (United States)
1896	Herman-Hollerith forms the Tabulating Machine Company. (United States)
1901	Guglielmo Marconi develops wireless telegraphy. (Italy)
1904	John Ambrose Fleming constructs the diodevalve (vacuum tube). (England)
	Elmore Ambrose Sperry develops the circular slide rule. (United States)
1906	Lee De Forest invents the triode vacuum tube (audion). (United States)
1908	Elmore Ambrose Sperry produces the gyrocompass. (United States)
1910	Sperry Gyroscope Company is established. (United States)
1912	Frank Baldwin and Jay Monroe found Monroe Calculating Machine Company. (United States)
1914	Leonardo Torres Quevado devises an electromechanical calculator, an electromechanical chess machine (End Move). (Spain)
	Thomas J. Watson Sr. joins the Computing Tabulating Recording Company (CTR) as General Manager. (United States)
1919	W. H. Eccles and F. W. Jordan develop the flip-flop (memory device). (England)
1922	Russian-born Vladimir Kosma Zworykin develops the iconoscope and kinescope (cathode ray tube), both used in electronic television for Westinghouse. (United States)
1924	The Computing Tabulating Recording Company (CTR), formed in 1911 by the merger of Herman Hollerith's Tabulating Machine Company with Computing

	Scale Company and the International Time Recording Company, becomes the IBM (International Business Machines).
1927	The Remington Rand Corporation forms from the merger of Remington Typewriter Company, Rand Kardex Bureau, and others. (United States)
1929	Vladimir Kosma Zworykin develops color television for RCA. (United States)
1931	Vannevar Bush develops the Differential Analyzer (an analog machine). (United States)
1933	Wallace J. Eckert applies punched card machines to astronomical data. (United States)
1937	Alan M. Turing proposes a Theoretical Model of Computation. (England)
	George R. Stibitz crafts the Binary Adder. (United States)
1939	John V. Atanasoff devises the prototype of an electronic digital computer. (United States)
	William R. Hewlett and David Packard establish the Hewlett-Packard Company. (United States)
1940	Claude E. Shannon applies Boolean algebra to switching circuits. (United States)
	George R. Stibitz uses the complex number calculator to perform Remote Job Entry (RJE), Dartmouth to New York. (United States)
1941	Konrad Zuse formulates a general-purpose, program-controlled computer. (Germany)
1942	John V. Atanasoff and Clifford Berry unveil the Atanasoff-Berry Computer (ABC). (United States)
1944	The Colossus, an English calculating machine, is put into use at Bletchley Park. (England)
	Howard Aiken develops, the Automatic Sequence Controlled Calculator (ASCC), the Harvard Mark I, which is the first American program-controlled computer. (United States)
	Grace Hopper allegedly coins the term "computer bug" while working on the Mark I. (United States)
1946	J. Presper Eckert Jr. and John W. Mauchly construct the ENIAC (Electronic Numerical Integrator and Computer), the first American general-purpose electronic computer, at the Moore School, University of Pennsylvania. (United States)
	J. Presper Eckert Jr. and John W. Mauchly form the Electronic Control Company, which later becomes the Eckert-Mauchly Computer Corporation. (United States)
1947	John Bardeen, Walter H. Brattain, and William B. Shockley invent the transistor at Bell Laboratories. (United States)
1948	F. C. Williams, Tom Kilburn, and G. C. (Geoff) Tootill create a small scale, experimental, stored-program computer (nicknamed "Baby") at the University of Manchester; it serves as the prototype of Manchester Mark I. (England)

1949	F. C. Williams, Tom Kilburn, and G. C. (Geoff) Tootill design the Manchester Mark I at the University of Manchester. (England)
	Maurice V. Wilkes develops the ED SAC (Electronic Delay Storage Automatic Calculator) at Cambridge University. (England)
	Jay Wright Forrester invents three-dimensional core memory at the Massachusetts Institute of Technology. (United States)
	Jay Wright Forrester and Robert Everett construct the Whirlwind I, a digital, real-time computer at Massachusetts Institute of Technology. (United States)
1950	J. H. Wilkinson and Edward A. Newman design the Pilot ACE (Automatic Computing Engine) implementing the Turing proposal for a computing machine at the National Physical Laboratory (NPL). (England)
	Remington Rand acquires the Eckert-Mauchly Computer Corporation. (United States)
1951	Engineering Research Associates develops the ERA 1101, an American commercial computer, for the U.S. Navy and National Security Agency (NSA). (United States)
	The UNIVAC I (Universal Automatic Computer), an American commercial computer, is created by Remington Rand for the U.S. Census Bureau. (United States)
	Ferranti Mark I, a British commercial computer, is unveiled. (England)
	Lyons Tea Co. announces Lyons Electronic Office, a British commercial computer. (England)
1952	UNIVAC I predicts election results as Dwight D. Eisenhower sweeps the U.S. presidential race. (United States)
	Remington Rand Model 409, an American commercial computer, is originated by Remington Rand for the Internal Revenue Service. (United States)
	Remington Rand acquires Engineering Research Associates. (United States)
1953	The IBM 701, a scientific computer, is constructed. (United States)
1954	The IBM 650 EDPM, electronic data processing machine, a stored-program computer in a punched-card environment, is produced. (United States)
1955	Sperry Corp. and Remington Rand merge to form the Sperry Rand Corporation. (United States)
1957	Robert N. Noyce, Gordon E. Moore, and others found Fairchild Semiconductor Corporation. (United States)
1957	Seymour Cray, William Norris, and others establish Control Data Corporation. (United States)
	Kenneth Olsen and Harlan Anderson launch Digital Equipment Corporation (DEC). (United States)

1958   Jack Kilby at Texas Instruments invents the integrated circuit. (United States)

1959   Robert N. Noyce at Fairchild Semiconductor invents the integrated circuit. Distinct patents are awarded to both Texas Instruments and Fairchild Semiconductor, as both efforts are recognized. (United States)

1960   The first PDP-1 is sold by Digital Equipment Corporation, which uses some technology from the Whirlwind Project. (United States)

            The UNIVAC 1100 series of computers is announced by Sperry Rand Corporation. (United States)

1961   The Burroughs B5000 series dual-processor, with virtual memory, is unveiled. (United States)

1964   The IBM/360 family of computers begins production. (United States)

            The CDC 6600 is created by Control Data Corporation. (United States)

1965   The UNIVAC 1108 from Sperry Rand Corporation is constructed. (United States)

1965   The PDP-8, the first minicomputer, is released by Digital Equipment Corporation. (United States)

            Robert N. Noyce and Gordon E. Moore found Intel Corporation. (United States)

1969   The U.S. Department of Defense (DoD) launches ARP ANET, the beginning of the Internet. (United States)

1970   The PDP–11 series of computers from Digital Equipment Corporation is put into use. (United States)

            The Xerox Corporation's Palo Alto Research Center (PARC) begins to study the architecture of information. (United States)

1971   Ken Thompson devises the UNIX Operating System at Bell Laboratories. (United States)

            Marcian E. (Ted) Hoff, Federico Faggin, and Stanley Mazor at Intel create the first microprocessor, a 4-bit processor, 4004. (United States)

1972   Seymour Cray founds Cray Research Inc. (United States)

            Intel releases the 8008 microprocessor, an 8-bit processor. (United States)

1974   Intel announces the 8080 microprocessor, an 8-bit processor. (United States)

            Motorola Inc. unveils the Motorola 6800, its 8-bit microprocessor. (United States)

            Federico Faggin and Ralph Ungerman co-found Zilog, Inc., a manufacturer of microprocessors. (United States)

1975   Bill Gates and Paul Allen establish the Microsoft Corporation. (United States)

The kit-based Altair 8800 computer, using an 8080 microprocessor, is released by Ed Roberts with MITS (Model Instrumentation Telemetry Systems) in Albuquerque, New Mexico. (United States)

MITS purchases a version of the BASIC computer language from Microsoft. (United States)

The MOS 6502 microprocessor, an 8-bit microprocessor, is developed by MOS Technologies, Chuck Peddle, and others, who had left Motorola, (United States)

1976   Gary Kildall creates the CP/M (Control Program/Monitor or Control Program for Microprocessors) Operating System of Digital Research; this operating system for 8-bit micro-computers is the forerunner of DOS 1.0. (United States)

Steven Jobs and Stephen Wozniak found Apple Computer, Inc. and create the Apple I. (United States)

Seymour Cray devises the Cray-1 supercomputer. (United States)

Commodore Business Machines acquires MOS Technologies. (Canada)

1977   The Commodore PET (Personal Electronic Transactor) personal computer, developed by Jack Tramiel and Chuck Peddle for Commodore Business Machines, features the 6502 8-bit Microprocessor. (Canada)

The Apple II personal computer from Apple Computer, Inc., is released featuring a 6502 microprocessor. (United States)

The TRS-80 personal computer from Tandy Radio Shack, equipped with the Zilog Z80 8-bit microprocessor from Zilog, is unveiled. (United States)

Intel announces the 8086 16-bit microprocessor. (United States)

1978   Digital Equipment Corporation launches the VAX 11/780, a 4.3 billion byte computer with virtual memory. (United States)

1979   Intel presents the 8088 16-bit microprocessor. (United States)

Motorola Inc. crafts the MC 68000, Motorola 16-bit processor. (United States)

1980   Tim Patterson sells the rights to QDOS, an upgrade operating system of CP/M for 8088 and 8086 Intel microprocessors, 16-bit microprocessor, to Microsoft. (United States)

1981   The IBM Corporation announces the IBM Personal Computer featuring an 8088 microprocessor. (United States)

The Microsoft Operating System (MS-DOS) is put into use. (United States)

The Osborne I, developed by Adam Osborne and Lee Felsenstein with Osborne Computer Corporation, invent the first portable computer. (United States)

1982   Scott McNealy, Bill Joy, Andy Bechtolsheim, and Vinod Khosla found Sun Microsystems, Inc. (United States)

1984	The Macintosh PC from Apple Computer Inc., running with a Motorola 68000 microprocessor, revolutionizes the personal computer industry. (United States)
	Richard Stallman begins the GNU Project, advocating the free use and distribution of software. (United States)
1985	The Free Software Foundation is formed to seek freedom of use and distribution of software. (United States)
	Microsoft releases Windows 1.01. (United States)
1986	Sperry Rand and the Burroughs Corporation merge to form Unisys Corporation. (United States)
1989	SPARCstation I from Sun Microsystems is produced. (United States)
1991	Tim Berners-Lee begins the World Wide Web at CERN. (Switzerland)
	Linus Torvalds builds the Linux Operating System. (Finland)
	Paul Kunz develops the first Web server outside of Europe, at the Stanford Linear Accelerator Center (SLAG). (United States)
1993	Marc Andreesen and Eric Bina create Mosaic, a Web browser, at the National Center for Supercomputing Applications (NCSA), University of Illinois-Urbana Champaign. (United States)
1994	Marc Andreesen and James H. Clark form Mosaic Communications Corporation, later Netscape Communications Corporation. (United States)
	Netscape Navigator is launched by Netscape Communications Corporation. (United States)
1995	Java technology is announced by Sun Microsystems. (United States)
1996	World chess champion Garry Kasparov of Russia defeats Deep Blue, an IBM computer, in a man vs. computer chess matchup, four to two. (United States)
1997	IBM's Deep Blue defeats world chess champion Garry Kasparov in a rematch, 3.5 to 2.5. (United States)
	An injunction is filed against Microsoft to prohibit the company from requiring customers to accept Internet Explorer as their browser as a condition of using the Microsoft operating system Windows 95. (United States)
1998	America OnLine (AOL) acquires Netscape. (United States)
	Compaq Computer Corporation, a major producer of IBM compatible personal computers, buys Digital Equipment Corporation. (United States)
	America OnLine (AOL) and Sun form an alliance to produce Internet technology. (United States)

1999	Shawn Fanning writes code for Napster, a music file-sharing program. (United States)
1998	The Recording Industry Association of America (RIAA) files a lawsuit against Napster for facilitating copyright infringement. (United States)
2000	Zhores I. Alferov, Herbert Kroemer, and Jack Kilby share the Nobel Prize in Physics for contributions to information technology. Alferov, a Russian, and Kroemer, a German-born American, share half the prize for their contributions to semiconductor-based technology used in high speed circuits. Kilby is awarded the other half of the prize for invention of the integrated circuit.
	Google becomes the first search engine to index one billion pages. (United States)
2001	Wikipedia, a free online user originated encyclopedia, comes online. (United States)
	Windows XP is introduced. (United States)
	Dell becomes the world's top computer systems provider. (United States)
2002	Hewlett Packard purchases Compaq. (United States)
2003	Apple creates and opens iTunes, an online music-buying application. (United States)
2004	Mark Zuckerberg creates and launches the online social network, Facebook. (United States)
	Google introduces Gmail, an Internet service. (United States)
2005	Video-sharing Web site, YouTube, comes online. (United States)
	Chinese company, Lenovo, acquires IBM's Personal Computing Division, making it the world's third-largest PC purveyor. (China)
2006	Apple switches all computers to Intel core processors. (United States)
	The first Twitter post is posted by co-founder Jack Dorsey at Twitter.com. (United States)
2007	Steve Jobs and Apple release the iPhone.
	Microsoft releases Windows Vista to the public. (United States)
	Apple announces that it will discontinue the use of the word "computer" in its title as it was working with products other than computers. It is now known as Apple, Inc. (United States)
2008	Bill Gates steps down as chairman of Microsoft to focus on philanthropic work. (United States)
2009	Intel unveils the "iA32 processor single-chip cloud computer," a CPU with 48 processing cores on a single chip. (United States)
2010	2010 Cyber-warfare and cyber-counterterrorism goes public: Stuxnet worm disrupts Iran's centrifuges dedicated to uranium enrichment.

2011   Social media, especially Facebook and Twitter, are credited with helping organizers form Arab Spring protests across Middle East. Revolution in Egypt results in resignation of President Hosni Mubarak and first free elections in Egypt's history.

         IBM's Watson supercomputer defeats human champions on the game show "Jeopardy."

2012   Facebook begins trading on NASDAQ as a private company (IPO).

         Facebook Facebook announces 'Graph Search' tool.

Timeline: The History of Programming, Markup, and Scripting Languages

The history of computer sciences has been filed with many creative inventions and innovations. Here are some of the milestones and achievements in the field of computer programming and languages.

c. 800   al-Khowarizmi, Mohammed ibn-Musa develops a treatise on algebra, his name allegedly giving rise to the term, algorithm.

1843   Ada Byron King, Countess of Lovelace, programs Charles Babbage's design of the Analytical Engine.

1945   Plankalkul is developed by Konrad Zuse.

1953   Sort-Merge Generator is created by Betty Holberton.

1957   FORTRAN is devised for IBM by John Backus and team of programmers.

FLOW-MATIC is crafted for Remington-Rand's UNIVAC by Grace Hopper.

1958   LISP is produced by John McCarthy at Massachusetts Institute of Technology.

1959   COBOL is formulated by the CODASYL Committee, initiated by the U.S. Department of Defense (DoD)

1960   ALGOL is the result of work done by the ALGOL Committee in the ALGOL 60 Report.

1961   JOSS is originated by the RAND Corporation.

GPSS (General Purpose Simulation System) is invented by Geoffrey Gordon with IBM.

RPG (Report Program Generator) is unveiled by IBM.

APL (A Programming Language) is designed by Kenneth Iverson with IBM.

1963   SNOBOL is developed by David Farber, Ralph Griswold, and Ivan Polonsky at Bell Laboratories.

1964   BASIC is originated by John G. Kemeny and Thomas E. Kurtz at Dartmouth.

PL/I is announced by IBM.

Simula I is produced by Kristen Nygaard and Ole-Johan Dahl at the Norwegian Computing Center.

1967   Simula 67 is created by Kristen Nygaard and Ole-Johan Dahl at the Norwegian Computing Center.

LOGO is devised by Seymour Papert at the MIT Artificial Intelligence Laboratory.

1971   Pascal is constructed by Niklaus Wirth at the Swiss Federal Institute of Technology (ETH) in Zurich.

1973	C developed by Dennis Ritchie at Bell Laboratories.
	Smalltalk is invented by Alan Kay at Xerox's PARC (Palo Alto Research Center).
1980	Ada is developed for the U.S. Department of Defense (DoD).
1985	C++ is created by Bjarne Stroustrup at Bell Laboratories.
1986	SGML (Standard Generalized Markup Language) is developed by the International Organization for Standardization (ISO).
1987	Perl is constructed by Larry Wall.
1989	HTML (HyperText Markup Language) is proposed by Tim Berners-Lee at CERN (Organization européenne pour la recherche nucléaire).
1991	Visual Basic is launched by the Microsoft Corporation.
1993	Mosaic is created by Marc Andreesen and Eric Bina for the National Center for Computing Applications (TSTCCA) at the University of Illinois-Urbana Champaign.
1994	A written specification of VRML (Virtual Reality Markup Language) is drafted by Mark Pesce, Tony Parisi, and Gavin Bell.
1995	Java is crafted by James Gosling of Sun Microsystems
1996	Javascript is developed by Brendan Eich at Netscape Communications co-announced by Netscape and Sun Microsystems.
1997	VRML (Virtual Reality Modeling Language), developed by the Web3D Consortium, becomes an international standard.
1998	XML (Extensible Markup Language) is originated by a working group of the World Wide Web Consortium (W3C).
2000	Microsoft publicly introduces the programming language C#.
2002	Perl 5.8 is released to the public.
2008	HTML5 is first introduced to the public as a working draft.

A

Agents

People have long dreamed of automated slaves that would do their every bidding, someone to run errands and do chores. Finally, with advances in computing and communications, some of those dreams are turning into reality. Whereas robotic slaves are still in development, software assistants are becoming quite popular. These are better known as agents, often called intelligent software agents. Software agents help to facilitate a more intelligent, accurate, and streamlined use of computers and their applications. They fall into a variety of categories from database management to daily personal assistance.

Software agents have been studied since the 1950s—the early days of computer science. However, interest in agents began to climb with the expansion of personal computing and local area networks (LANs)* in the 1980s, and then increased dramatically after the popularization of the Internet from 1995 onward.

Types of Agents

There are five main kinds of agents. The most well-known are personal assistants. These are often incorporated in desktop software products. Personal assistants try to understand what task a user is trying to perform and then help the user in performing that task. They might advise the user about the actions he or she might take to improve the quality of his or her work. A simple example is the Microsoft Clippy, who shows up when one starts an application program, such as Microsoft Word, and offers help on Word features that might be needed. Although some popular software assistants have a visual presence as a cartoon character, this is not necessary. An assistant may simply place text on a screen or interact through voice.

The second kind of agent is an information aggregating agent. These are used for searching for information or products on the web. The user can ask an agent to find the cheapest airline ticket from, say, Raleigh to the Bahamas, and the agent comes back with a set of options. These agents gather information from several sources on the web, but generally do not update it. They often combine with personal assistants that "learn" a user's preferences through the requests a user makes.

The third category of agents exists within information systems, typically of large enterprises. These software agents help correctly link and update information across related databases that often have subtle differences in meaning. For example, the payroll database in a company records salaries for all workers who are currently being paid, and the benefits

* **local area networks (LANs)** high-speed computer networks that are designed for users who are located near each other

* **distributed systems** computer systems comprised of many individual computers that are interconnected and act in concert to complete operations

database records health insurance premiums for current and former workers who are receiving health benefits. Such databases are designed to function independently, but people may need to receive interrelated information from them. For example, a manager might query for total monthly labor expenditures, which depend closely on the salaries and the health premiums paid out. However, if the manager queries for a list of permanent employees, neither database has the information. The payroll database includes temporary employees; the benefits database includes retirees. A possible solution is the set of workers who are listed in both databases. Software agents that can understand the information in the underlying "dumb" databases can prevent erroneous or misleading results from being computed. However, creating these agents is not an easy task and it gets more complex when the task requires that information be consistently updated in several places.

The fourth kind of agent functions within complex distributed systems*. Such agents are used to manage computer networks by keeping track of the status of various hosts and routers, monitoring traffic patterns, and attempting to detect security threats. They can analyze data transmissions that either do not fit the normal usage profile, or those that fit the profile of an attack, and take action to either stop an attack or alert a system administrator of a possible breach in security.

The fifth kind of agent provides services for the management and actions of a distributed system. These services include directories so that a software agent may find other agents and resources such as databases and web sites. The agent-location services can be more complex than a directory and may help find agents and provide additional support for negotiation among the agents. A practical agent system will typically include assistants for the various users, several agents to do the required work, and at least one directory or broker agent.

Connectivity and Communication

In most cases, an agent needs network connectivity to communicate with other agents or access remote resources. Only assistants for local applications such as Microsoft's Clippy can function without connectivity. Occasionally, one will see references to mobile agents, whose executing code moves from one computer to another. Although this is an interesting idea, it raises security concerns. A malicious agent running on one's computer could wreak havoc on one's data and use the computer to launch attacks on others. Moreover, in all practical applications, the effect of mobility can be achieved by having stationary agents reside on different computers and communicate securely with one another. For this reason, mobile agents are not used in practical applications.

There is no magic in computing. Ultimately, an agent is a software program, not completely unlike other programs. What makes agents interesting is that they provide programming abstractions that help users deal with complexity. Agents are programs that exhibit intelligence and autonomy, and can communicate with other programs. Unlike conventional programs, which must be explicitly invoked, agents can act proactively. Of these, the ability to communicate is central.

When these features are present, they enable the modular engineering of distributed systems. We create an agent for each major player in the system and set up the rules or protocols through which the agents can communicate and, presto, we have a distributed system. Virtually all serious applications of agents involve creating a multiagent system.

For example, designing an enterprise information system* from scratch is practically impossible, especially because real-life enterprises split and merge quite often. But when we build the components as agents, they can be composed together with the agents of different divisions or even different enterprises. Likewise, it is generally impossible to allocate resources centrally in a manner that will satisfy everyone competing for them. Often, a reasonable solution is to create a market for the given resource and let each interested party field its agents in that market. For example, agents can help people bid in auctions. Although present-day agents are simple, computational markets and agents for them are fast becoming a common feature of the business landscape, specifically, for trading in commodities* such as electrical power.

The power of software agents comes from their human-like traits of reasoning, acting autonomously, and communicating. Therefore, the study of agents not only incorporates traditional computing ideas of programming languages, objects, and concurrency, but also develops computational variants of cognitive, economic, ethical, legal, organizational, and social constructs. The science of agents is inherently interdisciplinary and one of the most exciting branches of computing.

 See also **Ergonomics • Interactive Systems**

Resources

Books

Bigus, Joseph, and Jennifer Bigus. *Constructing Intelligent Agents Using Java.* 2nd ed. New York: John Wiley & Sons, 2001.

Huhns, Michael N., and Munindar P. Singh, eds. *Readings in Agents.* San Mateo, CA: Morgan Kaufmann, 1998.

Amdahl, Gene Myron

American Computer Designer and Entrepreneur
1922–

Gene Myron Amdahl was born November 16, 1922, in Flandreau, South Dakota. He received a bachelor's degree in engineering physics from South Dakota State University (Brookings) in 1948 and a doctorate in

---

"Agents on the Web"

The Internet is host to a column about agents called "Agents on the Web." It appears in the *IEEE Internet Computing Online* magazine at <http://computer.org/internet>.

* **enterprise information system** a system of client and server computers that can be used to manage all of the tasks required to manage and run a large organization

* **commodities** raw materials or services marketed prior to being used

* **supercomputer** a very high performance computer, usually comprised of many processors and used for modeling and simulation of complex phenomena, like meteorology

theoretical physics from the University of Wisconsin (Madison) in 1952. His major contributions to the field of computer science have been in the design of computers and the founding of computer-related companies.

Prior to attending college, Amdahl served two years in the U.S. Navy during World War II (1939–1945), learning electronics and taking a computer programming course. This served him well academically and in his later entrepreneurial efforts. Amdahl's doctoral dissertation was on "The Logical Design of an Intermediate Speed Digital Computer." The computer itself was called the Wisconsin Integrally Synchronized Computer (WISC). Amdahl's design was implemented by successive classes of students at the University of Wisconsin.

Amdahl worked at the International Business Machines Corporation (IBM) from 1952 to 1955 and was a lead designer in the redesign of the IBM 701, which was later marketed as the IBM 704. After determining that he would not be made the manager of the IBM Stretch Project, a project aimed at developing advanced computer technology and a supercomputer* at IBM, Amdahl left the company for several years. He returned to IBM in 1960 after working at Ramo Wooldridge and Aeronautic, Inc., and became a leader in the design of the IBM System/360 series of computers.

Amdahl was made an IBM fellow in 1965, which meant he was able to pursue his own research projects. Introduced to the computer world in 1967, Amdahl is credited with originating Amdahl's law (sometimes also referred to as Amdahl's argument). The law is used to determine the maximum anticipated improvement to a computer system when only one part of the entire system is improved.

In 1969, Amdahl became the director of IBM's Advanced Computing Systems Laboratory in Menlo Park, California. IBM subsequently closed this laboratory on Amdahl's recommendation. In 1970, he left IBM and formed the Amdahl Corporation, based in Sunnyvale, California, a mainframe computer manufacturer in direct competition with IBM, with financial aid from the Japanese information technology equipment and services company, Fujitsu.

Amdahl computers could run the same software as the IBM series of computers, but they were priced more economically. They were, in a sense, IBM clones (near copies) in the mainframe computer market. A similar phenomenon later occurred in the personal computer market, when several manufacturers cloned or imitated the IBM personal computer. The cloning was done on the processors to run the software and on the peripherals as well, creating plug-to-plug compatible systems.

The first Amdahl computer was not shipped until 1975, but in subsequent years (1976–1978), the company was quite competitive, with between one and several hundred million dollars of product shipping per year. In 1979, Amdahl lost control of the company to Fujitsu, who continued to operate it as a wholly owned subsidiary as of 2012.

Amdahl resigned as chair of Amdahl Corporation in 1979, becoming chair emeritus, then left the company in 1980. That year he founded the Trilogy Systems Corporation with $230 million in start-up money.

His intent was to develop a high performance computing system with large scale integration (several hundred functions on a chip), fault tolerant wafer-scale chips, and a high performance central processing unit (CPU)*.

When Trilogy Systems encountered manufacturing problems, Amdahl acquired Elxsi, Ltd. in 1985 to obtain computer systems, and subsequently became its chair. In 1987, he founded Andor Systems to develop computers to compete with IBM's smaller mainframes. Amdahl formally left the merged company in 1989. However, Andor also suffered from manufacturing problems, and IBM came out with its own midsize computer, employing some of the same technology that Andor had developed. Hoping to remain a viable company, Andor turned to the manufacturing of peripheral systems and finally a data backup system, but by the mid-1990s, the company was forced to declare bankruptcy.

In 1996, at the age of 74, Amdahl helped found Commercial Data Servers, a company intended to produce IBM-compatible, PC-based mainframes. By 1998, people and companies worldwide had become concerned about what would happen to their computerized data as computer systems rolled over from the year 1999 to the year 2000. The so-called Y2K (Year 2000) problem caused uncertainty because traditionally only two digits had been used to identify the year in many applications, and programmers could not predict what would happen to time-sensitive systems when the year 99, for 1999, was followed by the year 00, for 2000 (not 1900). Commercial Data Servers developed the CDS2000E Enterprise Server to test applications for Year 2000 compliance, and provided it without affecting ongoing operations. It set the computer's clock ahead to simulate the start of 2000 and tested the software for problems. Many companies used this product to test their systems, rewrite programs, and adjust data storage accordingly. Few systems worldwide actually experienced any major Y2K problems. Amdahl eventually retired from Commercial Data Servers.

In 1987, Amdahl received the Eckert-Mauchly Award, bestowed jointly by the Association for Computing Machinery (ACM) and the Institute of Electrical and Electronic Engineers (IEEE) Computer Society for "outstanding innovations in computer architecture, including pipelining, instruction look-ahead, and cache memory." He also won the Computer Entrepreneur Award from the IEEE Computer Society in 1989, which is awarded to managers and leaders responsible for the growth of some segment of the computer industry whose efforts occurred at least fifteen years before the award and whose effects in the industry are easily recognizable.

In 1992, Amdahl was named one of the "1,000 Makers of the Twentieth Century" by the English newspaper *The Times*. In that same year, Amdahl was named by *Computerworld* magazine as one of the twenty-five people "who changed the world." In November 2004, Amdahl was appointed to the board of advisors of Massively Parallel Technologies, a software product developer. Three years later, Amdahl was recognized professionally with the SIGDA Pioneering Achievement Award for "his

central processing unit (CPU) the part of a computer that performs computations and controls and coordinates other parts of the computer

IBM 360 Series

The IBM 360 series of computers (System/360) was one of the first families of computers. The plan was to provide a wide range of computers, in price and performance, which were compatible with one another in what was termed upward compatibility. This meant that programs written on lower priced, less powerful models could be run on the more expensive, more powerful models. Customers could, for the first time, upgrade the power of their computing systems without having to rewrite programs for a new system. The concept proved extremely popular and was adopted by other computer manufacturers of the mid-1960s. Upward compatibility remains an industry standard.

outstanding contributions to the computing industry on the occasion of the 40th anniversary of Amdahl's Law." (SIGDA is the abbreviation for Special Interest Group on Design Automation, a part of the Association for Computing Machinery.) As of September 2012, Amdahl was a member of the Scientific Board of Advisors for Massively Parallel.

▶ *See also* **Generations: Computers • IBM Corporation • Mainframes • Supercomputers**

Resources

Books

Akera, Atsushi. *Calculating a Natural World: Scientists, Engineers, and Computers During the Rise of U.S. Cold War Research.* Inside technology. Cambridge, MA: MIT Press, 2007.

Bashe, Charles J., et al. *IBM's Early Computers.* Cambridge, MA: MIT Press, 1986.

Campbell-Kelly, Martin, and William Aspray. *Computer: A History of the Information Machine.* Boulder, CO: Westview Press, 2004.

Epstein, Robert, Gary Roberts, and Grace Beber. *Parsing the Turing Test: Philosophical and Methodological Issues in the Quest for the Thinking Computer.* New York: Springer, 2008.

Lee, J. A. N. *Computer Pioneers.* Los Alamitos, CA: Computer Society Press, 1995.

Web Sites

Massively Parallel Technologies. "Board of Advisors." http://massivelyparallel.com/company.php (accessed September 24, 2012).

SIGDA. "Pioneering Achievement Award." http://www.sigda.org/pioneer (accessed September 24, 2012).

Art

It would be difficult to exaggerate the impact of computers on the study and production of art. Not since the invention of photography has the art world been so radically transformed by a new technology.

Computers have changed methods of making art. Programs such as Adobe Photoshop can imitate the effects of watercolor, pastels, and paint through digital techniques and with greater flexibility than more traditional media such as oil or charcoal, because virtually every mark can be easily reversed or erased. Further, images produced with a program like Photoshop are much more transportable than images in traditional media because a digital image can be sent through e-mail or posted on a Web site with ease.

▲
Using digital 3D mapping technology, images are projected onto the walls of the Museum of Contemporary Art in Sydney, Australia. © *TORSTEN BLACKWOOD/AFP/Getty Images.*

There have been concerns about the alienating effects that such new technology might have on art and artists alike. With the production of images through traditional media such as oil paint, artists are able to leave physical marks on a surface such as canvas. Such imagery allows the presence of the artist to be recorded directly through brushstrokes or other gestures. With the mediating power of computer imagery, all artistic choices are filtered through a program. Thus, the direct relationship between the artist and his or her medium is compromised. Further, with digital images certain non-visual pleasures that accompany artistic production—the smell and feel of paint, for example—are lost. Other changes might be architectural and environmental, as artists occupy computer labs rather than the romanticized environment of the studio.

Nevertheless, many contemporary artists enjoy the new possibilities computers offer, far beyond the intended capabilities of image-producing software. Some artists use computer parts as sculptural elements. Janet Zweig, who lives in Brooklyn, New York, for example, sometimes produces kinetic (moving) sculpture with computer fragments to explore the ways in which new technologies change the way one understands processes of thought. In *Mind over Matter* (1993), as seen on her Web site, http://www.janetzweig.com, Zweig programmed a computer to generate all combinations of three sentences: "I think

* **permutations** significant changes or rearrangement

* **pixilation** the process of generating animation, frame by frame

therefore I am" (René Descartes); "I am what I am" (Popeye); and "I think I can" (the little engine that could). The resulting permutations* of sentences (such as "I think I can think") make it seem as if the computer truly contemplates its own existence. Further, a printer scrolls the resulting sentences out into a hanging basket. The basket is balanced by a hanging rock that rises as the paper-filled basket slowly descends. The computer's actions (thoughts) thus achieve a weighty presence and seem to have an effect on the world (the rock)—though not according to computers' usual methods of operating (working). In 2010, Zweig created Lipstick Enigma, a moving sculpture composed of 1,200 resin lipsticks, each driven by motors and controlled by circuit boards. Sentences are created and displayed on a sign, which the artist states is a mixture of the "language of engineering with the language of beauty advertising."

Other artists create Web sites. Mark Napier's (1961–) now canonical Web site http://www.potatoland.org, for example, offers a number of digital works that comment upon the notion of waste in cyberspace. At the site, one can visit Napier's "Digital Landfill," an ever-changing site to which people can contribute e-mail messages or other computer-generated documents that they wish to delete. One can then visit Napier's site to see how this digital landfill changes from day to day. The work is all the more interesting when one thinks about the ways in which waste works in a cyber environment. One usually thinks of waste as a pile of unpleasant refuse taking up physical space on the margins of a community. In some ways, this conceptualization of waste persists in cyberspace, as people delete files by moving them to the trash can or cleaning up their hard drives; but with cyberspace, the marginal location of a landfill changes. Because all Web sites are basically equal, the junkyard is just as likely to be next door to more pristine sites.

Still other artists create art with the use of robots, computers, and various high-tech devices. As an example, in 2012, American artist Pindar Van Arman developed a way to let Internet users control the creation of art using smart phones, tablets, and laptops. As described on his Web site (http://www.vanarman.com/), Van Arman calls the method Crowd Sourced Art.

Other artists use computers to produce digital photography. American artist Jason Salavon's (1970–) *Top Grossing Film of All Time, 1 × 1* (2000, http://salavon.com/work/TopGrossingFilmAllTime/) reduces each individual frame of the film *Titanic* down to one average color. Salavon then places each small frame in order from beginning to end in a rectangle. The resulting image references computer pixilation*, and supposedly allows the viewer to see (envison) the entire movie all in one shot (subsequent to Salavon's work, *Titanic* was replaced as the top-grossing film worldwide by the 2009 movie, *Avatar*; both films were directed by Canadian film director James Cameron [1954–]).

Jon Haddock's digital photography addresses the imagery of computer games. His *Lorraine Motel* (2000, http://asuartmuseum.asu.edu/2000/haddock/) shows the assassination of American civil rights activist Dr. Martin Luther King Jr. (1929–1968) as pictured according to the conventions of computer games like SimCity, and thus comments on the ways in which technology for children is intertwined with images of violence and social upheaval.

Digital images are transforming attitudes regarding the collection and exhibition of works of art. Once an image is digitally produced and posted on a Web site, virtually anyone with Internet access can gain access to that image and use it in whatever fashion one chooses. Images are ever more accessible, as major museums now offer Web sites cataloging their collections. Some museums have adopted this development directly. The Alternative Museum, for example, once occupied a building in Manhattan's Soho district. Now it only exists in cyberspace. The museum specializes in contemporary digital projects, Web sites, digital photography, links to scholarly sites, and chat rooms.

This widespread distribution of images seems to democratize the art world. More people have access to images, while museums maintain less control over reproductions of images in their collections. Further, artists are increasingly producing digital works of art outright. Such images are not reproductions but rather they are works of art in and of themselves. To download such an image from a Web site is, therefore, to possess the work—thus more people can gain access to original works (or to works that challenge the very distinction between original and reproduction). Such images may allow some to bypass institutions like galleries, auction houses, and museums that usually control traffic in art sales. These changes in the distribution and ownership of images have raised legal issues regarding copyright privileges.

Computers also facilitate art and art history research. Computerized databases such as *Art Abstracts* and *The Bibliography of the History of Art* (http://www.ebscohost.com/corporate-research/art-abstracts) can help researchers locate books and articles that have been written on art in the past several decades. Other online resources can also help researchers locate information on artists, galleries, current exhibitions, and reproductions of works of art. Even more impressive, the Getty Research Institute, in Los Angeles, California, offers one of the most complete collections of databases and other digital research facilities in all of cyberspace. Its site offers art-specific dictionaries, auction catalogs, and catalogs of archival holdings in the collection.

Such sites are only the beginning. Every day research institutes post new information on the web. Scanned primary documents, finders' aids, and more sophisticated research engines are making art history research more accessible and efficient. This process, however, is still incomplete. Although computers are tremendous tools for researching works of art, they are no replacement for physical trips to museums and research libraries.

Restoring a Masterpiece

Dirt, dust, and candle smoke covered the frescoes on the ceiling of the Sistine Chapel in Rome for centuries. To make the needed repairs, a team of art restorers worked on the frescoes for fifteen years to remove the age-old grime. Using sophisticated photographic equipment, spectrometers, and computers, the group located the areas needing the most work. Once the restoration was complete, the ceiling showed the brilliant colors and depictions created by Michelangelo in the fifteenth century. To ensure the long-lasting effects of the restoration work, a special air filtering system, like that used by the National Space and Aeronautics Administration (NASA) on the space shuttle fleet, was installed to monitor the amount of humidity and dust.

▶ *See also* **Digital Images • Fashion Design • Graphic Devices**

Resources

Books

Lopes, Dominic. *A Philosophy of Computer Art*. London, UK: London: Routledge, 2010.

Wands, Bruce. *Art of the Digital Age*. London, UK: Thames & Hudson, 2007.

Web Sites

Getty Research Institute. "Search Tools and Databases." http://www.getty.edu/research/tools/ (accessed September 27, 2012).

Artificial Life

Artificial life (also known as ALife) is an interdisciplinary study of life and lifelike processes by means of computer simulation and other methods. The goals of this activity include understanding and creating life and lifelike systems, and developing practical devices inspired by living systems. The study of artificial life aims to understand how life arises from non-life, to determine the potentials and limits of living systems, and to explain how life is connected to mind, machines, and culture.

▶ Museum conservator inspects cybernetic tortoise, an invention by Alan Turing, designed to study how animal brains function. © *AP Images/Geoff Caddick/ PA Wire.*

The American computer scientist Christopher Langton (c. 1948–) coined the phrase artificial life in 1987, when he organized the first scientific conference explicitly devoted to this field. Before there were artificial life conferences, the simulation and synthesis of lifelike systems occurred in isolated pockets scattered across a variety of disciplines. The Hungarian-born physicist and mathematician John von Neumann (1903–1957) created the first artificial life model (without referring to it as such) in the 1940s. He produced a self-reproducing, computation-universal entity using cellular automata*. Von Neumann was pursuing many of the questions that still drive artificial life today, such as understanding the spontaneous generation and evolution of complex adaptive structures.

Rather than modeling some existing living system, artificial life models are often intended to generate wholly new—and typically extremely simple—instances of lifelike phenomena. The simplest example of such a system is the so-called Game of Life devised by the British mathematician John Horton Conway (1937–) in the 1960s before the field of artificial life was conceived. Conway was trying to create a simple system that could generate complex self-organized structures.

The Game of Life is a two-state, two-dimensional cellular automaton. It takes place on a rectangular grid of cells, similar to a huge checkerboard. Time advances systematically, in a step-by-step manner. A cell's state at a given time is determined by the states of its eight neighboring cells according to the following simple birth-death rule: a dead cell becomes alive if and only if exactly three neighbors were just alive, and a living cell dies if and only if fewer than two, or more than three, neighbors were just alive. When all of the cells in the system are simultaneously updated again and again, a rich variety of complicated behavior is created and a complex zoo of dynamic structures can be identified and classified (blinkers, gliders, glider guns, logic switching circuits, etc.). It is even possible to construct a universal Turing machine* in the Game of Life, by cunningly arranging the initial configuration of living cells. In such constructions, gliders perform a role of passing signals. Analyzing the computational potential of cellular automata on the basis of glider interactions has become a major direction in research. Like living systems, Conway's Game of Life exhibits a vivid hierarchy of dynamical self-organized structures. Its self-organization is not a representation of processes in the real world, but a wholly novel instance of this phenomenon.

To understand the interesting properties of living systems, von Neumann and Conway each used a constructive method. They created simple and abstract models that exhibited the kind of behavior they wanted to understand. Contemporary artificial life employs the same constructive methodology, often through the creation of computer models of living systems. This computer methodology has several virtues. Expressing a model in computer code requires precision and clarity, and it ensures that the mechanisms invoked in the model are feasible.

The Turing Machine

Alan Turing's famous machine is an abstract automaton that can be in any one of a number of states and that is capable of moving back and forth on an infinitely long tape of instructions (customarily zeros and ones), reading and writing instructions on each segment of tape as it moves. A Turing machine's state at a given time is a finite function of both the machine's current state and the information on the currently scanned section of tape. A universal Turing machine is a Turing machine capable of executing any algorithm.

* **cellular automata** a collection or array of objects that are programmed identically to interact with one another

* **Turing machine** a proposed type of computing machine that takes inputs off paper tape and then moves through a sequence of states under the control of an algorithm; identified by British mathematician and computer scientist Alan Turing (1912–1954)

* **artificial intelligence (AI)** a branch of computer science dealing with creating computer hardware and software to mimic the way people think and perform practical tasks

* **neural networks** pattern recognition systems whose structure and operation are loosely inspired by analogy to neurons in the human brain

* **algorithm** a rule or procedure used to solve a mathematical problem—most often described as a sequence of steps

Artificial life is similar to artificial intelligence (AI)*. Both fields study natural phenomena through computational models, and most naturally occurring intelligent systems are, in fact, alive. Despite these similarities, AI and artificial life typically employ different modeling strategies. In most traditional artificial intelligence systems, events occur one by one (serially). A complicated, centralized controller typically makes decisions based on global information about all aspects of the system, and the controller's decisions have the potential to affect directly any aspect of the whole system.

This centralized, top-down architecture is quite unlike the structure of many natural living systems that exhibit complex autonomous behavior. Such systems are often parallel, distributed networks of relatively simple low-level agents, and they all simultaneously interact with each other. Each agent's decisions are based on information about only its own local situation, which they affect.

In similar fashion, artificial life characteristically constructs massively parallel, bottom-up-specified systems of simple local agents. One repeats the simultaneous low-level interactions among the agents, and then observes what aggregate behavior emerges. These are sometimes called agent-based or individual-based models, because the system's global behavior arises out of the local interactions among a large collection of agents or individuals. This kind of bottom-up architecture with a population of autonomous agents that follow simple local rules is also characteristic of the connectionist (parallel, distributed processing, neural networks*) movement that swept through AI and cognitive science in the 1980s. In fact, the agents in many artificial life models are themselves controlled internally by simple.

Computer simulation in artificial life plays the role that observation and experiment play in more conventional science. The complex self-organizing behavior of Conway's Game of Life would never have been discovered without computer simulations of thousands of generations for millions of sites. Simulation of large-scale complex systems is the single most crucial development that has enabled the field of artificial life to flourish.

Living systems exhibit a variety of useful properties such as robustness, flexibility, and automatic adaptability. Some artificial life research aims to go beyond mere simulation by constructing novel physical devices that exhibit and exploit lifelike properties. Some of this engineering activity also has a theoretical motivation because a full appreciation of life's distinctive properties can come only by creating and studying real physical devices. This engineering activity includes the construction of evolving hardware, in which biologically inspired adaptive processes control the configuration of micro-electronic circuitry. Another example is biologically inspired robots, such as those robotic controllers automatically designed by evolutionary algorithms*.

Although not without his critics, American author and futurist Raymond Kurzweil (1948–) has proposed that, by 2029 the computer would have the same capabilities as the human brain. In his book, *The Singularity is Near*, Kurzweil proposed that in the near future the human body could be supplemented with computers into what is called a super intelligence, or a technical singularity. Kurzweil proposed that this singularity could happen through the development of genetics, nanotechnology, and robotics, including the use of artificial intelligence.

 See also **Artificial Intelligence • Biology • Computer Vision • Neural Networks • Robotics**

Resources

Books

Angelov, Plamen, Dimitar P. Filev, and Nikola Kasabov, editors. *Evolving Intelligent Systems: Methodology and Applications*. Hoboken, NJ: John Wiley, 2010

Komosinski, Maciej, and Andrew Adamatzky, editors. *Artificial Life Models in Software*. 2nd ed. New York: Springer, 2009

Web Sites

International Society of Artificial Life. "Christoph Adami: Finding Life We Can't Imagine." http://www.ted.com/talks/christophe_adami_finding_life_we_can_t_imagine.html (accessed September 25, 2012).

TED. "ALife.org." http://alife.org/ (accessed September 25, 2012).

Assistive Computer Technology for Persons with Disabilities

The personal computer (PC) can be the backbone of independence for millions of individuals with sensory, physical, and learning disabilities. Computers and information technology can be modified with alternative input, alternative output, and other assistive technology to empower consumers who have disabilities. Computer vendors support persons with disabilities by incorporating accessibility utilities into operating systems such as Microsoft Windows, Apple OS X, Linux, and UNIX. Computers equipped with assistive technology permit individuals to function independently at school, work, and home, and allow access to great quantities of information from diverse sources such as compact disks (CDs) and digital versatile discs (DVDs), networks, electronic mail, instant messaging, the World Wide Web, and other Internet resources. For the purposes of this discussion, the term "assistive technology" will be used to describe any hardware device or software program that permits individuals with disabilities to operate PCs and access information technology independently. Moreover, this article uses the definition of disability as outlined in the United States by the Americans with Disabilities Act (ADA) and

Cellular Automaton

Cellular automaton is a regular spatial lattice of cells, each of which can be in any one of a finite number of states. The states of all the cells in the lattice are updated simultaneously and the state of the entire lattice advances in discrete time steps. The state of each cell in the lattice is updated according to a local rule that may depend on the state of the cell and its neighbors at the previous time step. Each cell in a cellular automaton could be considered to be a finite state machine which takes its neighbors' states as input and outputs its own state. The best known example is John Conway's Game of Life.

Advances in technology allow this young girl to communicate. Sensors trained on her eyes allow her to control a mouse pointer on a computer by looking left, right, up and down. © *AP Images/ Albanpix Ltd/Rex Features.*

* **central processing unit** the part of a computer that performs computations and controls and coordinates other parts of the computer

the Disabilities Discrimination Act in the United Kingdom—any permanent condition that impairs a major life function such as seeing, hearing, walking, or speaking.

Personal Computer Platforms

Since their advent in the early 1980s, PCs have become a vital tool for business and education applications, and are now common in many homes. Personal computer platforms are a combination of hardware and software, working together in synergy. The hardware is the physical structure of the system, and software is the set of instructions that control the hardware. PC hardware consists of several fundamental components, including the central processing unit*, memory units, disk drive storage, keyboard, mouse, speakers, and video monitor or screen.

For persons with disabilities, the keyboard, mouse, and monitor are of prime concern. PCs employ input devices like keyboards and mice for entering information and for controlling the system. Output devices, such as screens and printers, display processed information. Adapting PCs for use by persons with disabilities involves the modification of these standard input and output devices with assistive hardware or software. For example, adapting a computer's output systems to produce synthesized speech or Braille printouts can make the computer accessible for persons with disabilities. Software allows the timing and responsiveness of computer keys, trackpads, and touchscreens to be modified to better reflect the intended actions of the user.

Technology for Persons with Vision Impairments

The screen or monitor is a standard output device for PCs. By its nature, the monitor relies on the visual sense to convey information. For persons with vision-related disabilities, the monitor can present a significant barrier, depending on the nature of the vision loss. The output of a standard computer printer is also fundamentally inaccessible for persons with vision impairments. Several assistive technologies that can help compensate for visual impairments include video magnification, screen readers, Braille keys and printers, voice-assisted technology, intelligent agents, and optical character recognition systems.

Magnification software enlarges text and graphics displayed by PCs. Magnification programs are widely used by persons with poor vision or who have difficulty reading. They focus a larger image on the retina, making text and graphics more visible. Most magnification programs can magnify either the whole screen, or just a select region of the screen. Some basic magnification utilities magnify just the mouse pointer or cursor. Most comprehensive packages allow the user to change the screen contrast and font or adjust the magnification in steps. Some programs provide speech output and magnification at the same time. Magnification software can enlarge the output from commercial applications such as word processors, databases, spreadsheets, browsers, e-mail, ebooks, and other applications.

Screen readers are software programs that provide either speech or Braille output, and are commonly employed by persons who are blind or visually impaired. Screen readers require a computer sound card* and speakers to provide voice output. For Braille output, a screen reader requires a Braille display. Braille displays connect to the PC and contain a row of mechanical Braille dots that pop up and down under computer control. The user employs arrow keys to scroll text for reading. Braille displays allow vision-impaired users to control the operating system and application programs.

For persons with vision impairments, the printed word can present a formidable barrier to independence. Optical character recognition* (OCR) software can help overcome this barrier. OCR software requires a flatbed or handheld scanner to be connected to the host PC in order to function.

OCR systems are used to scan printed materials directly into the PC to accommodate many types of disabilities. Once scanned, the text can be read using a screen reader, magnification software, or Braille display or printer. OCR software can also help users with learning disabilities scan and format information in ways that help them process the information. In addition, the technology empowers those with motor-related disabilities to process and access information.

* **sound card** a plug-in card for a computer that contains hardware devices for sound processing, conversion, and generation

* **optical character recognition** the science and engineering of creating programs that can recognize and interpret printed characters

Technology for Persons with Motor Impairments

For persons with motor-related disabilities, the computer keyboard and mouse can present a significant barrier. There is a wide range of assistive technology available to compensate users who have motor disabilities. Several common input modifications include adapted keyboards, on-screen keyboards, alternative communication programs, and voice recognition.

Keyboard adaptations designed to assist users who have difficulty using the standard keyboard come in many different forms. Models exist that can be used with one hand, or with another part of the body. There are adapted keyboards that allow the keys to be rearranged to suit the user's needs. Some models allow the keyboard to be adjusted for the most suitable ergonomic fit. These can be adjusted to lay flat on the desk in the traditional manner or they can be used in a vertical configuration, if that best suits a user's preferences and needs.

On-screen keyboards display a pictorial representation of a standard keyboard on the computer screen. The on-screen keyboard can be configured to respond to human touch (as is common in all tablet computers) or scan through the keys one at a time through software. Software-controlled adapted switches come in many configurations: They can respond to one's breath, a hand, or another part of the body. Voice-recognition software also allows for word processing without use of a keyboard.

Many motor disabilities can impact one's ability to speak, so software engineers have developed alternative communications systems to assist persons with communications tasks at home, school, or in the workplace. Alternative communications systems range from picture boards to laptop and tablet computers equipped with speech synthesis systems capable of an unlimited vocabulary. Such systems can facilitate communications with friends, family members, and co-workers, as well as tasks such as delivering presentations.

Voice recognition and dictation systems are powerful assistive technologies that allow persons with disabilities to control a computer and dictate documents verbally using spoken commands. Voice recognition software requires a computer with a sound card and a microphone to accept verbal input. Voice recognition software must be trained by the user to recognize the speaker's voice accurately. The software stores recorded voice patterns from the training process, and matches these stored templates against the incoming verbal command stream from the microphone. Voice recognition can be used for applications such as e-mail, web browsing, and word processing.

Technology for Persons with Hearing Impairments

Numerous forms of adaptive and non-assistive technologies are available to increase independence and quality of life for individuals who are deaf or hard of hearing. For persons with hearing-related disabilities, access to the spoken word often can present a significant barrier. Assistive technology to support users with hearing-related disabilities focuses on accessing the spoken word at home, in the classroom, or at the work site. Technologies to assist the hearing-impaired include such systems as TTYs, text messaging, Internet messaging, video internet conferencing, text-to-voice technology, amplification systems, and applications such as e-mail.

TTYs, or text telephones, enable people to type messages back and forth over the telephone using a keyboard and printer or visual display. They access the telephone system using standard connectors, and can be used for home, school, or business applications. There are also portable TTYs suitable for a mobile environment, but text messaging using cellular phones has become more a popular and common mobile communication option.

Amplification systems increase the volume and clarity of the spoken word, making it more accessible for persons with limited hearing ability. These devices range from hearing aids that fit inside the ear to assistive listening devices that can be carried in a pocket or purse and used for large gatherings. Most cellular phones have built-in amplification systems to boost volume and clarity, and offer visual and vibrating ringers for users with limited hearing.

Non-assistive computer programs such as electronic mail, Internet messaging, text messaging, and online video conferencing empower individuals with hearing-related impairments to communicate over the Internet. The widespread availability of electronic mail contributes greatly to the independence of persons with hearing impairments. Messaging allows for expanded communication in much the same manner as electronic mail does, with an immediacy similar to that of a telephone conversation, and its wide availability to all computer and cell phone users makes it attractive as a means of communication.

Technology for Persons with Learning Disabilities

The term learning disabilities covers many impairments that impact the ability to process information. Technologies to assist persons with learning disabilities include speech systems that read printed material aloud, digital assistants to maintain schedules and lists of tasks, software to correct spelling, and task management software to guide users through the successful completion of projects. Many of these are standard productivity software programs used in business and education.

The Internet

The Internet is a vast network that spans the globe, linking together everything from individual computers, to private and public networks and Intranets. This global network allows persons with disabilities to share and exchange information in an accessible form. The Internet supports applications like e-mail, chat messaging, and the World Wide Web. PCs connected to the Internet can be adapted with a wide variety of technologies to allow access to applications such as e-mail, web browsers, and online databases. The Internet empowers persons with disabilities to access information using speech, magnification, or some other form of

Americans With Disabilities Act

The Americans with Disabilities Act (ADA), which went into effect in 1992, attempts to end discrimination practices against persons with physical or mental impairments. The ADA was updated in 2008 with passage of the ADA Amendments Act (ADAAA). At times, disabled people experience difficulties when job hunting, not because they cannot do a particular job but because prospective employers assume that they cannot. Assistive computer technology has opened many new avenues for the disabled, making once difficult tasks now easily achievable.

The TTY

TTY technology helps people with hearing and speech impairments communicate by telephone. Short for "Teletypewriter for the Deaf," the device is also referred to as a "text telephone" because the TTY permits users to send and receive text messages.

assistive technology. The Internet increases independence for people with mobility issues to interact, work, and socialize. Assistive software can be loaded onto a network to allow that software to be shared by all users belonging to the network.

Assistive Technology and Computer Operating Systems

Accessibility utilities are being integrated into computer operating systems such as Windows and OS X. While these accessibility utilities differ from one platform to another, most operating systems include utilities to magnify text and graphics, convert text into synthesized speech, and help users control the keyboard and mouse functions. Over the years, operating systems have grown more compatible with assistive technology. For example, Microsoft Active Accessibility (MSAA) was an Application Programming Interface (API) program that helped assistive technologies (consisting of both hardware devices and software) work together with the Windows operating system and application programs. MSAA first appeared as an add-on to Microsoft's Windows 95 operating system, and thereafter in subsequent versions of Windows. In 2005, Microsoft released a successor to MSAA called User Interface Automation (UIA). Beginning with the release of Windows 7 in 2009, UIA became a subset of the Windows Automation API framework.

Future Technology

Legislation such as the Americans with Disabilities Act in the United States and the Disabilities Discrimination Act in the United Kingdom is fostering the development of assistive technology for persons with disabilities. Section 508 of the Rehabilitation Act in the United States helped to make the World Wide Web more accessible as well. The development of computer platforms of increasing speed and power also contributes to the ongoing evolution of assistive technology. As computers get more powerful, assistive technology also increases in capacity and potential, driven by the advancement of microprocessor-based technology. The increasing miniaturization of powerful computer components will lead to assistive technologies that are more portable, lightweight, and cost effective, allowing for increased independence and improving the overall quality of life for persons with disabilities.

▶ *See also* **Human Factors: User Interfaces • Input Devices • Internet: Applications • Robotics**

Resources

Books

Bryant, Diane P., and Brian R. Bryant. *Assistive Technology for People with Disabilities*. 2nd ed. Boston: Pearson, 2012.

Internet Resources

Hawking, Stephen, and the Alliance for Technology Access. *Computer Resources for People with Disabilities: A Guide to Assistive Technologies, Tools and Resources for People of All Ages.* 4th ed. Alameda, CA: Hunter House, 2004.

Seale, Jane. *E-Learning and Disability in Higher Education: Accessibility Research and Practice.* New York: Routledge, 2006.

Web Sites

ABLEDATA. "Assistive Technology Products." http://www.abledata.com/ (accessed November 5, 2012).

Asynchronous Transfer Mode (ATM)

The physical infrastructure supporting data communications has improved its ability to transmit data quickly with advances such as optical fibers. As this physical capacity increases, there is a need to utilize effectively the bandwidth* to carry a variety of traffic (voice, video, data) in an efficient manner. Traditionally, circuit switching is used to support the real-time delivery needed for voice and video. Packet switching* is used to support intermittently heavy data traffic. Asynchronous Transfer Mode (ATM) has emerged as a technology that efficiently utilizes the bandwidth while carrying one or more traffic types. ATM is a high-speed packet switching technology that is capable of supporting both real-time voice and video and the kind of data traffic that has peaks and plateaus in its transmission.

ATM uses fixed size packets (called cells) to reduce processing and switching delays. The cell size is kept small, at 53 bytes, to allow for fast preparation and transmission. ATM allows different users to request varying amounts of resources to support the desired quality of transmission. It supports several traffic classes with differing quality-of service-requirements.

A user requests a connection to another user with a desired quality of service. The ATM switches use signaling protocols* to communicate with one another about the availability of resources needed for the requested connection. ATM allocates bandwidth dynamically, so if some users are not transmitting their cells for some time, lower priority traffic with higher tolerance for delays can be transmitted.

History of ATM

ATM has grown out of the need for a worldwide standard to allow interoperability of information, regardless of the end-system or type of information. There have been separate methods used for the transmission of information among users on a local area network (LAN)*, versus users

bandwidth a measure of the frequency component of a signal or the capacity of a communication channel to carry signals

Packet switching an operation used in digital communications systems whereby packets (collections) of data are dispatched to receivers based on addresses contained in the packets

signaling protocols protocols used in the management of integrated data networks that convey a mix of audio, video, and data packets

local area network (LAN) a high-speed computer network that is designed for users who are located near each other

Higher Layers
ATM Adaptation Layer
ATM Layer
Physical Layer

▲

Figure 1. ATM architecture. © *Gale, Cengage Learning. Reproduced by permission of Gale, a part of Cengage Learning.*

* **wide area network (WAN)** an interconnected network of computers that spans upward from several buildings to whole cities or entire countries and across countries

on a wide area network (WAN)*. This has added to the complexity of networking as users' needs for connectivity expand from the LAN to metropolitan, national, and finally worldwide connectivity.

Today separate networks are being used to carry voice, data, and video information due to their different characteristics. Data traffic tends to be "bursty"—not needing to communicate for an extended period of time and then needing to communicate large quantities of information as fast as possible. Voice and video, on the other hand, tend to be more even in the amount of information required, but are very sensitive to when and in what order the information arrives. With ATM, separate networks are not required. ATM is the only standards-based technology that has been designed from the beginning to accommodate the simultaneous transmission of data, voice, and video. Although some technologies today are scalable in terms of one of the factors (size or bit-rate or number of users), only ATM is truly "scalable" in terms of bit-rate, network size, and number of users.

ATM Cells

An ATM cell is 53 bytes long with a 5-byte header possessing information for control and signaling, and 48 bytes of data payload. Having fixed-size cells may reduce queuing delays for high priority cells. Because one knows the size of a cell beforehand, it becomes easier to implement the switching mechanism in hardware for efficient switching. The header information is generated in the ATM Layer, while the ATM Adaptation Layer (AAL) breaks the entire message into 48-byte data chunks. The cell header contains fields to help deal with congestion, maintenance, and error control problems. It is broken up into the following fields:

- Generic Flow Control (GFC), a mechanism used to alleviate short-term overload conditions in the network. It is intended to provide efficient and equal utilization of the link between all the users.

- Virtual Path Identifier (VPI), which allows for more virtual paths to be supported within the network.

- Virtual Channel Identifier (VCI), which functions as a service access point as it is used for routing to and from the end user.

- Payload Type (PT), which is used to distinguish between user information and connection-associated layer management information.

- Cell Loss Priority (CLP), which is used to provide guidance to the network to discard the cell in case of congestion.

- Header Error Control (HEC), which contains the information that can be used by the physical layer for error detection or correction. It is calculated from the first 32 bits of the header.

VCI/VPI Connections

The entire ATM network is based on virtual connections set up by the switches upon initialization of a call. Virtual Channel Identifiers (VCI) and Virtual Path Identifiers (VPI) are used to identify these virtual connections. They are used to route information from one switch to another. VCI and VPI are not addresses; they are explicitly assigned to each segment within a network.

A Virtual Channel Connection (VCC) is set up between two end users through the network and used for full-duplex flow of cells. They are also used for user-network exchange (control signaling) and network-network exchange (network management and routing). The VCI label identifies a VCC between two ATM switches and may change at intermediate nodes within a route.

Virtual channels having the same endpoints are often grouped together to form a Virtual Path Connection (VPC). This grouping of channels makes the task of network management easier without losing flexibility. Usually many virtual channels share a physical link at the same time, allowing asynchronous interweaving of cells from multiple connections. VPI connections share a common path through the network and thus network management actions need to be applied to only a single virtual path as opposed to all of the individual virtual channels.

Layers and Their Functions

ATM is a layered architecture allowing multiple services—voice, data, and video—to be carried over the network. It consists of three layers: the physical layer, the ATM layer, and the ATM adaptation layer. Layers are as shown in Figure 1 and their functionality is summarized in Figure 2.

Physical Layer   The physical layer of ATM is similar to layer 1 of the Open Systems Interconnections (OSI)* model and performs bit level functions. It defines electrical characteristics and network interfaces. It is further divided into two layers: Physical Medium (PM) and Transmission Convergence (TC) sub-layer.

The PM sublayer contains physical medium (e.g. optical fiber, coaxial, or twisted pair) dependent functions and provides bit transmission capability including bit alignment.

The TC sublayer performs five primary functions as shown in Figure 2. The lowest function is the generation and recovery of the transmission frame. Transmission frame adaptation adapts the cell flow according to the used payload structure of the transmission system in the sending direction, and extracts the cell flow from the transmission frame in the receiving direction.

The cell delineation function enables the receiver to recover the cell boundaries. The Header Error Control (HEC) sequence generation is done in the transmit direction and its value is recalculated and compared with the received value. Cell rate decoupling inserts the idle cells in the transmitting direction in order to adapt the rate of the ATM cells to the payload capacity of the transmission system. It suppresses all idle cells in

* **Open Systems Interconnections (OSI)** a communications standard developed by the International Organization for Standardization (ISO) to facilitate compatible network systems

Figure 2. ATM functionality. *Reproduced by permission of Gale, a part of Cengage Learning.*

Upper layer functions		upper layers	
Convergence	CS		AAL
Segmentation & Reassembly	SAR		
Generic Flow Control Cell header generation/extraction Cell VPI/VCI Translation Cell multiplex and de-multiplex		ATM	
Cell rate Decoupling HEC generation & verification Cell delineation Transmission frame adaptation Transmission frame generation & recovery	TC		Physical Layer
Bit timing Physical Medium	PM		

the receiving direction. Only assigned and unassigned cells are passed to the ATM layer.

ATM Layer   The ATM layer is next above the physical layer. The ATM layer takes the data to be sent and adds the 5-byte header information. It performs the following four actions:

■ Cell header generation/extraction, which adds the appropriate ATM cell header to the received cell information field from the upper layer in the transmit direction. It does the opposite in the receive direction.

■ Cell multiplex and demultiplex function, which multiplexes cells from individual virtual channels and virtual paths into one resulting cell stream in the transmit direction. It divides the arriving cell stream into individual cell flows to VCs or VPs in the receive direction.

■ VPI and VCI translation, which is performed at the ATM switching and/or cross-connect nodes.

■ Generic Flow Control (GFC), which supports control of the ATM traffic flow in a customer network.

ATM Adaptation Layer   The AAL performs the adaptation of OSI higher layer protocols, as most applications cannot deal directly with cells. The Adaptation Layer assures the appropriate service characteristics, and divides all types of data into the 48-byte payload that will make up the ATM cell. AAL is further divided into two sublayers: Segmentation and Reassembly (SAR) and Convergence Sublayer (CS).

The SAR sublayer performs segmentation of the higher layer information into a size suitable for the payload of the ATM cells of a virtual connection and, at the receiving side, it reassembles the contents of the cells of a virtual connection into data units to be delivered to the higher layers. The CS sublayer performs functions like message identification and time/clock recovery.

Key Benefits of ATM

ATM offers significant benefits to users and those who design and maintain communications networks. Because network transport functions can be separated into those related to an individual logical connection (virtual connection) and those related to a group of logical connections (virtual path), ATM simplifies network management. ATM also allows for the integration of networks, improving efficiency and manageability and providing a single network for carrying voice, data, and video.

ATM increases network performance and reliability because the network is required to deal with fewer aggregated entities. There is also less processing needed and it takes less time to add new virtual channels because capacity is reserved beforehand on a virtual path connection. Finally, ATM offers a high degree of infrastructure compatibility. Because ATM is not based on a specific type of physical transport, it can be transported over twisted pair, coaxial, and fiber optic cables.

 See also **Internet • Network Design • Networks • World Wide Web**

Resources

Books

Stallings, William. "Asynchronous Transfer Mode (ATM)." *Data and Computer Communications*. 5th ed. Upper Saddle River, NJ: Prentice Hall, 1997.

Sudkamp, Thomas A. *Languages and Machines: An Introduction to the Theory of Computer Science*. Indianapolis, IN: Addison Wesley, 2005.

Wah, Benjamin W. *Wiley Encyclopedia of Computer Science and Engineering*. Hoboken, NJ: John Wiley, 2009.

Periodicals

ATM Forum. "Asynchronous Transfer Mode Technology: The Foundation for Broadband Networks" *NSDL Scout Report for Math, Engineering, and Technology* (July 19, 2002).

Web Sites

Cisco Connection Online. "Asynchronous Transfer Mode (ATM) Switching." http://www.cisco.com/en/US/docs/internetworking/technology/handbook/atm.html#wp1020552 (accessed October 4, 2012).

* **retinal scan** a scan of the retina of the eye, which contains a unique pattern for each individual, in order to identify (or authenticate) someone

* **encrypted** coded, usually for purposes of security or privacy

Authentication

Authentication is the process of verifying the identity of something or someone, often for security purposes, through some unique characteristic. Although the term has a specific meaning in the context of computer use, authentication is something people do on a regular basis. An object may be identified to an expert as an "authentic" antique by its manufacturer's mark or signature. An individual will be "authenticated" to family and friends by face recognition, or in the case of speaking, voice recognition. So for instance, in a telephone call to a friend, the caller is granted access to information that the call recipient regards as appropriate based on the recipient's recognition of the caller's voice. This is a basic form of authentication. In the computer world, authentication is the process by which a user (a person or a device) is granted access to a computer, a computer network, an application, or another form of information that is contained in or protected by a device or software.

Authentication can take numerous forms, and can require several factors. There are one-, two-, and three-factor authentication methods. A factor is a single representation of a user's identity. For example, in two-factor authentication, a user is required to provide two pieces of information in order to be verified by the requestor. The most common method of two-factor authentication is the use of a user identification name or account, and a password. The more factors that are involved, the higher the reliability of the verification process.

To be permitted access to a computer, a database, or a web site, for example, a user must provide unique credentials in response to a query from a device or requesting resource. This unique information could be a user identifier (userid or ID) and password combination, as mentioned earlier. It could also be a one-time use password or passcode, a token to be read by a special reader or application, or a biometric device used to read biological information that is obviously unique to the user, such as a fingerprint or retinal scan*.

In the case of userid and password combinations, the resource being asked to provide access requires that the user present an ID and password that is supposed to be unique to that individual or user. This information has been previously stored in a database or other application, and is generally encrypted* for added security. When requesting access to the resource, the user provides this combination of ID and password so that it can be compared to the combination that was previously stored. If they match, then access is granted. If not, the system may prompt the user several times for the correct information, and will not grant access until the correct combination is entered. if the number of failed attempts exceeds a predetermined amount, access can be blocked until cleared by an authorized service person. The purpose of this indefinite blocking is to reduce the possibility of access by a non-authorized user who guesses at enough possible combinations to manage an accidental match.

A one-time use passcode or password requires some form of synchronization between the user and resource. For example, a computer system or application performs the duty of generating a passcode at a predetermined interval. The user has a token or other device that also generates the same password or passcode at precisely the same time. When users request access, they must present the generated password or passcode. This passcode or password is generally valid for a predetermined period of time that usually varies from 30 seconds up to 30 minutes. A security benefit with this method is that the passcode is continually changing and one code is valid only within a limited and specific period of time.

A biometric scanner works differently. It may or may not require a userid. Instead, users, via some device, have a small portion of their bodies scanned—most commonly a fingerprint. This information has been previously recorded, as in the case of the userid/password combination described earlier. The requested resource then compares this information with what is on file. This information can be stored in itself or on another resource, and it is generally encrypted for added security. This form of authentication makes it more difficult for someone to impersonate or masquerade as an authorized user by attempting to pass along credentials belonging to someone else. Biometric devices can be expensive. One of the primary hurdles in their widespread use is arguably the societal fear of having a system or organization that possesses biometric data, such as fingerprints.

Another method of authentication involves the use of a token, which is a device or file that contains information permanently stored on or in it. For example, a typical Automated Teller Machine (ATM) requires the use of a card. The card stores the user's account number, along with other information. In addition to using an ATM card to initiate the transaction—neither a driver's license nor a credit card would work, for example—one must also be authenticated by the machine with the use of a personal identification number (PIN). Without the PIN, the user's ATM card will not provide the desired results, and without the card, the PIN is insufficient to identify the user with the bank's computers.

Another form of a token is a digital certificate. This is a file that contains information pertaining to a user or resource. It is stored on a computer or in an application, and it "invisibly" allows a user authorized access to something like an account, web site, or another computer. Digital certificates are becoming more popular as a form of user authentication for web site access or usage. An organization called Certificate Authority (CA) issues a certificate and, in doing so, verifies the identity of the owner. CAs can issue certificates to individuals, computers, or other CAs. Certificates are usually issued for a specific period of time, after which they expire; however, they can generally be renewed.

Authentication can be accomplished by various means. The most widely used method is by using the operating system of the resource a user wishes to access. Virtually all operating systems are able to require users to verify their identity through authentication mechanisms. Organizations

Facial Scans

In the wake of the terrorist attacks on September 11, 2001, in the United States, airport security personnel tested out new technologies designed to improve safety measures. One of the methods was a facial recognition system, which scans people's faces and digitally compares the images against those of suspected terrorists. The technology, however, is not new. Some casinos use such devices to identify people who have been known to cheat.

such as large companies and the government may elect to install additional software programs with more advanced authentication mechanisms built in. This adds another layer of security to the authentication process.

The advent of mobile devices and smartphones poses a new challenge to authentication. These devices are functionally small, portable computers, carrying priceless amounts of sensitive information, from bank account numbers to media to personal memos. Many of them have PIN, pattern and fingerprint recognition installed as security measures. Unfortunately many users find these to be obstructions to their personal use and do not utilize them.

 See also **E-Commerce • Networks • Security**

Resources

Books

Oppliger, Rolf. *Authentication Systems for Secure Networks*. Boston: Artech House Inc., 1996.

Smith, Richard E. *Authentication: From Passwords to Public Keys*. Boston: Addison-Wesley, 2002.

Web Sites

PC World Magazine "Authentication Takes Center Stage for Mobile Device Security" http://www.pcworld.com/article/2011294/authentication-takes-center-stage-for-mobile-device-security.html (accessed November 3, 2012).

B

Bandwidth

Communication channels are classified as analog or digital. Bandwidth refers to the *data throughput capacity* of any communication channel. As bandwidth increases, more information per unit of time can pass through the channel. A simple analogy compares a communication channel to a water pipe. The larger the pipe, the more water can flow through it at a faster rate, just as a high capacity communication channel allows more data to flow at a higher rate than is possible with a lower capacity channel.

In addition to describing the capacity of a communication channel, the term "bandwidth" is frequently, and somewhat confusingly, applied to information transport requirements. For example, it might be specified that a broadcast signal requires a channel with a bandwidth of six MHz to transmit a television signal without loss or distortion. Bandwidth limitations arise from the physical properties of matter and energy. Every physical transmission medium has a finite bandwidth. The bandwidth of any given medium determines its communications efficiency for voice, data, graphics, or full motion video.

Widespread use of the Internet has increased public awareness of telecommunications bandwidth because both consumers and service providers are interested in optimizing the speed of Internet access and the speed with which web pages appear on computer screens.

Analog Signals

Natural signals such as those associated with voice, music, or vision, are analog in nature. Analog signals are represented by a sine wave*, and analog channel capacities are measured in hertz (Hz) or cycles per second. Analog signals vary in amplitude (signal strength) or frequency (signal pitch or tone). Analog bandwidth is calculated by finding the difference between the minimum and maximum amplitudes or frequencies found on the particular communication channel.

For example, the bandwidth allocation of a telephone voice grade channel, which is classified as narrowband*, is normally about 4,000 Hz, but the voice channel actually uses frequencies from 300 to 3,400 Hz, yielding a bandwidth that is 3,100 Hz wide. The additional space, or guardbands, on each side of the voice channel serve to prevent signal overlap with adjacent channels and are also used for transmitting call management information.

* **sine wave** a wave traced by a point on the circumference of a circle when the point starts at height zero (amplitude zero) and goes through one full revolution

* **narrowband** a general term in communication systems pertaining to a signal that has a small collection of differing frequency components (as opposed to broadband which has many frequency components)

Connectivity kits can aid in the development of high bandwidth applications © *AP Images/PRNewsFoto/ Xilinx, Inc.*

* **modem** the contraction of MOdulator DEModulator; a device which converts digital signals into signals suitable for transmission over analog channels, such as telephone lines

Digital Signals

Signals in computing environments are digital. Digital signals are described as discrete, or discontinuous, because they are transmitted in small, separate units, each of which is called a bit (a contraction of *b*inary dig*it*). Digital channel capacities are measured in either bits per second (bps) or signal changes per second, which is known as the baud rate. Although these terms are frequently used interchangeably, bits per second and baud rate are technically not the same. Baud rate is an actual measure of the number of signal changes that occur per second rather than the number of bits actually transmitted per second. Prefixes used in the measurement of data transmission speeds include kilo (thousands), mega (millions), giga (thousands of millions; or billions), and tera (thousands of billions; or trillions). To describe digital transmission capabilities in bits per second, notations such as Kbps, Mbps, Gbps, and Tbps are common.

The telephone system has been in a gradual transition from an analog to a digital network. In order to transmit a digital signal over a conventional analog telephone line, a modem is needed to *modulate* the signal of the sender and *demodulate* the signal for the receiver. The term modem* is an abbreviation of *modulate-demodulate*. Although the core capacity of the telephone network has experienced an explosion in available bandwidth, local access to homes and businesses, referred to as the local loop in the telephone network, frequently is limited to analog connections. Digital transmission is popular because it is a reliable, high-speed service that eliminates the need for modems.

Broadband Communications

Financial and other business activities, software downloads, video conferencing, and distance education have created a need for greater bandwidth. The term broadband is used to refer to hardware and media that can support a wide bandwidth. Coaxial cable and microwave transmission are classified as broadband. Coaxial cable, used for cable television, has a bandwidth of 500,000,000 Hz, or 500 megahertz (MHz), and microwave transmission has a bandwidth of 10,000 Hz (or 10 KHz).

The capacity potential of broadband devices is considerably greater than that of narrowband technology, resulting in greater data transmission speeds and faster download speeds, which are important to Internet users. Data transmission speeds range from a low of 14,400 bps on a low speed modem to more than ten gigabits per second on a fiber optic* cable. On the assumption that 50,000 bits represents a page of data, it takes 3.5 seconds to transmit the page at 14,400 bps, but only 8/10 of a second at 64,000 bps. If a page of graphics contains one million bits per page, it takes more than a minute to transmit the page at 14,400 bps, compared to 16 seconds at 64 Kbps. Full motion video requires an enormous bandwidth of 12 Mbps.

Upload versus Download Bandwidth

Among Internet Service Providers (ISPs)* and broadband cable or satellite links, there is considerable difference in upstream, or upload, bandwidth, and downstream, or download, bandwidth. Upstream transmission occurs when one sends information to an ISP whereas downstream transmission occurs when information is received from an ISP. For example, a broadband cable modem connection might transmit upstream at one Mbps and downstream at ten Mbps.

Typical media used to connect to the Internet, along with upstream and downstream bandwidths include: T3 leased lines, T1 leased lines, cable modems, asymmetric digital subscriber lines (ADSLs), integrated services digital networks (ISDNs), and dial-up modems. As noted in Gary P. Schneider and James T. Perry's book *Electronic Commerce*, T3 leased lines provide the fastest speeds (44,700 kbps—equivalent to 44.7 Mbps—for both upstream and downstream speeds) while the rates for T1 leased lines are 1,544 kbps, ISDNs are 128 kbps, and dial-up modems are 56 kbps. ADSL upstream and downstream speeds are 640 kbps and 9,000 kbps (9 Mbps), respectively, while cable modem speeds are 768 kbps upstream and 10,000 kbps (10 Mbps) downstream.

There have been upgrades to many of the specifications for various Internet-delivery technologies. For instance, the first ADSL standard was released back in the 1990s. Improved techniques have led to a number of revisions to the original ADSL standard. ADSL2 and ADSL2+ are upgraded versions of the original ADSL specification. The latest ADSL2+ version, approved in 2008, supports ADSL upstream data rates of 3.5 Mbps and downstream rates of 24 Mbps; those data rates are considerably higher than those supported by the original ADSL specification.

Each of the connections has advantages and disadvantages. As the speed of the medium increases in the broadband media beginning with T1 lines, costs increase substantially. Although classified as broadband,

* **fiber optic** transmission technology using long, thin strands of glass fiber; internal reflections in the fiber assure that light entering one end is transmitted to the other end with only small losses in intensity; used widely in transmitting digital information

* **Internet Service Providers (ISPs)** commercial enterprises which offer paying subscribers access to the Internet for a fee

What is a URL?

The description of the location of an item (document, service, or resource) on the Internet and the means by which to access that item is known as the URL, or Uniform Resource Locator. The URL contains the protocol that will be used to access the item (for example, Hypertext Transfer Protocol, http://), the domain name of the computer that holds the item (for example, www.loc.gov), and the hierarchical description of the location on the computer where the file exists (for example, /foldername/filename.html). Each URL is a precise "address" that is connected to one specific resource.

* **client** a program or computer often managed by a human user, that makes requests to another computer for information

* **Hypertext Transfer Protocol (HTTP)** a simple connectionless communications protocol developed for the electronic transfer (serving) of HTML documents

cable modems are often considered as possessing the optimal in price and performance for the home user.

History of Bandwidth Research

Researchers have studied the effects of bandwidth on network traffic since the 1920s. Research objectives have always focused on the development of encoding techniques and technology enhancements that allow more bits to be transmitted per unit of time. In 1933 Harry Nyquist discovered a fundamental relationship between the bandwidth of a transmission system and the maximum number of bits per second that can be transmitted over that system. The Nyquist Intersymbol Interference Theorem allows one to calculate a theoretical maximum rate at which data can be sent. Nyquist's Theorem encourages data communications professionals to devise innovative coding schemes that will facilitate the maximum transmission of data per unit of time.

In 1948, noting that Nyquist's Theorem establishes an absolute maximum not achievable in practice, Claude Shannon of Bell Labs provided refinements to the theorem to account for the average amount of inherent noise or interference found on the transmission line. Shannon's Theorem can be summarized as saying that the laws of physics limit the speed of data transmission in a system and cannot be overcome by innovative coding schemes.

 See also **Fiber Optics • Networks • Shannon, Claude E. • Telecommunications**

Resources

Books

Comer, Douglas E. *Computer Networks and Internets*. 5th ed. Upper Saddle River, NJ: Prentice Hall, 2009.

Schneider, Gary P. *Electronic Commerce*. 9th ed. Boston: Course Technology Cengage Learning, 2011.

Browsers

A browser is a computer program that allows a computer to display information from the Internet. It also provides a way for the user to access and navigate through this information space.

A browser can also be thought of as a client*, sending requests to Web servers using Hypertext Transfer Protocol (HTTP)*. Whenever a browser is started, or a user clicks on a hyperlink, or a Uniform Resource Locator (URL) is typed in, the browser sends a message to a Web server (based on the address indicated by the URL) to have a file transferred. The browser interprets the information in the file so that it can be viewed in the browser

A popular Web browser. © *Chris Ratcliffe/Bloomberg via Getty Images.*

window, or if necessary, through another program. The information displayed may be text or images. The browser interprets information written in Hypertext Markup Language (HTML)* and displays this information in the browser window.

Files that have sounds or animation may require different programs to enable the information to be heard or seen. Most capabilities are built into the browser but sometimes the computer needs special equipment or programs. To hear sounds, for example, the computer needs a sound card, speakers, and software that enable the sounds to be heard. Some other files need a type of program called a plug-in* in order to be viewed. For example, to read files written in Portable Document Format (PDF), users need to download the Adobe Acrobat program to their computers so the documents can be displayed in the browser window.

Browser Features

More than 100 different browsers exist, and most of them are available to download from the Internet for free; however, not all of them are usable on all computer platforms. There are specialized browsers, for example, that are designed to work only on devices such as personal digital assistants (PDAs)* (e.g., Palm Pilots). Others only work on Macintosh computers, Windows operating systems, or UNIX computers.

As of 2012, the most popular browsers were Microsoft Internet Explorer, Mozilla Firefox, and Google Chrome. Combined, these three browsers, which are all compatible with Windows and Mac, accounted for more than 92 percent of the market share for internet browsers. Internet Explorer, with its 53.6 percent market share, continues to enjoy a significant lead over its opponents. Firefox, by comparison, is second,

* **Hypertext Markup Language (HTML)** an encoding scheme for text data that uses special tags in the text to signify properties to the viewing program (browser) like links to other documents or document parts

* **plug-in** a term used to describe the way that hardware and software modules can be added to a computer system, if they possess interfaces that have been built to a documented standard

* **personal digital assistants (PDAs)** small-scale handheld computers that can be used in place of diaries and appointment books

accounting for 20 percent of desktop computer internet access. Chrome is a close third at 18.9 percent. Since 2009, however, Chrome has made significant gains on both its competitors. That year, Internet Explorer had a 59 percent market share, Firefox had 23 percent, and Chrome sat at just 11 percent.

Most browsers share similar characteristics and elements, and employ many of the same options and techniques. In addition to providing ways for the user to navigate between web pages, browsers also generally allow a user to search for words in an individual web page. A browser also keeps a history of the web pages the user has already visited, and allows the user to organize what has been accessed. Users may save locations of web pages for easy future retrieval. Netscape's Bookmarks and Internet Explorer's Favorites organize URLs into files and save them indefinitely.

A browser allows the user to move between web pages by going back and forward, and features a scrolling device so that the user can move up and down a web page. Most browsers display the title of the current web page being viewed at the very top of the browser window. Browsers have menus with several elements available that can help the user manage the information found on the web. There are options such as saving a web page, sending a page, printing a page, and more. In addition, there are options that allow the user to copy text and other information from the current web page and paste it in other applications. Also included is the ability to search a web page for a word or phrase.

A web browser also provides a way for the user to view the HTML source of the current web page. This is a useful function for web page developers who want to know how a particular page was constructed and which HTML tags and elements were used in its design. The user may also view the vital information about a page, including the date the page was modified or updated, and whether it is a secure document for private transactions.

The option to reload a web page is also provided, as is the option to stop loading a page. Stopping is a useful option when a page is taking a long time to load.

History of Browsers

The browser as it is known today owes its development to Tim Berners-Lee, director of the World Wide Web Consortium (W3C) and a researcher at the Laboratory for Computer Science at the Massachusetts Institute of Technology. It was while working at CERN, the European Particle Physics Laboratory near Geneva, Switzerland, in the 1980s and early 1990s, that Berners-Lee developed the groundwork for the World Wide Web.

Crucial to the web's development was Berners-Lee's work in defining Hypertext Transfer Protocol (HTTP), a set of rules that enable a web page to be browsed using hypertext, and the language computers use to communicate with each other over the Internet. Hypertext, a term coined by Ted Nelson in 1965, and a concept invented by Vannevar Bush in 1945, is defined as a way of presenting information non-sequentially. It includes hyperlinks, or selections of text or images, that when activated by a point-and-click with a mouse, take the user to other related text or images. As the information linked to can include images and sounds as well as text, the term is more aptly named hypermedia.

Berners-Lee completed his work on the first World Wide Web browser in 1990 on a NeXT machine, a personal computer developed by Steve Jobs, founder of Apple Computer. Special features of the NeXT platform made it easier for him to try his idea of programming a hypertext client program on it, and combining it with the Internet.

While there were several hypertext projects being worked on in several countries at the time, none of the projects fit Berners-Lee's vision of what he wanted this system to look like, so he developed his own. He wrote the code for HTTP and invented the Universal Resource Identifier (URI), the scheme for document addresses. The most common type of URI is the URL. The browser he developed was called WorldWideWeb. He later renamed the browser Nexus so as not to confuse it with the World Wide Web itself. He also wrote Hypertext Markup Language (HTML) that contains the rules for formatting pages with hypertext links, or hyperlinks.

The problem with the WorldWideWeb browser was that it only ran on the NeXT computer. Browser clients were needed for use on PCs, Macintosh computers, and UNIX platforms. Universities in Europe and the United States were urged to take on browser creation projects. In 1992 students at Helsinki University developed a browser called Erwise that ran on a UNIX machine. At about the same time, Pei Wei, a student at the University of California, Berkeley, created Viola-WWW, a web browser for UNIX computers that was able to display HTML with graphics, load animations, and download small, embedded applications. Viola-WWW was a precursor to the popular software Hot Java, which was not in use until a few years later.

Mosaic, developed by Marc Andreessen and Eric Bina at the National Center for Supercomputing Applications (NCSA) at the University of Illinois at Urbana-Champaign, was the first widely distributed browser that was compatible with several platforms. It was also the first web browser with a graphical user interface (GUI)*. It was released in 1993 as free, downloadable software on the Internet.

Mosaic introduced the Internet and the World Wide Web to a wide audience. The graphical interface made the web appear more exciting and made the information more accessible to people. Lynx, a text-only browser, was developed at the University of Kansas at around the same time. Lynx is still used by people who are not able to use graphical browsers due to their computers' limitations. It is also useful for users who want to view information only in text format, or those who are visually impaired and find that Lynx is ideal for use with Braille or screen reading software.

Many of the features of Mosaic were integrated into a new browser developed by Netscape Communications, a company formed with Andreessen and other people from the NCSA. In October 1994 Netscape released the first version of its browser, called Mozilla, as a beta, or test

* **graphical user interface (GUI)** an interface that allows computers to be operated through pictures (icons) and mouse-clicks, rather than through text and typing

Hypertext and Hyperlinks

Hypertext is information organized so that it can be connected to other related information in a non-sequential way. The information is linked together by hyperlinks. By clicking on hyperlinks, users can choose various paths through the hypertext material. A hyperlink is a word, phrase, image, or region of an image, often highlighted, that can be selected from a web page. Each hyperlink represents another web page, a location in the current web page, an image or multimedia file, or some other resource on the World Wide Web. When a user clicks on a hyperlink, the browser sends a message to the web server that holds the resource to send it to the user's browser window.

version. The commercial version, Netscape Navigator 1.0, was released in December of 1994 as a free, downloadable software package on the Internet. In August 1995 Microsoft released Windows 95 and the Internet Explorer browser. In the spring of 1998 Microsoft provided the Windows 98 operating system along with Internet Explorer 4.0, which came as an integral part of the operating system. Netscape Navigator and Microsoft Internet Explorer continue to compete with each other as the dominant software options in the web browser market.

Browser Development

The World Wide Web Consortium and other developers continue to try to create speech recognition software that will allow users to interact with the Internet using spoken words. People with visual impairments or those who access the web in situations where their eyes and hands are occupied, will find these browsers helpful. Also possible are browsers that talk back to the user. Other browser developments will include the full support of Extensible Markup Language (XML) and Resource Description Framework (RDF), both of which advance the organization of web information in a structured way. Browser programmers will continue to work on projects that increase the browser's capability to improve human-computer information processing in the complexity of the web environment.

 See also **Bandwidth** • **Internet** • **Internet: Applications** • **World Wide Web**

Resources

Books

Ackermann, Ernest, and Karen Hartman. *Internet & Web Essentials: What You Need to Know.* Wilsonville, OR: Franklin, Beedle, and Associates, 2001.

Berners-Lee, Tim, with Mark Fischetti. *Weaving the Web: The Original Design and Ultimate Destiny of the World Wide Web.* New York: Harper Collins, 2000.

Periodicals

Head, Milena, Norm Archer, and Yufei Yuan. "World Wide Web Navigation Aid." *International Journal of Human-Computer Studies* 53, no. 2 (August 2000): 301–330.

Mintz, Bridget. "Graphics on the Internet." *Computer Graphics World* 23, no. 10 (October 2000): 32–44.

Web Sites

Nermarketshare.com. "Desktop Browser Market Share." http://www.poynter. org/latest-news/top-stories/190586/new-data-show-shifting-patterns-as-people-seek-news-across-platforms/ (accessed October 19, 2012).

C

Censorship: National, International

Censorship is a practice that limits public access to materials, including text, photographs and art, music and video, or other multimedia, based on the value judgments or prejudices of the censoring individuals or groups. According to psychologist Sara Fine, censorship is essentially a defense mechanism triggered by fear of threats of some sort. Whether this fear is based on a real threat, an exaggeration of some actual danger, or an unconscious reaction to some dark, hidden impulse is irrelevant. Thus, just about any material can be censored. Materials most likely to be censored in the United States are those that deal with sex and sexuality, challenge the authority of adults, or differ from the censor's beliefs and traditions.

Librarian Lester Asheim points out that censorship is different from *selection,* which is the process of deciding which resources to include in a museum or library collection, for example, in that censorship favors the control of thought whereas selection favors the liberty of thought. Censorship's approach to materials is negative, seeking vulnerable characteristics within or outside the work, and often without considering the work as a whole. Selection's approach is positive, seeking the merits of the work by examining the entire document. Censorship seeks to protect others from images, ideas, or language deemed by the censor to be negative in some way, whereas selection seeks to protect people's right to read, view, or otherwise experience the material in question. Censors trust only their own intelligence; selectors have faith in the reader's intelligence. In sum, censorship is authoritarian while selection is democratic.

The primary argument against censorship is that it infringes on the First Amendment to the U.S. Constitution which reads: "Congress shall make no law respecting an establishment of religion, or prohibiting the free exercise thereof; or abridging the freedom of speech, or of the press, or the right of the people peaceably to assemble, and to petition the government for a redress of grievances."

Whereas some citizens are strongly against censorship of any kind, believing it is undemocratic, others advocate some censorship on the Internet for several reasons. Chief among them are Web sites featuring adult or child pornography as well as those with racist or hate speech. Many of the concerned people are parents who do not want their kids exposed to such material, which they believe is easily accessible via the Internet. They fear their children might stumble onto such sites while innocently surfing the Web.

An activist supporting the group Anonymous holds a poster as they protest against the Indian government's increasingly restrictive regulation of the Internet. © *STRDEL/AFP/Getty Images.*

* **protocol** an agreed understanding for the sub-operations that make up a transaction, usually found in the specification of inter-computer communications

Censorship and Computers

As it pertains to the world of computing—and to the Internet, in particular—censorship may be accomplished by the use of filtering or blocking software. There are several types of filtering software available: keyword blocking, host or site blocking, and protocol* blocking. These filters generally are promoted as ways to limit access to material deemed undesirable available via the Internet. Parents, schools, and public libraries are the target customers for filtering software.

Keyword blocking indiscriminately targets individual words or strings of words to be blocked; the vocabulary usually consists of taboo words related to parts of the body, sex, political speech, etc.

Host blocking targets specific Internet sites for blocking; the block could include the entire site or only files on that site. Host blocking sometimes results in the politically motivated exclusion of sites dealing with feminism, political opposition, social unrest, or the environment.

Protocol filtering blocks entire domains, such as YouTube or Facebook, which many authoritarian governments believe may be used to disseminate anti-government messages or organize political dissent. This, of course, also limits user access to a wide range of benign content that would not otherwise be censored.

Examples of commercial filtering products are CyberPatrol and NetNanny. These filters have their own web sites and most have test software that can be downloaded. In each case, vendors determine the blocking language and decide which sites should be blocked. However, each offers a password that can turn off the system, and various options for custom configuration of categories.

Censorship Abroad

There are constitutional guarantees and a strong commitment to the full exercise of free speech in the United States. However, this is not the case in many countries of the world. The international organization, Human Rights Watch, issued a report on the global attack on free speech on the Internet. In the document's summary, the threat is clearly stated: "Governments around the world, claiming they want to protect children, thwart terrorists and silence racist and hate mongers, are rushing to eradicate freedom of expression on the Internet ...."

Since 2006, Reporters without Borders, a nongovernmental organization that advocates free speech rights for journalists and citizens, has issued an annual report on countries that severely restrict access to the Internet.

Conclusion

Should cyberspace receive the full freedom of speech and press that is accorded to print materials in the United States, or are there valid arguments for increased restrictions? One might ask: Is a teen more likely to take up smoking because he or she sees pictures of celebrities on the

Internet with cigarettes in hand? Is a child more likely to find lewd pictures on the Internet than in a bookstore or library? These are the types of questions that need to be raised when considering whether the risks of offensive texts or images on the Internet are greater than those from printed materials, and whether they are worth weakening the freedom of speech that is important to protecting political, religious, and personal freedom in the United States.

▶ *See also* **Internet • Internet: Applications • Privacy • Security • World Wide Web**

Resources

Books

Deibert, Ronald, ed. *Access Denied: The Practice and Policy of Global Internet Filtering.* Cambridge, MA: Harvard University Press, 2008.

MacKinnon, Rebecca. *Consent of the Networked: The Worldwide Struggle for Internet Freedom.* New York: Basic Books, 2012.

Morozov, Evgeny. *The Net Delusion: The Dark Side of Internet Freedom.* New York: PublicAffairs, 2011.

Periodicals

Asheim, Lester. "Not Censorship but Selection." *Wilson Library Bulletin* 28 (September 1953): 63–67.

———. "Selection and Censorship: A Reappraisal." *Wilson Library Bulletin* 58, no. 3 (November 1983): 180–184.

Fine, Sara. "How the Mind of a Censor Works: The Psychology of Censorship." *School Library Journal* 42., no. 1 (January 1996): 23–27.

Web Sites

Xindex: The Voice of Free Expression. http://www.indexoncensorship.org/about-free-expression/ (accessed November 7, 2012).

Monitoring Censorship

Various organizations monitor attempts to censor print and electronic materials worldwide. They include: American Civil Liberties Union <http://www.aclu.org/>; Center for Democracy and Technology <http://www.cdt.org/>; Computer Professionals for Social Responsibility <http://www.cpsr.org/>; Electronic Frontier Foundation <http://www.eff.org/>; and Reporters without Borders <http://www.rsf.org>.

Chemistry

The field of chemistry requires the use of computers in a multitude of ways. Primarily, computers are useful for storing vast amounts of data for the researcher or student to use. From facts about the periodic table to displaying 3-D models of molecules for easy visualization, computers are vital in the modern chemistry lab.

Equally important, many aspects of chemistry are explained in mathematical terms, and mathematicians have applied the laws of physics to much of chemistry. The result of this work is a diversity of equations

Technology being used in a university chemistry lab. © *AP Images/The Idaho Press-Tribune, Mike Vogt.*

* **mass spectrometers** instruments that can identify elemental particles in a sample by examining the frequencies of the particles that comprise the sample

that define chemical properties and predict chemical reactions. Because of these equations, for example, one can figure out the volume and density of gases. Equations are also used to calculate atmospheric pressures or to figure out the molecular weight of a solute (dissolved substance) in a solvent.

Typically, chemistry software applications include a multitude of equations. Some equations are quite complex. Using an equation engine, much like using a search engine, allows the user to search for equations and bring them to the desktop in a format that allows for the insertion of values. Because the chemist does not need to recopy complex equations and constants, equation engines save time as well as decrease the chance of errors. Computers then allow the easy and accurate processing of this information.

Computers are so necessary in chemistry that some colleges and universities require chemistry majors to take courses in computer science. The chemist must gain proficiency in using word processors and constructing spreadsheets for presentations. Statistics, statistical methods, and scientific graphing are also important elements in chemistry. Many students learn computer programming to become comfortable with a variety of operating systems. Familiarity with utility programs, networking, and network software is essential. Some knowledge of graphic design allows for the demonstration and manipulation of chemical principles, for example, in molecular modeling.

More and more instruments for chemists are being designed to work seamlessly with computers. Tools such as mass spectrometers* are being interfaced with computers to allow for fast and accurate presentation of complex data. A thorough knowledge of computer architecture allows the chemist to interface these instruments if such interfacing is not readily available. The field of chemistry is also ideally suited to computer assisted instruction. Some universities, such as the Massachusetts Institute of Technology, provide free general chemistry courses online.

Not only are computers helpful as a resource but they can also cut costs, time, and errors in the classroom. For instance, biochemistry students might want to participate in an experiment to study the structure-function relationship of a polypeptide* (including the study of the structure of the using an amino acid analyzer and peptide sequencer). The cost of conducting such an experiment (approximately $200,000) can be a major drawback. The time constraints, even if the study runs smoothly, can also exceed the limits of a single semester course. Computer simulation, however, can make the process much easier and more cost effective. Also, the student's attention can be focused on a specific point of interest instead of being distracted by the endless details involved in the actual experiment.

Computational chemistry is similar to molecular modeling*. Both consist of the interactive combination of visualization and computational techniques. Molecular modeling keeps the emphasis of the work on the visualization of the molecule. Computational chemistry concentrates on the computational techniques. A fine illustration of the use of computers and the Internet with molecular (DNA) modeling was constructed by American molecular biologist James Watson (1928–) of Clare College and British molecular biologist and physicist Francis Crick (1916–2004) of Gonville and Caius College, in Cambridge, England, who had previously received Nobel Prizes for their discovery of the structure of DNA.

Chemists, like scientists in other fields, are growing increasingly dependent upon the Internet. The World Wide Web, and especially e-mail, allows instant mass communication between teachers and students, as well as the isolated chemist and his or her colleagues. Online professional journals are becoming more common, allowing scientists to review literature more easily. The first online chemistry conference was held in 1993 by the American Chemical Society. Online classes are being offered more frequently. The Internet also allows scientists to collaborate on projects with each other without necessarily working in the same building, or even the same continent. The Internet makes it far easier for individuals to participate in professional organizations.

Database management is essential to chemistry. Many databases evolve too quickly and are too extensive to be maintained by a single chemist. The National Institutes of Health (NIH) is a major supplier of resources for molecular modeling for researchers. The Center for Molecular Modeling is part of the Division of Computational Bioscience, Center for Informational Technology. At this Web site, computational chemists work with researchers on the relationships between structure

*polypeptide the product of many amino acid molecules bonded together

*molecular modeling a technique that uses high performance computer graphics to represent the structure of chemical compounds

Chemometrics

Chemometrics, an advanced field of chemistry, utilizes the application of mathematics and statistics to clinical information. One example of chemometrics is pyrolysis mass spectrometry, in which an unidentified material is fixed to a metal strip and heated to a specific temperature. At this temperature, the electrostatic bonds holding the atoms together break. Using the light components given off by the atoms, the mass spectrometer creates a chemical profile, or chemical fingerprint. With these statistics, the chemist is able to identify the material.

and function of molecules. This allows researchers to develop a greater understanding of chemical interactions, enzyme production, ion bonds, and other properties of molecules.

The Internet is also a wonderful resource for students and educators of chemistry. Web resources include tutorials and reference sites for almost all fields and levels of chemistry students, from high school and college. One site, the Schlumberger Excellence in Educational Development, or SEED, Web site, promotes the science and technology to students by introducing lab experiments, providing science news, offering help to teachers, and hosting a question and answer forum. This site offers another forum for one-on-one communication between future scientists and those actively working in the field.

Some chemists have decided that the computer and Internet can allow them to make chemistry entertaining. For example, John P. Selegue and F. James Holler of the University of Kentucky have put their research and technical skills to use by composing a web page that explores the use of the elements of the periodic table (even molybdenum [Mo]) throughout the history of comic books. This site was one of the winners of the 2001 Scientific American's Sci/Tech Web Awards.

The Royal Society for Chemistry Publishing (RSC) is developing a system through which chemistry publications will have added information that enables a computer to understand the meaning of the content. The initiative, Project Prospect, began development in February 2007 with articles being published in a way such that their "data can be read, indexed, and intelligently searched by a machine." This type of information, and similar non-chemistry articles published in the same manner, is indexed together into what is called the semantic web. Technical editors use computer programs to enrich scientific articles with extra information, termed "metadata", which is written in a computer-readable language and hidden. Researchers can click on a compound, a scientific concept, or even data in an enriched article to download structures, get more information on related topics, or link to electronic databases such as the International Union of Pure and Applied Chemistry's (IUPAC) Compendium of Chemical Terminology (or Gold Book).

 See also **Computer Assisted Instruction • Molecular Biology • Physics • Scientific Visualization**

Resources

Books

Kumari, Ramesh. *Computers and Their Applications to Chemistry*. 2nd ed. Oxford: Alpha Science International, 2005.

Random House Reference. *Random House Concise Dictionary of Science & Computers*. New York: Random House, 2004.

* **robotics** the science and engineering of building electromechanical machines that aim to serve as replacements for human laborers

* **photosensitive** describes any material that will change its properties in some way if subjected to visible light, such as photographic film

Web Sites

MIT Open Courseware. "Chemistry." Massachusetts Institute of Technology (MIT), http://ocw.mit.edu/courses/chemistry/ (accessed October 7, 2012).

Schlumberger Excellence in Educational Development. "Student Center." Schlumberger, http://www.planetseed.com/node/3804 (accessed October 7, 2012).

Van Noorden, Richard. "Computers Learn Chemistry." Royal Society of Chemistry (RSC) (February 2007), http://www.rsc.org/chemistryworld/News/2007/February/01020701.asp (accessed October 9, 2012).

Computer Vision

Computer vision is a technical capability that enables a computer to recognize or understand the content of a picture. Robotics* is a field that is particularly affected by the development of computer vision. A robot with vision capability will be much more effective in its workspace than a non-sighted one. Robots with vision can be programmed to respond to unstructured or random changes. For example, imagine that a robot is needed to pick up and use bolts that are lying loose in a box. The bolts can be at any orientation with respect to the gripper and only a sighted robot will have the ability to adapt to this random configuration. A robot with no vision system would have to be pre-programmed by somebody to know exactly where every bolt was lying in the box—not a very cost-effective solution.

Human vision, which is what one would normally expect a computer to be able to mimic, is actually a more complex process than most people might imagine. The human eye is composed of a flexible lens. Muscles around the periphery of the lens can stretch the lens so that it becomes thinner and its focal length increases, or the muscles can compress the lens so that it becomes thicker as its focal length decreases. These adjustments all take place automatically as far as humans are concerned; people make no conscious effort to adjust the focal length of the lenses of the eyes. Instead, whether people look at distant objects or those nearby, the eye automatically adjusts to focus accordingly. A vision system connected to a computer cannot function this way; the machine must be designed and programmed to distinguish between far and near objects and then have the capacity to adjust its focus accordingly.

As well as managing lens adjustment, the human eye has an intricately structured light sensitive film at the back of the eye called the retina. The retina is photosensitive*, so it collects the focused light and converts it into signals that are dispatched to the brain. The light-sensitive elements are classified as either cones or rods. There are approximately six to seven million cones in the retina, mostly grouped around its center. The cones

* **isosceles triangle** a triangle that has two sides of equivalent length (and therefore two angles of the same size)

* **ultrasonic** the transmission and reception of sound waves that are at frequencies higher than those audible to humans

* **radar** the acronym for RAdio Direction And Ranging; a technique developed in the 1930s that uses frequency shifts in reflected radio waves to measure distance and speed of a target

* **pixel** a single picture element on a video screen; one of the individual dots making up a picture on a video screen or digital image

are responsive to variations in the wavelength of the light that reaches them—this means they are the receptors of color. The cones can also sense a variation in light intensity and as such are the principle enablers of daylight vision.

The function of rods is slightly different. There are about 130 million of them and they are predominantly found around the periphery of the retina. Rods are really only sensitive to the amount of light and tend to be more useful in assisting with night vision. The rods and cones are connected by minute nerve endings that all tend to gather at one point on the retina, where the optic nerve connects the eye and the brain. Arranging for a computer to incorporate a device that could act in a way that is anything like a retina is challenging.

The fact that humans have two eyes that are forward-facing makes it possible, with the help of the brain, to perceive depth. The two lines of sight between each eye and one object in focus, together with the line between the two eyes, form an isosceles triangle*. The height of the triangle provides a perception of the distance between the plane that contains the eyes, and the object itself. A computer vision system attempting to simulate human vision would also have to try to deal with distance perception. It is possible, though, that distance measurement might be attained in other ways in a computer system; for example, a computer's sensory system could be augmented with extra facilities that use ultrasonic* or radar* techniques.

Components of Computer Vision

A computer vision system requires one or more television cameras that are capable of digitizing an image so that these can be stored in memory. A processor will then be commanded to analyze the information by identifying and defining any objects that may be significant. It then deals with primary objects differently than it does with objects from the scene or background. There are several commonly used camera types, but in all cases, they operate by transferring an image into horizontal scan lines that make up a picture. In most cases, the cameras and the central processor will be assisted by two other elements: a frame-grabber and an image pre-processor.

The frame-grabber is a special device that can take an image from the camera, digitize it if it has not already been digitized, and make it available as one object to the remainder of the system. The digitized images tend to be rather large blocks of data. Each individual pixel* in the image will have parameters for brightness, and perhaps color, associated with it. Thousands of these are found in just one static picture, and as soon as either the scene or the camera position changes, some or all of the data associated with the pixels changes and must therefore be updated.

In order to help with the management of these large amounts of data, the pre-processor assists by discarding parts of the image that are not considered useful, thereby reducing the image size and the computational effort involved in dealing with the image. It does this by various means, but one common way is to group together collections of pixels that have almost the same color or brightness values and changing them so that they are all the same. This obviously distorts the original image, but it can be a successful optimization technique if none of the important image information is lost. Unfortunately, it is difficult to guarantee that all the important information will always be safeguarded.

Steps of Computer Vision

Once an image has been captured by the camera and set up for further operations by the pre-processor, then the real business of computer vision can begin. One of the important results of the pre-processing operations is known as edge-detection. Here, the pre-processor identifies areas of the image that possess regions of clearly differing light intensity. This is the first step in providing the vision system with a way of recognizing objects.

The next step is called image segmentation. Segmentation is an operation whereby the vision system tries to identify particular shapes or regions by differentiating them from their backgrounds. It does this by choosing an intensity threshold level and organizing the image so that all pixels darker than this level are sectioned off from all those that are lighter. This breaks the image up into segments that will correspond directly to the main features and objects in the field of view. The difficulty is in selecting the most suitable threshold level; normally there will be a way to adjust the threshold so that the most satisfactory segmentation results can be produced.

Image segmentation can be artificially enhanced, if the environment is conducive to it, by intentionally selecting bland and uniform backgrounds that contrast in color and brightness with objects in the foreground. Image segmentation can also be carried out using attributes of the image other than light intensity such as color or texture.

After segmentation has been completed, the next step is image extraction and recognition. Segmentation permits regions of the image to be isolated, but getting the computer system to recognize what it is looking at requires further effort. This operation requires training the computer system to be aware of certain specific objects and shapes that it is expected to encounter. This is easier to do if one limits the nature of the working environment of the machine. The computer can be given data sets of standard objects called templates and then can be asked to ascertain similarities among these templates and the segments of the images that it captures. It uses statistical techniques to attempt to determine what types of objects it is looking at, based on the templates that it has been given.

Computer vision is important in manufacturing and other industry areas that use robotic technology, but it is also being developed to assist with pattern recognition* and provide support to visually impaired people.

* **pattern recognition** a process used by some artificial-intelligence systems to identify a variety of patterns, including visual patterns, information patterns buried in a noisy signal, and word patterns imbedded in text

NESSY Demonstrates Visual Learning

Some researchers at the University of Bielefeld (Germany) have produced a computer-based system called NESSY, which demonstrates object recognition at the Heinz Nixdorf Museums Forum. Assisted by neural networks, NESSY learns about the shape and form of various objects and then recognizes them automatically. Visitors to the demonstration are invited to move the objects about in a small enclosure so that NESSY can be seen to observe and recognize them.

Driverless Cars

An autonomous car, one that does not need a human driver, is able to drive itself by sensing the environment around it in order to make appropriate navigational moves. To do so, the driverless cars use a combination of radar, LIDAR (LIght Detection And Ranging), GPS (global positioning system), and computer vision. As of October 2012, the states of Nevada, Florida, and California have passed laws to permit driverless cars on their roads and highways. In fact, American Internet-related product and service provider, Google, lobbied California to pass the state law because it has already developed driverless cars for its employees to use while commuting to work. According to the California law, autonomous cars are allowed in California as long as a licensed driver occupies the driver seat in case the technology fails.

Competition Involving Computer Vision

The Defense Advanced Research Projects Agency (DARPA) sponsors a competition involving autonomous vehicles called the DARPA Grand Challenge. The objective of the competition is to promote the technology of driver-less vehicles in order to meet the U.S. military's stated goal of having one-third of its vehicles supporting its ground forces functioning autonomously (i.e., without the direct intervention or guidance of humans) by 2015. Competitions were held in 2004, 2005, and 2007. Many teams that entered autonomous vehicles in those competitions made use of some sort of computer vision in order to supply information about the terrain to their vehicle's onboard computer(s). Those vehicles used the visual data they gathered to help navigate the vehicle over a route from start to finish. Competitions in different years emphasized different environments, from the twisting, bumpy terrain that characterizes an off-road course, to the urban setting; indeed, the November 3, 2007, competition was called the DARPA Urban Challenge. The $2 million top prize went to the Tartan Racing team, which used a modified Chevy Tahoe nicknamed Boss. The Tartan team states that Boss "is equipped with more than a dozen lasers, cameras and radars to view the world." DARPA management has announced that its next Grand Challenge would be called the DARPA 2012 Robotics Challenge.

Using humanoid robots, the goal of this challenge is to develop ground-based robotics capable of executing complicated tasks in dangerous environments. Launched in October 2012, the Robotics Challenge will extend for about 27 months, with one virtual competition in June 2013, followed by two live competitions in December 2013, and December 2014. According to the Federal Business Opportunities (FBO) article *Sole Source Intent Notice for Humanoid Robot Systems for the DARPA Robotics Challenge Program*, the American engineering and robotics design company Boston Dynamics Inc. (BDI), headquartered in Waltham, Massachusetts, will build all eight of the robots used in the competition. The FBO article states, "This effort will develop approximately eight identical platforms consisting of two legs, torso, on board computing, two arms with hands, and a sensor head. BDI will deliver these robots to DARPA so they can be provided to the top software development teams based on the results of the Virtual Disaster Challenge. Boston Dynamics will also provide in the field support and as required maintenance to the delivered systems."

▶ See also **Artificial Intelligence** • **Optical Technology** • **Pattern Recognition** • **Robotics**

Resources

Books

Szeliski, Richard. *Computer Vision: Algorithms and Applications*. New York: Springer, 2010.

Yoshida, Sota R., ed. *Computer Vision*. Hauppauge, NY: Nova Science, 2011.

Web Sites

Federal Business Opportunities. "Sole Source Intent Notice for Humanoid Robot Systems for the DARPA Robotics Challenge Program." https://www.fbo.gov/index?s=opportunity&mode=form&id=1a693d7823dcc435068066b4637c516a&tab=core&_cview=0 (accessed October 1, 2012).

Forbes and Joann Muller. "With Driverless Cars, Once Again It Is California Leading The Way." http://www.forbes.com/sites/joann-nmuller/2012/09/26/with-driverless-cars-once-again-it-is-california-leading-the-way/ (accessed October 1, 2012).

University of California at Berkeley, and Jitendra Malik. "Computer Vision: The Fundamentals." https://www.coursera.org/#course/vision (accessed October 1, 2012).

Cookies

In the World Wide Web, a computer "cookie" is a small piece of data that a Web server sends to an Internet user's computer along with the requested Web page. The Web browser is supposed to save the cookie and send it together with all future requests to the same server (or group of servers). Although there are privacy and security concerns that cause some Internet users to block cookies, there is no danger that cookies will damage data on a user's computer or server; cookies cannot contain viruses since they are not executable files.

When a user clicks on a hyperlink, the browser sends a request to the web server specified in the Uniform Resource Locator (URL)* underlying the hyperlink. The formal syntax* for such requests and the corresponding answer (response) is regulated by the Hypertext Transfer Protocol (HTTP)*. For performance reasons, HTTP was designed to be "stateless"—which means that each request is treated in isolation. After a Web server answers a request, the connection between the browser and the server is closed within seconds. The HTTP protocol has no notion of a session (with logon and logoff). For some Internet activity this is a serious limitation; therefore, cookies were invented by Netscape as an extension to the HTTP protocol.

What Does a Cookie Do?

Cookies identify and track users of Web sites. For instance, in an online shop, a user navigates through a number of pages to fill a "shopping basket." The Web server tracks user activity by means of cookies. The very first time a user enters an online shop, the Web server notices that no identifying cookie was received with the request for Web page access. Therefore, the Web server generates a new unique number and sends it in a cookie, along with the response. In future requests from that user

* **Uniform Resource Locator (URL)** a reference to a document or a document container using the Hypertext Transfer Protocol (HTTP); consists of a hostname and path to the document

* **syntax** a set of rules that a computing language incorporates regarding structure, punctuation, and formatting

* **Hypertext Transfer Protocol (HTTP)** a simple connectionless communications protocol developed for the electronic transfer (serving) of HTML documents

to the same server, the browser will automatically include the cookie, which will alert the server that the user is continuing with his/her shopping session. The contents of the shopping basket are stored on the Web site's server, indexed by the cookie. When the user purchases something from the shopping basket, thus identifying him or herself by name and address, that information, along with the number of the cookie, is stored on the server.

Personalized Web pages also depend on cookies: Some online shops make special offers to returning customers based on their previous buying behavior or suggest new products that are similar to previous purchases. Other Web sites allow their users to customize the appearance or contents of the page as it appears on their computer screen.

Search engines can use cookies to track users and build up a list of search terms the user has entered previously. This information can be used to display advertisements to the user, related to his or her interests. Normally, the search engine will not know the name and address of the user, only the unique number linked to the user's computer.

Cookie Concerns

Advertisements on web pages are often managed by specialized agencies, rather than by the companies that operate the web servers. Such agencies can send cookies alongside the images containing the advertisement. Agencies that manage advertisements on a relatively large subset of the World Wide Web can build up quite a detailed profile of interests for users. As long as they do not know the names and addresses of the users, this might be acceptable. However, through collaboration with online shops, the information of the shop and the advertising agency can be brought together. Technically, the shop refers to images stored on the Web server of the advertising agency. In the URLs referencing the images, the unique identifications of users in the shop are included. The server of the advertising agency then gets its own cookies together with the name and address information from the online shop.

Because of such possible privacy problems, web browsers allow users some options to switch cookies off. If a user so chooses, the browser will simply throw away the cookies sent by a server and will not include them in future requests. However, some online shops will not work without cookies. Other shops add the unique number to the hypertext links embedded in the pages. This works only as long as the user stays within the shop; subsequent visits appear as being from a new user.

Internet Explorer stores cookies in "C:\WINDOWS\COOKIES" or "C:\WINDOWS\Temporary Internet Files." Netscape stores cookies in a file called "cookies" or "cookies.txt." A text editor like Wordpad will show the name of the cookie, the contents of the cookie, and the domain of the originating Web server plus some additional data (e.g., expiration time). The same server can define several cookies. It is possible for users to delete cookies (the browser must be closed first), but if a user returns later to a web site for which cookies have been deleted, the site's server will not recognize personalized options.

Some cookies contain passwords. This is a security risk, especially if different people have access to the same computer. In addition, the cookie and history folders on a PC give a good picture of the kind of Web pages that were viewed by previous users of that PC.

▶ *See also* **Internet • Internet: Applications • Privacy • Security • World Wide Web**

Resources

Books

Ladd, Eric, Jim O'Donnell, et al. *Using HTML 4, XML, and Java 1.2, Platinum Edition.* Indianapolis: Que, 1999.

Periodical

Kristol, David M. "HTTP Cookies: Standards, Privacy, and Politics." *ACM Transactions on Internet Technology* 1, no. 2 (2001): 151–198.

Web Sites

Adhikari, Richard. TechNewsWorld "Internet Explorer Flaw Lets Hackers Into the Cookie Jar." http://www.technewsworld.com/story/72539.html (accessed October 16, 2012).

Electronic Privacy Information Center (EPIC). "Cookies." http://www.epic.org/privacy/internet/cookies (accessed October 22, 2012).

Whalen, David. "The Unofficial Cookie FAQ." *Cookie Central.* http://www.cookiecentral.com/faq (accessed October 22, 2012).

Copyright

Copyright is a legal framework that protects some forms of intellectual property, including works of the mind such as music and art. Copyright includes not only the right to make copies of a work—called the right of reproduction—it also includes several other rights, including the right to distribute, adapt, publicly perform, and publicly display a work. By allowing authors to control reproduction and other uses of their creative works for a period of time, copyright enables authors to make money by charging for such uses during the copyright term. This in turn creates a financial incentive for authors to invest time and effort to produce new works.

In the United States, the period of copyright control lasts for different periods of time, depending upon who the author may be. The copyright

Privacy Threat

In the communication between Web browsers and Web servers, cookies are used to link together several page requests to one session. They are useful because otherwise each time a user clicks on a Web link, the page request is treated in isolation. However, cookies can endanger the privacy of the Web server.

In 2011, Italian internet security researcher Rosario Valotta discovered a flaw in Microsoft's Internet Explorer Web browser that allowed hackers to access a victim's computer by tricking them into sending the hacker their browser's cookies. Once the cookie was acquired, a hacker could use the information to access the victim's security credentials, which reveals private information and, potentially, more websites with more information. Valotta dubbed the process "cookiejacking."

Kim Dotcom, founder of Megaupload.com, speaks to the media as he leaves the high court in Auckland, New Zealand in 2012. Dotcom was indicted by the U.S. for orchestrating the country's biggest copyright infringement conspiracy. © *Brendon O'Hagen/Bloomberg via Getty Images.*

term for a work created by a natural person is the lifetime of the author plus seventy years. The copyright term for a work created by a corporation, through its employees, is 120 years from the date of creation or 95 years from the date of publication, whichever first expires. After a copyright expires, the work falls into the public domain for anyone to use.

The proliferation of computer technology posed several problems for traditional copyright owners. Computer technology typically functions by reproducing copies of something in memory devices: when a computer file, such as a digitized music file, is digitally transmitted or downloaded, a copy is being made. Computers therefore make reproduction and distribution of digitized works cheap and easy, and the technology to do so has become widely available at a low cost.

This is good news for information consumers, because the cost of access to creative works becomes minimal; nearly everyone can afford access. But this is bad news for information producers, because they make no money from virtually free, unauthorized digital copies, and so they have less incentive to produce the works in the first instance. Copyright law, which provides artists and authors the legal right to prohibit unauthorized digital reproduction, is more difficult to enforce when the technology to make such reproductions is widespread. Much of the public controversy over copyright and the Internet, such as the debate that took place over the Napster peer-to-peer music trading service during 2000, revolves around this clash between the interests of information consumers and those of information producers. In the Napster controversy, a lawsuit filed against the company led to the termination of its online services in 2001, which in turn forced the company into liquidation in late 2002. Eventually, Napster was reconstituted as an online fee-based music subscriber service (in contrast to its original free download service, which was found to violate copyright laws), and in 2008 was purchased by the consumer electronics company Best Buy for 121 million dollars. In 2010, Napster could boast of having more than 10 million songs available for download to its paying subscribers, but was eclipsed in popularity by iTunes (the service that made paid digital media profitable and popular) and online music streaming subscription and free services such as Pandora and Spotify. Napster merged with the online music subscription service Rhapsody 2011.

Some digital copying has been justified on the basis of "fair use," which is a limited user right that allows unauthorized use of portions of a copyrighted work for certain select purposes. The fair use privilege is especially important in allowing study, scholarship, commentary, and criticism of copyrighted works. For example, quoting a few lines of a book in a book review would be a classic example of fair use. Without the fair use privilege, copying the lines out of the book would constitute infringement, and could not be done without the permission of the copyright owner.

In the United States, the standard for fair use is extremely flexible, depending upon the circumstances of the use: In some instances, using an entire work without permission might be a fair use, whereas in many instances, fair use might permit the use of only a small portion. However, the fair use privilege is not unlimited, and many instances of unauthorized digital copying exceed the privilege. Other countries recognize a much more narrow user right of "fair dealing," which allows a few specific unauthorized uses of a copyrighted work, such as for news reporting.

Establishing Copyright

Such controversies are likely to be widespread because the majority of creative works, including those found in digital format on the Internet or elsewhere, are likely to be copyrighted. Unlike patents for inventions, which must be applied for and approved, copyrights arise spontaneously when the work is fixed. As soon as pen is set to paper, or brush to canvas, or fingers to keyboard, the author holds rights in the resulting work. No application or registration is necessary. The work may be registered with the Copyright Office if the author wishes, and doing so affords the author the ability to pursue copyright violators in the courts, but this is optional.

There are benefits for choosing to register the work. In particular, the copyright cannot be enforced in a U.S. court unless it has been registered. There are also benefits to placing a copyright notice on the work. Many creators use digital watermarks to note copyrighted material (such as photographs) on the Internet, but the author is not required to do so to protect their work legally. This presents a problem for consumers who wish to use a work, as it may be copyrighted even though there is no notice of copyright attached to the work. Because copyright arises automatically, it is likely that any given work is copyrighted unless the work is old enough for the copyright to have expired, or unless it falls into a category of uncopyrightable subject matter.

Computer Sciences, 2nd Edition

* **intangible** a concept to which it is difficult to apply any form of analysis; something which is not perceived by the sense of touch

* **tangible** of a nature that is real, as opposed to something that is imaginary or abstract

What Is Covered? What Is Not?

Copyright traditionally has covered literary works, such as books, plays, and poems; musical works; sound recordings; pictorial and graphic works, such as paintings, drawings, cartoons, and photographs; and audiovisual works, such as motion pictures and graphic animation. Court decisions and international treaties have recognized that these types of works are protected by copyright, whether they are in digital format or in hardcopy. Additionally, in the United States since 1978, copyright covers computer software, which has been considered a kind of literary work. The 1996 Digital Millennium Copyright Act (DMCA) further extended protection of digital works by prohibiting the use and distribution of technology and services that circumvent digital rights management (DRM) schemes including copyrights in digital materials. Most other countries around the world have added software to the list of copyrightable works. Copyright also covers the original selection and arrangement of collections or compilations of information, including databases. Thus, a great deal of the content found in digitized formats falls within the subject matter of copyright.

Copyright does not cover facts, short phrases or words, ideas, processes, or "unfixed" works. For example, an improvisational theater performance or musical "jam session" will not be covered by copyright if it is not recorded because if it is unrecorded, the work is unfixed. At the same time, if a concert goer were to record the session without authorization and publish that recording, he or she likely would be in violation of the author's rights with respect to their performance. Similarly, a measurement or a law of nature cannot be copyrighted because they are facts that did not originate from an author, but which simply exist as part of the world. Business names or book titles usually are not copyrightable because they are short phrases or words. Individual recipes and game rules usually are not copyrightable because they simply describe processes. Thus, the copyright on a work such as a computer program extends to the original expression of the program—the software code—but not to the underlying computer functions or processes.

The fundamental premise of copyright law is the distinction between a copy and the work. The work is the abstract, intangible*, intellectual work that is embodied in a tangible* copy. Works may be embodied in paper, canvas, stone, celluloid film, computer memory devices, digital medium, or almost any other kind of material. Copyright grants authors the right to control the underlying work but does not necessarily grant the copyright holder rights in a particular copy. This contrast is perhaps best illustrated in U.S. copyright's "First Sale" doctrine. The purchaser of a particular copy does not by virtue of the purchase gain rights in the work. The copyright in the work still rests with the author or copyright owner, so the purchaser of the copy is still precluded from, for example, reproducing the work by creating additional copies embodying the work. But the purchaser does generally have the right to dispose of his copy as

* **intellectual property** the acknowledgement that an individual's creativity and innovation can be owned in the same way as physical property

he wishes, by reselling it, giving it away, or even destroying it. The copyright owner may, of course, also sell the copyright to the work, but that is a different matter from selling copies of the work. And here again, digital technology has changed the interpretation and implementation of copyright protection. When the purchaser or owner of a traditional hardcopy embodiment of a copyrighted work, such as a sound recording, gave away or sold the copy, no new copies were created; the purchased unit itself passed from one person to another. In contrast, transfer of ownership of a digital work usually means no physical object is handed over; instead, a digital copy is rendered to the recipient.

International Copyright and Computer Technology

The international nature of the Internet poses certain challenges for copyright law. As in the case of patents, there is no international copyright or universally recognized copyright; copyright laws differ from nation to nation. When digitized works are transmitted from one country to another, it may be very difficult to determine which country's copyright law should apply. This situation is not as problematic as it could be because many nations have signed an international treaty, the Berne Convention, which sets minimum standards for copyright protection. It also requires nations to accord the citizens of other signatory nations the same rights that it gives to its own citizens. Additionally, the standards of the Berne Convention have been adopted as part of the series of intellectual property* treaties accompanying membership in the World Trade Organization (WTO). Consequently, the basics of copyright are similar among most nations, although variations are possible. Interestingly, in 2009 a WTO panel ruled that China had failed to uphold its obligations properly under the WTO to enforce rights sufficently, including violations of copyright laws. Shortly thereafter, Chinese government officials pledged to increase their enforcement of both domestic and international rights.

Owners of copyrighted works may also use technological measures to prevent unauthorized uses of their works in digital form. These may include software or hardware devices that prevent reproduction or use of the protected content unless a password or other access code is obtained from the owner of the content. Many countries have adopted laws making it illegal to disable, tamper with, or "hack" around such content management devices. A 2012 survey of 15,000 computer users in 35 countries by lobbying group Business Software Alliance found that 57 percent of respondents admitted to using pirated software (software that is unlicensed, illegally copied, or illegally obtained.) The organization estimated that digital piracy cost the software industry $63.4 billion (USD) in 2011.

To facilitate the sharing and use of digital content, the U.S. nonprofit organization Creative Commons (CC) developed a free-of-charge copyright licensing scheme. Creative Commons licenses allow creators to communicate precisely which rights they reserve, such as author attributions or limiting commercial use. Authors can even elect to waive all rights, signaling to others that an item is free to use without restriction. The standard CC designations have become popular with Internet users internationally, even though underlying copyright laws vary from country to country.

▶ *See also* **Internet: Applications • Patents • Security • World Wide Web**

Resources

Books

Klemens, Ben. *Math You Can't Use: Patents, Copyright, and Software.* Washington, DC: Brookings Institution Press, 2006.

LaFrance, Mary. *Copyright Law in a Nutshell.* 2nd ed. St. Paul, MN: West Publishing, 2011.

McJohn, Stephen M. *Copyright: Examples & Explanations.* 3rd ed. New York: Wolters Kluwer Law &amp Business, 2012.

Web Sites

U.S. Copyright Office. "Laws and Regulations." http://www.copyright. gov/laws/ (accessed November 5, 2012).

Credit Online

Credit online can have two meanings. It refers to services that provide online credit verification on companies that conduct business over the Internet. It can also refer to online credit card applications and obtaining credit reports for individuals.

With the enormous growth of the Internet and electronic commerce, online credit, or trust, has become an increasingly important issue. Although the Internet offers tremendous new opportunities in business and other areas, there are also great uncertainties and risks in the online world. Concerns about an online store's credit history, security features, reliability, and customer service for online purchases should be addressed before submitting personal information and payment.

Credit can be defined as a belief and a confidence in the reliability of the other party. A potential creditor can check the credit of an individual or a company by assessing the party's past behavior. A lender also may be able to infer a party's credit by examining its ability to meet its obligations; for example, by looking at a company's financial information—such as assets, earnings, and stock price—to have a better understanding of the company's trustworthiness.

In the world of the Internet, consumers often deal with a distant party that can be identified only by an Internet address. Vendors can set up a secure Web site for conducting transactions to protect customers' financial information from being intercepted by a third party. However, this does not prevent the vendor from abusing the customer's credit. An online business must have a good reputation in order for consumers to have confidence in doing business with the company. Credit between long-term business partners can develop through past business experiences. Among strangers, however, trust is much more difficult to build because strangers lack known past histories. Given these factors, the temptation for someone to cheat over the Internet could outweigh the incentive to cooperate. Two types of credit systems can help consumers overcome these concerns.

Building Online Trust

An Internet reputation system allows a customer to verify a company's credit even though the customer has never interacted with the firm before. At eBay, the largest person-to-person online auction site, although the company offers limited insurance and buyers and sellers have to accept significant risks, the overall rate of fraud remains astonishingly low. eBay attributes this to its reputation system. After a transaction is complete, buyers have the opportunity to rate the seller and leave comments. The reputation system at eBay serves as a credit system for its customers. Before purchasing an item, a new buyer can check the seller's credit by examining its ratings from past customers. Such reputation systems are not limited to eBay and other auction sites, however. For example, Bizrate.com rates online retailers by asking consumers to complete a survey after each purchase.

Online credit can also be established through third-party endorsement and assurance. Usually, the third party has a good reputation and is highly trusted in society. For example, the Better Business Bureau (BBB) offers two programs to endorse companies that have met the BBB's standard. The reliability program confirms that a company is a member of a local Better Business Bureau, that it has been reviewed to meet truth-in-advertisement guidelines, and that it follows good customer service practices. The privacy program can confirm that a company stands behind its online privacy policy and has met the program requirements regarding the handling of personal information that is provided through its website. The BBB gives qualifying companies a seal of endorsement. The seal can then be displayed on the qualifying company's Web site, encouraging users to check BBB information on the company.

Companies such as eBay and the BBB that provide online credit services utilize the Internet and World Wide Web to collect information on online merchants and make the credit information available on the Internet. For example, customers at eBay can easily submit comments on a particular seller online. eBay then collects the comments electronically, saves them in a database, and makes the compiled information available to all potential buyers. In order to get a BBB seal of endorsement, companies can go to the BBB website and apply electronically. Consumers can

Online Fraud

According to MSNBC, research companies that conduct studies about credit card fraud disagree regarding the extent of the problem. While some analysts cite the occurrence of online credit card theft as about 3.5 times higher than non-Internet credit card fraud, others claim the rate to be about ten times greater.

*Hypertext Markup Language (HTML) an encoding scheme for text data that uses special tags in the text to signify properties to the viewing program (browser) like links to other documents or document parts

also use the Internet to file complaints with the BBB if they are unsatisfied with the service of a company.

For these online credit systems, the Internet is the interface through which consumers can access credit information and submit comments or complaints. The information is written in Hypertext Markup Language (HTML)* so that Web browsers can display the multimedia information consistently. Companies that provide credit information use Web servers, database management systems, and Web software programs written in Java, C++, VBScript, or other programming languages to build such applications.

Credit Cards and Credit Reports Online

Consumers can also apply for credit cards online and obtain their credit reports over the Internet. Banks and credit companies such as Citibank and American Express allow customers to apply for credit cards online and receive an instant response. This is made possible because individual credit information is stored electronically in large databases, and financial companies can access the information and make quick decisions. Companies such as annualcreditreport.com provide credit reports to individuals over the Internet. In the United States, companies such as Equifax maintain consumer and commercial credit information on file. However, errors sometimes occur in these credit profiles, which may cause problems for the affected individuals. By checking their credit profiles, consumers can manage their own credit by correcting credit reporting errors and finding out how to improve their credit rating, if necessary. In the United States, the Fair Credit Reporting Act (FCRA) requires nationwide credit reporting companies to provide individuals with a free copy of their credit report once a year at the individual's request.

Security is a major concern for both online credit card application and access to credit profiles because sensitive personal information is involved. The transmission of private information is protected using Secure Socket Layer (SSL), an encryption technology that allows the web browser to encrypt or scramble data automatically before sending the data through the Internet.

 See also **E-Commerce • Privacy • Security**

Resources

Books

Charlton, Kate, and Natalie Taylor. *Online Credit Card Fraud against Small Businesses*. Research and public policy series, no. 60. Canberra: Australian Institute of Criminology, 2004.

Schneider, Gary. *Electronic Commerce*, 9th ed. Boston: Course Technology Cengage Learning, 2011.

Weston, Liz Pulliam. *Your Credit Score: How to Fix, Improve, and Protect the 3-Digit Number That Shapes Your Financial Future.* 2nd ed. Upper Saddle River, NJ: Pearson Prentice Hall, 2007.

Cryptography

Cryptography, the science of encoding communications so that only the intended recipient can understand them, is ancient. In the modern world where computers, the internet, and technology transmit and store a great deal of sensitive information, cryptography is used widely in daily life as a necessary security measure.

In almost every civilization, cryptography appeared almost as soon as there was writing. For example, in 1500 B.C.E. a Mesopotamian scribe, using cuneiform* signs that had different syllabic interpretations (akin to spelling "sh" as "ti," as in nation), disguised a formula for pottery glazes. According to the Greek historian Herodotus, in the fifth century B.C.E. a Greek at the Persian court used steganography, or hiding one message within another, to send a letter urging revolt against the Persians. In the fourth century B.C.E. the Spartans developed a transposition algorithm* that relied on wrapping a sheet of papyrus around a wooden staff; in the same period, the Indian political classic the *Arthasastra* urged cryptanalysis* as a means of obtaining intelligence. In the fifteenth century, the Arabic encyclopedia, the *Subh al-a 'sha*, included a sophisticated discussion of cryptanalysis using frequency distributions.

The increasing use of digitized information and the rise of the Internet has made cryptography a daily tool for millions of people today. People use cryptography when they purchase an item via the World Wide Web, when they call on a European (GSM) cell phone, or when they make a withdrawal from a bank machine. Cryptography provides confidentiality (assurance that an eavesdropper will not be able to understand the communication), authenticity (proof of the message's origin), and integrity (guarantee that the message has not been tampered with in transit). Modern communications—phone, fax, or e-mail—are frequently in digital form (0s and 1s), and the unencrypted string of bits, or plaintext, is transformed into ciphertext by an encryption algorithm.

There are two parts to any encryption system: the algorithm for doing the transformation and a secret piece of information that specifies the particular transformation (called the key). (In the Spartan system described earlier, the key is the width of the wooden staff. If someone were to intercept an encrypted message, unless the interceptor had a staff of the correct width, all the spy would see would be a confused jumble of letters.) Each user has a personal key. This private chunk of information enables many people to use the same cryptosystem, yet each individual's communications are confidential.

Crytographic telegraph operators at Strategic Air Command, in Omaha, Nebraska, 1973. © *AP Images.*

* **cuneiform** in the shape of a wedge

* **algorithm** a rule or procedure used to solve a mathematical problem—most often described as a sequence of steps

* **cryptanalysis** the act of attempting to discover the algorithm used to encrypt a message

* **cipher** a code or encryption method

* **cryptanalyst** a person or agent who attempts to discover the algorithm used to encrypt a message

In modern cryptography the encryption algorithm is public and all secrecy resides in the key. Researchers can study the cryptosystem, and if they are unable to break the system, this helps establish confidence in the algorithm's security.

In theory an eavesdropper should be unable to determine significant information from an intercepted ciphertext. The Caesar cipher*, developed by the Roman general Julius Caesar (c. 100–44 B.C.E., shifts each letter three to the right ("a" is encrypted as "D," "b" becomes "E," "z" becomes "C," and so on), and fails this test. Indeed, systems which replace letters of the alphabet by others in a fixed way—called simple substitution s—do not produce random-looking output. As any Scrabble player knows, letters do not appear equally often in English text. For example, "e" occurs 13 percent of the time, "t" 9 percent, and so on. If "W" crops up as 13 percent of the text, it is a likely bet that W is substituting for e. The complex patterns of a language provide grist for the cryptanalyst*, who studies such characteristics as the frequency of each letter's appearance at the beginning and end of a word and the frequency of occurrence of pairs of letters, triples, etc. If a message is encrypted under a simple substitution, a trained cryptanalyst can usually crack the message with only twenty-five letters of the text.

The development of polyalphabetic ciphers in fifteenth- and sixteenth-century Europe signified a major advancement in encryption. These ciphers employ several substitution alphabets and the key is a codeword that indicates which alphabet to use for each letter of the plaintext. Both polyalphabetic ciphers and transposition ciphers, in which the letters of the plaintext trade positions with one another, also fall prey to frequency analysis.

Despite its fame, for 4,000 years cryptography remained relatively unimportant in the context of wartime communications. That changed with the advent of the radio. Radio technology gave military commanders an unparalleled means to communicate with their troops, but this ability to command at a distance came at a cost: transmissions could be easily intercepted. Encrypted versions of a general's orders, troops' positions, and location and speed of ships at sea were available for friend and foe alike, and cryptanalysis became a critical wartime tool. However, errors made by cipher clerks were cryptography's greatest weakness. A single error, by substantially simplifying the breaking of a cryptosystem, could endanger all communications encrypted under that system. This led to the development of automatic cryptography, a part of the mechanized warfare that characterized World War II.

American Gilbert Vernam (1890–1960) developed encryption done directly on the telegraph wire, eliminating error-prone cipher clerks. This was done using "one-time" pads, a string of bits that is added, bit by bit, to the numeric version of the message, giving a completely secure cryptosystem. One-time pads can be used only once; if a key is ever reused, the system becomes highly vulnerable. The constant need for fresh keys, therefore, eliminates much of the advantage of one-time pads.

After the war inventors designed automated polyalphabetic substitution systems. Instead of looking up the substitutions in a paper table, they could be found by electric currents passing through wires. Rotor machines, in which the plaintext and ciphertext alphabets are on opposite sides of an insulated disk and wires connect each letter on one side to a letter on the other, were simultaneously developed in Europe and the United States. A single rotor is a simple substitution cipher. Automation can provide more. After encrypting a single letter, the rotor can shift, so that the letters of the plaintext alphabet are connected to new letters of the ciphertext alphabet. More rotors can be added and these can shift at different intervals. Such a system provides far more complex encryption than simple polyalphabetic substitution. These were also the principles behind the most famous rotor machine, the Enigma, used by the Germans during World War II. The Allies' ability to decode the Japanese cryptosystem Purple and the German Enigma dispatches during World War II played crucial roles in the battles of the Pacific and control of the Atlantic. The Colossus, a precursor of the first electronic, general-purpose computer, was built by the British during the war to decode German communications.

While substitution and transposition used by themselves result in weak cryptosystems, combining them properly with the key can result in a strong system. These were the operations used in the design of the U.S. Data Encryption Standard (DES), an algorithm with a 56-bit key that became a U.S. cryptography standard in 1977. With the exception of web-browser encryption and relatively insecure cable-TV signal encryption, DES was the most widely used cryptosystem in the world in the late 1990s. It was used for electronic funds transfer, for the protection of civilian satellite communications, and—with a small variation—for protecting passwords on computer systems.

For a cryptosystem to be secure, the difficulty of breaking it should be roughly the time it takes to do an exhaustive search of the keys. In the case of DES, this would be the time it takes to perform 2^{56} DES encryptions. By 1998, however, the speed of computing had caught up with DES, and a $250,000 computer built by the Electronic Frontier Foundation decrypted a DES-encoded message in 56 hours. In 2001 the National Institute of Standards and Technology, whose predecessor (the National Bureau of Standards) certified DES, chose a successor: the Advanced Encryption Standard algorithm Rijndael (pronounced "Rhine Dahl"). This algorithm, which works in three key lengths (128, 192, and 256 bits), was developed by two Belgian researchers. Used even at its shortest key length, a message encrypted by Rijndael is expected to remain secure for many billions of years.

DES and Rijndael are "symmetric," or "private-key," systems; the same key is used for encryption and decryption and is known to both sender and receiver. But electronic commerce requires a different solution.

* **digital signature** identifier used to authenticate the sender of an electronic message or the signer of an electronic document

What happens when a shopper tries to buy an item from an Internet merchant? The parties may not share a private key. How can the customer securely transmit credit information? The answer is public-key cryptography.

Public-Key Cryptography

Public-key cryptography operates on the seemingly paradoxical idea that one can publish the encryption algorithm and the key, and yet decryption remains computationally unfeasible for anyone but the correct recipient of the message. The concept, invented by Whitfield Diffie and Martin Hellman in 1975, relies on the existence of mathematical functions that are fast to compute but which take an extremely long time to invert. Multiplication and factoring form one such pair. Using processors available in 2001, the product of two 200-digit primes can be determined in under a second. Even with the world's fastest computers in 2002, factoring a 400-digit integer was estimated to take trillions of years. The well-known public-key algorithm RSA, named after its inventors Ronald Rivest, Adi Shamir, and Leonard Adleman, relies on the difficulty of factoring for its security.

Public-key cryptography is sometimes called "two-key" cryptography, since the public encryption key is different from the decryption key. By enabling two parties communicating over an insecure network to establish a private piece of information, public-key cryptography simplifies the problem of key distribution. Public-key systems run much slower than private-key ones, and so they are primarily used to establish an encryption key. This key is then used by a private-key system to encode the communication. Public-key cryptography also enables digital signatures*, which verify the identity of the sender of an electronic document.

The great increase in the use of the Internet for commercial and social purposes has presented many opportunities to unscrupulous people to steal private information through malicious hacking. Moreover, the ever-increasing use of portable computers means that personal or business information can be lost or stolen along with the laptop or tablet computer in which it is stored. To address such concerns, modern computer operating systems typically have built-in encryption capabilities. For instance, Microsoft's Windows 7 operating system, released in 2009, enables the user to encrypt files. If an unauthorized person then gains access to the user's computer—either remotely through the Internet, or by physical possession of the computer itself—then the selected files will be protected by the applied encryption.

As of 2012, the increasing use of and reliance on mobile devices for storing and communicating important information presents security with a conundrum. Because so many mobile devices, such as smartphones and tablets, are relatively new, it is difficult to have them all conform to a secure cryptographic standard. Many mobile devices emit keys that make it easy for hackers to compromise them. As newer technology appears it will become increasingly vital that these devices invest in cryptographic security.

Although cryptography has been studied and used for thousands of years by mathematicians, politicians, linguists, and lovers, it became the province of national security in the half century following World War I. And while humans have always sought to keep information from prying eyes, the Information Age has intensified that need. Despite controversy, cryptography has returned from being a tool used solely by governments to one that is used by ordinary people, everyday.

▶ *See also* **Internet: Applications • Security • World Wide Web**

Resources

Books

Sinkov, Abraham, and Todd Fell. *Elementary Cryptanalysis: A Mathematical Approach*, 2nd ed Washington, D.C.: Mathematical Association of America, 2009.

Stinson, Wade. *Cryptography: Theory and Practice*. 3rd ed. New York: Chapman & Hall, 2006.

Trappe, Wade, and Lawrence C. Washington. *Introduction to Cryptography: With Coding Theory*. 2nd ed. Upper Saddle River, NJ: Prentice Hall, 2006.

Web Sites

Information Week. Chicakowski, Ericka. "Mobile Cryptography's Conundrums." http://www.informationweek.com/security/mobile/mobiles-cryptography-conundrums/232602311 (accessed October 8, 2012)

Cybercafe

Cybercafes, also termed Internet cafes, are places where people can pay by the minute or hour to access the Internet. By combining two modern essentials, coffee and the Internet, cybercafes have merged the need for public computer access with the age-old practice of meeting socially in cafes. At a cybercafe, people can meet to chat with friends in the room or sip beverages at a terminal while chatting with friends long-distance over the Internet.

Cafe Cyberia (now named Be the Reds), one of the oldest Internet cafes in existence, is located in London. It was one of the first to coin the term cybercafe. In the early 1990s fewer than one hundred cybercafes existed, but that number quickly grew to an estimated 15 hundred world-wide by 1997. By 2001 there were an estimated 34 hundred cybercafes in 160 countries. They have proved popular with a wide range of patrons,

Fooling The Enemy

Unlike the Germans' infamous Engima code, one of the most successful codes used during World War II was not produced by a machine. Instead, it was developed and implemented by Navajo Indians serving in the U.S. Marines. Based on the ancient language of the Navajo, the code was unbreakable because so few people in the world then knew or understood the language. The contributions of the servicemen, now referred to as the "Navajo Code Talkers," were vital in keeping the enemy unaware of the activities and plans of American forces during the war.

Surfing at a cybercafe in Kenya.
© *TONY KARUMBA/AFP/Getty Images.*

including vacationers accessing e-mail, travelers using online banking services, students creating class assignments, gamers interested in multiplayer video gaming, and researchers browsing international databases.

Types of cybercafes vary, but, according to the International Association for Cybercafes, the only requirement is that the establishment offers public access to computers. Some cybercafes provide a sparse selection of snacks and vending machine drinks, while others are renowned coffeehouses, bistros, or bars that offer a full menu as well as access to computers. Most cybercafes prefer a relaxed atmosphere to draw customers. Almost all cybercafes host a web page where anyone can learn more about the services provided by the cafe they are visiting.

Cybercafes collect payment in a variety of ways. At some, customers are timed by the minute and then asked to bring their tab to a cashier when they are done. At others, users pay in advance for a certain amount of time, using the computer until the screen goes blank. Some cafes have a daily or monthly pass for purchase for unlimited access. Many cybercafes are connected through a network to other cybercafes around the world and offer their customers e-mail addresses from their domain. Most also provide a selection of desktop computer brands with a choice of keyboard layouts to support a variety of popular international languages. Others feature telephone connections for laptop computers as well as printers, scanners, web cameras, microphones, and other peripheral devices.

Because cafes are popular in Europe, the largest number of cybercafes can be found throughout that continent. Cybercafes are extremely useful in countries where domestic Internet service is commonly slow and expensive. In many parts of the world, the average person goes to a cybercafe to use a computer instead of buying and installing one in the home, although the precise reason for frequenting the establishment varies from place to place.

- In the United Kingdom, cybercafes take the form of Internet-equipped pubs that allow patrons to enjoy a pint while using a computer.

- In Bosnia and Herzegovina, many customers are drawn to cybercafes for the arcade-like atmosphere provided through computer gaming.

- In France, many students used go to cybercafes to type and print school papers. However, most French students did not use cybercafe computers to explore the Internet, preferring instead to use their Minitel console at home for those tasks. Minitel was a countrywide network that preceded the Internet, electronically connecting most French homes, businesses, cultural organizations, and government offices. This service came to a close on June 30, 2012.

- In Malaysia, one political party set up a cybercafe in each of its one hundred territorial divisions to encourage party members to master the new technology. In the capital of Kuala Lumpur, a cybercafe was set up in a police training center to help officers and their families learn to use the Internet and multimedia applications.

- In Japan, where computers are widely available and inexpensive to own, cybercafes are frequented primarily by out-of-town tourists or visitors away from home.

- In Mexico, where international telephone calls can be very expensive, cybercafes offer Mexicans and visitors a cheap way to communicate long-distance.

- In Colorado, one cybercafe even promotes jazz concerts and gourmet dishes while offering Internet access as an added convenience.

Cybercafes also appeal to businesses marketing new products. They are especially valuable for software developers because customers can familiarize themselves with new software before choosing to buy it. Most cybercafes that are promoting a software program will also have a resident expert on hand for quick answers. For this reason, many companies offer promotional deals to cybercafes in the hope of attracting a wider consumer audience. Many cybercafe owners also take advantage of their computer expertise by offering classes or seminars in computer or software use.

The cybercafe is evolving from a meeting place to a learning center, where members of many communities can use new technologies as they expand their horizons.

With the availability of Internet access on cellular phones, in public libraries, and wireless Internet (Wi-Fi) access available at many restaurants, coffee shops, and retail establishments, it is no longer necessary to visit an Internet cafe for online access. Additionally, computers have become affordable enough that many people have computers at home.

Cafe Cyberia

London's Cafe Cyberia Internet cafe opened its doors in 1994. It offers food, coffee, and tea along with access to the Internet and e-mail. Cafe Cyberia also provides photocopying, fax, scanning, and CD burning services. Cafe Cyberia was purchased from its founder by Korean investors that renamed the establishment, Be The Reds, and served sushi and Korean dishes. Other Cafe Cyberia locations include Bangkok, Thailand, and Dublin, Ireland.

---

* **robotics** the science and engineering of building electromechanical machines that aim to serve as replacements for human laborers

* **Turing machine** a proposed type of computing machine that takes inputs off paper tape and then moves through a sequence of states under the control of an algorithm; identified by Alan Turing (1912-1954)

▶ *See also* **Embedded Technology (Ubiquitous Computing)** • **Home Entertainment** • **Home System Software** • **Integrated Software** • **World Wide Web**

Resources

Books

Adomi, Esharenana E., ed. *Security and Software for Cybercafes.* Hershey, PA: Information Science Reference, 2008.

Bell, Mary Ann, Mary Ann Berry, James L. Van Roekel, and Frank W. Hoffmann. *Internet and Personal Computing Fads.* New York: Haworth Press, 2004.

Sahay, A., and Mahavir S. Chhikara. *New Vistas of Entrepreneurship: Challenges & Opportunities: Analysis of Cyber Cafes.* New Delhi: Excel Books, 2007.

Web Sites

Schofield, Hugh. "Minitel: The Rise and Fall of the France-wide Web" http://www.bbc.co.uk/news/magazine-18610692 (accessed October 14, 2012).

Cybernetics

The term *cybernetics* is much misused in the popular media. Often used to convey notions of high-technology, robotics*, and even computer networks like the Internet, in reality, cybernetics refers to the study of communications and control in animal and machine.

Great mathematicians of the past such as Wilhelm Leibniz (1646–1716) and Blaise Pascal (1623–1662) had been interested in the nature of computing machinery long before these machines had ever been realized. They concerned themselves with philosophizing over what special peculiarities might be present in machines that had the ability to compute. In the mid-1930s Alan Turing (1912–1954) developed the idea of an abstract machine (later to become known as the "Turing Machine*"). Turing machines introduced the possibility of solving problems by mechanical processes that involved a machine stepping through a sequence of states under the guidance of a controlling element of some sort. This laid the fundamental groundwork that was then developed by Norbert Wiener (1894–1964) into what has become cybernetics.

In 1948 Wiener concluded that a new branch of science needed to be developed. This field would draw from the realms of communication, automatic control, and statistical mechanics. He chose the word cybernetics, deriving it from the Greek word for "steersman" which underlines one of the essential ingredients of this field—that of governance or control. He defined cybernetics to be "control and communication in the animal and the machine." What really makes cybernetics stand apart from other fields in science and engineering is that it focuses on what machines do rather than the details of how they actually do it.

Classically, the study of a particular piece of conventional mechanical machinery—for example, a typewriter—would not be considered complete until all of the intricacies of the physics of movement of the constituent parts had been accounted for. This constitutes a Newtonian view* of systems—one that commences with a perspective of Newtonian mechanics and builds from there. Cybernetics, on the other hand, accentuates the behavior and function of the machine as a whole. The result of this stance is that cybernetics is not restricted to dealing with mechanical or perhaps electrical machines only; instead it applies to anything that might possibly be viewed in some way as a machine—including organisms. That is, cybernetics looks at all the elements that are common denominators in that class of entities that might be described as machines. Wiener concluded that for a system to be classed as cybernetic, communication between parts of a system was a necessary characteristic, as was feedback from one part to another. The presence of feedback means that a cybernetic system is able to measure or perceive a quantity of some sort, then compare this to a required or desired value, and then instigate some strategy or behavior that affects change in that quantity. This is as much true of a heater and thermostat used to regulate temperature in a house, as it is of a bird that seeks refuge in a bird bath on a hot day.

Historically, the human body, in particular the human brain, has been viewed by many as a type of machine. This perception was generated by people who were hopeful of finding a way of modeling human behavior in the same way that they could model human-made machines—an approach with which they were comfortable. Much effort was directed toward understanding the operation of the human brain in this light.

Throughout the nineteenth and early twentieth centuries, significant advances were made in understanding the physiology of the human brain. Research into the structure of the cerebral cortex, the discovery of the brain as the center of perception, and the identification of neurons and synapses were all contributors to the conclusion that the brain is the regulator, controller, and seat of behavior of the human species. Because these ideas are fundamental to cybernetics, the human brain and the notion of intelligence are also considered as subjects that are within the realm of the cybernetic field. As a consequence, a great deal of research has been carried out in the areas of biological control theory, neural modeling*, artificial intelligence (AI)*, cognitive perception, and chaos theory* from a perspective that resulted from the development of cybernetics.

With respect to computer systems, cybernetics has been prominent in two areas. The first is artificial intelligence, where computer algorithms* have been developed that attempt to exhibit some traits of intelligent

* **Newtonian view** an approach to the study of mechanics that obeys the rules of Newtonian physics, as opposed to relativistic mechanics; named after Sir Isaac Newton (1642-1727)

* **neural modeling** the mathematical study and the construction of elements that mimic the behavior of the brain cell (neuron)

* **artificial intelligence (AI)** a branch of computer science dealing with creating computer hardware and software to mimic the way people think and perform practical tasks

* **chaos theory** a branch of mathematics dealing with differential equations having solutions which are very sensitive to initial conditions

* **algorithm** a rule or procedure used to solve a mathematical problem—most often described as a sequence of steps

Human Plus Machine

Researchers at British Telecommunications have worked on a radical project called "Soul Catcher." The goal of the project, led by Peter Cochrane, is to develop a computer that can be implanted into the human brain in order to support memory and computational skills. The work is complex and introduces ethical as well as technological problems.

behavior—initially by playing games and later by processing speech and carrying out complex image and pattern manipulation operations. The second is in robotics, which frequently encompasses artificial intelligence and other cybernetic areas such as communication and automatic control using feedback. Early robotic systems were nothing more than complex servo-mechanisms that carried out manual tasks in place of a human laborer; however, the modern cybernetic approach is to attempt to construct robots that can communicate and be guided toward acting together as a team to achieve a collective goal. This has generated interest in a new type of adaptive machine that has the capacity to re-organize its strategies and behavior if its environment or mission changes.

Finally, beyond a computing context, cybernetics offers some advantages in our understanding of nature. First, it permits a unified approach to studying and understanding machine-like systems. This results from the distinct way in which the cybernetic viewpoint of systems is formulated; it is not restricted to particular machine or system types. For example, we can draw a correspondence between an electro-mechanical system like a collection of servo-motors and linkages that give a robot locomotion, and a biological system like the nervous and musculo-skeletal systems of a caterpillar. One is not required to undertake greatly differing analyses to gain an appreciation of both. Secondly, it offers a manageable way of dealing with the most predominant type of system—one that is highly complex, non-linear, and changes over time.

 See also **Artificial Intelligence • Robotics • Space Travel and Exploration**

Resources

Books

Conway, Flo and Jim Siegelman. *Dark Hero of the Information Age: In Search of Norbert Wiener The Father of Cybernetics*. New York: Basic Books, 2005.

Wiener, Norbert. *Cybernetics: Or, Control and Communication in the Animal and the Machine*. 2nd ed. Cambridge, MA: MIT Press, 1961.

Web Site

George Washington University. "Definitions of Cybernetics." http://www.gwu.edu/~asc/cyber_definition.html (accessed November 4, 2012).

D

Data Mining

Data mining is the process of discovering potentially useful, interesting, and previously unknown patterns from a large collection of data. The process is similar to discovering ores buried deep underground and mining them to extract the metal. The term knowledge discovery is sometimes used to describe this process of converting data to information and then to knowledge.

* **demographics** the study of the statistical data pertaining to a population

Data, Information, and Knowledge

Data is any facts, numbers, or text that can be processed by a computer. Many organizations accumulate vast and growing amounts of data in a variety of formats and databases. This data may be loosely grouped into three categories: operational or transactional data, such as company sales, costs, inventory, payroll, and accounting; non-operational data, such as industry sales, forecast data, and macro-economic data; and metadata, which is data about other data, such as elements related to a database's design or query protocol.

The patterns, associations, and relationships among all these data can provide information. For example, analysis of retail point-of-sale transaction data can yield information on which products are selling and when. Information can then be converted into knowledge about historical patterns and future trends. For example, summary information on retail supermarket sales can be analyzed in light of promotional efforts to provide knowledge of consumer buying behavior. Thus, a manufacturer or retailer could determine which items to combine with promotional efforts for the best sales or profit results.

Applications of Data Mining

Data mining is used today by companies with a strong consumer focus, such as retail, financial, communication, and marketing organizations. Data mining enables these companies to identify relationships among internal factors such as price, product positioning, or staff skills, and external factors such as economic indicators, competition, and customer demographics*. It enables them to determine what impact these relationships may have on sales, customer satisfaction, and corporate profits. Finally, it enables them to drill down into summary information to view detailed transactional data and to find ways to apply this knowledge for business improvement.

With data mining, a retailer can use point-of-sale records of customer purchases to send targeted promotions based on an individual's purchase

* **terabyte** one million million (one trillion, or 10^{12}) bytes

* **artificial intelligence (AI)** a branch of computer science dealing with creating computer hardware and software to mimic the way people think and perform practical tasks

* **data reduction technique** an approach to simplifying data, e.g. summarization

history. By mining demographic data from comment or warranty cards, retailers can develop products and promotions to appeal to specific customer segments. For example, Netflix can mine its DVD rental and online streaming history database to recommend rentals to individual customers, and American Express can suggest products to its cardholders based on an analysis of their monthly expenditures.

Data mining has many applications in science and medicine. Astronomers use data mining to identify quasars from terabytes* of satellite data, as well as to identify stars in other galaxies. It can also be used to predict how a cancer patient will respond to radiation or other therapy. With more accurate predictions about the effectiveness of expensive medical treatment, the cost of health care can be reduced while the quality and effectiveness of treatment can be improved.

The data mining process is interactive and iterative, and the user is able to make many decisions. Data mining is not an automatic process; it does not simply happen by pushing a button. Rather, data mining requires an understanding of the decision-maker's intentions and objectives, the nature and scope of the application, and the limitations of data mining methods. Data mining is research: a process that requires one to develop knowledge about every task at hand, to review possibilities and options, to apply the best data mining methods, and to communicate the results in a comprehensible form. Armed with solid information, researchers can apply their creativity and judgment to make better decisions and get better results. A variety of software systems are available today that will handle the technical details so that people can focus on making the decisions. Most of these systems employ a variety of techniques that can be used in several combinations. Advanced techniques yield higher quality information than simpler ones. They automate the stages of information gathering to enhance the decision-making process through speed and easily understood results.

Techniques for Data Mining

Just as a carpenter uses many tools to build a sturdy house, a good analyst employs more than one technique to transform data into information. Most data miners go beyond the basics of reporting and On-Line Analytical Processing (OLAP), also known as multi-dimensional reporting, to take a multi-method approach that includes a variety of advanced techniques. Some of these are statistical techniques while others are based on artificial intelligence (AI)*.

Cluster Analysis Cluster analysis is a data reduction technique* that groups together either variables or cases based on similar data characteristics. This technique is useful for finding customer segments based on characteristics such as demographic and financial information or purchase behavior. For example, suppose a bank wants to find segments of customers based on the types of accounts they open. A cluster analysis may result in several groups of customers. The bank might then look for differences in types of accounts opened and behavior, especially attrition, between the segments. They might then treat the segments differently based on these characteristics.

Linear Regression   Linear regression is a method that fits a straight line through data. If the line is upward sloping, it means that an independent variable such as the size of a sales force has a positive effect on a dependent variable such as revenue. If the line is downward sloping, there is a negative effect. The steeper the slope, the more effect the independent variable has on the dependent variable.

Correlation   Correlation is a measure of the relationship between two variables. For example, a high correlation between purchases of certain products such as cheese and crackers indicates that these products are likely to be purchased together. Correlations may be either positive or negative. A positive correlation indicates that a high level of one variable will be accompanied by a high value of the correlated variable. A negative correlation indicates that a high level of one variable will be accompanied by a low value of the correlated variable.

Positive correlations are useful for finding complementary products, products that tend to be purchased together. Negative correlations can be useful for finding substitute products, products that tend to fulfill the same purpose as another, or diversifying across markets in a company's strategic portfolio. For example, an energy company might have interest in both natural gas and fuel oil since price changes and the degree of substitutability might have an impact on demand for one resource over the other. Correlation analysis can help a company develop a portfolio of markets in order to absorb such environmental changes in individual markets.

Factor Analysis   Factor analysis is a data reduction technique. This technique detects underlying factors, also termed latent variables, and provides models for these factors based on variables in the data. For example, suppose you have a market research survey that asks the importance of nine product attributes. Also suppose that you find three underlying factors. The variables that load highly on these factors can offer some insight about what these factors might be. For example, if three attributes such as technical support, customer service, and availability of training courses all load highly on one factor, we might term this factor service. This technique can be very helpful in finding important underlying characteristics that might not be easily observed but which might be found as manifestations of variables that can be observed.

Another good application of factor analysis is to group together products based on similarity of buying patterns. Factor analysis can help a business locate opportunities for cross-selling and bundling. For example, factor analysis might indicate four distinct groups of products in a

* **neural networks** pattern recognition systems whose structure and operation are loosely inspired by analogy to neurons in the human brain

company. With these product groupings, a marketer can now design packages of products or attempt to cross-sell products to customers in each group who may not currently be purchasing other products in the product group.

Decision Trees   Decision trees separate data into sets of rules that are likely to have different effects on a target variable. The decision tree seeks to list all possible combinations of data as different paths in a tree. Each contributing piece of data is represented by a layer in the tree. Each leaf node corresponds to a unique combination of all the data evaluated for the tree. Each leaf node can be evaluated for its effect on the target variable, and leaf nodes that exhibit the desired properties represent the rules for what data is required to influence a variable in a specific way. For example, we might want to find the characteristics of a person likely to respond to a direct mail piece. These characteristics can be translated into a set of rules. Imagine that you are responsible for a direct mail effort designed to sell a new investment service. To maximize your profits, you want to identify household segments that, based on previous promotions, are most likely to respond to a similar promotion. Typically, this is done by looking for combinations of demographic variables that best distinguish those households who responded to the previous promotion from those who did not.

This process gives important clues as to who will best respond to the new promotion and allows a company to maximize its direct marketing effectiveness by mailing only to those people who are most likely to respond, increasing overall response rates and increasing sales at the same time. Decision trees are also a good tool for analyzing attrition (churn), finding cross-selling opportunities, performing promotions analysis, analyzing credit risk or bankruptcy, and detecting fraud.

Neural Networks   Neural networks* mimic the human brain and can deduce information from examples to find patterns in data or to classify data. Neural networks can be trained to recognize patterns by processing data sets for which the result is already known, and correcting the network when the computed answer differs from the known result. Done repeatedly with a diverse enough training set, the network will be tuned to recognize a specific pattern in the data (if one exists). The advantage is that it is not necessary to have a model specific to the problem when running the analysis as most share very similar models. A representative training set becomes the most important element for a high-quality network. Also, neural networks can find interaction effects (such as effects from the combination of age and gender) which must be explicitly specified in regression. The disadvantage is that it is harder to interpret the relationship between the data calculated by the neural network. The neural network model is represented by layers of weights and arcane transformations, which represent the relationship between inputs to the network. Neural networks are therefore useful in predicting a target variable when the data is highly non-linear with interactions, but they are not very useful when these relationships in the data need to be explained. They are considered good tools for such applications as forecasting, credit scoring, response model scoring, and risk analysis.

Association Models Association models examine the extent to which values of one field depend on, or are predicted by, values of another field. Association discovery finds rules about items that appear together in an event such as a purchase transaction. The rules have user-stipulated support, confidence, and length. The rules find things that are associated in some way. These models are often referred to as Market Basket Analysis when they are applied to retail industries to study the buying patterns of their customers.

The Future of Data Mining

One of the key questions raised by data mining technology is not a business or technological one, but a social one: where does personal privacy come into play? Data mining makes it possible to analyze routine business transactions and glean a significant amount of information about individuals' buying habits and preferences, and even postulate about identity. A set of web search data released by America Online in 2006 was sanitized for user information, but researchers using data mining techniques were able to guess the identity of a user by correlating the content of their searches.

Another issue is that of data integrity. Clearly, data analysis can only be as good as the data that is being analyzed. A key implementation challenge is integrating conflicting or redundant data from different sources. For example, a bank may maintain credit card accounts on several different databases. The address (or even the name) of a single cardholder may be different in each. Software must translate data from one system to another and select the address most recently entered.

Finally, there is the issue of cost. While system hardware costs have dropped dramatically within the past five years, data mining and data warehousing tend to be self-reinforcing. The more powerful the data mining queries, the greater the usefulness of the information being gleaned from the data, and the greater the pressure to increase the amount of data being collected and maintained. The result is increased pressure for faster, more powerful data mining queries. These more efficient data mining systems often cost more than their predecessors.

▶ *See also* **Data Warehousing • Database Management Software • E-Commerce • Electronic Markets • Privacy**

Resources

Books

Berthold, Michael, and David J. Hand. *Intelligent Data Analysis: An Introduction.* 2nd ed. Berlin and London: Springer, 2011.

Data Mining and Wal-Mart

In 1995 Wal-Mart computers processed more than one million complex data queries. The company's data mining efforts are transforming its supplier relationships. Wal-Mart captures point-of-sale transactions from more than 29 hundred stores in six countries and continuously transmits this data to its massive 7.5 terabyte Teradata data warehouse. Wal-Mart allows more than 35 hundred suppliers to access data on their products and perform data analysis. These suppliers use this data to identify customers' buying patterns at the store level. They use the information to manage local store inventories and identify new merchandizing opportunities.

Data Mining and Sports

The National Basketball Association (NBA) has a data mining application that is used in conjunction with image recordings of basketball games. A data mining system analyzes the movements of players to help coaches orchestrate plays and strategies. For example, an analysis of the game played between the New York Knicks and the Cleveland Cavaliers on January 6, 1995, revealed that when American professional basketball player Mark Price (1964–) played the guard position, American professional basketball player John Williams (1962–) attempted four jump shots and made each one. Data mining techniques also recognized that Williams's performance during the game was exceptional—the average shooting percentage for the team on that day was 49.30 percent.

* **relational database** a collection of records that permits logical and business relationships to be developed between themselves and their contents

* **intranet** an interconnected network of computers that operates like the Internet, but is restricted in size to a company or organization

Han, Jiawei, and Micheline Kamber. *Data Mining: Concepts and Techniques.* 3rd ed. Amsterdam: Elsevier/Morgan Kaufmann, 2011.

Kargupta, Hillol, ed. *Next Generation of Data Mining.* Boca Raton, FL: CRC Press, 2009.

Larose, Daniel T. *Discovering Knowledge in Data: An Introduction to Data Mining.* Hoboken, NJ: Wiley-Interscience, 2005.

Lawrence, Kenneth D., Stephan Kudyba, and Ronald K. Klimberg, eds. *Data Mining Methods and Applications.* Boca Raton, FL: Auerbach Publications, 2008.

Myatt, Glenn J. *Making Sense of Data: A Practical Guide to Exploratory Data Analysis and Data Mining.* Hoboken, NJ: Wiley-Interscience, 2007.

Sumathi, Sai, and S. N. Sivanandam. *Introduction to Data Mining and Its Applications.* Berlin and New York: Springer, 2006.

Wang, Hsiao-Fan, ed. *Intelligent Data Analysis: Developing New Methodologies through Pattern Discovery and Recovery.* Hershey, PA: Information Science Reference, 2009.

Web Sites

University of Texas at Austin and Doug Alexander. "Data Mining." http://www.laits.utexas.edu/~anorman/BUS.FOR/course.mat/Alex/#6 (accessed October 31, 2012).

Data Warehousing

With the advent of the information age, the amount of digital information that is recorded and stored has been increasing at a tremendous rate. Common data formats for storage include commercial relational database* engines, often interconnected via an intranet*, and more recently World Wide Web sites connected via the Internet. The interconnectivity of these data sources offers the opportunity to access a vast amount of information spread over numerous data sources. Modern applications that could benefit from this wealth of digital information abound, and they range over diverse domains such as business intelligence (e.g., trade-market analysis or online Web access monitoring), leisure (e.g., travel and weather), science (e.g., integration of diagnoses from nurses, doctors, and specialists about patients), libraries (e.g., multimedia online resources like museums and art collections), and education (e.g., lecture notes, syllabi, exams, and transparencies from different Web sites). The one common element among all these applications is the fact that they must make use of data of multiple types and origins in order to function most effectively. This need emphasizes the demand for suitable integration tools that allow such applications to make effective use of diverse data sets by supporting the browsing and querying of tailored information subsets.

* **paradigm** an example, pattern, or way of thinking

In contrast to the on-demand approach to information integration, where applications requests are processed on-the-fly, the approach of tailored information repository construction, commonly referred to as data warehousing, represents a viable solution alternative. In data warehousing, there is an initial setup phase during which relevant information is extracted from different networked data sources, transformed and cleansed as necessary, fused with information from other sources, and then loaded into a centralized data store, called the data warehouse. Thereafter, queries posed against the environment can be directly evaluated against the pre-computed data warehouse store without requiring any further interaction and resultant processing delay.

Data warehousing offers higher availability and better query performance than the on-demand approach because all data can be retrieved directly from one single dedicated site. Thus, it is a suitable choice when high-performance query processing and data analysis are critical. This approach is also desirable when the data sources are expensive to access or even sometimes become unavailable, when the network exhibits high delays or is unreliable, or when integration tasks such as query translation or information fusion are too complex and ineffective to be executed on-the-fly.

However, such a static snapshot of the data kept in a data warehouse is not sufficient for many real-time applications, such as investment advising. Hence updates made to the data in individual sources must be reflected in the data warehouse store. This can be accomplished by a complete reload of the data warehouse store on some periodic schedule, say once a day during the off-peak business time. Given the size of many modern data warehouses, such a reload is often too time consuming and hence not practically feasible. This has led to the development of strategies for incremental database maintenance, a process whereby a data warehouse is updated more efficiently with information that is fed into an existing database.

Many types of systems benefit from such a data warehousing paradigm*. The first category includes monolithic systems, where one organization controls both the single data source providing the data feed as well as the back-end data warehouse store. An online purchasing store such as Amazon.com has, for example, the web-based front end that handles high-performance transactions by customers, whereas the underlying data warehouse serves as a container of all transactions logged over time for offline analysis. The second category includes distributed yet closed environments composed of a small number of independent data sources controlled by trusted owners with a joint cooperative goal. An example would be a hospital information system that attempts to integrate the data sources maintained by different units such as the

* **SGML** the acronym for Standard Generalized Markup Language, an international standard for structuring electronic documents

* **XML** the acronym for eXtensible Markup Language; a method of applying structure to data so that documents can be represented

personnel department, the pharmacy, and the registration system. Large-scale open environments such as the World Wide Web represent the third category where unrelated sources come and go at unpredictable times and the construction of temporary data warehouses for new purposes are common.

These data warehousing systems often feature a multi-tier architecture. The individual data sources in a networked environment are at the bottom tier. These sources often are heterogeneous, meaning that they are modeled by diverse data models and each support different query interfaces and search engines. This may include legacy systems, proprietary application programmer interfaces, traditional relational database servers, or even new technology such as web sites, SGML* (Standard Generalized Markup Language) or XML* (eXtensible Markup Language) Web documents, news wires, and multimedia sites. Due to the heterogeneity of the data sources, there is typically some wrapper software associated with each data source that allows for smoother communication between the queries and processes associated with both the new data and the data warehousing system.

The software tools in the middle tier, collectively referred to as the data warehouse management system, are dedicated to diverse integration services. These software tools offer services beyond those common to a traditional database engine. For example, there may be tools for filtering and cleansing information extracted from individual data sources, for intelligently fusing information from multiple sources into one integrated chunk of knowledge, or for incrementally keeping the data warehouse up-to-date under source changes.

Finally, the actual data warehouse store is (at least logically) a centralized database repository that must support complex analysis queries at high levels of performance. In current systems, such a data warehouse store is built using standard relational database servers due to the maturity of this technology. Such complex decision and analysis query support on databases is commonly referred to as online analytic processing. Depending on the requirements of the application, additional data analysis services may be built on top of the integrated data warehouse store. This may include graphical display systems, statistics and modeling packages, and even sophisticated data mining tools that enable some form of discovery of interesting trends or patterns in the data.

 See also **Data Mining • Database Management Software • E-Commerce**

Resources

Books

Kimball, Ralph, Margy Ross, Warren Thornthwaite, and Joy Mundy. *The Data Warehouse Lifecycle Toolkit.* 2nd ed. Indianapolis, IN: Wiley, 2008.

Web Sites

Rensselaer Polytechnic Institute. "Rensselaer Data Warehouse
Project."http://www.rpi.edu/datawarehouse/dw-links.html(accessed
November 4, 2012).

Digital Filmmaking

The rise of computer technology and the Internet has prompted new
demands for storytelling techniques. Filmmaking has continued to
hold its own in the area of storytelling where technology and art blend
into visual narrative. Growing with new technological advances, the
process of filmmaking inevitably has evolved to the creation of digital
filmmaking.

This new method of motion picture and consumer video production has resulted in greater opportunities for filmmakers. It makes the art
affordable to a wider market, resulting in new genres and industry—for
example, the emergence of indie (or independent) films, wedding videog-
raphy, and online web series. The accessibility of digital filmmaking has
blurred the line between consumers and professional filmmakers for the
first time since the advent of the film industry.

Digital filmmaking specifically refers to the process of recording live
action onto digital video formats, and then capturing those images digitally. The first all-digital video camera was introduced by Sony in 1995,
and it used innovative 3-CCD and firewire technology. It stood apart from

A participant in the Ten-Second Film
Challenge in Minneapolis, Minnesota.
Only nontraditional sources for making
the mini-movies is acceptable—such as
digital cameras and cell phones.
© *AP Images/Jim Mone.*

* non-linear editing systems
systems that allow for video footage to be edited together digitally, without the need for cutting and splicing the actual film.

all other preceding cameras. In the years leading up to the digital movement cameras recorded either onto film or onto video tapes. Afterwards the footage was captured for post-production using digitization methods. The introduction of the digital camera removed the tedious, and costly, process of converting film or analog images into digital ones able to be edited on computers using non-linear editing systems*. Firewire technology enabled the camera to be connected directly to a computer, and for the footage to be captured digitally. The addition of 3-CCD technology meant the camera was able to interpret each color on the RGB scale individually to produce a significantly higher quality of image compared to its single-CCD predecessors.

The VX-1000 was one of the first cameras to bridge the gap between consumers and professionals creating the new market of "prosumers." These new users were able to take advantage of its affordable price point and hand-held design. In addition, the camera sparked the development of original third-party accessories. Its wide use amongst action sports videographers caused lens maker Century Optics to create a fisheye lens specifically for the VX-1000. With 180 degrees of diagonal viewing capability, videographers were able to record and view extreme sports in quality never experienced previously.

As digital filmmaking expanded the consumer market and flooded the industry with new content, pressure was placed on the professionals in the movie business to up their game. Although digital visual effects had been augmenting Hollywood films for decades, it wasn't until non-linear editing was coupled with high-definition digital video that filmmakers could really harness all the benefits of computerized visual effects.

One of the pioneers of this movement was George Lucas (1944–), director and producer of Star Wars. When the first film of the series (*Star Wars Episode IV: A New Hope*) was released in 1977, it implemented cutting-edge visual effects techniques: most notably, the use of motion control to produce the fighter jet/spaceship sequences. Lucas's motivation to utilize new technology consistently in the art of storytelling led him to be among the first major Hollywood filmmakers to shoot an entire movie digitally. His film *Star Wars Episode II: Attack of the Clones*, released in 2002, was shot using high-definition 24p digital video technology. Being shot in 24p digital technology meant that Lucas was able to get an initial image somewhat similar to film, and yet after applying numerous digital effects and then outputting the movie to a digital format for theatrical viewing, the image would retain much of its original quality over time. Lucas had experimented with this on his previous Star Wars film and decided the ease of use and the preservation of image quality made it worth the switch.

Since this time, the move from film to digital has continued to cause controversy amongst filmmakers in Hollywood. Advocates for digital such as directors George Lucas, James Cameron ([1954–] *Titanic*, *Avatar*), and

Danny Boyle ([1956–] *28 Days Later*, *Slumdog Millionaire*) argue the benefits of lossless image capturing, size, and efficiency of digital cameras. Those loyal to film, such as directors Christopher Nolan (1970–) and Paul Thomas Anderson (1970–), claim that digital images will never match the beauty of those captured on film. Despite the introduction of high-definition cameras that shot at 24 frames per second like film did, there was a noticeable difference in image resolution between early models of digital cameras compared to film cameras. This was mostly due to the fact that the number of pixels used to record high-definition images (1920x1080) was simply not enough to provide a high dynamic range, i.e., a large amount of information held between the light and dark areas of the image.

The divide amongst filmmaking professionals was quite firm until the founder of Oakley, Jim Jannard (1949–), decided to create a digital camera that would provide more dynamic range by shooting at a higher resolution than ever before. In 2007, he introduced the RED ONE, which was capable of groundbreaking 4K pixel resolution. The doubling of the number of pixels enabled the camera to capture more information and greater variances of light resulting in an immensely improved image. Jannard's company, RED Digital Cinema was also one of the first camera companies to listen and respond to the needs of professionals almost instantaneously. For example, when it was necessary to make the camera lighter in order to film the rowing scenes of David Fincher's (1962–) *The Social Network*, the company modified the body and used carbon fiber to reduce the weight. These new benefits of digital filmmaking were noticed throughout the industry and caused many filmmakers to move to digital and not look back since.

On the consumer, and prosumer level, the use of DSLR cameras* has been a digital video standard since the introduction of the Canon 5D in 2005. Originally it was created to offer news photojournalists an option of recording video on location, but it was picked up quickly by a larger audience due to its compact size, price, and quality of image. The 5D offered a full-frame sensor that recorded at 12.8 megapixels. With a full-frame sensor the camera was able to capture an image with a similar depth of field to that of film cameras. It also was compatible with a wider number of lenses. This was a huge advancement for indie filmmakers, who needed to produce high-quality video with the flexibility of camera size and lens options at a reasonable price.

Just as growing technologies pushed the need for digital filmmaking, the increasing popularity of digital filmmaking has in turn been a motivating factor for the rapid development of new technologies. Although producers continue to shoot movies on film, major camera companies have stopped manufacturing any new film cameras. Thus, as digital filmmaking becomes the ever-increasing norm, there will continue be a need for better, faster, and cheaper digital cameras and digital processing systems.

* **DSLR cameras** digital single-lens reflex cameras that allowed for the use of interchangeable lenses.

*pixel a single picture element on a video screen; one of the individual dots making up a picture on a video screen or digital image

Resources

Books

Hughes, Michael K. *Digital Filmmaking for Beginners: A Practical Guide to Video Production*. New York: McGraw-Hill, 2012.

Shaner, Pete. *Digital Filmmaking: An Introduction*. Dulles, VA: Mercury Learning and Information, 2011.

Web Sites

"American Cinematographer: George Lucas Interview." http://www.theasc.com/ (accessed November 11, 2012).

"Sony Global—Product & Technology Milestones." http://www.sony.net/ (accessed November 11, 2012).

Digital Images

A digital image is a representation of a real two-dimensional image as a set of zeros and ones that can be stored and displayed by a digital computer. In order to translate the image into numbers, it is divided into small areas termed pixels* (picture elements). For each pixel, the imaging device records a number, or a small set of numbers, that describe some property of this pixel, such as its brightness (the intensity of the light) or its color. The numbers are arranged in an array of rows and columns that correspond to the vertical and horizontal positions of the pixels in the image. Digital images can either be created using a camera or from an analog image such as a printed photograph by using an image scanner. Digital cameras are widely used to create digital images of a physical landscape and are incorporated into many cellular phones and personal digital assistants (PDAs). Many digital cameras also integrate digital image processing software to automatically adjust brightness and color, such as color correction for red eye in images of people and pets.

Digital images have several basic characteristics. One is the *type* of the image. For example, a black and white image records only the intensity of the light falling on the pixels. A color image can have three colors, normally RGB (Red, Green, Blue) or four colors, CMYK (Cyan, Magenta, Yellow, Black). RGB images are usually used in computer monitors and scanners, while CMYK images are used in color printers. There are also non-optical images such as ultrasound or X-ray in which the intensity of sound or X-rays is recorded. In range images, the distance of the pixel from the observer is recorded. *Resolution* is expressed in the number of pixels per inch (ppi). A higher resolution gives a more detailed image. A computer monitor typically has a resolution of 100 ppi, while a printer has a resolution ranging from 300 ppi to more than 1440 ppi. This is why an image looks crisper in print than on a monitor.

The *color depth* (of a color image) or bits per pixel is the number of bits* in the numbers that describe the brightness or the color. More bits make it possible to record more shades of gray or more colors. For example, an RGB image with eight bits per color has a total of twenty-four bits per pixel (true color). Each bit can represent two possible colors so we get a total of 16,777,216 possible colors. A typical GIF image* on a Web page has eight bits for all colors combined for a total of 256 colors. However, it is a much smaller image than a twenty-four-bit one so it downloads more quickly. A fax image has only one or two colors, black and white. The *format* of the image gives more details about how the numbers are arranged in the image file, including what kind of compression is used, if any. Among the most popular of the dozens of formats available are TIFF, GIF, JPEG, PNG, and Post-Script. SVG format, a World Wide Web Consortium (W3C) standard for two-dimensional vector graphics, is increasingly used on the Web.

Digital images tend to produce big files and are often compressed to make the files smaller. *Compression* takes advantage of the fact that many nearby pixels in the image have similar colors or brightness. Instead of recording each pixel separately, one can record information about which pixels share the same color (e.g., the 100 pixels around a certain position are all white). Compression methods vary in their efficiency and speed. The GIF method has good compression for eight bit pictures, while the JPEG (Joint Photographic Experts Group)* is lossy*, meaning that it causes some image degradation. JPEG's advantage is its efficient compression, which can be configured for low compression and high image quality or high compression and smaller file size at the expense of file quality.

One of the advantages of digital images over traditional ones is the ability to transfer them electronically almost instantaneously and convert them easily from one medium to another such as from a web page to a computer screen to a printer. A bigger advantage is the ability to change them according to one's needs. There are several programs available now that give a user the ability to do that, including Adobe Photoshop, Corel Photo-paint, and Gimp. With these programs, a user can change the colors and brightness of an image, delete unwanted visible objects, move others, and merge objects from several images, among many other operations. In this way a user can retouch family photos or even create new images. Other software, such as word processors and desktop publishing programs, can easily combine digital images with text to produce books or magazines much more efficiently than with traditional methods.

A very promising use of digital images is automatic object recognition. In this application, a computer can automatically recognize an object shown in the image and identify it by name. One of the most important uses of this is in robotics*. A robot can be equipped with digital cameras that can serve as its eyes and produce images. If the robot could recognize

* **bit** a single binary digit, 1 or 0—a contraction of Binary digIT; the smallest unit for storing data in a computer

* **GIF image** the acronym for Graphic Interchange Format where a static image is represented by binary bits in a data file

* **JPEG (Joint Photographic Experts Group)** organization that developed a standard for encoding image data in a compressed format to save space

* **lossy** a nonreversible way of compressing digital images; making images take up less space by permanently removing parts that cannot be easily seen anyway

* **robotics** the science and engineering of building electromechanical machines that aim to serve as replacements for human laborers

an object in these images, then it could make use of it. For instance, in a factory environment, the robot could use a screwdriver in the assembly of products. For this task, it has to recognize both the screwdriver and the various parts of the product. At home a robot could recognize objects to be cleaned. Other promising applications are in medicine, for example, in finding tumors in x-ray images. Security equipment could recognize the faces of people approaching a building. Automated drivers could drive a car without human intervention or drive a vehicle in inhospitable environments such as on the planet Mars or in a battlefield.

To recognize an object, the computer has to compare the image to a database of objects in its memory. This is a simple task for humans but it has proven to be very difficult to do automatically. One reason is that an object rarely produces the same image of itself. An object can be seen from many different viewpoints and under different lighting conditions, and each such variation will produce an image that looks different to the computer. The object itself can also change; for instance, a smiling face looks different from a serious face of the same person. Because of these difficulties, research in this field has been rather slow, but there are already successes in limited areas such as inspection of products on assembly lines, fingerprint identification by the FBI, and optical character recognition (OCR). OCR is now used by the U.S. Postal Service to read printed addresses and automatically direct the letters to their destination, and by scanning software to convert printed text to computer readable text.

▶ *See also* **Art • Digital Libraries • Fashion Design • Optical Technology • Photography**

Resources

Books

Burger, Wilheim, and Mark J. Burge. *Introduction to Digital Image Processing*. Goldaming, UK: Springer London, 2009.

40 Digital Photography Techniques. 3rd ed. Seoul: Youngjin.com, 2007.

Galer, Mark. *Digital Photography*. 4th ed. Amsterdam and Boston: Elservier 2008.

Gonzalez, Rafael C., and Richard E. Woods. *Digital Image Processing*. 3rd ed. Upper Saddle River, NJ: Prentice Hall, 2008.

Sheppard, Rob. *Kodak Guide to Digital Photography*. New York: Lark Books, 2008.

Web Sites

Vsellis.com. "Understanding DPI, Resolution and Print vs. Web Images" http://www.vsellis.com/multimedia/understanding-dpi-resolution-and-print-vs-web-images/(accessed September 24, 2012).

Digital Libraries

In the age of the Internet, the wealth of available information can seem overwhelming. Information does not, however, need to be messily distributed across the Iinternet's vast digital landscape. Just as libraries sort and categorize books and information in a way that makes it easier to find, digital libraries enable information to be stored in a manageable location and shared on computers and over the Internet.

The term digital library was coined relatively recently and is used to describe distributed access to collections of digital information. The terms electronic library and virtual library are sometimes also used. According to the Digital Library Federation (DLF), digital libraries are "organizations that provide the resources, including the specialized staff, to select, structure, offer intellectual access to, interpret, distribute, preserve the integrity of, and ensure the persistence over time of collections of digital works so that they are readily and economically available for used by a defined community or set of communities." The DLF is a consortium of libraries and organizations that attempt to identify standards and best practices, coordinate research and development in the field, and initiate cooperative projects <http://www.diglib.org/dlfhomepage.htm>. The DLF has thirty-seven partners, many of which are college and university libraries. Sometimes the term digital library is used to refer to the content or collection of materials (a digital library of historic photographs), whereas at other times it refers to the institution or service provided (the digital library provided electronic reference).

A unique characteristic of a digital library is that it is a collection of material organized for access by the users of the electronic documents.

Many library systems offer both books and digital versions of much of their collections. © *AP Images/Alex Brandon.*

* **Library of Congress Classification** the scheme by which the Library of Congress organizes classes of books and documents

* **metadata** data about data, such as the date and time created

The material is in digital form and may consist of or incorporate various media, such as photographs, video, sound recordings, as well as text and page images. Access is provided through search engines that search the actual text of the materials, or more formal cataloging such as Library of Congress* Classification or Subject Headings. Bibliographic and descriptive information about the contents is usually referred to as metadata*, making the information accessible for use. Once users locate information in the form of digital documents, they are able to view or download them.

The users for whom the digital library is intended are a defined community or group of communities. They may be scattered around the world, or may be in the same geographical location but wish to access the information from off-site. Therefore, another key aspect of the digital library is that it can be accessed remotely, usually through a web browser. In general, the information contained in the World Wide Web is not considered to be a digital library (though it is sometimes referred to as such) because it lacks the characteristics of a collection organized for a specific purpose.

Because the development of digital libraries is a relatively new undertaking, research and development is being conducted even as new digital library projects are being launched. A number of organizations have taken a leadership role in integrating research and practice. For example, the National Science Foundation (NSF), along with other government bodies, funded a series of Digital Library Initiatives in order to help create a number of large-and medium-sized digital library projects with a research focus. The Association for Computing Machinery (ACM) and Institute of Electrical and Electronics Engineers (IEEE) sponsor the Joint Conference on Digital Libraries, which brings together researchers and practitioners. The Institute of Museum and Library Services, a federal agency, provides funding for digital library projects at various levels.

Advantages of the Digital Library

The digital library increases access to information in a number of ways. First, in many cases, the digital library enables users to search documents based on content that is indexed automatically. This is true not only for text but also to some extent for images, video, and sound because content-based retrieval techniques have been developed to index digital characteristics such as image color and texture. Documents that have not received formal cataloging may still be located in a digital library, and even if cataloging information is available, the content-based information provides extra ways to search it. Once the relevant material has been found, access is again improved because the user can view the material online, or even download and view or print it at the user's location. This means that scholars need not travel to a distant library, or request an interlibrary loan. Instead, they have instantaneous access to the information at their desktop. Access is also improved because in many cases, through the medium of the World Wide Web, the information in the digital library is available not just to the local population, but to anyone who wishes to use it. Researchers benefit from digital libraries as they no longer have to leave the office or laboratory to obtain publications needed for their projects.

An additional advantage of the digital library is that because the digital information can be viewed and copied without access to the original document, it prevents wear and tear on library materials. This is particularly important when the original is valuable or fragile. The digital library, however, is not primarily concerned with preserving the original document because digitization changes the format of the document and the digital form itself may be difficult to preserve.

Types of Digital Libraries

There are many different types of digital libraries, ranging from simple collections to large-scale projects. The national libraries in many countries have been leaders in developing digital libraries of historical materials. In the United States, for example, the Library of Congress has an ongoing digital library project named American Memory, which includes many historically important and interesting collections of photographs, sound recordings, and video. The materials are cataloged in ways similar to the library's physical collections in Washington, D.C., but, unlike those collections, they are available for viewing and downloading by anyone with a web browser and an Internet connection. The digital collection includes everything from baseball cards to Civil War photographs to video clips of Coca-Cola advertisements.

University and college libraries and many public libraries around the world are also undertaking digital library projects to make their materials more readily and widely available. The libraries of ten University of California campuses have initiated a co-library, the California Digital Library, which provides access to faculty and students around the state. Materials include reference material such as encyclopedias and dictionaries, electronic journals, databases, and a digital archive of important manuscripts, photographs, and works of art held in libraries, museums, archives, and other institutions across California. Carnegie Melon University has scanned and digitized over 1.5 million books as of 2007 for its Million Book Project, funded in part by the NSF. Google Inc., Yahoo!, and MSN are also working on large digitization projects.

Technological Issues

The enabling technologies for digital libraries are economical storage of large quantities of data, high-speed connectivity and networking, and technologies related to digitizing, indexing, retrieving, and using multimedia. As digital libraries evolve, many technological issues remain to be solved. Desirable characteristics of digital libraries are scalability, interoperability,

Impact of Digital Libraries

Digital libraries, which provide widespread access to collections of electronic materials, are changing popular and scholarly use of textual and multimedia information. Their continued growth depends on the solution of technological problems, particularly the development of standards, as well as underlying legal, social, and economic questions.

* **protocol** an agreed understanding for the sub-operations that make up a transaction, usually found in the specification of inter-computer communications

* **interface** a boundary or border between two or more objects or systems; also a point of access

* **intellectual property** the acknowledgement that an individual's creativity and innovation can be owned in the same way as physical property

* **digital watermarks** special data structures permanently embedded into a program or other file type, which contain information about the author and the program

and sustainability—they need to be able to grow, to interact with other digital libraries, and to continue to function as organizations and technologies change.

Builders of digital libraries consider the identification of standards important to ensure the smooth development and growth of their products. For example, standard formats are needed for digitization so digital products can be universally distributed and read. For content, metadata standards are needed for cataloging, and encoding standards for indicating. Because digital libraries are often federations of individual sites, standards for digital library architecture are also important. Often, an open architecture is specified, in which the digital library is considered to be a set of services and functions, with a specific protocol* specifying what the interface* to that function will be.

Social, Legal, and Economic Issues

In this new field, many questions related to social, legal, and economic issues need to be addressed. Some considerations include charges (if any) for accessing the digital materials; ownership of these materials; copyrights for digital images, sound, and text; intellectual property* rights protection through digital watermarks*, who will be able to access the materials, and privacy and security settings. These concerns, like those of developing standards, are still open to research and debate.

▶ *See also* **Data Mining • Database Management Software • Information Technology Standards • Library Applications**

Resources

Books

Ali, Amjad. *Digital Libraries and Information Networks*. New Delhi: Ess Ess Publications, 2007.

Agosti, Maristella, ed. *Information Access through Search Engines and Digital Libraries*. Berlin: Springer, 2008.

Dahl, Mark, Kyle Banerjee, and Michael Spalti. *Digital Libraries: Integrating Content and Systems*. Chandos information professional series. Oxford, UK: Chandos Publishing, 2006.

Kresh, Diane, ed. *The Whole Digital Library Handbook*. Chicago: American Library Association, 2007.

Lesk, Michael. *Understanding Digital Libraries*. 2nd ed. Boston: Elsevier, 2004.

Miller, William, and Rita M. Pellen, eds. *Libraries and Google*. Binghamton, NY: Haworth Information Press, 2005.

Papy, Fabrice, ed. *Digital Libraries*. London: ISTE Ltd, 2008.

Web Sites

Clir.org and Daniel Greenstein and Suzanne E. Thorin. "The Digital Library: A Biography" http://www.clir.org/pubs/reports/pub109/pub109.pdf (accessed October 29, 2012).

Digital Photography

The early twenty-first century is a time of rapid and tremendous technological transition for photography and journalism. The addition of cameras to cell phones has altered the photographic landscape radically, making it possible for anyone, anywhere to take pictures or videos and upload them immediately to the internet. Never before have images of daily life been created so easily and cheaply, and distributed so widely.

The impact on journalism (including photojournalism) is profound, creating "citizen journalists" who can use their cell phones to photograph natural disasters, police brutality, and random events not covered by professional photojournalists.

From Film to Digital

From the 1930s to the 1990s, a professional photographer's career often included time in a chemical lab. Most photographers learned to shoot black and white film, followed by hours in the darkroom processing the negatives and printing the images on paper. Many photojournalists got their start working for a local newspaper, moving gradually to bigger papers if their careers took off. A lucky few might graduate to magazine

Scanning technician uses Photoshop to restore a badly damaged picture from the vast collection of historic photographs in the Hulton Archive (London, UK). © *Oli Scarff/Getty Images.*

photography, still practicing photojournalism, but shooting in color. The most ubiquitous black and white film was TRI-X 400. The standard color slide film was Kodachrome 64, so popular that Paul Simon referred to it in his 1973 hit song, "Kodachrome."

There were many popular general interest magazines and newspapers in the United States during this period, including *Life*, *Look*, *National Geographic*, *Sports Illustrated*, *Newsweek*, *Time*, *Reader's Digest*, *The New York Times*, *Washington Post*, *San Francisco Chronicle*, *Chicago Tribune*, *Boston Globe*, *Philadelphia Inquirer*, and *Seattle Times*, in addition to hundreds of smaller papers and magazines across the country that offered both employment and markets for photographers. These publications relied on revenue not only from sales to the public, but from advertising and classified ads. Anyone wanting to sell something—whether a large car manufacturer such as Ford Motor Company or a neighbor with a used car—had to advertise in the local media to reach an audience. A free online listing with publishing platforms such as Craig's List was not an option. Since the 1970s, many small to medium sized newspapers and magazines have shut down.

Typically a photographer did not see the results of his or her shoot until after leaving the field and getting the film processed. If the photographer worked locally, the wait time might average a few hours to a few days. For foreign correspondents, the delay could range from weeks to months. Often the photographer would go to great lengths to telephone from the field to learn the results of a shoot, or would wait to receive a tersely worded telegram from headquarters.

These factors conspired to make photojournalism the realm of professionals. Photographers covered society, daily life, the environment, and wars. They recorded local news and national politics, and shot fashion, food, portraits, sports, or weddings. Many photographers were staff members of the publications they worked for, earning retirement benefits like other office workers. Freelance photographers relied on the resale of their images through photo agencies such as Magnum, Gamma, *Agence France Press*, and National Geographic to augment their incomes.

Democratized Photography

In 2002, the first DSLR (Digital Single Lens Reflex) cameras manufactured by Canon and Nikon reached a price point and quality that allowed professional photographers to adopt them and give up film. The transition was costly, because digital cameras initially were much more expensive than film cameras, but the benefits were apparent immediately. With the advent of digital photography, a photographer knows instantly whether a shot is successful, simply by looking at a screen on the back of the camera. If adjustments to exposure or other settings are needed, the photographer can make them while still shooting.

Furthermore, digital cameras are much more sensitive to light than traditional film, enabling photographers to shoot in much darker situations without the need for flash. Tri-X film, with an ISO rating of 400, had been considered a high-speed film, but cameras of the 2010s can shoot at an ISO of up to 102,400.

Instant feedback and immediate processing also has democratized photography, making it more popular than ever before. Inexpensive and automatic "point and shoot" cameras make it convenient and easy to shoot fairly decent images. In the past good cameras and lenses were expensive, film was not very sensitive to light, and processing the film was an additional cost and delay.

With digital equipment, a photographer need not be concerned with bringing enough film into the field, or the correct type of film. Digital cameras can adjust color balance for the type of lighting in a scene. Airport security guards using x-ray machines no longer degrade the unprocessed film which traveling photographers bring home with them after a shoot.

Technological Advances

Most professional photographers record their images on compact flash cards in a large digital file format called RAW (uncompressed), whereas amateurs shoot in a compressed format called JPEG (the initials of the Joint Photographers Experts Group, which created the standard). The processing of film has shifted from a darkroom to a light room. Photographers use computers and software such as Adobe Photoshop, Lightroom, or Aperture to organize, caption, and "process" the images. Amateur photographers tend to use programs such as iPhoto, a basic version of powerful editing software. Photographers have transitioned to an entirely different workflow and acquired new computer skills.

Another tremendous technological advance has been the addition of video to digital photographic cameras. A single camera can shoot both photographic stills or video with sound. As the technology improves, the distinction between videographers and photographers is blurring, creating a new kind of video journalist adapted for the Web.

The rapid development of the Internet coincided with the advent of digital photographic technology. As photographers switched from shooting film to digital cameras, publishers migrated from products printed on paper to publication on the Internet. The Internet has created a glut of information, images, and video available to the public. Anyone can self-publish, independently of newspapers, magazines, and books. This technological revolution has created many more creative possibilities for photographers, while at the same time eroding their earnings from stock sales of images, and reducing photographic assignments from magazines and newspapers.

Impacts of Digital Photography

Digital photography is just one aspect of the digital world, but images still carry profound impact and both define and shape events and society. During the Arab Spring and civil war in Syria, citizen journalists uploaded thousands of photos and videos to the Internet. Nicknamed "vee-jays," they risked their lives to expose the harsh crackdown on protesters by the Assad regime.

At times the impacts of photographs are unintended. In 2004, digital photos casually taken by soldiers at Abu Ghraib prison in Iraq became evidence of U.S. military human rights abuses of Iraqi prisoners. The photos, shocking to the public when disclosed, resulted in courts-martial for many of the U.S. soldiers involved, and undermined the credibility of then Secretary of State Donald Rumsfeld (1932–) and others the chain of command.

The Kodak company manufactured the last roll of Kodachrome 64 film in 2009. The 131-year-old company, an icon of the twentieth century, declared bankruptcy in 2012. The word "Kodachrome" will have less and less resonance with the public as time goes on. Perhaps it will feel as historic and unfamiliar as the word "daguerreotype" does today.

Resources

Books

Caputo, Robert, and Boris Weintraub. *National Geographic Guide to Digital Photography*. Washington, DC: National Geographic Society, 2006.

Dickman, Jay, and Jay Kinghorn. *Perfect Digital Photography*. 2nd ed. New York: McGraw-Hill, 2009.

Hacking, Juliet. *Photography, The Whole Story*. New York: Prestel, 2012.

Light, Ken. *Witness in Our Time, Working Lives of Documentary Photographers*. Washington, DC: Smithsonian Books, 2010.

Martin, Bob. *Ultimate Field Guide to Photography*. Washington, DC: National Geographic, 2009.

Olsenius, Richard. *National Geographic Photography Field Guide: Digital Black & White: With Film Techniques Included*. Washington, DC: National Geographic, 2005.

Digital Signatures

A digital signature is an identifier that can be used to authenticate the sender of an electronic message (e-mail) or the signer of an electronic document. This technology can also be used to ensure the integrity of the message or document (that no alterations have been made since it was signed) as well as to date/time-stamp the document at signing. Finally, the signatory cannot easily repudiate or refuse to acknowledge his digital signature, nor can the document be easily forged.

Due to these criteria, a digital signature can be trusted and used like a written signature. On October 1, 2000, the Electronic Signatures in Global and National Commerce Act (known as the E-Signature Act) became effective in the United States. This act basically states that a signature cannot be denied simply because it is electronic, and an electronic signature must be considered as legally valid as a written signature. Not all electronic signatures, however, are digital signatures, so it is worth noting the following electronic signature examples that are *not* digital signatures:

- a biometric identifier;
- a written signature on a document that has been scanned into an electronic file; or
- a signature on a document that has been faxed (transmitted by facsimile).

So what *is* a digital signature? A digital signature uses cryptographic* technology to create an electronic identifier, but it can be used with any message, whether the message is encrypted* or not. Thus, digital signatures can accompany an unencrypted or an encrypted message. For example, the Computer Emergency Response Team (CERT) broadcasts

▲

A German TV station gets new digital studio. © *AP Images/Michael Probst.*

* **cryptography** the science of understanding codes and ciphers and their application

* **encrypted** coded, usually for purposes of security or privacy

Computer Sciences, 2ⁿᵈ Edition

This man's signature is seen on a monitor as he signs on an electronic pad while applying for the new identification card. © *ODD ANDERSEN/AFP/Getty Images.*

* **public key infrastructures (PKIs)** the supporting programs and protocols that act together to enable public key encryption/decryption

messages of computer vulnerabilities in clear text (unencrypted) to everyone on its mailing list. To allow its recipients to verify that these messages come from the CERT and are not spoofed (counterfeited into looking like messages from CERT) or modified in transit, the CERT signs all of its messages with its digital signature. Yet a government employee protecting classified information or a company employee protecting trade secrets would not only digitally sign his document but would encrypt the base message as well.

Many different software packages can be used to create a digital signature, from freeware to PC-based, shrink-wrapped software to large server-based systems, also known as public key infrastructures (PKIs)*. The process for sending a digitally signed unencrypted message is the same regardless of the package used as follows. A user creates a digital signature with a private key that he keeps to himself. He then attaches this signature to a document and sends it to others. His private key is mathematically linked to a public key that he posts on a public key server. He then tells the recipient(s) where his public key is stored. The recipient can then retrieve the sender's public key and reverse the process to determine the authenticity of the document.

The process for sending a digitally signed encrypted message is similar. In this case, the sender must retrieve the recipient's public key from a public key server. She then uses it to encrypt the message and send it to the recipient. The recipient then uses her own private key to decrypt the document, and the sender can be sure that only the recipient can read it.

Although there are many advantages to using digital signatures, several problems also exist:

■ Anyone can create a public/private key pair and contact the recipient, claiming to be the sender. Without knowing the sender by voice or another method, there is no way to guarantee that the owner of the key is indeed the person sending the document.

■ If someone other than the owner of the computer has had physical or logical access to the computer that houses the encryption software, malicious code could be inserted into this software to enable other actions, such as collecting the owner's private key and mailing it to the author of the code.

■ A computer may legitimately have a person's digital signature resident on it, but if that computer is stolen or used by another and the private key guessed, then a document created on that computer may not have been "signed" by the digital signature's owner.

In other words, the integrity of a digital signature can be compromised if someone gains improper access to the computer that runs the encryption software.

Regardless of the problems, digital signatures have great potential. However, for electronic business to reach its full potential, the end user must feel secure in signing or receiving a document electronically. Digital signature technology has the potential to create that level of trust.

▶ *See also* **Authentication • Cookies • Security**

Resources

Books

Katz, Jonathan. *Digital Signatures*. 2nd ed. New York: Spring Publishing, 2010.

Web Sites

US-Cert. "Understanding Digital Signatures." http://www.us-cert.gov/cas/tips/ST04-018.html (accessed September 24, 2012).

What is a Digital Signature?

A digital signature can be trusted and used like a written signature. Not all electronic signatures, however, are digital signatures.

Federal Government Saves Paper and Lowers Costs with Digital Signature

According to the U.S. Government Printing Office (GPO), in 2008 the Federal government's Budget for fiscal year 2009 was transmitted electronically. According to GPO head Robert C. Tapella, the GPO provided "authentication for the Budget via digital signature. This authentication verifies to anyone who downloads the Budget that the content has not been changed or altered. GPO's authentication capability ushers in a new era for Federal publications in terms of digital capability. Along with ongoing programs for the use of recycled paper and vegetable-based ink, digital also helps promote environmental sustainability in the Government's publishing and information dissemination activities." People can still obtain printed versions of each year's Federal Budget, but they must pay a fee to do so.

E

E-banking

Traditional banks offer many services to their customers, including accepting customer money deposits, providing various banking services to customers, and making loans to individuals and companies. Compared with traditional channels of delivering banking services through physical branches, e-banking uses the Internet to make traditional banking services available to bank customers, such as opening accounts, transferring funds, and electronic bill payment.

Financial institutions can offer e-banking in two main ways. First, an existing bank with physical offices can also establish an online site and offer e-banking services to its customers in addition to the regular channel. For example, Citibank is a leader in e-banking, offering walk-in, face-to-face banking at its branches throughout many parts of the world as well as e-banking services through the World Wide Web. Citibank customers can access their bank accounts through the Internet, and in addition to the core e-banking services such as account balance inquiry, funds transfer, and electronic bill payment, Citibank also provides premium services including financial calculators, online stock quotes, brokerage services, and insurance.

E-banking from banks such as Citibank complements those banks' physical presence. Generally, e-banking is provided without extra cost to customers. Customers are attracted by the convenience of e-banking through the Internet, and in turn, banks can operate more efficiently when customers perform transactions by themselves rather than going to a branch and dealing with a branch representative.

In addition to traditional banks that have both a physical and online presence, there are several e-banks that exist only on the Internet, allowing users to work with a virtual bank. First Internet Bank of Indiana is one of the first Internet-only banks. Another online-only bank is ING Direct. Without physical branches, these banks can cut operating costs and can potentially offer higher deposit rates to its customers and waive many fees normally charged by a bank with a large network of physical branches. The challenge for Internet-only banks is to provide quality customer services without physical offices. One way in which ING Direct is dealing with this issue is through the establishment of cafes, which are locations in both Canada and the United States where free coffee and Internet access are available to customers. Seminars on managing money, retirement plans, mortgages, and credit management are offered at both cafe locations and online.

E-banking in China is on the rise.
© *AP Images/Imaginechina.*

* **Hypertext Markup Language
(HTML)** an encoding scheme for
text data that uses special tags
in the text to signify properties to
the viewing program (browser)
like links to other documents or
document parts

E-banking services are delivered to customers through the Internet
and the Web using Hypertext Markup Language (HTML)*. In order to
use e-banking services, customers need Internet access and Web browser
software. Multimedia information in HTML format from online banks
can be displayed in Web browsers. The heart of the e-banking application
is the computer system, which includes Web servers, database management systems, and Web application programs that can generate dynamic
HTML pages.

Bank customers' account and transaction information is stored in a
database, a specialized piece of software that can store and retrieve large
amounts of data in high speed. The function of the Web server is to process requests for Web pages and deliver information to users through
the Internet. When the Web server receives a request such as an account
inquiry from an online customer, it requires an external Web application
to interact with the bank's infrastructure to retrieve the account information. C, Visual Basic, VBScript, and Java are some of the languages that
can be used to develop web applications to process customer requests,
interact with the database, and generate dynamic responses. Then, the
Web server will forward the HTML describing the response to the Web
browser of e-banking customers. Several banks, such as NationsBank, also
use state-of-the-art imaging systems, allowing customers to view images
of checks and invoices over the Internet.

One of the main concerns of e-banking is security. Without great
confidence in security, customers were initially unwilling to use a public network, such as the Internet, to view their financial information

online and conduct financial transactions. Some of the security threats include invasion of individuals' privacy and theft of confidential information. Banks with e-banking service offer several methods to ensure a high level of security: (1) identification and authentication, (2) encryption, and (3) firewalls*. First, the identification of an e-banking Web site takes the form of a known Uniform Resource Locator (URL) or Internet address, while a customer is generally identified by his or her login ID and password to ensure only authenticated* customers can access their accounts. Many e-banking Web sites are also identified with an HTTPS certificate, which ensures that the website is who it claims to be, and has not been hijacked by a hacker. Second, messages between customers and online banks are all encrypted* so that a hacker cannot view the message even if the message is intercepted over the Internet. The particular encryption standard adopted by most browsers is termed Secure Socket Layer (SSL). SSL is a protocol, which defines how to perform authentication and encryption over a network in a secure manner without being susceptible to eavesdropping or message tampering by a third party in between. SSL encryption is built into most Web browsers, and users do not have to take any extra steps to set up the browser to use SSL encryption for Web sites which support it. Third, banks have built firewalls, which are software or hardware barriers between the corporate network and the external Internet, to protect the servers and bank databases from outside intruders. For example, Wells Fargo Bank connected to the Internet only after it had installed a firewall and made sure the firewall was sufficiently impenetrable.

The range of e-banking services has since increased. Use of electronic money has skyrocketed. Completely Web-based payment services such as Paypal are extremely popular for both businesses and for personal exchanges of money. According to a "Wired" article, by 2009 about 15 percent of all online monetary transactions were through Paypal alone. Electronic money can be stored in computers or smart cards*, and consumers can use the electronic money to purchase small value items over the Internet. Further, banks seek to offer their customers more products and services such as insurance, mortgage, financial planning, and brokerage. This delivers more value to the customers but also help banks to grow business and revenues. The added convenience and perks of online banking has made it extremely popular. In a 2012 survey by the American Bankers Association, 39 percent of respondents said online banking on a computer was their preferred method, making it the most popular banking method by a wide margin. Banking at a physical bank branch came in a distant second at 18 percent. Additionally, banking via smartphones and mobile devices has increased in popularity, with six percent of respondents citing mobile banking as their favorite method.

* **firewall** a special purpose network computer or software that is used to ensure that no access is permitted to a sub-network unless authenticated and authorized

* **authentication** the act of ensuring that an object or entity is what it is intended to be

* **encrypted** coded, usually for purposes of security or privacy

* **smart card** a credit-card style card that has a microcomputer embedded within it; it carries more information to assist the owner or user

* **encrypted** coded, usually for purposes of security or privacy

* **ASCII** an acronym that stands for American Standard Code for Information Interchange; assigns a unique 8-bit binary number to every letter of the alphabet, the digits (0 to 9), and most keyboard symbols

▶ *See also* **E-Commerce • Privacy • Security • World Wide Web**

Resources

Books

New Century Publications. *New Century's Dictionary of Banking and Finance: Including a Glossary of E-Banking Terms*. New Delhi, India: New Century Publications, 2008.

Shah, Mahmood, and Steve Clarke. *E-Banking Management: Issues, Solutions, and Strategies*. Hershey, PA: Information Science Reference, 2009.

Uppal, R. K. *Banking with Technology*. New Delhi, India: New Century Publications, 2008.

Web Sites

Geffne, Marice. "Online Banking Tops Again." Bankrate.com. http://www.bankrate.com/financing/banking/online-banking-tops-again/ (accessed October 27, 2012).

Wolman, Daivd. "Time to Cash Out: Why Paper Money Hurts the Economy." Wired.com. http://www.wired.com/culture/culturereviews/magazine/17-06/st_essay (accessed October 27, 2012).

E-books

E-books, or electronic books, are books stored in digital format that are created, delivered, and read by electronic methods. This means that the book's text may be available on CD-ROM through a computer or encrypted* and delivered through a handheld device. The term "e-book" is also used to refer to a dedicated handheld device used to read electronically based text, although these devices should more properly be referred to as e-book readers.

The term "e-text" is sometimes used in relation to e-books; it is usually used to refer to any digitized text that a person can read by means of a computer, e-book reader, or other electronic device. E-text can come in a variety of digital formats, such as ASCII* code, and various versions of Unicode (which possess a much greater depth of supported characters than). It is important to note that a given e-book may, or may not, be available in an e-text form such as. That is because many e-books are recorded by companies in a proprietary electronic form, or code, that is generally intended to be read only using a particular company's e-book reader.

The availability and delivery of the text of books in electronic format is not new. Project Gutenberg (www.gutenberg.net/) has been providing

Sony presents new e-reader. © *Daniel Acker/Bloomberg via Getty Images.*

the text of public domain books free since 1971. But advances in computer technology, especially laptop and handheld computer technology, coupled with near-ubiquitous Internet access, brought about the conditions necessary for e-book readers to gain the widespread acceptance of consumers that they now enjoy.

Computerized texts have several advantages. Compared to a print volume, a computer can store much more text. Computerized text is also much easier to search, and hyperlinks* can move the reader easily throughout the text, or from one text to another. Even after the personal computer (PC) became commonplace in the 1980s, many people still preferred reading from a printed page. They disliked scrolling down a screen rather than flipping pages, and they also found that reading text from a conventional computer monitor to be somewhat tedious. Those preferences resulted in numerous attempts to try to create an electronic reading experience that mimicked that of reading a printed book.

There are many types of e-book readers currently available for purchase. A couple of the more popular e-book brands (as of 2010) are Amazon's *Kindle* (first released in late 2007) and Barnes and Noble's *Nook* (initially released in late 2009—often referred to in the lower-case as "nook"). Throughout the 2000s, the price of e-book readers tended to decrease, while their capabilities generally increased. The downward cost trend can be seen in the Kindle and Nook readers. When the *Kindle 2* version was released by Amazon in early 2009, it cost a little over $350; by mid-2010 its price had fallen to about $190. A similar price drop occurred for the Nook, which was introduced in late 2009. Its initial retail price was listed at about $260; but by mid-2010 its price was reduced to around

* **hyperlinks** connections between electronic documents that permit automatic browsing transfer at the point of the link

$200, with a strictly Wi-Fi version being offered for approximately $150. The Kindle and Nook have proven to be very popular. In 2011, Nook device and e-book sales generated $1.3 billion in revenue. Meanwhile, in 2012, Amazon reported that e-book sales had eclipsed sales of printed books on its UK website.

It is important to note that tablet PCs, laptop computers, and other portable computers are fully capable of being used to display digitized books. For instance, Apple's iPad is a tablet PC first introduced in the spring of 2010. It provides the capability to view e-books, but is also a fully functioning computer, albeit one without a keyboard, mouse, or stylus for input. Instead, it incorporates a multi-touch screen system. The advantage of a tablet PC or laptop computer for viewing e-books is that, generally-speaking, they can perform a wider array of functions. Whether one decides to purchase a tablet PC or e-book reader is largely dependent upon what uses the user has in mind for the device—if one is mainly interested in reading electronic books, then an e-book reader is probably the right device to purchase.

The first e-book readers were introduced into the consumer market-place in the late 1990s. Many different versions of these readers have been created, but most share a common set of attributes. For instance, most readers are more or less the size of a large paperback book, and are fairly lightweight (weighing about the same as a hardcover book, or even less). Because they store text digitally, these readers can hold numerous books worth of text. They use touch-screen technology, provide built-in diction-aries, have the capability to highlight text and store notes made by the reader, and also offer keyword searching. Pages can be bookmarked for easy reference, and battery life is more than sufficient for the reading of a complete book. Other options include varying font sizes and adjustable screen backlighting to meet users' needs.

There are several advantages of being able to access books in digital format from a relatively small, lightweight reader. Students can access all their textbooks on one small device. By linking to the Internet, users of reference books can enjoy the advantages of having a text that never goes out of date since updated versions can be uploaded. And travelers can enjoy having only one small device to carry, rather than multiple books.

Most publishers see the field of digital publishing as one more way they can reach readers. Both publishers and authors have tried different ways of selling books online. One well known example of this is Stephen King's novella *Riding the Bullet*, which was published only electronically. King's novella can be considered the first e-book bestseller since more than 50,000 copies were downloaded. A later novella, called Ur, was written by King for release in early 2009, and once again was available only in electronic format; in this instance King's novella was restricted to Amazon's Kindle platform.

See also **Assistive Computer Technology For Persons With Disabilities • Digital Libraries • World Wide Web**

Resources

Books

Angel, Edward. *Interactive Computer Graphics: A Top-Down Approach with Shader-Based OpenGL*, 6th ed Boston: Addison-Wesley, 2012.

Brinkmann, Ron. *The Art and Science of Digital Compositing: Techniques for Visual Effects, Animation and Motion Graphics*. Amsterdam and Boston: Morgan Kaufmann Publishers/Elsevier, 2008.

Sutcliffe, Alistair. *Multimedia and Visual Reality: Designing Usable Multisensory User Interfaces*. Mahwah, N.J., and London: Lawrence Erlbaum, 2003.

Web Sites

Alter, Alexandra.. "Your E-Book is Reading You." *The Wall Street Journal,*, July 19, 2012. http://online.wsj.com/article/SB10001 424052702304870304577490950051438304.html (accessed November 4, 2012).

Shiv Malik. "Kindle ebook Sales Have Overtaken Amazon Print Sales, Says Book Seller." *The Guardian*, 5 August 2012. http://www.guardian.co.uk/books/2012/aug/06/amazon-kindle-ebook-sales-overtake-print (accessed November 4, 2012).

E-commerce: Economic and Social Aspects

E-commerce is technology-enabled buying and selling that occurs over telecommunications networks such as the Internet. As in physical marketplaces, these exchanges can occur between businesses, between a business and a consumer, or even between consumers. E-commerce has grown dramatically since it emergence in the late 1990s. This transition from traditional physical marketplaces to technology-enabled ones has important economic and social implications.

One significant economic effect is the reduction of transaction costs compared to traditional commerce. In the 1930s, economist Ronald Coase (1910–) defined transaction costs as the costs associated with organizing a transaction, starting with searching for a product, then negotiating for a price, and finally making the exchange. E-commerce can reduce transaction costs by removing many of the geographic and time barriers that buyers and sellers previously faced. Customers who had to drive to

E-Books versus Hardcover and Audio Books

By the close of the 2000s, consumers had widely embraced e-book technology. The Association of American Publishers, which gathers book industry statistics, reported that 2009 was the first year in which e-books had outsold audio books. And in 2010, Amazon.com, which is the largest online retailer in the United States, announced that sales of its Kindle-based e-books had overtaken sales of hardcover books for the first time. Indeed, e-book sales at Amazon (in mid-2010) were running at almost twice the rate as sales of hardcover titles. However, sales of paperback books are still much greater than those of both hardcover and e-books combined.

* **XML** the acronym for eXtensible Markup Language; a method of applying structure to data so that documents can be represented

a physical store location during business hours, park, and manually do comparison shopping before buying, can now do this for many products online, anytime. For information products, such as digital music, e-books, and movies, which can be both bought and delivered online, e-commerce also reduces the product delivery cost. However, initial delivery costs may rise in situations where parcels of goods are shipped to individual consumer addresses rather than commercial stores.

For businesses, the potential cost savings are even greater. Most industries are organized into supply chains that integrate supply and demand requirements across manufacturers, suppliers, warehouses, and stores so that merchandise shows up on time and at the right location. Business rules provide the glue that binds the various producers together by specifying company policies on pricing, payment, returns, and other contractual information. By automating business rules using technologies such as XML*, e-commerce platforms provide fast, synchronized exchange of supply and demand information between supply chain members thereby reducing both labor and inventory costs, as well as increasing customer satisfaction. Joint work between and within companies is also fostered by Internet-based technologies that allow easy communication across different time zones and collaboration using communal web sites.

Privacy

Internet technologies also have an effect on social issues, such as privacy. Physical and technological barriers to gathering personal information about consumers are rapidly disappearing. While companies have always gathered and resold information about their customers' purchasing habits, the Internet simplifies this process and allows new types of information to be collected. Internet market research firms compile consumer information across multiple stores, search engines, and even some social media sites.

Privacy issues exist concerning who owns and controls the use of this information and how it may be gathered. Laws generally require that companies with access to personal information, including email and physical addresses, post privacy policies on web sites that detail where and how personal information can be used.

Companies can also collect customer information to provide more personalized service and to speed up online transactions. Amazon.com's recommendation services combine information about a customer's past purchases with those of other customers with similar interests. Since these data detail not only how much merchandise was sold, but also where and to which demographic groups, marketing campaigns can use these data to target their advertisements to people most likely to buy their products.

Security

While privacy addresses the customers' control over the confidentiality of their transaction information, security considers how such transactions can be protected from assault or corruption. Customers must be confident that credit card numbers will remain secure before providing them on the Internet. To reduce the possibility of theft, companies use digital certificates* to authenticate* that they are who they claim to be, and not some fraudulent site stealing customer credit card numbers. Certificate authorities, such as VeriSign, act as trusted third parties to issue to companies. Using industry-standard Secure Sockets Layer (SSL) technology, employ encryption-based protocols to protect the integrity of customer data exchanged online. Once the transaction data resides on the merchant site, a firewall* can be used to restrict Internet access.

Finding the Niche

E-commerce businesses may be completely online enterprises such as Expedia which sells airline tickets and other travel services. These are known as click enterprises. Alternatively, a business venture may comprise a mixture of online and traditional business, wherein the Internet adds another channel for reaching the consumer. Many traditional stores, for example, avoid a purely Internet-based strategy and e-commerce with traditional brick-and-mortar stores. This strategy is known as brick and click. Other traditional retailers who traditionally relied on catalog sales, such as Land's End, have capitalized on Internet sales channels and advertising while minimizing formerly sizable printing and distribution costs.

Some fully web-based businesses have become profitable, creating new market categories in the process. In the travel industry, travel agents traditionally served as intermediaries between the airlines and customers. As more online services such as Priceline are available to connect customers with the products and services they want, the Internet effectively disintermediates travel agents. Most travel companies such as airlines and hotels sell tickets and bookings directly to consumers. The fully web-based online auction site eBay effectively launched the online auction market.

Finding the right mixture of on-and-offline commerce is always a challenge. As is the case in traditional business ventures, the experience gained by the successes and failures of one generation of entrepreneurs can serve as case studies for the e-commerce leaders of the future.

▶ *See also* **E-Commerce • Internet: Applications • Privacy • Security • World Wide Web**

Resources

Books

Developers DevZone. *Building eCommerce Applications*. Cambridge, MA: O'Reilly, 2011.

Laudon, Kenneth and Carol Guercio Traver. *E-Commerce 2012*. 8th ed. Upper Saddle River, NJ: Prentice Hall, 2011.

Travelocity.com

Many travelers are turning to online vendors in the hope of getting discounted or bargain rates. One of the e-businesses specializing in travel is Travelocity.com, founded in 1996. Headquartered in Fort Worth, Texas, Travelocity.com provides reservation services in over 80 countries. This e-commerce company also offers tour packages and travel magazines, as well as luggage and other sundries—articles that a traveler might need while on vacation or a business trip.

* **digital certificates** certificates used in authentication that contain encrypted digital identification information

* **authenticate** the act of ensuring that an object or entity is what it is intended to be

* **firewall** a special purpose network computer or software that is used to ensure that no access is permitted to a sub-network unless authenticated and authorized

* **dynamic links** logical connections between two objects that can be modified if the objects themselves move or change state

* **Uniform Resource Locators (URLs)** references to a document or a document container using the Hypertext Transfer Protocol (HTTP); consist of a hostname and path to the document

* **server** a computer that does not deal directly with human users, but instead handles requests from other computers for services to be performed

Web Sites

U.S. Federal Government. "BusinessUSA." http://business.usa.gov (accessed November 4, 2012).

E-journals and E-publishing

Electronic journals (e-journals) published on the World Wide Web provide users with online access to various journals. E-journals may be digitalized images or text of older issues of a journal, a digitalized version of a journal that also appears in print, or a journal that is published only on the Internet. Unlike traditionally published journals, e-journals often are optimized with keyword searchable articles, searchable indices, and linked cross-references. E-journal databases, such as JSTOR, provide users with a single searchable database for many journals.

E-journals have numerous benefits compared to their print versions. For example, most e-journals can be accessed twenty-four hours a day, seven days a week, making it unnecessary for users to visit libraries in order to make copies of articles. E-journals eliminate the need to track down missing hardcopies or wait for a group of issues to be bound together at the bindery to preserve them for later use. Another benefit is that many e-publishers allow users to download or print most articles. E-journals are also often an enhanced version of their print counterparts, with embedded links that add value to the journal. Some publishers make particular articles of an e-journal available electronically before the entire issue is available. One of the most important benefits is that multiple users at one location can access the same article at the same time.

Many libraries are making tough choices to save shelf space and labor costs by canceling their print subscriptions and subscribing to electronic versions only. Whereas print journals are limited to traditional static text and two-dimensional graphics, e-journals can include sound, video, or other multimedia options. They can be optimized for easy navigation on e-readers or app-enabled devices such as smartphones. References in articles can be linked dynamically to other online works as well. Articles also can list dynamic links* to various examples and other sources, rather than just being limited to the standard citations or images seen in the print versions.

There are two primary criticisms of e-journals: their instability in the publishing market and the lack of a permanent archive (backlog) for many journals. Common complaints include Uniform Resource Locators (URLs)* that change frequently and servers* that crash. Some journals lack a consistent archive of issues that are made available on the Web, choosing instead to only feature a limited number of past issues (back issues). This is a matter of great concern to libraries, especially if they choose to cancel print subscriptions in favor of access to e-journals or if publishers stop printing the bound version of the journal.

Relationship to Traditional Research

Many scholarly journals are available as e-journals. In fact, some scholarly e-journals that have a significant impact on their respective fields are available for free. Attitudes toward papers published in e-journals are gradually changing, making them more accepted. At the same time, scholars continue to have concerns about how to view e-journals in the peer review process, the integrity of publishing in e-journals, and the use of such publications for tenure and promotion decisions. This process is evolving and changing, largely due to a movement underway between various scientific societies and universities to transform and have an impact on scholarly publishing. Leading this movement is an initiative called "Scholarly Publishing and Academic Resources Coalition (SPARC)" <http://www.arl.org/sparc> with the goal of "returning science to scientists."

Authentication and Verification

There are primarily two methods for accessing e-journals: by password and by Internet Protocol (IP)* authentication. Passwords work well for people with individual subscriptions, but in a library setting, it becomes cumbersome to keep patrons apprised of password information. Therefore, although passwords are an effective way to provide users with access when they are using the journals from off-site, IP authentication* is the most efficient way for an institution to provide access to its e-journals for users who want to access the information while on-site. If organizations use the IP authentication method, they have to inform the publisher of all the possible IP addresses for their institution. IP authentication works by providing the user with a certificate or token that certifies their identity within an organization. When the identity of the user is verified, the user is either passed on to the publisher's server or to a server that acts as a proxy. This method can sometimes be expensive and complex, and there is a need for an organization to maintain a local server with an access control list of eligible users. Another challenge is that some publishers limit the number of simultaneous users, which can present its own set of problems.

Kerberos is also an authentication scheme based on encrypted* credentials. It was created at Massachusetts Institute of Technology (MIT) and is freely available. Kerberos uses hidden tickets that can be used over open networks for authentication. A central server with account information authenticates each ticket and then passes the user through to the resources on that server. Kerberos was developed with an important emphasis on security and uses a strong cryptography protocol* that can be used on insecure networks.

Proxy Servers

Proxy servers are important for organizations with a dispersed group of users. An example would be a university whose faculty and students travel worldwide for conferences, internships, and other events. These people may need access to their university library's e-journals while off-campus, and proxy servers provide them with this common means of access.

*Internet Protocol (IP) a method of organizing information transfer between computers; the IP was specifically designed to offer low-level support to Transmission Control Protocol (TCP)

*authentication the act of ensuring that an object or entity is what it is intended to be

*encrypted coded, usually for purposes of security or privacy

*protocol an agreed understanding for the sub-operations that make up a transaction, usually found in the specification of inter-computer communications

SPARC

The Scholarly Publishing and Academic Resources Coalition (SPARC) was founded to offer an affordable alternative to the high-priced scientific and high-tech journals on the marketplace. By publishing the latest scientific discoveries and research findings through print and online articles, SPARC helps meet the needs of the library market, as well as the scientific, technical, and medical fields.

* **PDF** the acronym for Portable Document Format, developed by Adobe Corporation to facilitate the storage and transfer of electronic documents

A proxy server works by masking remote users with the accepted IP address needed to access an e-journal restricted by an IP address. Users configure their browsers to access a proxy server and are prompted to authenticate themselves when they link to an e-journal. Authentication may require a user's name, social security number, student identification number, or other unique piece of information that will identify a user. The most attractive feature of the proxy server is that a user can access a restricted resource from any location. The most important problem with a proxy server, however, is that some publishers refuse access to their e-journals by a proxy server. Also, if all users are funneled through a proxy server, it may create a bottleneck, especially if the proxy server goes down.

Technology and Software

The primary formats used for e-journals are HTML and Adobe Acrobat PDF*, which has become somewhat of a standard for many e-journals because it is readily available, flexible, inexpensive, and prevents unwanted copying and pasting of journal text in some instances.

Organizations

For computer sciences, some of the key organizations that publish e-journals are as follows.

- ACM (Association for Computing Machinery) Digital Library: <http://dl.acm.org/dl.cfm>
- American Mathematical Society Journals: <http://www.ams.org/mathscinet/searchjournals>
- Cambridge Journals Online: <http://journals.cambridge.org/>
- JSTOR: <http://www.jstor.org/>
- Springer: <http://www.springer.com/?SGWID=5-102-0-0-0>
- MIT Journals Online: <http://www-mitpress.mit.edu/>
- Oxford University Press Journals: <http://www.oxfordjournals.org>

▶ *See also* **Desktop Publishing • Document Processing • Educational Software**

Resources

Web Sites

E-Journals.org. http://www.e-journals.org (accessed November 4, 2012).

University of Edinburgh. "Finding e-Journals." http://www.ed.ac.uk/schools-departments/information-services/services/library-museum-gallery/finding-resources/find-ejournal/search-ejourn (accessed November 4, 2012).

University of Michigan Press. "Journal of Electronic Publishing." http://www.journalofelectronicpublishing.org (accessed November 4, 2012).

Electronic Campus

The traditional classroom lecture, supplemented with blackboard and chalk, has stood for centuries as the prevailing model for formal instruction. The term lecture is based on the Latin *lectura*, meaning a reading, and classroom design has traditionally reflected the format where lecturers read from texts or notes held before them on a lectern. Educational institutions are now replacing blackboards and lecterns with hardware and software solutions that provide rich multimedia support for instructional presentations and help engage students in active learning experiences.

Early attempts to supplement the classroom lecture experience involved adding equipment such as 16 millimeter (mm) film and 35mm slide projectors to allow students to view previously prepared images. The film projectors were difficult to run, often requiring an equipment operator and the purchase or rental of expensive films, but had the advantage of offering high quality images and sound. Similarly, 35mm slides were difficult and time-consuming to create, but offered excellent viewing quality.

The technology that had the greatest impact in the classroom from the 1950s through the 1990s was borrowed from the bowling alley—the overhead projector. The overhead projector allowed the instructor to prepare a presentation in advance, print it on clear transparencies, and project it onto a screen. More importantly, it allowed the instructor to be spontaneous and write notes, draw illustrations, or scribble equations with a grease pencil and save them for future classes. The overhead projector became an indispensable classroom aid, particularly in large classrooms where the chalkboard cannot be seen from a distance.

Large classrooms present other problems as well, particularly with audio. Program audio from films, audiotapes, and videocassettes must be amplified and broadcast over a system of speakers. Typically, instructors in large lecture halls must have their voices amplified through audio reinforcement, captured by a microphone. Wireless lavaliere microphones* free instructors from the confines of the lectern and allow them to walk around the room while their voices are still picked up by the audio system.

With the advent of videocassette recorders (VCRs), videotapes replaced films in the classroom except in special circumstances requiring large, high quality displays. The video display unit was typically a standard television monitor, heavy and limited in size, but with the advantage of being viewable in normally lit rooms. Some institutions experimented with video distribution networks that allowed video to be distributed from a centralized source, such as a media center, to the classroom, using fiber optic* cable. As VCRs reached commodity prices, however, most institutions found it more cost-effective to build individual VCRs and monitors into classrooms. Some institutions combine the two forms of technology. This allows for centralized distribution of announcements or special presentations, as well as for classroom-level use and control of videotaped material.

* **wireless lavaliere microphones** small microphones worn around the speakers' necks, which attach to their shirts

* **fiber optic** transmission technology using long, thin strands of glass fiber; internal reflections in the fiber assure that light entering one end is transmitted to the other end with only small losses in intensity; used widely in transmitting digital information

* **microcomputer** a computer
that is small enough to be used
and managed by one person
alone; often termed a personal
computer

* **liquid crystal display (LCD)** a
type of crystal that changes
its level of transparency when
subjected to an electric current;
used as an output device on a
computer

* **infrastructure** the foundation
or permanent installation
necessary for a structure or
system to operate

* **lumens** a unit of measure of light
intensity

* **digitizes** converts analog
information into a digital form for
processing by a computer

When microcomputers* became popular, instructors sought the ability to display the contents of their computer screens to the entire class. In the 1980s, liquid crystal display (LCD)* units became available that could be placed on top of overhead projectors, building on existing infrastructure*. Although early models had limited screen resolution and required the room to be darkened, making it difficult for students to take notes, this new capability provided instructors with several clear advantages. It reduced the need for preparing overhead transparencies and allowed live demonstrations of computer-related content. The wide availability of network access further increased their value.

By the end of the twentieth century, LCD projection technology had evolved to allow a single projector to display both data and video material adequately. By 2001 projectors could output in excess of 4,000 lumens*, sufficient for viewing under normal classroom lighting conditions. The wide availability of quality display technology now allows virtually all material to be viewed digitally in many schools and institutions.

Components of the Electronic Classroom

Today's general-purpose electronic classrooms, sometimes referred to as smart classrooms, typically provide at least one LCD data/video projector and offer the ability to connect to a wide range of source input devices, including built-in or portable microcomputers equipped with network communications ports, videocassette recorders, digital video disc (DVD), compact discs (CDs), and document cameras. The document camera digitizes* two- and three-dimensional objects placed on its stand and displays an image via an LCD projector. This setup provides all of the functionality associated with the old overhead projectors and also allows the digitized images to be transmitted to remote sites or recorded.

Smaller classrooms can utilize a touch-sensitive display panel, such as Smart Technologies' SMART Board interactive whiteboard, that connects to a computer and digital projector and allows the instructor to make annotations on a presentation or create new images spontaneously. Teachers can use their finger on the interactive whiteboard to manage computer applications, write notes, draw images, pull up charts and images, search the Internet, play videos, and save any of these actions. The newest models of SMART Boards enable instructors to switch modes automatically through touch recognition. This allows instructors to write with a pen, erase using a palm, and move objects using a finger. The created images can be retained for subsequent printing, posted to a class Web page, or edited for future use. The end result provides the instructor with virtually unlimited whiteboard space and an electronic recording of the class displays. The SMART Board 600 Series, for instance, can be used with other SMART products, such as the SMART document camera and the SMART Response interactive response system. The 600 Series can also be updated to include a wireless Bluetooth connection and other accessories.

In the classroom, as in most other areas, necessity often proves to be the mother of invention. Innovators at the University of Pittsburgh combined technologies to address two related problems: allowing instructors who use wheelchairs to make use of SMART Board-like capabilities and providing a means for students in large lecture halls to view the instructors' ad hoc notes, drawings, and illustrations. The solution pairs a small, touch-sensitive LCD panel with a laptop computer and an LCD projector. The LCD panel doubles as graphics tablet and preview screen, allowing the instructor to stand or sit, facing the class, and make drawings and annotations that the entire class can view on the large projection screen.

The needs of some academic disciplines often require more specialized classroom designs, including:

- Electronic tally systems, or classroom response systems, provide hardware and/or software solutions to allow the class to respond electronically to the instructor's questions and view the results on the classroom display equipment. These systems, used in many colleges and some secondary schools, generally consist of a personal response system (PRS) clicker or wireless remote either purchased by the student or provided by the school system. These clickers can be used to monitor attendance, comprehension of the subject matter through results from students' answers, for student polling to facilitate discussion, and to administer exams and quizzes during class, thus eliminating the need to collect papers and grade manually. The real-time results can be accessed during classes to monitor students' understanding of course topics as the lecture progresses or can be downloaded later to calculate grades.

- Computers at every seat, or ports and power outlets to allow the connection of networked laptops and other devices. Many institutions are moving to wireless networks to accomplish this goal.

- Hardware or software to network the monitors, keyboards, and mouse inputs from the classroom microcomputers. This setup allows the instructor, from the console, to redirect and control any individual computer display so the entire class can see the example.

- Interactive Television (ITV) capabilities, which use video compression algorithms to create two-way audio, video, and data interactions between similarly equipped classrooms. Such facilities use Integrated Services Digital Network (ISDN), Asynchronous Transfer Mode (ATM), or other high-bandwidth network connections to provide real-time support for distance education programs between the instructor and students at one or more remote sites.

Classroom technology continues to evolve at a rapid pace. For example, networked LCD projectors can now display content stored in Web pages, allowing an instructor to make presentations without having a local microcomputer. Tomorrow's classroom will be an exciting place for learning with and about technology.

No More Blackboards!

Educational institutions are replacing blackboards and lecterns with hardware and software solutions that provide rich multimedia support for instructional presentations and help engage students in active learning experiences.

In 2012, Harvard University, Massachusetts Institute of Technology (MIT), and University of California Berkeley launched the "edX" technology platform for distance education. The technology allows students around the world access to select classes from the renowned schools. As of 2012, students cannot earn degree credit but can be awarded certificates of completion for coursework. Harvard and MIT, the founding schools, announced that more than 100 universities located around the world expressed interested in joining edX and the network is expected to grow.

▶ *See also* **Distance Learning** • **E-Books** • **Educational Software** • **Telecommunications**

Resources

Books

Blake, Robert J. *Brave New Digital Classroom: Technology and Foreign Language Learning*. Washington, DC: Georgetown University Press, 2008.

Gura, Mark, and Kathleen P. King. *Classroom Robotics: Case Stories of 21st Century Instruction for Millennial Students*. Charlotte, NC: IAP, 2007.

SMART Technologies, Inc. *SMART Board: Interactive Whiteboard Learner Workbook*. Calgary, AB: SMART Technologies, 2006.

Tomei, Lawrence A. *Integrating Information and Communications Technologies into the Classroom*. Hershey, PA: InfoSci, 2007.

Web Sites

Office of the Chief Information Officer, The Ohio State University. "Clickers." http://ocio.osu.edu/elearning/toolbox/depth/clickers (accessed October 2, 2012).

SMART Technologies. "SMART Board 600 series interactive whiteboard." http://www.smarttech.com/us/Solutions/Education+ Solutions/Products+for+education/Interactive+whiteboards+ and+displays/SMART+Board+interactive+whiteboards/600+for+ education (accessed October 2, 2012).

Electronic Markets

Markets are a fundamental feature of modern capitalism and have a long history behind them. During the Middle Ages in England, for example, fairs and markets were organized by individuals under a franchise from the king. Organizers of these markets not only provided the physical facilities for the markets, but also were responsible for security and settlement of disputes in the trading. Throughout history, some traditional markets have diminished in importance while new ones have gained in importance. For example, stock and commodities* markets, previously not significant, now play a vital role in the world economy. Regardless of changes, the fundamental functions of markets remain the same: to match buyers and sellers, enforce contracts, and provide a price mechanism to guide the trade.

Electronic markets are markets connected through modern communications networks and powered by high-speed computers. In an electronic marketplace, buyers and sellers do not have to be in the same physical location in order to interact. A classic example of electronic markets is the Nasdaq stock market. Nasdaq was launched in the 1970s, long before the widespread use of the Internet. It does not have an exchange floor where traders interact and conduct business in person. Essentially, Nasdaq is a huge electronic network connecting investors, brokers, and dealers, allowing various parties to exchange information and buy and sell securities. With the development of the Internet, electronic markets play an increasingly important role in people's everyday lives. The World Wide Web has become the universal interface* for electronic markets. People can use the Web to access various electronic markets virtually from anywhere at any time. Ordinary investors can use the Internet to conduct online trading through online brokerage firms, and customers can bid for various products at online auction houses such as eBay.

The availability of online trading fundamentally changed the dynamics of investment. Before the advent of web-based technologies, an investor who wanted to place an order with a broker had to either walk to the local office of the broker or call by phone. Then, sometime later, a second call was necessary to get a confirmation of the transaction. A number of brokerage firms currently offer Internet-based services that contrast sharply with the traditional scenario. Online investors can simply log onto the web site of the brokerage firm. The following are some of the typical functions of the online trading application offered by most online brokers to investors:

- Place buy and sell orders and receive electronic confirmations as soon as the order is executed;
- Check account balances;
- Receive real-time price updates;
- View historic account activities;
- Track the portfolio performance on a real-time basis.

Online trading is not only flexible and easy to use, in many instances, it also incurs lower costs. Online brokerage firms may be able to charge customers lower commission fees since they no longer have to employ a large staff to field phone calls from customers. The savings in overhead costs from replacing human brokers with Internet-based communication

Digital Cash

Digital cash (known by a variety of other labels, such as "electronic money") is simply a series of bits and bytes representing money. In order to use digital cash, users first need to purchase some digital cash tokens from digital cash providers. The digital cash provider maintains a central database to keep track of the digital cash tokens that have been issued. Once a token is spent, the token is deleted from the database to prevent it from being duplicated.

* **commodities** raw materials or services marketed prior to being used

* **interface** a boundary or border between two or more objects or systems; also a point of access

systems are passed on to investors in the form of lower fees. The growth of online trading resulted in a new category of traders known as day traders. Some individual investors use online brokers to make dozens of trades per day, many times on the same security.

New Avenues

Electronic markets have had an impact that reaches far beyond the financial world. Entrepreneurs have created new markets to better match buyers and sellers, and they have also introduced innovative products for trading. Two examples, eBay and the catastrophe insurance market, illustrate such developments.

eBay eBay is the world's leading online person-to-person auction market. Individual buyers and sellers can register at eBay and exchange products and services; besides individuals, many businesses use eBay to sell their products as well. Founded in 1995, eBay had more than 29 million registered users in 2001. By 2010, the number of active users worldwide had grown to 90 million, and the company reported that the total value of goods sold the previous year (2009) was some $60 billion—that works out to nearly $2,000 of merchandise sold *per second!* eBay has created a worldwide central marketplace that lists millions of items such as computers, antiques, coins, and furniture. Such a large-scale market has never existed before, and without the Internet, it would have been impossible to create such a market.

Although there are several other auction sites on the Internet, eBay is by far the most successful. Since the beginning, eBay management endeavored to be the dominant player in the online market environment. eBay has taken full advantage of the network effect in electronic markets. Without geographical barriers in the Internet, buyers and sellers would like to visit the dominant market because it is the place where sellers will find the most buyers and buyers will find the most sellers. The network effect is simple: more buyers and sellers will attract even more buyers and sellers to the same market. By providing a central marketplace, eBay has lowered the costs of trading for millions of buyers and sellers.

Catastrophe Insurance Another successful online offering is the catastrophe insurance market, showing how electronic markets can bring innovative products for trading and fundamentally change the way existing companies do business. Risk and insurance are integral parts of modern-day life. Insurance companies provide protection against loss in value of human capital, physical property, and financial assets. However, almost any insurance company is limited in the amount of insurance it can write on any one risk. The law of averages makes it safer to insure a large number of small risks than to insure a few large risks. For example, a catastrophe as big as Hurricane Katrina, which struck New Orleans in 2005 and caused $81 billion in damage making it the costliest natural disaster in

U.S. history, can bankrupt insurers. Because of the great monetary damage claims that such disasters can invoke, insurance companies have to seek ways to reduce large risks.

A catastrophe insurance market tries to share risks between insurance companies and other institutions. Risk is the product that is traded in a catastrophe market. The process to convert risks to tradable products is called securitization, which transforms illiquid* assets into liquid financial securities in a financial market. Securitizing insurance risk enables institutions and individuals who are not in the insurance business to participate in the insurance market. Currently, the products that are openly traded include Cat (catastrophe) bonds and Cat options.

The Catastrophe Risk Exchange (CATEX) is a New Jersey-based electronic market that allows property and casualty insurers, reinsurers, and brokers to swap or trade risk exposure to natural disasters. Developed in reaction to events such as Hurricane Andrew and the Northridge Earthquake, the exchange is designed to allow insurers to protect themselves against severe losses by geographically distributing risk and diversifying across different perils through an electronic marketplace. Trading operations on CATEX started in 1996. In 1998, CATEX was launched over the Internet. Meanwhile, CATEX began evolving from the initial swap exchange to a more complete insurance market, which supported the reinsurance transactions of marine, energy, and political risk.

Growth of Electronic Banking

Rapid growth in electronic market applications requires secure and efficient electronic banking and payment services. If one buys shares of a company listed on a stock exchange, she has to send in her payment within three days of the date of purchase. She can either send a check by express mail or make a bank transfer. Both options are relatively expensive. Many brokers require that she maintain sufficient funds with them to cover the cost of any such purchase, but there can be situations when she would prefer not to leave money sitting idle in her brokerage account. Payment systems that allow the investor to make payments directly out of her bank account would be far superior in a number of ways.

Individuals can have better control over the movement of cash in and out of their accounts. Check-based systems are also generally more expensive—for both financial institutions, as well as for consumers—than most electronic payment systems. Safer and more efficient payment systems such as debit cards, digital checks, digital wallets, or electronic money continue to gain in acceptance and use. The bottom line is that the trend is toward electronic payment and real-time settlement of transactions. Electronic payment systems allow transactions to be settled on a real-time basis as soon as the transaction is executed, or at least on the same day. Faster settlements lower the risks of default by the counterparty in the transaction.

Digital Wallets

A digital wallet is a software component that a user can install on his or her computer. A user can store credit card, digital cash, and other personal information in the digital wallet. Every time the user shops at merchants who accept digital wallets, he or she does not need to enter personal information again. The digital wallet automatically fills in the payment information and allows the user to perform shopping effortlessly.

Digital Checks

A digital check is simply the electronic version of a paper check and works the same way that a paper check works. When a customer pays a merchant with a digital check, the check information, including the check's routing number, account number, and check number, is sent to the clearing network and the transaction is settled electronically. Digital checks can be processed more quickly and at less cost compared to paper checks. Many banks have created a system to digitally process paper checks, allowing for users to deposit checks by submitting photos of the checks via online banking applications on their smartphones.

* **illiquid** lacking in liquid assets; or something that is not easily transferable into currency

See also **E-Banking** • **Internet: Applications** • **World Wide Web**

Resources

Books

Standing, Craig, ed. *The Information Superhighway and Electronic Commerce: Effects of Electronic Markets.* New York: Palgrave Macmillan, 2009.

Standing, Craig, ed. *Electronic Markets: Benefits, Costs and Risks.* New York: Palgrave Macmillan, 2009.

Entrepreneurs

In general, entrepreneurs are enthusiastic and bright risk takers who are willing to take a chance and create new markets. In the computer industry, some have become very wealthy, very fast. During the last half of the twentieth century, the vision and daring of computer entrepreneurs generated one of the most extensive technological revolutions ever.

This article contains, in alphabetical order, brief biographical sketches of eleven of those entrepreneurs and their contributions: Tim Berners-Lee, Jeff Bezos, Bill Gates, Steven Jobs, Mitchell Kapor, Sandra Kurtzig, Pierre Omidyar, Larry Page, John W. Thompson, Jerry Yang, and Mark Zuckerberg.

The Weekly Standard editor, William Kristol (left) shakes hands with PayPal co-founder and former CEO, Peter Thiel. © *Chip Somodevilla/Getty Images. New/Getty Images*

Tim Berners-Lee

Timothy "Tim" John Berners-Lee was born in England in 1955, graduated from Oxford University with a degree in physics, and is generally acknowledged as the originator of the World Wide Web. During his adolescence, he was influenced by British science fiction author Arthur C. Clarke's (1917–2008) short story "Dial F for Frankenstein." This possibly influenced his later vision that the Web could truly seem alive.

While consulting at CERN (the acronym derives from the original title Conseil Européen pour la Recherche Nucléaire—in English, the European Council for Nuclear Research) he created a program called Enquire to master CERN's intricate information system and his own mental associations of information. With this program, he could enter several words in a document, and when the words were clicked, the program would lead him to related documents that provided more information. This is a form of hypertext, a term coined by Theodor "Ted" Nelson (1937–) in the 1960s to describe text connected by links.

In collaboration with colleagues, Berners-Lee developed the three cornerstones of the Web: the language for encoding documents—Hypertext Markup Language (HTML)*; the system for transmitting documents—Hypertext Transfer Protocol (HTTP)*; and the scheme for addressing documents—Uniform Resource Locator (URL)*.

Berners-Lee heads up the nonprofit World Wide Web Consortium (W3C)—which he also founded—which helps set technical standards for the Web. Its members come from industry, such as Microsoft, Sun, Apple, and International Business Machines (IBM), some universities, and some government research centers, both from the United States and elsewhere, for example, CERN. As of March 2012, W3C had over 350 members. As director of W3C, he brings members together to negotiate agreement on technical standards. In 2009, Berners-Lee and Dr. Nigel Shadbolt began work on the data.gov.uk (http://data.gov.uk/) Web site, a U.K. project to open to the public almost all data acquired by the government. As of October 2012, over 5,400 datasets were available to the public.

In May 1998, Berners-Lee was awarded one of the prestigious MacArthur genius fellowships, freeing him to do about whatever he wanted for a few years. In 2004, Berners-Lee was knighted by Queen Elizabeth II (1926–) for his pioneering work with computers. In April 2009, he was honored by election to the National Academy of Sciences (NAS) of the United States. In 2011, Berners-Lee was inducted into the Institute of Electrical and Electronics Engineers (IEEE) Intelligent Systems' AI's Hall of Fame for his significant work in the field of artificial intelligence (AI) and intelligent systems. In 2012, the Internet Society inducted him into the Internet Hall of Fame.

Jeff Bezos

Jeffrey "Jeff" Preston Bezos was born in New Mexico in 1964. He was raised by his mother and his stepfather, Mike Bezos, who had emigrated from Cuba. Bezos became famous for using the Internet as the basis for the Seattle-based bookseller Amazon.com.

* **Hypertext Markup Language (HTML)** an encoding scheme for text data that uses special tags in the text to signify properties to the viewing program (browser) like links to other documents or document parts

* **Hypertext Transfer Protocol (HTTP)** a simple connectionless communications protocol developed for the electronic transfer (serving) of HTML documents

* **Uniform Resource Locator (URL)** a reference to a document or a document container using the Hypertext Transfer Protocol (HTTP); consists of a hostname and path to the document

After graduating from Princeton University summa cum laude in electrical engineering and computer science in 1986, he joined FITEL, a high-tech startup company in New York; two years later, he moved to Bankers Trust Company to develop their computer systems, becoming their youngest vice-president in 1990. He then worked at D. E. Shaw & Co., an investment firm. It was there that he got the idea to start an online company based on the Internet.

In 1994, Bezos left Wall Street to establish Amazon.com. He had no experience in the book-selling business, but, after some research, realized that books were small-price commodities that were easy and relatively inexpensive to ship and well-suited for online commerce. More than three million book titles are in print at any one time throughout the world; more than one million of those are in English. However, even the largest bookstore cannot stock more than 200,000 books, and a catalog for such a large volume of books is too large for a mail-order house to distribute. Bezos had identified a strategic opportunity for selling online.

Amazon.com has continued to extend its product line offerings, which now include a variety of consumer goods, including electronics, software, art and collectibles, housewares, and toys. In December 1999, *Time* magazine chose Bezos as its Person of the Year.

In 2000, Bezos founded the fledgling spaceflight company Blue Origin. With its launch facility in Culberson County, Texas, Blue Origin is working within the National Aeronautics and Space Administration (NASA) Commercial Crew Development (CCDev) program to develop technologies to support human spaceflight. The company's Launch Abort System has been one such technology of interest to NASA. In addition, Blue Origin is developing its new Shepard suborbital spacecraft for commercial flights into space.

Bill Gates

As a teenager, William "Bill" Henry Gates III (born in 1955 in Seattle, Washington) was a devoted hacker. He knew how to make computers work and make money. Together with his friend (and later co-founder with Gates of Microsoft), Paul Allen (1953–), he designed a scheduling program for their school, Lakeside School, in Seattle. Later, the two designed a program to perform traffic analysis that reportedly earned their company, Traf-O-Data, $20,000.

Gates entered Harvard University (Cambridge, Massachusetts) in 1973, and while there was impressed by an article that Allen had shown him in *Popular Electronics* about the Micro Instrumentation and Telemetry Systems (MITS) *Altair* home computer. He recognized that these computers would need software and that much money could be made writing such programs. He and Allen developed a full-featured Beginner's All-purpose Symbolic Instruction Code (BASIC) language interpreter that required only 4 kilobytes (KB) of memory. BASIC made the Altair an instant hit; in 1975, Allen and Gates formed Microsoft Corporation.

Much to the disappointment of his parents, Gates dropped out of Harvard to pursue his software development dreams.

Gates's biggest break came when the International Business Machines (IBM) Corporation decided to enter the personal computer (PC) business. He convinced IBM that his small company could write an original operating system that would take advantage of the disk drives and other peripherals that IBM had planned.

By 1998, Gates had turned Microsoft into the world's largest and most dominant computer software company. In 2008, Gates resigned from Microsoft to dedicate himself to the Bill & Melinda Gates Foundation. By 2011, Microsoft had revenues of $73.72 billion and employed about 94,000 people worldwide.

Steve Jobs

Orphaned shortly after his birth in California in 1955, Steven "Steve" Paul Jobs (1955–2011) was adopted by Paul and Clara Jobs in Mountain View, California, and was raised there and in Los Altos, California. His interest in electronics started in high school. In order to build his projects, he had to beg for parts, going as far as asking William Hewlett (1913–2001), president of Hewlett-Packard, for the parts he needed to build a computer device. His boldness landed him a summer job at Hewlett-Packard where he befriended electronics wizard Stephen "Steve" Wozniak (1950–).

Jobs was thirteen years old and Wozniak was eighteen when they met. They built the prototype of the Apple I in Jobs's garage, and together founded Apple Computer in 1976. They sold their first computers to a local electronics store, one of the first computer stores. Wozniak eventually left Hewlett-Packard to work at Apple full time.

From the day it opened for business in 1976, Apple prospered, first with the Apple I, and then the Apple II. The introduction of the VisiCalc spreadsheet introduced Apple products to the business world, and in 1982 Jobs made the cover of *Time* magazine.

When sales of Apple computers dropped off after the introduction of the IBM-PC, Jobs set to work on the design of a new computer, the affordable and hugely successful Apple Macintosh. Jobs left Apple in September 1985, in a dispute over management, to found a new company, NeXT, Inc., which built workstations for university and business environments. However, despite a revenue of $60 million in 1996, NeXT was unsuccessful as a hardware company and was sold to Apple later that year for $400 million. Jobs later returned to Apple and became its chairperson. From the late 1990s and continuing throughout the 2000s, Jobs continued to oversee a new and, overall, highly successful series of new product launches including the iMac personal computer, the iPod portable music player, iPhone series of multi-touch display cell phones, and the iPad. After his return in the 1990s, Apple went on to become one of the world's most valuable companies. Jobs' personal wealth consistently placed him in the ranks of the world's wealthiest individuals.

The Gates Foundation

Improving health care in developing nations throughout the world is one of the main goals of the Gates Foundation, begun by Bill and Melinda Gates and currently headed (2012) by chief executive officer Jeff Raikes. According to the Gates Foundation Web site, the foundation had assets of $33.5 billion available for charitable activities as of September 2011. Among the group's goals is to help poor countries, which carry the burden of 90 percent of disease worldwide, but have few health care resources to combat it. The foundation seeks to provide medications to fight easily curable diseases, make vaccinations for measles and other childhood diseases readily available, and improve conditions and thereby significantly lessen infant and maternal mortality rates. They seek to make quality health care a basic human right.

* **Silicon Valley** an area in California near San Francisco, which has been the home location of many of the most significant information technology orientated companies and universities

Jobs died of complications from pancreatic cancer on October 5, 2011.Of the numerous awards and honors presented to Jobs the following are a few: the National Medal of Technology (1985), the Samuel S. Beard Award (1987), Inc. magazine's Entrepreneur of the Decade (1989), induction into the California Hall of Fame (2007), Fortune magazine's CEO of the Decade award (2009), and Financial Times newspaper's Person of the Year award (2010).

Mitch Kapor

Mitchell "Mitch" David Kapor was born in Brooklyn in 1950 and raised in Freeport, New York, on Long Island. He graduated from Yale University in 1971 with a bachelor of arts (B.A.) in psychology. Kapor spent several years doing odd jobs until 1978, when he became interested in personal computers and purchased an Apple II. Kapor became a serious programmer and created VisiPlot, an application that would plot and graph the results of a spreadsheet, and VisiTrend. Before long, Kapor's royalty checks were running into the six-figure range.

In 1982 Kapor and American programmer Jonathan Sachs (1947–) went on to establish Lotus Corporation to make and market his multipurpose Lotus 1-2-3, a program that combined some of the best features of a then well-known and widely used spreadsheet program, VisiCalc, with graphics and database management capabilities.

Lotus 1-2-3 was designed to work on IBM's sixteen-bit processor rather than on the eight-bit processor, which was the standard for other microcomputers. Kapor felt that this new processor would soon become the standard throughout the personal computer industry, giving his program a head start. By the summer of 1986, Kapor left Lotus, and in 1987 he established ON Technology; he later founded Kapor Enterprises, Inc. Lotus was sold to IBM in 1997.

In 2001, Kapor founded the Open Source Applications Foundation. In 2006, he founded the San Francisco, California-based Foxmarks (later renamed as Xmarks), which produced the add-on Xmarks for Web browsers. The company was acquired by LastPass in 2010.

Sandra Kurtzig

Sandra Kurtzig was born in Chicago in 1946. She received a bachelor's degree from the University of California at Los Angeles (UCLA) in 1967 and later a master's degree from Stanford University. In 1971, she used $2,000 to found a software company, ASK Computer Systems, Inc., which went public in 1974.

ASK started as a part-time contract software programming business based in her second bedroom. She received $1,200 from her first client, a telecommunications equipment manufacturer that needed programs to track inventory, bills of material, and purchase orders. ASK grew into a company that had $450 million in annual sales in 1992.

Kurtzig could not convince venture capitalists in Silicon Valley* to invest in her company, so she launched it on her earnings alone. At one point, she needed a computer to run a manufacturing program under development. She managed to gain access to a Hewlett-Packard facility where her colleagues could test the program during off hours. It was here that they developed computer software that was packaged with Hewlett-Packard computers.

In 1994, ASK was purchased by Computer Associates, a software company founded by Charles Wang, Judy Cedeno, and Russ Artzt; Wang and Artzt attended Queens College, in New York, at the same time. The company is based in Long Island, New York, but is a worldwide enterprise.

Kurtzig later became chairperson of the board of E-benefits, a San Francisco insurance and human resources service provider, founded in 1996 by one of her sons. ASK stands for Arie (the name of her ex-husband), Sandy, and Kurtzig.

In 2011, Kurtzig founded the company Kenandy Inc. (http://www.kenandy.com/), a manufacturing management software company. As of October 2012, she served as the company's chief executive officer (CEO) and its chairperson.

Pierre Omidyar

Pierre Morad Omidyar (1967–) is the founder of eBay, the online marketplace where anyone, according to its mission, can buy or sell just about anything. Omidyar was born in Paris, France, in 1968 and lived there until he was six years old when his family emigrated to the United States. He admits that his interest in computers started in high school and continued in college. He graduated with a bachelor of science in computer science from Tufts University in 1988.

The auction Web site, eBay, founded in 1995, was not his first venture; in 1991 he was the co-founder of Ink Development Corp., one of the pioneers in online shopping. It was bought by Microsoft in 1996 under the name of eShop.

Omidyar also worked as a developer for Claris, a subsidiary of Apple Computer, and, while he was launching eBay, he was working for General Magic, Inc., a mobile telecommunications company. Omidyar started eBay hoping to provide people with a democratic opportunity to trade goods, and to fulfill the wishes of his wife-to-be to find people who collected and wanted to trade Pez candy dispensers.

The 2011 revenue of eBay was approximately $11.651 billion, and the company, with about 27,700 employees, could boast of hundreds of millions of registered users. Currently Omidyar spends much of his time on philanthropic projects. As of March 2012, Omidyar was worth about $6.7 billion in U.S. dollars.

Larry Page

Lawrence "Larry" Page was born in 1973. Along with Russian-born American entrepreneur Sergey Brin (1973–), Page founded Google Inc. in September 1998. The original concept that eventually became Google began as a research project that the two men collaborated on as doctor of philosophy (Ph.D.) students at Stanford University in California. Page and Brin developed improved methods for performing searches of databases. Google began posting keyword-based advertisements to its Internet search service as of the year 2000. In order to prevent slow response times for their users, as well as to keep webpage clutter to a minimum, the ads were only allowed to appear in text form (e.g., no advertising pictures or videos).

Beginning in the early 2000s, Google began acquiring smaller companies to expand the number and quality of the services it offered. The company raised significant capital through a public offering of its stock in August 2004. From a company focused upon one service, namely, an Internet search engine, Google eventually expanded into a variety of Web-based products and services. For instance, in late 2006, Google finalized the acquisition of YouTube, a highly popular video-sharing website. As of 2011, Google operated in excess of one million servers in various facilities worldwide, and processed over a billion online search requests every day. Google's 2011 revenue was approximately $37.905 billion, with total company assets pegged at approximately $72.574 billion. Some of its subsidiaries include AdMob, DoubleClick, Motorola Mobility, On2 Technologies, Picnik, YouTube, and Zagat.

John W. Thompson

John W. Thompson (1949–) received a bachelor's degree in business administration from Florida A&M University and a master's degree in management science from MIT's Sloan School of Management. Upon graduation he joined IBM, where he spent twenty-eight successful years, advancing to general manager of IBM Americas, a 30,000 employee division, where his major responsibilities were in sales and support of IBM's products and services.

In 1999, he left IBM to join Symantec, a world leader of Internet security technology. As chief executive officer (CEO) of Symantec, Thompson transformed the company from a publisher of software products to a principal provider of Internet security products aimed at individuals as well as large businesses.

Probably the company's most well-known product is their Norton line of security systems, which for the year 2012 included such popular software applications as Norton Internet Security, Norton360, Norton AntiVirus, Norton Utilities, and Norton Mobile Security. However, it also provides much needed security to most of the leading corporations.

Thompson retired from his position as CEO for Symantec in 2009. In 2012, he was the CEO of Virtual Instruments.

Jerry Yang

Jerry Yang, born in Taiwan in 1968, emigrated to the United States with his mother when he was ten years old. He graduated from Stanford University (California) in 1990 with a bachelor's of science and a master's of science degree in electrical engineering in four years. There he met and formed a close friendship with David Filo (1966–), who had also earned a master's in electrical engineering at Stanford.

Yang and Filo entered the doctorate program at Stanford and, after Filo developed the Web browser Mosaic, they became addicted to surfing the World Wide Web. Their addiction developed into a list of links to their favorite Web sites, which was stored on Yang's home page and was called *Jerry's Guide to the World Wide Web*.

Knowledge of *Jerry's Guide* spread fast and his site began to experience thousands of hits every day. Yang and Filo quickly realized that the guide had market potential and decided to form a company to promote it. The name Yahoo! is a takeoff on the UNIX program YACC, short for Yet Another Compiler Compiler, and stands for Yet Another Hierarchical Officious Oracle. The hierarchical part of the term comes from its categorization scheme of Web sites. Yahoo! is one of the few search engines that use the intelligence of human labor to categorize the sites found.

Yahoo! Inc. went public in 1996. As of 2011, Yahoo! claims that about 700 million people visit its Web sites each month. The company had a total revenue of $4.98 billion in 2011. Yang resigned from Yahoo!'s board of directors in January 2012. That year, his estimated worth was $1.2 billion. Yang is currently a member of the board of directors of Cisco Systems and the Asian Pacific Fund. He is also a member of the board of trustees at Stanford University.

Mark Zuckerberg

Mark Elliot Zuckerberg, born in 1984, attended Harvard University starting in 2002. In early 2004, he launched the social networking Web site, Facebook, from his Harvard dorm room. Initially, Facebook was intended for the use by Harvard students only. But, later on, Zuckerberg teamed with classmates Dustin Moskovitz, Chris Hughes, and Eduardo Saverin to make Facebook available to other universities. Facebook eventually became the world's leading social networking Web site, and in October 2012 surpassed one billion active users globally. Anyone aged 13 years or older can become a registered user of Facebook. In 2010, Zuckerberg's 24 percent share of Facebook meant that he was the world's youngest billionaire, with a net worth in the company estimated to be about $4 billion in 2010. As of October 2012, Zuckerberg was the chair and chief executive officer of Facebook, Inc. That year, his net worth had risen to $9.4 billion. As of June 2012, it was reported that Facebook had over 955 million active users.

Epilogue

The list of entrepreneurs is never-ending. Others that merit special mention are: Daniel Bricklin and Robert Frankston (VisiCalc), Nolan Bushnell (Atari), Steve Case (AOL), Larry Ellison (Oracle), and Ross Perot (EDS).

Yahoo's David Filo

Born in 1966 in Wisconsin, David Filo grew up in Louisiana in an alternative community (a commune-like atmosphere) with six other families. He received his bachelor's of arts (B.A.) degree from Tulane University in New Orleans before relocating to California to attend Stanford University. At Stanford, Filo met Jerry Yang and the pair went on to create Yahoo. In time, the pair's road map to the Internet, called *Jerry's Guide to the World Wide Web*, was renamed *Jerry and David's Guide to the World Wide Web*. Yang has received more notoriety for Yahoo because he has served as its spokesperson while Filo has preferred to stay behind the scenes.

▶ *See also* **Distance Learning • E-Commerce • Educational Software • Internet: Applications**

Resources

Books

Isaacson, Walter. *Steve Jobs* New York: Simon & Schuster, 2011.

Lusted, Marcia Amidon. *Mark Zuckerberg: Facebook Creator* Edina, MN: ABDO, 2012.

McPherson, Stephanie Sammartino. *Sergey Brin and Larry Page: Founders of Google* Minneapolis: Twenty-First Century Books, 2011.

Stewart, Melissa. *Tim Berners-Lee: Inventor of the World Wide Web* Chicago: Ferguson, 2001.

Strother, Ruth. *Bill Gates* Edina, MN: ABDO, 2008.

Weston, Michael R. *Jerry Yang and David Filo: Founders of Yahoo!* New York: Rosen, 2007.

Wright, Robert. *Jeff Bezos: Business Executive And Founder Of Amazon.com* New York: Ferguson Publishing Company, 2005.

Web Sites

The Wall Street Journal. "Silicon Valley Pioneer Sandra Kurtzig Back In Start-Up Game With Kenandy." http://blogs.wsj.com/venturecapital/2011/08/29/silicon-valley-pioneer-back-in-start-up-game-with-new-company-kenandy/ (accessed October 3, 2012).

Ethics

Ethics is system of thought that allows choices, often described as value or moral choices, based on a preexisting structure of collective thought. Formally, ethics is a branch of philosophy that involves the study of morality on society as a whole and specifically within the individual. Ethics is involved indirectly in all facets of computer science. Education for professionals in the computing disciplines includes, but is not limited to, degree tracks called computer science, computer engineering, software engineering, information systems, and information technology. Major professional organizations for the computing disciplines include the Association for Computing Machinery (ACM), the Institute of Electrical and Electronics Engineers Computer Society (IEEE-CS), and the Association for Information Technology Professionals (AITP). Each of these professional organizations has published a code of ethics. The complete, current versions of these codes can generally be found on the organizations' Web sites. These codes are designed to establish a framework for judging the ethical quality of professional behavior, and anyone who aspires to be a professional in the computing disciplines should be aware of them.

One important general principle contained in these codes is that a professional has a responsibility to society as a whole. For example, the AITP standards of conduct lists six items under the heading of obligation to society. These include informing the public about computing technology, ensuring that work products are used in socially responsible ways, and making information public when it is relevant to a situation of public concern. The ACM code and the joint ACM/IEEE-CS Software Engineering Code of Ethics each include similar concerns. This overall obligation to society is the foundation for a responsibility to blow the whistle if one's company engages in illegal or unethical activities.

Rights and Responsibilities

Another important general principle is to respect intellectual property* laws and ensure that credit is fairly assigned for the results of intellectual work. For example, the General Moral Imperatives in the ACM code of ethics contains the statements "Honor property rights, including patents and copyrights" and "Give proper credit for." The honoring of existing laws can be a controversial issue. Sharing, or facilitating the sharing of, copyrighted digital audio and video files on the World Wide Web (sometimes simplified as the Web) is certainly a violation of existing copyright laws. Some users of the Web believe strongly in the right to such activity. However, the codes clearly label this behavior as unethical. Existing copyright law also labels it as illegal! Many computing professionals who do not agree with existing copyright law suggest that the more appropriate action is to change copyright laws.

The codes of ethics also touch on general principles regarding software development. These are most fully detailed in the joint ACM/IEEE-CS Software Engineering Code of Ethics. Two elements listed under the Product section of this code are the following: (1) "Ensure that specifications for software on which you work have been well documented, satisfy the users' requirements and have the appropriate approvals." (2) "Ensure adequate testing, debugging, and review of software and related documents on which you work." One classic case study of failures in software design, implementation, and testing is that of the Therac-25 radiation therapy machine. The Atomic Energy of Canada Limited (AECL) produced the machine. Between 1985 and 1987, massive amounts of radiation were accidently given to several patients as a direct result of software failures in this AECL system. Some of these patients died as a result. Concern about the quality of software development, especially software for safety-critical systems, is one of the factors behind the movement to license software engineers.

In general, a code of ethics cannot be used as a means to avoid serious thought and judgment. In particular, codes should not be used to search

*intellectual property the acknowledgement that an individual's creativity and innovation can be owned in the same way as physical property

for proof text, or the practice of using an isolated piece of information for a desired conclusion. Consider the situation of a technician who accidentally discovers that his or her manager has used an office computer to collect a large amount of pornography downloaded from the Web. The question is whether the technician should report the pornography or keep it private. One element of the AITP standards of conduct states, "Protect the privacy and confidentiality of all information entrusted to me." But, other elements of the same code state "Take appropriate action in regard to any illegal or unethical practices that come to my attention" and "Protect the proper interest of my employer at all times."

So if people use the code to search for justification for what they already want to do, they will likely find it. Instead, the correct approach is to look at the code of ethics and the particular situation as a whole, and to make a judgment based on careful consideration of all the relevant facts. In this example, the use of a company-owned computer to collect pornography for personal enjoyment seems to be outside the bounds of acceptable professional behavior, making it something that should be reported to upper management.

Social Issues

There are several important and controversial social issues at the forefront of ethics and computing. One issue involves missile defense systems. In 1983, U.S. President Ronald Reagan (1911–2004) proposed a Star Wars (formally called the Strategic Defense Initiative) missile defense system that would protect the United States from attack by the Soviet Union. The goal of the proposed system was to use space-based sensors to detect missiles launched by the Soviet Union, to track the missiles on their way toward the United States, and to direct anti-missile weapons to destroy the missiles before they hit the United States. This proposal was eventually abandoned. In 2001, U.S. President George W. Bush (1946–) renewed the call for a scaled-down version of the system to meet the perceived threats of the time. Computer programs designed to operate a missile defense system are an extreme example of safety-critical software, and concerns about specifications and testing raise important ethical issues.

Many experts argue that it is not possible to create missile defense software that would have a high reliability of working. One reason for this is that identifying the software specifications requires knowing how the enemy will choose to attack. Therefore, it is difficult to know the specifications with any certainty. Another reason is that it is difficult to envision how the software could be realistically tested. As a result of these and other concerns, many programmers and designers feel that working on such software would go against the values embedded in the code of ethics governing their profession.

Another issue at the cutting edge of ethics and computing is freedom of speech. The first amendment to the U.S. Constitution provides a general protection against the government regulating the speech of its citizens. The United States has perhaps the strongest protections for freedom of speech of any country. For instance, some hate speech Web sites that are legal in the United States would be illegal in Canada, England, France, Germany, and other countries. But, it is still unclear how to enforce national laws in cyberspace, and perhaps the free speech tradition as it is known in the United States is not the only workable alternative. Some people argue that traditional free speech rights in the United States should be restricted in the modern world of cyberspace.

The introduction and use of computing technology continues to raise important ethical and social concerns. The professional societies have developed codes of ethics to help provide a framework for ethical decision-making in the computing disciplines. It is the responsibility of each individual computing professional to be aware of and to integrate a code of ethics into their professional behavior.

▶ *See also* **E-Commerce • Privacy • Security • World Wide Web**

Resources

Books

Tavani, Herman T. *Ethics and Technology: Controversies, Questions, and Strategies for Ethical Computing.* Hoboken, NJ: Wiley, 2011.

Woodbury, Marsha Cook. *Computer Information and Ethics.* Champaign, IL: Stipes, 2003.

Parnas, David L. "Software Aspects of Strategic Defense Systems." *Communications of the ACM* 28 (1985): 1326–1335.

Web sites

Association for Computing Machinery. "What is ACM?" http://www. acm.org/about (accessed October 3, 2012).

Association of Information Technology Professionals. "History of AITP." http://www.aitp.org/?page=AITPHistory (accessed October 3, 2012).

Department of Computer Science, Virginia Polytechnic Institute and State University; Nancy Leveson and Clark S. Turner. "An Investigation of the Therac-25 Accidents." http://courses.cs.vt.edu/ cs3604/lib/Therac_25/Therac_1.html (accessed October 3, 2012).

Electronic Frontier Foundation. "About EFF." https://www.eff.org/about (accessed October 3, 2012).

IEEE Computer Society. "About Us." http://www.computer.org/portal/ web/about (accessed October 3, 2012).

F

Feynman, Richard P.
American Physicist
1918-1988

Richard P. Feynman was born in 1918 in Far Rockaway, New York. He graduated with a bachelor of science degree from Massachusetts Institute of Technology in 1935, and he received a Ph.D. in physics from Princeton University in 1942. It was during this time that he began working on the Manhattan Project* at New Mexico's Los Alamos Scientific Laboratory, which resulted in the development of the first atomic bomb. While working on this team, he had his first experience with computers.

The project required many implosion calculations, which had to be done quickly and correctly. At the start, the group used Marchand hand calculators, but the devices kept breaking down and were very cumbersome. To speed up the process, one of the group's members, Stanley Frankel, decided to order some IBM business machines—adding machines called tabulators, for listing sums, and a multiplier, which used cards for input. This scheme would have worked out just fine if Frankel had not succumbed to the "disease" that afflicts many who work extensively with computers. Feynman described it in these words, as noted in *Surely You're Joking, Mr. Feynman!* "It's a very serious disease and it interferes completely with the work. The trouble with computers is you *play* with them. They are so wonderful. You have these switches—if it's an even number you do this, if it's an odd number you do that—and pretty soon you can do more and more elaborate things if you are clever enough, on one machine."

After a while Frankel spent less time doing his job and more time playing with the computers. Those who have worked with computers have probably experienced the feeling of delight in being able to do just one more thing with the computer; hence, they can understand the "disease." However, this situation was delaying the final results, so Feynman was put in charge of the group that worked with the computers. To speed things up and meet deadlines, he devised a way to work out two problems in parallel. His group also realized that errors made in one of the program cycles would affect nearby data values, so they used smaller sets of data to test the program and correct the errors as they occurred, making the work go faster. Feynman never contracted the computer disease.

Feynman was known for his irreverent nature and general disregard for official rules and regulations. During his years with the Manhattan Project, he learned how to break into filing cabinets where classified

* **Manhattan Project** the U.S. project designed to create the world's first atomic bomb

Physicist Richard Feynman during a panel investigation of President's commission on fatal explosion of *Challenger.* © *Diana Walker//Time Life Pictures/Getty Images.*

information was stored. Although he never took any of the secret documents, he left behind notes and evidence that made it clear to those responsible for the files that someone had managed to bypass their security efforts.

After Los Alamos, Feynman never worked with the military again, but taught physics at Cornell University where he worked on reconstructing and restating quantum mechanics and electrodynamics in terms of particles. In 1951 he left Cornell for the California Institute of Technology, where he continued to teach until shortly before his death.

Feynman received the Albert Einstein Award in 1954, and the Lawrence Award in 1962. In 1965 he was one of three scientists to receive the Nobel Prize for work done on the theory of quantum electrodynamics. His contributions to the field included simplification of the rules of calculation and a diagrammatic approach to analyzing atomic interactions, both of which became standard tools of theoretical analysis.

In addition to his work in teaching and research, Feynman was an author. *The Feynman Lectures on Physics,* published in 1963, remained a favorite textbook for physics students for more than three decades. A writer in *The Economist* magazine called it "one of the best physics texts, as well as the most readable." In 1985 his popular book, *Surely You're Joking, Mr. Feynman!*, began a 15-week run on the *New York Times* list of bestselling non-fiction titles. In 1986 he wrote *QED: The Strange Theory of Light and Matter* to introduce the theory of quantum electrodynamics to a general, non-academic audience.

His fame in the scientific and academic world as a teacher, theoretician, and author expanded when in 1986 he was appointed to the President's Commission on the Space Shuttle Challenger Accident. Feynman's impatience with the bureaucracy of the hearings process led him to offer a simple, but dramatic illustration of the effect of cold on the ill-fated space shuttle's O-rings*, which were supposed to seal the joints of the shuttle's rocket booster segments. During televised testimony, he used ice and water to show that a piece of the O-ring material would rapidly harden when submerged in low temperatures. Typical of his direct approach to explaining the properties and behavior of physical matter, this simple experiment crystallized a key point of the commission's investigative conclusions.

Feynman, who is remembered by students and peers as a man who was curious about everything and light-hearted in his dealings with others, died on February 15, 1988 of abdominal cancer. His legacy includes his innovative approach to problem solving and his ability and desire to make the study of complex science accessible to students and the general public alike.

▶ *See also* **Physics** • **Programming**

Resources

Books

Feynman, Richard P. *Surely You're Joking, Mr. Feynman!* New York: Bantam Books, 1985.

Lee, J. A. N. *Computer Pioneers.* Los Alamitos, CA: IEEE Computer Society Press, 1995.

Periodical

Chandler, David L. "Richard Feynman, Nobel Laureate in Physics: Probed Shuttle Disaster." *The Boston Globe*, February 17, 1988.

Fiction, Computers in

Computers appeared in fiction centuries before they materialized as working devices, helping to inspire the creation of real computers and also warning of their dangers. The first fictional computer appears in Irish author Jonathan Swift's (1667–1745) 1726 satire *Gulliver's Travels.* An inventor has made a machine that allowed people to write books about

The Manhattan Project

Beginning in June 1942 during World War II, the United States' Manhattan Project brought together scientists and military experts to create the world's first atomic bomb. The project began following concerns that the Nazis were close to creating effective atomic weapons of mass destruction. Led by Gen. Leslie Groves and J. Robert Oppenheimer, the Manhattan Project successfully detonated the first atomic bomb at the Trinity test site in New Mexico in July 1945.

* **O-rings** 37-foot rubber circles (rings) that seal the joints between the space shuttle's rocket booster segments

* **automaton** an object or being that has a behavior that can be modeled or explained completely by using automata theory

various topics, such as mathematics, politics, and poetry. This computer, or Engine as it is called by Swift, contained numerous Bits that contained all the words of language. These "Bits" were turned by wires and cranks. Within the story, scribes made hard copy by recording any sequence of words that seemed to make sense, thus showing the absurdity of valuing machine-generated texts more than human thought.

Actual mechanical automata, common in the eighteenth century, suggested the possibility of lifelike creatures with mechanical brains. An influential fictional automaton* of the early nineteenth century was Olympia, who slavishly dotes on her human lover in German author E. T. A. Hoffman's (1776–1822) story *The Sandman* (1816). There is a direct connection between Olympia and the slavish women constructed by computer scientists to replace their uppity wives in American author Ira Levin's (1929–2007) novel (1972) and film (1975) *The Stepford Wives*.

The tendency to conceive of thinking machines as humanoid in appearance was dominant until the advent of the first actual electronic digital computers in the 1940s, huge machines that did not look at all like people. But, some fiction did project computers based on the evolving automated mechanisms of industry. For example, American writer George Parsons Lathrop's (1851–1898) 1879 story *In the Deep of Time* imagines vast automated future factories run by a person at a keyboard. French author Jules Verne (1828–1905) prophesied, in his 1863 manuscript *Paris in the Twentieth Century*, giant "calculating machines" resembling huge pianos operated by a "keyboard" and hooked to "facsimile" machines; banks used the most advanced models of these computers to coordinate the activities of this hypercapitalist future.

By the early twentieth century, the standard fictional computer was the brain of a robot, usually conceptualized as a metal man. The archetype was Tik-Tok, the "Thought-Creating, Perfect Talking Mechanical Man" equipped with "Improved Combination Steel Brains" in American author L. Frank Baum's (1856–1919) *Ozma of Oz* (1907) and *Tik-Tok of Oz* (1914). When asked whether he is alive, Tik-Tok responds: "No, I am only a machine. But I can think and speak and act."

To some, the evolution of machines seemed menacing. English writer E. M. Forster's (1879–1970) novella *The Machine Stops* (1909) imagines a future earth run by a global computer that caters to every physical human need (except sex) through its automated appendages. Living in a mechanical environment, people rarely come into contact with each other because they communicate as individuals and chat groups through the machine's Internet.

By the 1930s, fiction about human overdependence on computers or the replacement of humans by intelligent machines was quite commonplace. Examples include: American author Edmond Hamilton's (1904–1977) *The Metal Giants* (1926) featuring an atom-powered metal brain that constructs a rampaging army of 300-foot-tall robots; British writer S. Fowler Wright's (1874–1965) "Automata" (1929), in which machines take over all human activities and then eliminate our species; and British author Lionel Britton's (1887–1971) 1930 play "The Brain" where an enormous mechanical brain ends up as the only form of intelligence left on a doomed Earth.

The most influential shaper of robot fiction was Russian-born American author and biochemist Isaac Asimov (1920–1992), who conceived of all-purpose mechanical beings with "positronic brains" governed by his Three Laws of Robotics, first articulated in his 1942 story *Runabout.* According to these Laws, all robots' brains were preprogrammed to guarantee that they would never harm humans, would obey orders, and would protect themselves, in that order. Asimov later wrote the *I, Robot* (1950) book and still later the Robot Series of books: *The Caves of Steel* (1953), *The Naked Sun* (1956), *The Robots of Dawn* (1983), and *Robots and Empire* (1985). The 2004 motion picture *I, Robot*, starring American actor Will Smith (1968–), was loosely based on Asimov's book by the same name.

The computers created during World War II and its aftermath invited an avalanche of fictional computers. Because the supercomputers of the 1940s and 1950s were gigantic, their fictional descendants were commonly imagined as colossal masses of panels, buttons, switches, relays, and vacuum tubes*.

Some fictional computers were global and malevolent. The computer in British author D. F. Jones' (1917–1981) 1966 novel *Colossus* (filmed in 1970 as *Colossus—The Forbin Project*) takes over the world. In American writer Harlan Ellison's (1934–) 1967 story *I Have No Mouth, and I Must Scream,* the American, Russian, and Chinese supercomputers* waging thermonuclear war merge into a single conscious entity that destroys the entire human race except for five people it saves to torture forever.

Two memorable 1960s visions of computers came in masterpieces of American film director Stanley Kubrick (1928–1999). In *Dr. Strangelove; Or How I Learned to Stop Worrying and Love the Bomb* (1964), civilization ends because a U.S. atomic attack activates a computerized Soviet doomsday weapon. The most memorable character in *2001: A Space Odyssey* (1968) is HAL (short for Heuristically programmed ALgorithmic computer), the spaceship's psychotic supercomputer.

As computers have become commonplace features of everyday life, their cultural representations have spread from science fiction into other literature and film. Indeed, fiction about normal existence, at least in industrial societies, could exclude computers no more than it could ignore automobiles, telephones, airplanes, and television. This has been especially true for movies. When functioning as more than background in non-science-fiction movies, computers are often presented as a menacing power of the all-seeing bureaucratic state, as in *Enemy of the State* (1998). The main character in *The Net* (1995), a lonely computer hacker, has her actual identity deleted from all records by the computers of government conspirators.

Computer games had become a familiar fictional topic by the early 1980s. After it was revealed that malfunctions of an U.S. Air Force

* **vacuum tube** an electronic device constructed of a sealed glass tube containing metal elements in a vacuum; used to control electrical signals

* **supercomputers** very high performance computers, usually comprised of many processors and used for modeling and simulation of complex phenomena, like meteorology

Robotic Mayhem

In the 1973 movie *Westworld*, vacationers arrive at a new futuristic amusement park where they can live out their fantasies as gunslingers. During their stay, guests live in a recreated Old West town and fight humanlike robots, dressed as outlaws, who are programmed to lose. Then, one day, the robots begin to malfunction and start killing their human challengers. In the end it is every man and robot for himself as the battle between human and machine is waged.

WALL-E

As of 2012, sales remain strong for Pixar Animation Studios' 2008 robot romance, "WALL-E." Directed by Andrew Stanton, the animated movie's star, a waste clean-up robot named WALL-E assigned to a heavily-polluted and human-less future Earth, develops human-like emotions as he falls in love with a technically more sophisticated EVE reconnaissance robot designed to signal when Earth is finally clean enough for humans to return from their space exile.

* **progenitor** the direct parent of something or someone

supercomputer had, on numerous actual occasions, almost precipitated global thermonuclear war, the 1983 movie *WarGames* portrayed a teenage boy who nearly causes the apocalypse by playing what he thinks is a game with an Air Force computer programmed for global thermonuclear war.

The possibilities of organic computers are explored in fiction from the mid–1980s on. For example, in American author Greg Bear's (1951–) *Blood Music* (1985), medical biochips accidentally convert DNA (the acronym for deoxyribonucleic acid) molecules into living computers that transmute the human species into the progenitor* of "an intelligent plague" designed to reshape some of the fundamental principles of the universe. During the 1980s, computers also became central in the science fiction known as cyberpunk, especially the work of American-Canadian author William Gibson (1948–), where action often takes place in cyberspace and some characters even metamorphose into beings who exist solely as cyber phenomena.

The concept of existing in cyberspace became widespread. In *Tron* (1982), one of the first commercial films to depend on computer animation, a video-game designer is sucked inside a computer, where he becomes a character in a computer game. In the *Max Headroom* movie (1985) and TV series (1987–1988), a reporter continues his career after being uploaded to become a computerized character. The Matrix trilogy, including *The Matrix* (1999), *The Matrix Reloaded* (2003), and *The Matrix Revolutions* (2003), focused old and new images into a nightmare vision of a future where the only human function is supplying energy for computers, which have created a virtual reality where humans imagine they live real lives.

In the twenty-first century, fictional films featuring computers focus mainly on hacking. In *Antitrust* (2001), a corporation hires a young and talented programmer to develop code for a global satellite communication system. The chief executive officer (CEO) of the company provides the programmer with source code necessary to complete the project. The source code is later discovered to be stolen code obtained through the company's worldwide surveillance system. A hacker in *Swordfish* (2001) is on parole for infecting the Federal Bureau of Investigation (FBI) Carnivore e-mail monitoring initiative with a debilitating computer virus when he is offered $10 million to write a worm (a self-replicating computer program) that will seize money from a government reserve fund. In *Live Free or Die Hard* (2007), a group of hackers infiltrates the FBI's computer systems in an effort to shut down the computer-dependent infrastructure of the United States.

In 2008, the movie *The Day the Earth Stood Still* (a remake of the 1951 movie of the same time) was released. It contained the humanoid robot Gort, who uses a deadly beam through his visor to vaporize whoever is before it. The 2009 science fiction movie *Moon* introduces GERTY, a robot that helps an astronaut (Sam Bell) mine helium-3 on the far side of the Moon. However, the robot and Bell have problems when clones of Bell are found, and the real Bell is discovered to have never left Earth. *Prometheus* is a 2012 movie set in the late twenty-first century. The crew of the spaceship *Prometheus* is seeking the origins of humanity on a distant planet, but finds an advanced civilization that may cause the inevitable destruction of the human race. An android called David is used to service the needs of the crew, however, it develops insecurities while on the mission.

▶ *See also* **Asimov, Isaac • Robotics • Scientific Visualization • World Wide Web**

Resources

Books

Bould, Mark. *Science Fiction*. Milton Park, England: Routledge, 2012.

Cavallaro, Dani. *Cyberpunk and Cyberculture: Science Fiction and the Work of William Gibson*. London: Continuum, 2007.

Perkowitz, S. *Hollywood Science: Movies, Science, and the End of the World*. New York: Columbia University Press, 2007.

Telotte, J. P., and Gerald Duchovnay. *Science Fiction Film, Television, and Adaptation: Across the Screens*. New York, Routledge, 2012.

Youngman, Paul A. *We Are the Machine: The Computer, the Internet, and Information in Contemporary German Literature*. Rochester, NY: Camden House, 2009.

Web Sites

Film Site. "Robots in Film: A Complete Illustrated History of Robots in the Movies." http://www.filmsite.org/robotsinfilm.html (accessed October 3, 2012).

Total Film. "50 Greatest Movie Robots." http://www.totalfilm.com/features/50-greatest-movie-robots (accessed October 3, 2012).

Wired.com, and Charlie Sorrel. "The Five Most Powerful Movie Computers." http://www.wired.com/gadgetlab/2008/06/the-five-most-p/ (accessed October 3, 2012).

Firewalls

In computer terms, a firewall is a boundary system that sits between two networks and enforces a security policy that determines what information is allowed to pass between them. The networks in question are typically a corporate, or private, local area network (LAN)* and the public Internet. The security policy can be very simple, allowing most communication to pass through, or can be very complex, allowing only specifically designated traffic from specifically designated hosts to cross the boundary.

* **local area network (LAN)** a high-speed computer network that is designed for users who are located near each other

* TCP/IP protocol suite
Transmission Control Protocol/
Internet Protocol; a range of
functions that can be used to
facilitate applications working on
the Internet

A firewall acts like a security guard that monitors all incoming and outgoing traffic and makes decisions about whether or not certain traffic is allowed. These decisions are based on the security policy. Under the simplest, least restrictive security policy, everything is allowed except that which is explicitly denied. Under the most complex, most restrictive policy, everything is denied except that which is explicitly allowed. What this means in practical terms is that a firewall may be relatively simple to configure and manage, or it can be very complex and time-consuming to maintain.

Firewalls can be implemented at the *network, transport,* or *application* layers of the TCP/IP Protocol Suite*. The level of sophistication that a security policy can enforce depends on the layer at which the firewall is implemented. The, sometimes referred to as the DoD (Department of Defense) model, divides the network into four layers. From the bottom up, they are the *physical* or *hardware* layer, which describes the way networks are connected together; the *network* layer, which defines the addresses of the network and its hosts (computers that are part of the network, whether workstations or servers) and manages the routing of packets between networks; the *transport* layer, which provides end-to-end communication between services and establishes the reliability of the connection between networks and hosts; and the *application* layer, which is responsible for the actual services provided by a network such as e-mail, authentication method, and file transfer capability.

Network Layer Firewalls

At the network layer, a firewall controls access by examining the addresses or ports that the data packet is coming from or going to. This is the most basic type of firewall and is called a *packet filtering firewall.* Not only can packets be filtered based on the IP address of a host, they can also be filtered based on the port number of the service desired. For example, a security policy for a packet filtering firewall might be configured to allow all incoming packets from any address only if they are destined for SMTP (Simple Mail Transfer Protocol) port 25, which is the service that processes e-mail. This would allow the network to accept incoming e-mail from anywhere on the Internet. But anyone trying to access the FTP (File Transfer Service) that operates on port 21 would be denied.

On the other hand, if it was determined that a network called "spam-me.com" was sending unwanted e-mail, the security association could be extended to deny any incoming packets from that specific network, while still allowing SMTP traffic from all other networks. At this layer, the firewall does no analysis of the data contained in the packets, nor does it provide any ability to hide the addresses of the internal systems on outgoing packets. A packet filtering firewall is the least effective of all the types of firewalls available.

Transport Layer Firewalls

For firewalls at the transport layer, the decisions made by the security policy can be more complex and therefore offer more security. Sometimes referred to as circuit level or proxy firewalls, these types of firewalls can verify the source and destination of the communicating devices before opening the connection. After that initial verification, it is assumed that all further communication is allowed until the session is closed.

With this type of firewall, the addresses for the internal or private network can be hidden behind the address of the device providing the proxy service. The result is that only the address of the firewall is made public, preventing unauthorized individuals or hosts from knowing too much about the private network. The hiding of the internal addresses is called Network Address Translation (NAT) and is the feature most commonly implemented on firewalls at this level. This type of firewall can also provide proxy port IDs for network services, so that on the private network, common service destination ports can be changed but the sources trying to communicate with those services are unaware of the change.

As an example, incoming e-mail destined for the firewall's IP address and Port 25 is transparently routed to a host with a different IP address that may even have the SMTP service assigned to a port other than Port 25. This effectively hides the e-mail server so intruders cannot find it. But even if they do discover the address of the mail server, they would still need to discover the port number to which the service has moved. This makes the job of attacking the mail server much more difficult.

Application Layer Firewalls

Firewalls that operate at the application layer offer the most security of all possible configurations. Sometimes called Stateful Packet Filtering firewalls, these devices can perform an analysis on the contents of an individual data packet in order to do a more thorough job determining what is to be allowed or denied. For example, if the firewall allowed incoming Hypertext Transfer Protocol (HTTP)* packets to be passed to the network, a malicious user could hide a Trojan Horse in a web page. A Trojan Horse is a malicious program hidden inside of a program that the network accepts as harmless. In this case, it could be an applet* embedded in a Web page. When the Web page reaches its destination, the applet is released and causes harm to the network or host. A simple Packet Filtering Firewall would let the packet in because it appears to be on the allowed list but the Stateful Packet Filtering Firewall would look inside the packet and see that there is an embedded application and choose to deny that packet entry to the network.

Regardless of which layer the firewall functions at, the actual firewall can be either a software solution or a dedicated appliance. There is typically degradation in performance when running a firewall as software on a computer that runs other applications. Also, the firewall is typically exposed to the Internet so the computer and its other applications will be exposed as well. Dedicated appliances generally offer the most secure solution as a firewall, and provide the best performance. But they are more costly and can be more complicated to configure. Software or hardware, application, transport or network layer, no matter the type or level of implementation, a firewall is a necessary part of twenty-first-century

* **Hypertext Transfer Protocol (HTTP)** a simple connectionless communications protocol developed for the electronic transfer (serving) of HTML documents

* **applet**, a program component that requires extra support at run time from a browser or run-time environment in order to execute

Addresses for Security and Identity

A computer offering a service to the network is like an apartment building. The building itself has only one street address; in the case of the network server, that would be the IP address. But each apartment inside has a number that differentiates it from the others. In this analogy, each service offered by the server has a specific number, as each apartment does. In the case of the network server, that number is called a port ID.

* **protocol** an agreed understanding for the sub-operations that make up a transaction, usually found in the specification of inter-computer communications

* **TCP** the acronym for Transmission Control Protocol; a fundamental used in the networks that support the Internet (ARPANET)

* **Internet Protocol (IP)** a method of organizing information transfer between computers; the IP was specifically designed to offer low-level support to Transmission Control Protocol (TCP)

networking technology to provide a measure of security and privacy for data and the people who use it.

▶ *See also* **E-Commerce • Security • Security Software • World Wide Web**

Resources

Books

Blacharski, Dan. *Network Security in a Mixed Environment.* Foster City, CA: IDG Books Worldwide, Inc., 1998.

Strebe, Matthew, and Charles Perkins. *Firewalls 24seven.* 2nd ed. San Francisco: Sybex Books, 2002.

Periodical

Smith, Gary. "A Brief Taxonomy of Firewalls." *SANS Institute.* (May 18, 2001).

Web Sites

Tyson, Jeff. "How Firewalls Work." http://www.howstuffworks.com/firewall.htm (accessed October 4, 2012).

FTP

File transfer protocol (FTP) is an Internet-standard application for transferring files. The objectives of FTP are to promote file-sharing between different file systems, to promote use of remote computers across the Internet, and to enable effective file transfer. FTP transmits copies of files between two computers. It allows users to upload and download file copies between local and remote computers. FTP is an elastic application that is sensitive but adjustable to traffic fluctuations over the Internet. User expectation of file transfer delay is not only proportional to file size but also sensitive to changes caused by Internet traffic load.

Historical Development

FTP was first developed in 1971 as part of the U.S. Department of Defense's ARPANET protocols* and thus predates both TCP* and Internet Protocol (IP)*. FTP is currently documented for use with TCP in RFC 959, which became the standard in 1985. However, there have been several amendments to RFC 959, the latest being Proposed Standard 5797, dated March 2010. The Internet Engineering Task Force (IETF) maintains those documented standards.

Although the World Wide Web became the major application for transferring files in 1995, FTP can still be used with most web browsers, and many organizations still maintain an FTP repository for public and/ or restricted access. The convention for public FTP access is popularly referred to as anonymous FTP because the username is "anonymous."

Protocol

FTP is an interactive, connection-oriented client/server protocol that relies on TCP for transferring files. After a user invokes an FTP application, he or she receives a prompt that signals the application is ready for user commands. A username and password are requested by the remote FTP server in order to determine ownership and limit file system access. After successful authentication*, the local FTP client accepts user requests.

After receiving each request from the client, the remote FTP server responds by interacting with its local file system to execute each request as if it had been locally generated. Throughout each session, the remote FTP server maintains state information on each control connection and restricts file system access according to defined security permissions. Normally a single client can support multiple users and an FTP server can respond to multiple clients concurrently, but keeping track of each session can significantly constrain the total number of simultaneous sessions.

Technique

Different FTP packages have different commands available, and even those with similar names may operate differently. To access an FTP site, users must know three pieces of information: the remote computer domain name, the file system path location of desired file(s) (folders/directories and/or subfolders/subdirectories), and the name of the file(s) to be transmitted. The general command for initiating an FTP session to a specific remote computer is FTP *remote_computer_domain_name_or_IP_address*. If FTP is already executing, OPEN *remote_computer_domain_name_or_ IP_address* can be used. This opens an FTP control connection dedicated to sending commands and receiving responses for the entire session.

A separate data transfer connection is needed for each file transfer. Two parallel connections are necessary: a first connection for control information, and a second connection for the actual data transfer. Although one control connection exists for an entire session, many data connections come and go. The local FTP client does not pass user keystrokes directly to the remote FTP server but instead interprets user input. Only if a user command requires interaction with the remote FTP server does the local FTP client send an FTP request to the remote FTP server. Because FTP uses a separate control connection, it is said to send its control information out-of-band*, which provides extra functionality. For example, a client can abort a transfer while FTP is executing.

After a file transfer connection begins, files are transferred over the data connection without the overhead of any headers or control information at the application layer. When an end-of-file condition indicates a file transfer has finished, the control connection is used to signal completion and

Transferring files using FTP. © *AP Images/Houston Chronicle, Nick de la Torre.*

* **authentication** the act of ensuring that an object or entity is what it is intended to be

* **out-of-band** pertaining to elements or objects that are external to the limits of a certain local area network (LAN)

FTP vs. Telnet

Telnet, a TCP application for remote login, was developed between 1969 and 1971 and was the first application developed for packet-switching. Telnet, like FTP, is also a message transfer protocol. A telnet connection is a TCP connection used to transmit data with interspersed (in-band) control information. Rather than being limited to transferring files, a telnet login session appears to the user as a virtual terminal directly attached to a remote computer. However, telnet does not directly provide file system interaction between local and remote computers.

to accept new FTP commands. Because the server does not tell the client how much data to expect in advance, the file can grow during transfer. An FTP session between a local/remote pair of computers is closed with a BYE (CLOSE) command, and the FTP application is terminated with a QUIT command.

The two most common FTP commands are GET (or RETRieve) and PUT (or STORe). The GET command downloads, or copies, a file from a remote computer to a local computer. The FTP server locates the file that the user requested and uses TCP to send a copy of the file across the Internet to the client. As the client program receives data, it writes the data into a file on the user's local disk. The PUT command uploads a file from a local computer to a remote computer in a reversal of the GET command. Other FTP commands address the additional complexity introduced by file systems. For instance, data representation can be text (ASCII characters) or binary (nontext). FTP assumes that data transfers are text transfers unless the TYPE command is used to change the transfer mode to binary. FTP has the following commands for file system navigation: cd (move down a directory), cdup (move up a directory), dir (show contents of present directory), ls (show contents of present directory), and pwd (present working directory).

FTP accommodates diversity—it can be used to transfer a copy of a file between any arbitrary pair of computers. It hides the details of individual computer systems from users by providing a common set of services similar to those found on most operating systems, such as list directory, create new files, read an existing file, and delete files.

 See also **Distance Learning • Electronic Campus • Telecommunications**

Resources

Books

Comer, Douglas E. *The Internet Book: Everything You Need to Know about Computer Networking and How the Internet Works.* 4th ed. Upper Saddle River, NJ: Pearson Prentice Hall, 2007.

G

Global Positioning Systems

The Global Positioning System (GPS) is undoubtedly one of the most practical of all satellite projects. It provides navigation and location information to other satellites, commercial airliners, cruise ships, land surveyors, mapmakers, bicyclists, hikers, and drivers. GPS is based on a very simple theoretical principle that is complex to achieve practically.

The basic principle behind GPS is the measurement of distance—in this case, the distance between satellites and receivers on the ground. The satellites transmit a radio message. Their distance from the receiver can be easily calculated using the speed at which the message travels (the speed of light) and the time it takes to complete its travel. By comparing the time the signal was sent and received, the distance from the satellite can be calculated as: Distance = Speed (C) × Time Difference. If the satellite were directly overhead, the time for the signal to travel to the receiver would be 0.6 seconds. However, the actual dynamic satellite orbits, ionospheric distortion of the radio signal, and inaccuracies in timing measurements complicate the realization of this simple principle.

GPS Components

In order to achieve accurate, real-world measurements, the GPS is composed of three segments: space, control, and user. The space segment consists of GPS satellites in orbit around the Earth. The control segment is made up of ground stations that monitor the satellites. The user segment is comprised of the receivers used to make the measurements.

Space Segment The space segment is a constellation of thirty Navigation Satellite Timing and Ranging (NAVSTAR) satellites orbiting the Earth in circular orbits at 20,278 kilometers (12,600 miles). The constellation is composed of six orbital planes, each tilted 55 degrees with respect to the equator. Each orbital plane has four satellites spaced 60 degrees apart so that a minimum of five satellites are viewable from any location on the Earth. Although the constellation was designed to operate with twenty-four satellites, there are typically some extra (spare) satellites in orbit that take over as older models are decommissioned.

The GPS satellites are manufactured and launched in groups, called "blocks." As of 2012, Block IIF-series satellites are the most recent model of GPS satellite to be placed in orbit. The U.S. government has contracted for a total of thirteen Block IIF satellites to be placed in orbit,

Volunteers in Wyoming work together with a GPS device as they participate in a local "mapping party" designed to raise awareness area geography and promote geographic literacy. © *AP Images/Laramie Boomerang, Katie Glennemeier.*

* **ephemeris** a record showing positions of astronomical objects and artificial satellites in a time-ordered sequence

the first of which was launched in May 2010. Over the years, the GPS constellation of satellites has been repeatedly upgraded. The next major upgrade will take place with the Block III satellites, with first launch due in 2014. Block III GPS satellites will provide additional transmitted signals for civilian use, while at the same time increasing the capabilities for secure military navigation, targeting, and location.

Each satellite transmits precise time, position, and orbit information. In order to minimize or eliminate ionospheric distortion, the satellites transmit two signals with binary codes at different frequencies. The binary signals use a pseudo-random code (i.e., a binary signal with random noise-like properties), which obviates the need for great power or large antennas.

Control Segment The control segment, consisting of a master control station near Colorado Springs, Colorado, and additional ground stations around the world, keeps the space segment operational and accurate. This segment, properly known as the Operational Control System (OCS), is a vital part of the GPS system but is basically invisible to the GPS user. The control segment constantly measures and calculates detailed orbits, monitors satellite clock accuracy, and assesses the health status of all satellites to determine if any repositioning is required. Updated satellite orbital (ephemeris*) information, clock information, and routine maintenance commands are transmitted once or twice a day to the satellites from uplink antennas at three of the ground stations.

* **ionosphere** a region of the upper atmosphere (above about 60,000 meters or 196,850 feet) where the air molecules are affected by the sun's radiation and influence electromagnetic wave propagation

User Segment The user segment consists of users and their receivers. The GPS receiver contains a processor that calculates the location based on the satellite signals. The user does not transmit anything to the satellite and the satellite does not know the user is there. There is no limit to the number of users who can use the system at any time.

The GPS receiver detects and converts the signals transmitted by the satellites into useful information. It measures the time it takes for the signal to reach the receiver. This information is used together with satellite ephemeris data to compute position in three dimensions. In a perfect world, spherical trigonometry would require only three measurements to locate a point in three-dimensional space. However, four or more measurements are used in the GPS to eliminate any timing error. Dimensions are computed in Earth-Centered, Earth-Fixed X, Y, and Z coordinates. Position in XYZ is converted in the receiver to geodetic latitude, longitude, and elevation.

It should be noted that GPS signals are very weak, subject to atmospheric distortion, subject to signal bounce and diffusion, and difficult to access in dense forests and dense urban environments.

GPS Measurements

A typical hand-held receiver can provide a measurement of location that is accurate to around 7.8 meters (about 25.5 feet). However, this is not accurate enough for many applications such as mapmaking and surveying. Those who need them can use more complex (and expensive) receivers and alternative measurement techniques to improve locational accuracies up to a range of a few centimeters.

One of the most common techniques for achieving improved accuracies is differential GPS measurements. This is a method of eliminating errors in a GPS receiver to make the output more accurate. This technique is based on the principle that most of the errors seen by GPS receivers in a local area are common errors such as clock deviation or changing radio propagation conditions in the ionosphere*. In the differential approach, two receivers are employed, with one called a base station placed at a location for which the coordinates are known and accepted. The base station constantly monitors the difference between the known coordinates and the GPS-calculated coordinates to provide a measure of the error.

There are two ways of utilizing the base station data to perform differential GPS. In post processing, data at the base station and the surveying receiver, or rover, are recorded and processed together at a later time. In real-time processing, data are transmitted from the base station to the rover and the error is calculated in real time. Many commercial, private, and government base stations have data that can be used in either post processing or real-time processing. Commercial satellite services also provide correction signals for real-time processing of data.

Another effort to improve upon GPS accuracy is known as the Wide Area Augmentation System (WAAS). Originally developed to provide

GPS Use in Sports

Tracking the movement of athletes has become a common occurrence in sporting events and for training. GPS devices can be carried by runners, attached to bicycles, and mounted on golf carts or bags. In the game of golf, for instance, GPS units can tell the golfer the distance to the next hole from the bag or cart. In this age of global terrorism, security in sports is a top priority. Sporting events that capture worldwide attention, such as the Olympic Games, present a tempting target to terrorist groups. In the 2010 winter Olympics held in Vancouver, British Columbia, GPS units attached to buses and other vehicles were used by security personnel to monitor the real-time movements of Olympic athletes as they were shuttled around the competition site.

aircraft with improved navigation capabilities, WAAS uses techniques in common with differential GPS to produce an improved navigational or position result. Using a variety of ground stations that receive GPS signals all over North America, subtle variations in the received GPS signals are measured and eventually uplinked to satellites in geostationary orbit, from where the signal is transmitted back to Earth for the benefit of WAAS-enabled GPS units. Several countries are developing similar systems to the U.S.-developed WAAS. At the end of 2009, a regularly-scheduled passenger airline flight was the first to utilize WAAS as an integral part of its navigation system.

A discussion of GPS would not be complete without mentioning GLOSNASS, which is made up of twenty-four satellites, eight in each of three orbital planes. GLOSNASS was fully operational as of September 2010 (24 out of 24 satellites in orbit and working); the system was deployed by the Russian Federation and has much in common with the U.S. NAVSTAR GPS.

Besides Russia and the United States, governments of other nations are planning on having satellite constellations in orbit for navigation. Officials in the European Union plan to create an EU global navigation system consisting of thirty satellites, called Galileo. According to European Commission projections available in autumn 2012, Galileo's full navigation services will be available by 2019.

Another country interested in having its own navigation system is China. In 2009, the Chinese government announced plans to place a GPS-style satellite constellation into orbit by 2015. The Chinese project is called the BeiDou-2 Navigation System (BNS), also known as Compass.

 See also **Database Management Software • Geographic Information Systems • Telecommunications**

Resources

Books

Hofmann-Wellenhof, B., Herbert Lichtenegger, and Elmar Wasle. *GNSS—Global Navigation Satellite Systems: GPS, GLONASS, Galileo, and More.* Vienna and New York: Springer, 2008.

Misra, Pratap. *Global Positioning System: Signals, Measurements, and Performance,*, rev. 2nd ed. Lincoln, A: Ganga-Jamuna Press, 2011.

Van Sickle, Jan. *GPS for Land Surveyors.* 3rd ed. Boca Raton, FL: CRC Press, 2008.

Web Sites

European Space Agency "Galileo." http://www.esa.int/esaNA/galileo.html (accessed November 3, 2012).

GPS.gov. "Home." http://www.gps.gov (accessed November 3, 2012).

Global Surveillance

It has repeatedly been written that "information is power." Throughout history, the fate of nations has repeatedly hinged on the quality and timeliness of intelligence gathering and analysis. During a military or economic confrontation, knowing the capability of a friend or foe often means the difference between success and failure. Even during peacetime, global surveillance systems are utilized for verification purposes, preventing potentially dangerous conflicts.

The Space Age and Surveillance: A New Era

The onward march of technology has continued to drive intelligence gathering and surveillance. With the advent of the electronics and aerospace industries, the technology of intelligence gathering and analysis encountered significant change during the twentieth century. Declassified imagery and technology is now trickling down to private citizens and organizations outside the government.

The Space Age dawned in 1957, when the former Soviet Union launched Sputnik, the first artificial object to be placed in orbit around Earth. Since then, space has played a dominant role in global communication and surveillance. The vantage from outer space lets us see the planet in its entirety, or zoom in to examine select portions of the globe. Because of its numerous advantages, space has been accurately nicknamed the new "High Ground."

Space reconnaissance satellites are small, unmanned spacecraft fitted with cameras, sensors, radio receivers, and small rocket motors for maneuvering. They are generally launched into orbit atop a rocket booster or via one of the U.S. space shuttles. Once they are in orbit, they activate cameras, sensors, and receivers to begin their mission. Flight controllers on the ground can program the satellite to perform specific surveillance tasks, or to change the orbit to satisfy the requirements of the mission.

The National Reconnaissance Office (NRO) is responsible for designing, building, and flying space satellites for the U.S. Department of Defense (DoD) and the Central Intelligence Agency (CIA). The NRO was declassified in 1992, making 800,000 satellite reconnaissance photos available to the National Archives and placing them in the public domain.

Satellites are designed and built to accomplish specific missions including communications, weather forecasting, photographic reconnaissance, remote sensing, and signals intelligence. Satellites can be classified according to the type of orbit in which they travel around Earth. The two types of orbits most pertinent to this discussion are Low Earth Orbit (LEO), and the far higher Geostationary Earth Orbit (GEO). There are other important orbit types, such as Medium Earth Orbit (MEO), used by the Global Positioning System (GPS) satellites (which are about 20,000 kilometers, or roughly 12,500 miles, above Earth), and the high-inclination Molniya orbit, utilized by Soviet (now Russian) communications satellites.

Low Earth Orbit is the region of space from about 322 to 805 kilometers (200 miles to 500 miles) above the Earth's surface. Geostationary orbit is much higher, and is located at an altitude of approximately 36,000 kilometers (22,300 miles) above Earth. Satellites in GEO rotate at the same pace as the Earth rotates (more formally, the Earth and GEO satellites have the same angular velocity) and so to an Earth-based observer such satellites always remain over the same point on the ground, and take 24 hours for one orbit. By contrast, satellites in LEO move much more quickly from horizon to horizon as they orbit the Earth once every 90 minutes or so. For this reason, satellites in geostationary orbit can be permanently "parked" over a city or other fixed point on the surface (they only appear to hover above the Earth—in actuality, they simply orbit at the same angular rate as the Earth). Satellites in LEO do not stay over one point above Earth all the time, and are much closer to the planet. Satellites in LEO are able to photograph very detailed images of the surface, as well as closely intercept other forms of signal intelligence—so most spy satellites (but not all) are in LEOs.

Geographic Information Systems

Maps have long been a vital tool for exploring the globe and its physical resources. Geographic Information Systems (GIS) have their roots in traditional map making, but they offer a much higher degree of analysis and efficiency for the user. GIS systems are electronic databases containing maps of the Earth's surface, and are capable of providing advanced imagery and other information. GIS systems receive data from aircraft or space satellites. Because the electronic maps can be searched and sorted to provide solutions to questions and to solve real-world problems, they are useful in many different disciplines.

GIS systems can display data in a wide variety of formats according to user needs. Maps containing diverse data can be superimposed to show trends or to assist with prediction making. A time component can also be added to the information to determine future cause and effects. GIS systems can thus provide information for a diverse assortment of users: resource managers, development planners, environmentalists, and even emergency response personnel.

Recently declassified photographic intelligence from orbiting space satellites has been used to show the changes over time to the Antarctic ice flow. Using satellite imagery taken over multiple decades, scientists have been able to determine the patterns of ice flow on a continental scale. The declassified photographs have shown that the Antarctic ice is flowing at a different rate than had previously been assumed.

The Global Positioning System

The Global Positioning System is an important technology that aids a wide variety of users. The system consists of a string of Earth-orbiting satellites in Medium Earth Orbits that beam signals to ground-based receivers. The receivers translate the signals into exact time and location coordinates, showing the position of the user on the ground. The system was first developed for the U.S. military, but civilian devices are now widely available, and affordable, as well. The civilian GPS system is typically less accurate than the military version. Applications for GPS systems include navigation, scientific research, vehicle tracking, precision farming, map making, and the creation of travel aids for visually impaired persons.

CCTV Systems

Closed Circuit Television (CCTV) systems are used for a variety of security and surveillance-related applications. CCTV systems consist of video cameras that connect to video monitoring or recording equipment. These systems transmit images in real time to remote video monitors or recorders. Some CCTV systems are equipped with microphones, allowing them to transmit audio in addition to the video signal. CCTV systems are used by civil governments to oversee traffic and for security monitoring of public spaces. Home and business owners employ CCTV systems to monitor private property. CCTV systems can operate in a wireless mode, and can be monitored and controlled over standard computer networks or the Internet.

Surveillance and American Society

The power gained from global surveillance technology was once the private domain of rich and powerful governments, but now much of the technology belongs to private citizens as well. Consumer-oriented surveillance equipment empowers groups of users including automobile drivers, boaters, pilots, scientists, students, environmentalists, hobbyists, farmers, engineers, and persons with disabilities. Declassified reconnaissance photographs have helped environmentalists and scientists uncover the truth about the planet's ecology and biosphere. Surveillance technology permits the identification of threats from potential adversaries to prevent conflicts before they occur.

Many companies in the Internet age store extensive amounts of user information for the benefit of the company. This includes information such as IP addresses and Internet searches, down to where someone puts the cursor of his or her mouse. Often this is done to target Internet ads to specific users to enhance the browsing experience but it raises questions about privacy and security, and how much such corporate surveillance could be used against users.

Civil libertarians claim that surveillance technology may impede personal privacy, and many are concerned that the technology may be turned on the civilian population by a tyrannical regime. However, members of the intelligence community maintain that surveillance technology is vital for national security.

In the classic novel *1984,* author George Orwell described a tyrannical government run by "Big Brother" that routinely spied on its citizens, forcing personal freedom to fall by the wayside, reminding some critics

Surveillance Technology in Action

The Cuban Missile Crisis is the most prominent example of surveillance technology thwarting global thermonuclear war. In 1962 U.S. satellites and high flying U-2 reconnaissance aircraft saw that the Cuban military was building a nuclear missile strike force, a situation intolerable to the United States. The resolution of the crisis eventually led to a more stable relationship between the United States and the Soviet Union.

* **cybernetics** a unified approach to understanding the behavior of machines and animals developed by Norbert Wiener (1894-1964)

of the following statement by Benjamin Franklin on freedom: "They that can give up essential liberty to obtain a little temporary safety deserve neither liberty nor safety." Democratic societies such as the United States will continue to struggle to use surveillance technology to ensure domestic security while guarding against the possibility that such technology could be used to eliminate the very personal freedoms they wish to protect.

▶ *See also* **Geographic Information Systems • Global Positioning Systems • Privacy • Security**

Resources

Books

Graham Jr., Thomas, Keith Hansen, and Robert Huffstutler. *Spy Satellites: And Other Intelligence Technologies That Changed History*. Seattle: University of Washington Press, 2007.

Hofmann-Wellenhof, B., Herbert Lichtenegger, and Elmar Wasle. *GNSS—Global Navigation Satellite Systems: GPS, GLONASS, Galileo, and More*. Vienna and New York: Springer, 2008.

Johnson, Rebecca L. *Satellites*. Minneapolis, MN: Lerner Publications, 2006.

O'Day, Alan. *Cyberterrorism*. Aldershot, UK, and Burlington, VT: Ashgate, 2004.

Seeber, Gunter. *Satellite Geodesy*. 2nd ed. Berlin and New York: Walter de Gruyter, 2003.

Weimann, Gabriel. *Terror on the Internet: The New Arena, the New Challenges*. Washington, D.C.: United States Institute of Peace Press, 2006.

Periodical

Story, Louise. "F.T.C. to Review Online Ads and Privacy." *The New York Times*, November 1, 2007.

Glushkov, Victor M.

Soviet Mathematician and Computer Engineer
1923-1982

Victor M. Glushkov was a pioneer in cybernetics*, computer engineering, and mathematics. He initially made his reputation as the first mathematician to solve the fifth generalized problem of Hilbert but is better known as the force behind the U.S.S.R.'s Institute of Cybernetics that was of primary importance to the application of computers in the Soviet

Union. Glushkov is a holder of the Silver-Core award of the International Federation for Information Processing (IFIP). He issued more than 800 papers including thirty monographs, many of which have been translated into other languages.

Glushkov was born on August 24, 1923, in Rostov on the river Don. He attended and graduated from Rostov University (1947 to 1948) and Novocherkassk Polytechnic Institute (1943 to 1948). He started his career as a teacher at the Ural Timber-Technology Institute (Sverdlovsk) while performing research under two leading Soviet algebraists, S. N. Chernikov and A. S. Kurosh. In 1955 he received his Ph.D. from Moscow State University with a dissertation titled "Topological Locally Nilpotent Group." In 1956 Victor went to Kiev to become the head of the Computer Engineering Laboratory of the Institute of Mathematics of the National Academy of Sciences that became the basis for the Computer Center of the Academy of Sciences of Ukraine in 1957.

In 1961 the Computing Center became the Institute of Cybernetics of the Ukrainian Academy of Sciences and Glushkov became its director. His tenure lasted until his death. Under the leadership of Glushkov, the institute gained an international reputation for computer science research and the training of scientists (100 professors and 600 doctors of science under Glushkov). The year 1962 marked the release of Glushkov's classic book, *Synthesis of Computing Automata,* which he followed with *Introduction to Cybernetics* in 1964. Ten years later, Glushkov edited a compilation of all leading Soviet cybernetic scientists in the notable *Encyclopedia of Cybernetics*. When he died on January 30, 1982, after a long illness, he left behind a foundation that would eventually lead to the "informatization of Soviet society."

A scientist with a wide range of interests and talents, he was elected in 1961 as a member of the Ukrainian Academy of Sciences, and in 1962 he became the vice president of the same organization. In 1964 Glushkov was honored with the Lenin Prize for a series of contributions on discrete automata theory* and was elected a member of the Academy of Science of the U.S.S.R. In 1966 a team of designers headed by Glushkov was awarded the first state prize for the development of principles for the construction of small computers incorporating structural high-level languages for engineering calculations. In 1969, for achievements in the advancement of science and training of scientists, Glushkov was granted the title of "Hero of Socialist Labor," and the Institute of Cybernetics was awarded the Order of Lenin. In 1977 Glushkov and colleagues were awarded the U.S.S.R. State Prize for a series of contributions to the methods of computer-aided design of computers.

When computer science was a young discipline, Glushkov envisioned the use of a computer as more than just a calculator. He visualized the simulation of "brain-like" structures, evolutionary computing, automatic theorem proving, pattern recognition*, and the first robotic systems. He developed technologies for the design and construction of

* **automata theory** the analytical (mathematical) treatment and study of automated systems

* **pattern recognition** a process used by some artificial-intelligence systems to identify a variety of patterns, including visual patterns, information patterns buried in a noisy signal, and word patterns imbedded in text

Institute of Cybernetics

The Institute of Cybernetics, under the direction of Glushkov, was the leading organization in the field. Journals published by the Institute of Cybernetics and started under Glushkov's leadership have had consistently high ratings among computer scientists. Titles include *Automatica, Cybernetics (1965, called Cybernetics and Systems Analysis* from 1991), and *UsiM (1972)*.

computer components, including the joint design of computer hardware and software.

Glushkov was the first to formulate and document the concepts of computer design on the basis of automated algebraic models. He designed several special programming languages, such as ANALYTIC, for the translation of algebraic expressions on a computer. The personal computer MIR, a predecessor of present-day personal computers, was developed and mass produced under Glushkov. He is also associated with the publication of many books, journals, and scientific papers on cybernetics and computer science. The latter years of Glushkov's life were dominated by work on the Statewide Automated System or Data Collection and Processing (OGAS), which was designed to automate the management of the state economy.

▶ *See also* **Cybernetics**

Resources

Books

Lee, John A. N., ed. *International Biographical Dictionary of Computer Pioneers*. Chicago: Fitzroy Dearborn Publishers, 1995.

Periodicals

Zemanek, Heinz. "Eloge: Victor Mikhaylovich Glushkov." *IEEE Annals of the History of Computing* 4, no. 2 (1982): 100–101.

Web Sites

Glushkov Institute of Cybernetics. http://www.icyb.kiev.ua/ (accessed November 2, 2012).

Guru

Guru is a Hindi word that refers to a teacher or a religious and spiritual guide. Similarly, modern usage of the word in the West usually refers to a wise person—maybe a teacher—with knowledge and expertise about a particular subject, and its usage was made common first in computer circles. Gurus are typically people who are easy to get in touch with and are interested in sharing their knowledge with others. In computer jargon, a guru is someone who is extremely knowledgeable and has helped advance the world of computing significantly.

One of the early gurus in computer science was Jackson Granholm, who in 1962 coined the term kludge. This word initially referred to a poorly planned combination of parts put together while designing a computer. Therefore, a kludge is a machine that contains several features that are annoying to users and, in retrospect, are aspects that the designer wishes had been done differently. The term now encompasses programs, documentation, and even computing centers, so that the new definition describes systems that were hastily planned, patched together, and have proven themselves to be unreliable.

Another early computer guru was Canadian-American computer scientist H. R. J. Grosch (1918–), who, while working for the IBM Corporation in the 1950s, introduced Grosch's Law, which states that organizations can reduce the overall cost of their hardware if they strengthen their computing power because this will reduce the cost of performing computing functions. This means that the more powerful a computer system is, the lower its costs will be per unit of performance. So, if one spends twice as much on a new computer, one would anticipate its performance to be four times greater.

A third early guru was American chemist Gordon Moore (1929–), former chairman of the board of Intel, and the person who formulated Moore's Law in 1965 shortly after patenting the integrated circuit*. His hypothesis, which states that transistor densities on a single chip will double every eighteen months, has proven to be very accurate over the years. Moore's Law has had an impact on many aspects of modern computers. Increased transistor densities are directly attributable to the higher speed of modern processors, larger memory sizes, and lowering both the relative cost of electronics compared to performance and the absolute cost of computers, even without accounting for inflation. It is regularly predicted that Moore's Law will fail, that such progress cannot keep occurring. These predictions are always disproven, showing the foresight Moore possessed over forty years ago.

Some current computer gurus include:

- American computer scientist Peter J. Denning (1942–). His work on virtual memory systems helped make virtual memory a permanent part of modern operating systems.

- Canadian software developer James Gosling (1955–), creator of Java and developer of Sun's NeWS windowing system. He was also the principal investigator on the Andrew project while earning his Ph.D. in computer science from Carnegie Mellon University.

- British computer engineer and scientist Sir Tim Berners-Lee (1955–), originator of the World Wide Web. Together with colleagues, he developed Hypertext Markup Language (HTML), the language used for web documents; Hypertext Transfer Protocol (HTTP); and the Uniform Resource Locator (URL) used to uniquely identify anything on the web.

- Finnish software engineer Linus Torvalds (1969–). He developed Linux, an operating system originally designed to maximize the capabilities of the Intel 80386 microprocessor. Later, Linux became widely adopted in industry and educational markets around the world because of its power and flexibility.

* **integrated circuit** a circuit with the transistors, resistors, and other circuit elements etched into the surface of a single chip of semiconducting material, usually silicon

Guru or Wizard

Gurus are not necessarily programmers, and so, as a rule, they are not considered to be wizards. However, gurus usually are significant users of specific operating systems, user interfaces, or application software.

■ Bill Gates (1955–) helped found Microsoft. Microsoft was instrumental in creating computers for personal use at home or in an office. Gates also helped to create Corbis, a digital archive of images, videos, and more. Because of his work with Microsoft, Gates became one of the wealthiest people on Earth.

■ American businessman Steven Jobs (1955–2011) was co-founder of Apple Computer with American computer engineer Steve Wozniak (1950–). After bringing the first commercial desktop to market with the Macintosh, Jobs founded NeXT, another innovative computer company. Apple's subsequent purchase of NeXT brought Jobs back to the company, where he integrated NeXT's desktop environment into Apple to form the basis of their new OS X operating system. Although not considered as technically adept as some other computer gurus, he is recognized uniformly for his strong leadership and artistic vision in introducing innovative human-computer interaction technologies. Under the direction of Jobs, Apple created a string of innovative and successful multi-touch-interface products including the iPod, iPhone, and iPad.

▶ *See also* **Hacking • Invasive Programs • Procedural Languages • Programming • Security**

Resources

Books

Campbell-Kelly, Martin, and William Aspray. *Computer: A History of the Information Machine*. 2nd ed. Boulder, CO: Westview Press, 2004.

Young, Jeffrey S., and William L. Simon. *ICon: Steve Jobs, the Greatest Second Act in the History of Business*. Hoboken, NJ: Wiley, 2005.

Web Sites

Microsoft "Bill Gates: Chairman." http://www.microsoft.com/en-us/news/exec/billg/default.aspx (accessed October 17, 2012)

H

Hackers

Hacking emerged with the invention of computers. The term hacker has a variety of definitions. Among computer professionals, it is applied to someone who is proficient at software programming, debugging systems, or identifying vulnerabilities in a given computer, software application, or computer network. These are valuable skills for computer programmers and technicians. However hacker has taken on a negative meaning among the public and in the media. Outside the computer industry, the term is now generally used to describe a person with these skills who decides to apply them toward a damaging or illegal purpose.

The United States has two definitions of illegal hacking. First, it is illegal to have in one's possession the password to a computer or network without permission to possess that password. Secondly, it is a felony to enter a computer or network system without permission. If damage is caused in that system, the hacker is liable for additional legal charges.

The people who hack and the hacker organizations to which they may belong are as varied as their goals. Some hackers break into computer systems for bragging rights, causing no intentional damage. Others hack for political gain or protest. Still others release devastating codes called viruses, worms, or Trojan horses*. Many of these codes self-replicate and infect other computers, sometimes causing billions of dollars in damage worldwide. Hackers also have a variety of terms to describe themselves and classify what they do.

A well-known example of a hacker organization is Anonymous, a diverse, loosely organized group of hackers that is tied together by their opposition to Web censorship and surveillance. Members of the group have hacked numerous government and corporate Web sites, especially major security organizations. Anonymous members can be recognized in public by their wearing of masks in the likeness of English soldier Guy Fawkes (1570–1606), a member of the Gunpowder Plot of 1605, an unsuccessful attempt to blow up the House of Lords and assassinate King James I of England. He is the member most associated with the foiled attempt; with a Guy Fawkes Day annually held on November 5th to celebrate the failed attempt.

Anonymous members often use this date as a way to make themselves and their mission better known to the public. In 2012, according to the Huffington Post, they supposedly hacked a PayPal server and stole 28,000 customer passwords. They also supposedly hacked into the Web sites of Twitter, NBC (National Broadcasting Corporation), and

* **Trojan horses** potentially destructive computer programs that masquerade as something benign; named after the wooden horse employed by the Acheans to conquer Troy

Computer hacker and activist Jacob Appelbaum. © *Sean Gallup/Getty Images.*

Symantec, along with Lady Gaga's fan site Gagadaily.com. Although most of their activities are non-violent (primarily involving computer hacking) the group has threatened to bomb government buildings and perform other violent acts.

Types of Hackers

Phreakers are hackers who specialize in telephone networks. This was the first kind of hacker, as telephones used one of the first automated systems. Early phreakers developed a device called a Blue Box to use when placing free telephone calls, sometimes using several telephone lines and telephone numbers around the world. With the emergence of analog cellular phones, phreakers could hack literally from thin air. When a victim used his or her cell phone, phreakers intercepted the message along with the caller's identification code. The phreakers then supplied additional cell phones with the stolen identification code. The subsequent telephone bills went to the surprised victim. Digital cell phones make this practice impossible for phreakers.

Those who lack skills for hacking but attempt to access technology or information belonging to others are called Wannabes or Script Kiddies. Some experts say most of the world's hackers fall into this category. Elite hackers have proven their hacking abilities. Black Hat hackers reserve their skills for their own illegal profit.

White Hat hackers work legally. Ethical hackers are hired to break into computer networks to help improve security. In the past, many considered hiring ethical hackers to be a high-risk technique for companies, calling for strict supervision and solid insurance policies. Currently, however, it is considered a vital part of computer security for many organizations.

Another category of hackers, Warez Dudez, target software. They copy, or pirate, existing software, removing copy-preventing safeguards if necessary. An estimated 50 percent of software worldwide is illegally manufactured. In fact, more than 57 percent of computer users worldwide use this pirated software. Many times, hackers install their own viruses on pirated software before distribution.

Finally, criminal hackers, called Crackers, use hacking to complement their other illegal activities.

Consequences of Hacking

As computer technology becomes more complex and intricate, hackers need more specialized knowledge, experience, equipment, and money. In turn, the computers and information systems that hackers target require additional security features in order to counter the threat posed by illicit hackers.

With the growing dependence upon computer information systems and automation, many in the hacking world are increasingly drawn to corporate networks to engage in corporate espionage. In one study, 85 percent of businesses surveyed admitted that hackers had penetrated their computer security systems during the previous year, causing damage measured in hundreds of millions of dollars. Many times these businesses bear the cost quietly without prosecuting the hacker for fear of causing customer loss of confidence. However, they have the option of suing for damages in civil court without the publicity inherent in taking action in the criminal court system; many do.

Successful hacking depends upon experience and knowledge. Because of this, experts warn that devastating damage is increasingly likely to be caused by disgruntled and former employees. In many high-tech firms, dismissed employees are immediately escorted from the building upon termination and their computer system access codes are promptly changed. Companies that spend few, if any, resources to strengthen computer security, such as small businesses, and those lax about keeping discharged employees away from their business computer systems are vulnerable.

Any networked or online computer can be the target of hackers. Without adequate security measures, any computerized network—including those that power Wall Street, banks, and credit institutions, health institutions, educational institutions, air traffic control networks, power supply grids, traffic light systems, or municipal water supply systems—can become a prime target for domestic or international hackers.

Government-Sponsored Hackers

Hackers have been assembled into organized groups for the purpose of stealing the industrial and/or military secrets of other nations. In an April 2010 speech given at Lawrence Livermore National Laboratory, an important government facility involved in national defense research, James Olsen asserted that over 80 nations had either stolen, or attempted to steal, valuable intellectual property from the United States. Olsen is a former chief of counterintelligence within the U.S. Central Intelligence Agency (CIA). He listed the top three countries of state-sponsored Internet hacking as China, Russia, and Cuba. Olsen further claimed that "Every FBI or CIA counterintelligence official that I know considers China to be the No. 1 espionage threat to our country," with Russia not far behind.

According to Olsen, hackers directed by Chinese military intelligence were involved in attacks on computer systems at the Pentagon in 2007. The cyber attacks lasted for weeks and were able to overwhelm the defenses constructed by computer experts of the U.S. military. And in 2008, Chinese hackers penetrated the White House's computer network, with the result that e-mail messages between White House officials could be read by the perpetrators.

In May 2012, security analysts at Kaspersky Labs, a computer security company, announced the discovery of one of the most complex and sustained cyber attacks in history. Following a joint investigation with the United Nations' International Telecommunication Union, Kaspersky revealed that malware, known as Flame, had infected government, university, business, and individual computer systems in Iran, Israel, Sudan, Syria, Lebanon, Saudi Arabia, and Egypt since at least 2010. Flame collected private data and sent the information to the attackers. Flame even was capable of secretly recording video and audio using a computer's webcam and microphone before sending it back to the attackers. Kaspersky security analysts claim that the complexity of the attack and the systems targeted indicate that the cyber attack was state-sponsored. Computer security experts will spend years analyzing data from the attack in an attempt to identify the attackers.

Various branches of the U.S. government devote increasing portions of their budgets to defend against hackers; national security concerns include terrorist hackers. Experts speculate that the United States also uses hackers to advance its knowledge of other countries.

 See also **Guru • Hacking • Privacy • Security • World Wide Web**

Resources

Books

Avoine, Gildas, Pascal Junod, and Philippe Oechslin. *Computer System Security: Basic Concepts and Solved Exercises.* Computer and communication sciences. Lausanne, Switzerland: EPFL Press, 2007.

Barger, Robert N. *Computer Ethics: A Case-Based Approach.* Cambridge, U.K., and New York: Cambridge University Press, 2008.

Barthe, Gilles. and Cédric Fournet. *Trustworthy Global Computing: Third Symposium, TGC 2007, Sophia-Antipolis, France, November 5–6, 2007: Revised Selected Papers.* Berlin: Springer, 2008.

Bradley, Tony. *Computer Security 101: What You Need to Know to Secure Your Computer or Network.* San Francisco, CA: No Starch Press, 2005.

Buttyán, Levente, and Jean-Pierre Hubaux. *Security and Cooperation in Wireless Networks: Thwarting Malicious and Selfish Behavior in the Age of Ubiquitous Computing.* Cambridge, U.K.: Cambridge University Press, 2007.

Canetti, Ran. *Theory of Cryptography: Fifth Theory of Cryptography Conference, TCC 2008, New York, USA, March 19–21, 2008: Proceedings.* Berlin and New York: Springer, 2008.

Chen, Liqun, Yi Mu, and Willy Susilo. *Information Security Practice and Experience: 4th International Conference, ISPEC 2008, Sydney, Australia, April 21–23, 2008: Proceedings.* Berlin: Springer, 2008.

Dube, Roger. *Hardware-Based Computer Security Techniques to Defeat Hackers: From Biometrics to Quantum Cryptography.* Hoboken, NJ: Wiley, 2008.

Easttom, Chuck. *Computer Security Fundamentals.* 2nd ed. Indianapolis, IN: Pearson, 2012.

Himma, Kenneth Einar, ed. *Internet Security: Hacking, Counterhacking, and Society.* Sudbury, MA.: Jones and Bartlett Publishers, 2007.

Knapp, Kenneth J. *Cyber-Security and Global Information Assurance: Threat Analysis and Response Solutions.* Hershey, PA: Information Science Reference, 2009.

Lehtinen, Rick, et al. *Computer Security Basics.* Sebastopol, CA: O'Reilly Media, 2006.

Web Sites

Business Software Alliance. "2011 Piracy Study." http://portal.bsa.org/globalpiracy2011/index.html (accessed October 15, 2012).

Huffington Post, and Cavan Sieczkowski. "Anonymous Claims To Have Hacked 28,000 PayPal Passwords For Guy Fawkes Day." http://www.huffingtonpost.com/2012/11/05/anonymous-paypal-28000-password-hack-guy-fawkes-day_n_2076587.html (accessed November 5, 2012).

U.S. Government; science.gov. "Computer Hardware." http://www.science.gov/browse/w_117A1.htm (accessed May 29, 2012).

U.S. Government; science.gov. "Computer Security." http://www.science.gov/browse/w_117A4.htm (accessed May 29, 2012).

U.S. Government; science.gov. "Computer Software." http://www.science.gov/browse/w_117A3.htm (accessed May 29, 2012).

Home Entertainment

Home entertainment is the application of technology and the arts for private amusement and enjoyment. The proliferation of the microprocessor and digital media has produced a wide variety of innovative technologies for home entertainment. Digital entertainment systems found in many homes include portable music players such as iPods and wi-fi enabled audio receivers for listening to music; digital versatile disc (DVD), Blueray, digital video recorders (DVRs) or streaming content players such as Roku or Apple TV for movies and television programs; digital cameras, and gaming consoles.

Early Entertainment

The revolution in home entertainment technologies is a relatively new phenomenon. For centuries, most entertainment was almost exclusively a luxury for the wealthy or conducted in public. A major expansion of the traditional public arts such as plays and development of new forms of art such as opera followed the Renaissance period in Europe (c. 1350–1600). Prior to the development of electricity, the most advanced technology

A 1080p HD 3-D home theater system for sale. © *Jin Lee/Bloomberg via Getty Images.*
▼

used in performances was musical instruments such as the pipe organ and the piano (from which the modern concept of the computerized electronic keyboard is derived).

The use of modern technology for home entertainment is a product of the Industrial Revolution (c. 1730–1850) and extends back to the nineteenth century with the mass production of mechanical music boxes. These often-elaborate devices presaged the use of the computer as an entertainment component, with the use of punched holes in metal to program musical notes. Following mechanical music boxes, Hollerith cards, which were first used by the U.S. Census in 1890, were invented and were the precursor to the IBM punched card*.

Advent of Electricity

With the growth of the middle class in Europe and the United States beginning in the late 1800s, and the concurrent invention of electrical devices such as motors, new forms of entertainment for the home were developed. For example, Thomas A. Edison (1847–1931) was a prolific American inventor of entertainment systems such as the phonograph and the first movie projection system.

However, the first electronic system for home entertainment was the radio. Invented in 1895 by Italian inventor Guglielmo Marconi (1874–1937), the radio became a mass medium through the efforts of Russian-American businessman David Sarnoff (1891–1917) at RCA. The first musical broadcast was from the stage of the Metropolitan Opera in 1910. The key component of the radio—a vacuum tube* amplifier— spurred the creation of the first digital computers. For example, the Electronic Numerical Integrator and Analyzer Computer (ENIAC) developed by the University of Pennsylvania during World War II was composed of thousands of vacuum tubes. Similarly, the transistor*, invented at Bell Laboratories, saw its first application in small AM radios. It was later used as the basis for the development of the microprocessor, which powers computers and a myriad of electronics.

Television was an extension of broadcast radio technology. Like radio and the phonograph, television is now being transformed by the digital era. In the United States, over-the-air broadcast signals have traditionally been analog-based, meaning a signal that can vary continuously over a spectrum. However, they are now transmitted in digital form, meaning the signal is made up of discrete values with no possibility of signals falling in between values. This was mandated by the Federal Communications Commission (FCC), and allows for the same information to be broadcast in a more efficient form, which reduces the bandwidth required to distribute television signals. Beyond digital broadcast signals, high definition television (HDTV) is a form of digital television, which increases the amount of information per frame per second to give the viewer a more detailed picture. To decode such information in the amount of time necessary to display it on the screen, HDTVs and 3D HDTVs have

* **punched card** a paper card with punched holes which give instructions to a computer in order to encode program instructions and data

* **vacuum tube** an electronic device constructed of a sealed glass tube containing metal elements in a vacuum; used to control electrical signals

* **transistor** a contraction of TRANSfer resISTOR; a semiconductor device, invented by John Bardeen, Walter Brattain, and William Shockley, which has three terminals; can be used for switching and amplifying electrical signals

Personalized Entertainment

Technology has brought personalized entertainment within the grasp of many consumers. For example, DVRs, Apple TV, and Roku systems store or online-stream television programs for people to watch when they want. The systems also can be programmed to know a user's favorite types of shows and record, recommend, or queue for viewing similar programs that might be of interest to the user. Many of these devices allow a user's computer or app-enabled devices such as smartphones and tablets to manage content, mirror or play media from the remote device on a television screen, or act as a remote control.

* **encryption** also known as encoding; a mathematical process that disguises the content of messages transmitted

* **digital watermarks** special data structures permanently embedded into a program or other file type, which contain information about the author and the program

incorporated many microprocessors and have a processing power comparable to personal computers.

Video Games and Beyond

Following television, the invention of the video game in the early 1970s was the next great home entertainment system and the beginning of the digital era in the home. Game consoles were, in effect, the first home computers. Founded by American engineer Nolan Bushnell (1943–), Atari, Inc. produced the first hit video game in 1972. The game, Pong, used simple black and white graphics to represent a virtual Ping Pong (or table tennis) game. Atari also created the first console system for the home in 1975.

Game consoles rapidly grew more sophisticated and popular with the introduction of two-dimensional and three-dimensional graphics, digital sound, and a variety of input devices such as joysticks and game pads. Computer games also advanced modern graphics techniques such as texturing, and in fact almost single-handedly drove the development of advanced graphic chips, known as graphics processing units (GPUs). Later, more sophisticated game consoles included Nintendo 64 (developed with computer manufacturer SGI), the Sega Dreamcast, and the Sony Playstation with used compact discs (CDs) instead of specialized game cartridges to store games. The current generation of gaming consoles has made a radical leap in terms of processing power over their distant predecessors. The three major consoles (the Microsoft Xbox 360, the Nintendo Wii, and the Sony Playstation 3) all include custom processors, and the Xbox 360 and Playstation 3 actually include multiple processors to help handle the load modern games place upon the unit. The Playstation 3 also uses the Blu-ray disk optical storage medium to distribute games and play high definition movies. They are all Internet enabled and allow users to stream non-gaming media content to their televisions via services such as Netflix.

The relationship between entertainment and computing technologies is such that large-scale production tends to drive down the cost of manufacturing new systems and spur further advances. The convergence of entertainment with digital technology has given rise to many exciting possibilities, including the ability to obtain digital music and streaming video on the World Wide Web. In fact, many people use their personal computers, smartphones, and tablets for entertainment at home and work.

This new ability to make accurate reproductions of digital media has caused major controversies in copyright law and rules regarding encryption* and steganographic techniques such as digital watermarks*.

▶ *See also* **Bell Labs • Computer Vision • Copyright • Copyright • Graphic Devices • Hollerith, Herman • Home System Software • Marconi, Guglielmo • Robotics • Vacuum Tubes**

Resources

Books

Arnstein, Walter L., Christina Bashford, and Nicholas Temperley. *Victorian Entertainments: "We Are Amused": An Exhibit Illustrating Victorian Entertainment.* Urbana, IL: Rare Book & Manuscript Library, University of Illinois, 2007.

Blaszczyk, Regina Lee. *American Consumer Society, 1865–2005: From Hearth to HDTV.* Wheeling, IL: Harlan Davidson, Inc., 2009.

Cianci, Philip J. *HDTV and the Transition to Digital Broadcasting: Understanding New Television Technologies.* Amsterdam and Boston: Focal Press, 2007.

Wolf, Mark J. P. *The Video Game Explosion: A History from PONG to Playstation and Beyond.* Westport, CT: Greenwood Press, 2008.

Human Factors: User Interfaces

Every computer system has an interface that consists of software and hardware, which are needed for users interacting with the system. User interfaces allow people to input commands to the computer, read the computer's output, structure information, and complete certain tasks that may be related to business, education, government, medical, military, industrial, scientific, or home environments. Different types of interfaces allow users to perform a multitude of tasks on a computer, such as creating documents, searching the Internet, or sending and receiving e-mail messages. A user interface may enable a user to enter, locate, manipulate, analyze, monitor, or retrieve information.

Effective user interfaces are extremely important. Many users find computer interfaces difficult to use, and a user's ability to perform tasks on a computer is directly related to the effectiveness of the computer interface. Human-computer interactions should be structured and presented to ease learning, minimize errors, and facilitate use. A poorly designed interface display may lead to user mistakes, non-use of the computer system, and low user satisfaction. In general, interface design needs to answer questions about when, what, and how a user completes a task. User interface designers consider issues such as human memory, color perception, and task complexity to define the display requirements for a computer interface.

Computer games are very popular with people of all ages. Popular computer games include sophisticated interfaces using multimedia effects such as color and sound. Many schools use software programs in the classroom to teach skills and make lessons more interesting for students. The importance of a well-designed user interface is more important than ever as the number of people using computer systems has dramatically

* **virtual reality (VR)** the use of elaborate input/output devices to create the illusion that the user is in a different environment

increased over the last decade, fueled by the dramatic increase of the Internet on home computers.

Types of Displays

Humans interact with different computer interface displays, such as command line interfaces; menus; natural language; form-fill and spreadsheets; windows, icons, menus, and pointers (WIMP) interfaces; and three-dimensional interfaces. Displays vary in format, type, size, color, and content. Users find color displays attractive, which makes computer software easier to use.

Command line interfaces allow users to give instructions to the computer using commands and keywords. Most online search engines use command line interfaces. Menu-driven interfaces provide the user with a set of options from which to choose. For example, an automated teller machine (ATM) displays a list of options that allow users to deposit and withdraw money and check account balances. Natural language interfaces allow users to communicate with the computer through spoken or written sentences. For example, the Internet search engine "Ask Jeeves" allows users to ask questions when searching for information.

Fill-in forms or spreadsheets present users with a form to complete with numbers or words. For example, to book an airline ticket via the Travelocity website, a user must complete a form by providing destination and travel details. WIMP interfaces combine various display types and allow users to complete multiple tasks at the same time (known as "multitasking"), click on icons (or pictures), and use their mouse as a pointer. For example, Microsoft Windows allows users to use many software programs at the same time.

Three-dimensional (3D) interfaces are used in virtual reality (VR)*. For example, computer games have been created that utilize 3D interfaces and helmet-mounted displays. As the power of personal computer systems increases, the use of 3D interfaces becomes more practical. New types of heads-up displays can project information or images on the windscreen of a car or airplane.

Agents, Direct Manipulation

Computer interfaces may include software agents that perform tasks for users. Agents may perform tasks directly specified by a user, or watch and learn from a user's actions and perform tasks without the user present. For example, an e-mail agent may filter a user's e-mail. Direct manipulation means that specific tasks are represented as pictures to make the task easier for the interface user. For example, to print a document in Microsoft's word processing package Word, the user can click on a printer graphic to initiate printing.

Software

Software is the sequence of instructions in one or more programming languages or software tools that enable a computer application to automate a task. Computing languages, such as C++ or Java, are used by software engineers to create different types of interfaces with different features, depending on the task for which the interface was designed. Each software program provides users with an interface that allows them to complete a particular task or set of tasks. For example, a word processing interface that allows users to create and modify documents has different features than a web search engine interface. Better software design and software tutorials can make computer interfaces easier to use.

Hardware

Hardware refers to the computer itself (as well as any peripheral equipment, such as a printer) that interacts with a software program. Computer hardware also includes the keyboard, mouse, tablets, joysticks, and other input devices that allow the user to interact with the computer system. New technologies such as speech input, touch screens, and 3D displays increase interface usability. Advances in computer technology allow more powerful computational capabilities in a smaller package. Laptops, portable wireless computers, enable users to access the Internet from any of many locations at any time.

The hardware used in any given system has a significant impact on the user interface that can be designed. Improved computer hardware and software can allow users to complete tasks more quickly and effectively, reduce user errors, and minimize the training time and skill needed to use a computer. Specially designed user interfaces are helping younger, blind, elderly, and disabled people use computers. Better interface designs can continue to reduce the potential health risks of prolonged computer use. The interfaces of the future will take users into a 3-dimensional world of virtual reality sight, sound, smell, and touch.

 See also **Assistive Computer Technology For Persons With Disabilities • Ergonomics • Graphic Devices • Interactive Systems**

Resources

Books

Shneiderman, Ben. *Designing the User Interface: Strategies for Effective Human-Computer Interaction.* 5th ed. Reading, MA: Addison Wesley, 2010.

Realism in Multimedia

Some computer games use multimedia presentations that are so realistic, they are used to simulate the real experience. Take Microsoft's Flight Simulator game, for example. It has been used in pilot training programs at flight schools. The game helps students learn how to conduct flight safety checks as well as how to operate navigational tools. A new edition of the game underwent alterations, however, after the terrorist attack on New York City's World Trade Center (WTC) in 2001. Microsoft removed images of the WTC from its simulator game.

I

Information Access

Information access is the ability to identify, retrieve, and use information effectively. Access to information is vital to social, political, and economic advancement. Traditionally, information has been disseminated in a variety of formats that have been widely accessible, often through public libraries. Many individuals also relied on other people and the media for information. However, advances in computer technology have revolutionized information access, making vast stores of business, education, health, government, and entertainment information accessible on the World Wide Web. Yet, despite technology's dramatic impact on the extent and availability of digital information, many people do not have access to these resources.

The Digital Divide

The gap between those who have technological access, and those who do not, is known as the digital divide. It is attributed to constraints imposed by national and regional infrastructure, political limitations, educational attainment, resource availability, socioeconomic status, gender, ethnicity, age, disability, and geography. The disparity between the digital information "haves" and "have-nots" is reflected in access, content, literacy, and training, and is a global problem. Resolution of inequitable access is important particularly for developing nations because they cannot build and maintain economic independence without adequate information.

In the United States, the October 2000 Department of Commerce document, "Falling through the Net: Toward Digital Inclusion," reported increases in overall Internet access and use. However, the digital divide continued in some sectors of the American population, particularly among blacks, Hispanics, and Native Americans, individuals with disabilities, people fifty years of age or older, and single-parent households. For many, the cost of computer ownership and Internet Service Provider (ISP)* connections creates significant barriers and high-speed, broadband connections via cable, digital subscriber line (DSL)*, or satellite remained beyond reach. Geography was also a difficult constraint with many rural areas still not wired for Internet access. In some rural communities, the only access methods were through outdated and slow "dial-up" ISPs that did not have local access telephone numbers.

A 2010 report from the Department of Commerce focused specifically on people's access to high-speed Internet services. The 2010 report titled "Digital Nation: 21st Century America's Progress towards Universal Broadband Internet Access" was based on information gathered from a

* **Internet Service Provider (ISP)** a commercial enterprise which offers paying subscribers access to the Internet (usually via modem) for a fee

* **digital subscriber line (DSL)** a technology that permits high-speed voice and data communications over public telephone networks; it requires the use of a DSL modem

survey of some 54,000 U.S. households. Many of the patterns seen in the 2000 report were similar to those discussed in the 2010 report—older people, those with lower incomes, and minorities were all less likely to have at-home broadband Internet service than the general population. Interestingly, males and females were almost equal in broadband usage, at about 59 percent each.

In 2009, the Federal Communications Commission (FCC) created the National Broadband Plan (sometimes known as Connect America) to address digital divide issues in the United States. However, by 2012 only one quarter of U.S. citizens in rural areas had access to high-speed broadband connections and the U.S. ranked sixteenth globally in broadband connections per 100 citizens. Broadband connections in the United States remained more expensive than similar or faster connections in Europe in late 2012. An FCC study of 2011 rates found that consumers in Paris, France, paid less than about $35 (USD) for 100 Mbps broadband access whereas consumers in Lafayette, Louisiana, paid $65 for a 6 Mbps connection.

Effective use of information content requires a complex set of competencies. With the uneven quality of web resources, as well as the absence of a consistent organizational structure, locating relevant and reliable information can be difficult and time-consuming. Search and meta-search engines as well as hierarchical subject indexes and portals were developed to improve access to specific information. Virtual reference desks, some with access to experts through AskA services, were opened. However, search precision remains problematic because, even when used in combination, search engines neither examine the entire web nor return all types of files equally.

Information on the Internet requires basic reading proficiency, sometimes in a language not native to the user. Optimal use of the Internet also requires competency in navigation and searching; without appropriate instruction, these skills can be difficult to master. Adequate training is crucial because even the most poorly constructed search generally will produce some results. The challenge then is not only connecting to the Internet or retrieving information, but also effectively evaluating the results.

Modes of Access

Most people connect to the Internet from at home, work, or on public networks using computers, smartphones, tablets, laptops, gaming consoles, and web-enabled smartTVs. Others may use computers at public access sites such as libraries, schools, and community centers.

Applications

The need for improved access has led to the development and refinement of applications. Web browsers, like Google Chrome or Safari, use graphical interfaces with embedded hyperlinks for navigation, making the underlying commands transparent to the user. With these applications, the Internet became more accessible and it emerged as a global information source. Scholarly, scientific, and everyday research was transformed by access to full-text documents as well as by the digitization of primary sources. Text translation applications minimized language barriers and text-to-speech technology improved access for the visually impaired. Educational opportunities were extended to new audiences and business access to management information and market intelligence was improved.

Asynchronous applications, like e-mail, as well as real-time or synchronous applications, like instant messaging and video conferencing, altered communication patterns and changed the flow of information substantially. The gap between limited local information and highly specialized but distant resources was dramatically narrowed, particularly in agriculture and healthcare. With geographical information systems (GIS), maps can be individualized and produced on demand. Combining XML* applications with Global Positioning System (GPS)* led to the development of virtual advisers with a voice interface that provides drivers with personalized traffic and news reports, e-mail, stock market, and sports news. Intelligent agents, such as Apple's Siri, and push technology mine and filter user-specified data from the Web and push it out directly to cell phones and computers.

Impact on Society

Digital information access has affected virtually every aspect of modern life by opening new communication pathways and fostering greater individual participation in society. Technological access has changed everyday activities like banking, shopping, and travel as well as business, education, and the economy. Not only has the Internet eased traditional boundaries and opened access to global resources, it also has generated new questions as society struggles to adapt to rapid and often autonomous information access.

Copyright laws developed for earlier publication mediums have been difficult to adapt to electronic publishing and intellectual property* rights have been jeopardized by online piracy and plagarism. Legal questions related to filtering, censorship, and Internet freedom have emerged.

Although technology has opened exciting new avenues of information access, the full benefits of these advances will remain elusive until the digital divide is closed. Until that is accomplished, many individuals and communities will be barred from participation in an increasingly technological world.

Developing Nations and the Internet

Although the Internet has changed economic and social patterns in much of the world, access to the Internet remains poor throughout most of the world, especially in developing countries. For example, as of mid–2008

* **XML** the acronym for eXtensible Markup Language; a method of applying structure to data so that documents can be represented

* **Global Positioning System (GPS)** a method of locating a point on the Earth's surface that uses received signals transmitted from satellites to calculate position accurately

* **intellectual property** the acknowledgement that an individual's creativity and innovation can be owned in the same way as physical property

East Africa was connected to the Internet only by a few expensive satellite links and West Africa was connected only by a single fiber-optic cable, forcing five West African countries to share only 1.2 gigabits per second of bandwidth. Overall, sub-Saharan Africa had only 0.2 percent as much Internet bandwidth per person as the United States and only 1 percent as much as the global average. Universities throughout much of sub-Saharan Africa were therefore unable to download scientific and technical articles and economic activity over the Web was choked by lack of access.

Internet accessibility and capacity began to improve dramatically for many of the underserved regions in the world, including Africa, in the first decade of the twentieth century. In July 2009, the SEACOM undersea cable was completed, bringing much greater data capacity and lower costs to several countries in East Africa, which previously were connected to the Internet only by a few expensive satellite links. And a slightly higher-capacity undersea cable, known as EASSy, will further enhance sub-Saharan Africa's global connectivity; it began operations in 2010.

Computer scientists such as Tim Berners-Lee (1955–), inventor of the World Wide Web, were warning that the nature of the Internet was being threatened by the desire of internet service providers to begin favoring some types of messages over others, especially those from higher-paying customers. Since its beginnings in the 1970s, the Internet had been characterized by "net neutrality"—that is, all users had equal access to long-distance transmission equipment. Favoring certain corporate or higher-paying customers over others would result in slower access for non-favored clients, eliminating net neutrality, which Berners-Lee and others claim is essential to the Internet's continued growth and vitality.

▶ *See also* **Digital Libraries** • **Distance Learning** • **Home Entertainment** • **Home System Software**

Resources

Books

Cohen, Ellen S., ed. *Broadband Internet: Access, Regulation and Policy.* Hauppauge, NY: Nova Science Publishers, 2008.

Deibert, Ronald J., John G. Palfrey, Rafal Rohozinski, and Jonathan Zittrain, eds. *Access Denied: The Practice and Policy of Global Internet Filtering.* Cambridge, MA: MIT Press, 2008.

MacKinnon, Rebecca. *Consent of the Networked: The Worldwide Struggle for Internet Freedom.* New York: Basic Books, 2012.

Web Sites

Electronic Frontier Foundation. "Internet Governance Forum."https:// www.eff.org/igf (accessed November 2, 2012).

Information Overload

The world's total yearly production of digital information content amounts to over 1.5 billion gigabytes (GB) of storage, or 250 megabytes (MB) of information for every individual on the planet. Locating key strategic information, such as the latest market predictions for the tele-communications sector, is as easy as accessing the bus timetable for one's local area, at least in theory. However, defects are beginning to appear in this digital fabric, highlighting the problem of information overload in everyday life.

Information overload, a great contributor to which is the Internet, refers to the difficulty that users experience in trying to locate and process useful information quickly and easily. The ability to create new information content has far outstripped the ability to process and search it. Moreover, changes in how individuals access information are exacerbating the problem. Information overload also includes the experiences by people while using the Internet. For instance, distractions are plentiful while on-line, often including too many e-mail messages, e-mail spam, instant messages, updates from Facebook, and Tweets (from Twitter).

In the early stages of the online information age, personal computer based (PC-based) Internet access was the primary way of interacting with online information sources. Today, there are mobile computing devices such as personal digital assistants (PDAs)* and smart phones. These devices are designed to help people access and manage information. While they provide greater access to online information, they also suffer from significant limitations such as small screen-sizes. A typical cell phone screen is up to 200 times smaller than a standard PC monitor. This imposes limits on one's ability to locate and display the right information quickly at the right time, and therefore the information overload problem itself becomes even more acute. Because these access devices are becoming the norm rather than the exception, there is a need to make the next generation of information retrieval tools capable of actively reducing information overload.

Traditionally, the search engine has been the primary tool for information retrieval. Search engines operate by maintaining a comprehensive index of available information. Typically, an index represents an information item (such as a Web page or a document) in terms of a set of relevant index terms. For example, words that occur frequently in a Web page, but that are relatively rare in the Web as a whole, are likely to be chosen as relevant index terms for the page.

When an end-user submits query terms to a search engine, they are compared against index terms for relevant items in the search engine index. An overall relevancy score for each information item is computed according to how many of the user's query terms occur in its index, and how important these terms are for that item. The relevant items are then ranked according to their relevancy score before being presented to the user.

* **personal digital assistants (PDAs)** small-scale hand-held computers that can be used in place of diaries and appointment books

* **artificial intelligence (AI)** a branch of computer science dealing with creating computer hardware and software to mimic the way people think and perform practical tasks

Of course there are no guarantees that users will select the same terms for their queries as the search engine has used for its index. This vocabulary mismatch problem greatly limits the effectiveness of search engines. In addition, many search engines are incapable of resolving latent ambiguities in query terms. For example, does the query term jaguar refer to the cat or the car?

The usefulness of search engines in general is measured by their precision and recall characteristics. Ideally, search engines should have both high precision and high recall.

Precision refers to the proportion of retrieved items that are actually relevant to the user's query. Search engines tend to return very large result lists and many of these results may have been selected because of spurious matches with the query. For example, a user looking for information about Jaguar cars may submit jaguar as a query only to be overloaded with irrelevant pages about wild cats among the relevant car-related pages. In this case, precision is low.

The recall of a search engine refers to the proportion of relevant items that are actually retrieved in a search. For example, the jaguar search may miss many relevant Web pages that focus on the famous E-Type sports car (manufactured by Jaguar in the 1960s) but that fail to mention Jaguar explicitly. In this case, recall is low.

If search engines are limited in their ability to solve the information overload problem by their low precision and recall characteristics, then what does the future hold? What new technologies will provide a solution? One answer lies with recent artificial intelligence (AI)* research in the area of personalization. One of the fundamental problems with current search engine technologies is their inability to recognize the motivations and preferences of individual users when carrying out a search. Two users submitting the same query will receive the same results, irrespective of their individual preferences. Personalization techniques look at ways of learning about the preferences of individual users over time, by monitoring their online interactions for example, and then use this information to better direct their searches.

For example, a personalization system can learn that a user is interested in cars by noting that the term automobile tends to occur frequently in Web pages that they visit, and this can be used as an additional query term every time that user searches for information. Thus, the user's jaguar query becomes jaguar automobile and the search engine is better able to filter out the irrelevant wildlife pages that would otherwise be retrieved.

Personalized information services hold great promise when it comes to relieving the problem of information overload. There are technologies today that are capable of automatically and accurately learning about the information needs and preferences of individual users, and of using this information to guide searches. For example, Google.com can personalize a person's Web search (what it calls search history personalization) using past search activity on the Google Web site. This personalized Web search includes both the searches performed by a person and the results clicked on by that individual. Thus, Google can usually solve the information overload for PC, PDA, and smart phone users.

Information overload is a significant problem but personalization techniques provide a real solution at the technology level. However, personalization techniques must also provide a solution at the user level. Due care must be taken to recognize and respect the impact that these new technologies will have on end-users. By their very nature, personalization techniques are designed to learn about the preferences of users automatically—preferences that users may not be willing to reveal to others. Steps are being taken today to define standards for regulating the collection and usage of private user information. For instance, Google users can turn off the ability to make personalized Web searches. With these standards in place, the large-scale deployment of personalization technology may usher in a new information age free from the gridlock of information overload.

▶ *See also* **Digital Libraries • Ergonomics • Human Factors: User Interfaces • Information Access • Information Retrieval • World Wide Web**

Resources

Books

Baeza-Yates, Ricardo, and Berthier Ribeiro-Neto. *Modern Information Retrieval: The Concepts and Technology Behind Search.* New York: Addison Wesley, 2011.

Chowdhury, G. G. *Introduction to Modern Information Retrieval.* New York: Neal-Schuman, 2010.

Levene, Mark. *An Introduction to Search Engines and Web Navigation.* Hoboken, NJ: John Wiley, 2010.

Web sites

Salon. "Are We on Information Overload?" http://www.salon.com/2012/01/01/are_we_on_information_overload/ (accessed October 3, 2012).

World Wide Web Consrotium. "The Platform for Privacy Preferences 1.0 (P3P1.0) Specification." http://www.w3.org/TR/P3P (accessed October 4, 2012).

Information Theory

"Information" is a term used universally in fields associated with computing technology. It is often loosely applied when no other term seems to be readily at hand; examples of this are terms such as "information technology," "information systems," and "information retrieval." However, the

* **ethernets** a networking technology for mini- and microcomputer systems consisting of network interface cards and interconnecting coaxial cables; invented in the 1970s by Xerox Corporation

* **fiber optic** transmission technology using long, thin strands of glass fiber; internal reflections in the fiber assure that light entering one end is transmitted to the other end with only small losses in intensity; used widely in transmitting digital information

term "information" actually has a very real meaning in an engineering context. It does not mean the same thing as "knowledge" or "data," but instead is intertwined with elements of communication systems theory.

When computing systems are connected together, it is necessary to consider how they might exchange data and work cooperatively. Computing machines can formulate messages and dispatch them to other machines that receive them and then deal with the message contents. All of the issues that are involved with these transmission and reception operations constitute what is known as "information theory."

A communication channel is a connective structure of some sort that supports the exchange of messages. Examples are wired interconnections such as ethernets* or perhaps fiber optic* cables, or even wireless communications such as microwave links. These are all paths over which digital information can be transmitted.

Noise and Errors

Information theory has to do with how messages are sent via communication channels. When this field was first being studied, the common consensus was that it would be impossible to get digital machines to make exchanges in a way that was guaranteed to be error-free. This is because all the components used to construct computing machines are imperfect; they tend to distort the electrical signals they process as a side effect of their operation.

The components add extra electrical signals called "noise." In this instance, the term "noise" does not necessarily refer to something that can be heard. Instead, "noise" is used to describe the corruption of electrical signals, which makes them harder for devices in the computer system to understand correctly. This signal corruption might appear as extra voltage levels in the signal, or some signals may be completely missing.

Because communication channels inherently contain noise, exchanged messages are always being damaged in one way or another. When a particular message is dispatched from one machine to another, there is a chance that it might be distorted by imperfections in the channel and therefore not correctly interpreted by the recipient. Channel noise cannot be entirely eliminated. For this reason, early information theorists believed that it was a reality that messages transmitted digitally would not arrive at their destinations in exactly the way that the senders had sent them.

Information Defined

This pessimistic outlook all changed in 1947 with the publication of American mathematician Claude Shannon's (1916–2001) seminal study of information theory. He proposed that even in the presence of noise (which it had been agreed was unavoidable), it was possible to ensure error-free transmission. This effectively heralded the era of a new field of computing science and engineering: that of information theory. "Information" was granted a precise definition. It was related to the inverse of the probability of the content of a message. For example, if a person was told in a message that "tomorrow, the sky will be blue," that person would conclude that there was not much in that message that he or she had not already expected. In other words, there was not much information in that message, because it essentially reaffirmed an expectation. There is not much information in that message, because the probability of the outcome is high. Conversely, if one were told in a message that "tomorrow, the sky will be green," then he or she would be greatly surprised. There is more information in this second message purely by virtue of the fact that the probability of this event is so much lower. The information pertaining to a particular event is inversely proportional to the logarithm of the probability of the event actually taking place.

Information = log (1/p) where p is the probability of an event within the message.

Shannon's work led to a new field of engineering. Quantities such as the capacity of a channel to transmit information could be evaluated. This provided telecommunications specialists with a way of knowing just how many messages could be simultaneously transmitted over a channel without loss.

Encoding

In addition to this, ways of representing, or encoding, information during transmission from one place to another were explored; some approaches were better than others. Encoding simply means that some pieces of information that are normally represented by particular symbols are converted to another collection of symbols that might better suit their reliable transfer. For example, text messages are often represented by collections of alphabetic characters when created and read, but they are then converted into another form, such as ASCII* codes, for transmission over a communication channel. At the receiving end, the codes are converted back into text again.

The advantage these conversions offer is that some ways of representing information are more robust to the effects of noise in information channels than others, and perhaps more efficient, as well. So, the extra expense involved in carrying out these encoding and decoding operations is offset by the reliability they offer.

Information theory has become a mature field of engineering and computer science. It has enhanced the reliability of computer-based networks at all levels, from small local area networks (LANs)* to the Internet, and it has done so in a way that is unobtrusive, so that users are unaware of its presence. In addition to this, information theory has also assisted in the development of techniques for encoding digital information and sending this over analog communication channels that were not designed for handling computer-based transmissions, such as the public telephone networks. It is important to remember that these contributions of information theory to modern computing began with the ability to define information mathematically, and the work Claude Shannon did to understand communication channels and encoding schemes.

* **ASCII** an acronym that stands for American Standard Code for Information Interchange; assigns a unique 8-bit binary number to every letter of the alphabet, the digits (0 to 9), and most keyboard symbols

* **local area networks (LANs)** high-speed computer networks that are designed for users who are located near each other

* **peer-to-peer services** the ways in which computers on the same logical level can interoperate in a structured network hierarchy

* **Internet Service Providers (ISPs)** commercial enterprises that offer paying subscribers access to the Internet (usually via modem) for a fee

* **personal digital assistants (PDAs)** small-scale hand-held computers that can be used in place of diaries and appointment books

▶ *See also* **Cybernetics • Networks • Privacy • Shannon, Claude E.**

Resources

Books

Cover, Thomas M., and Joy A. Thomas. *Elements of Information Theory.* 2nd ed. Hoboken, NJ: Wiley-Interscience; 2006.

Gleick, James. *The Information: A History, a Theory, a Flood.*. New York: Pantheon Books; 2011.

Web Sites

Schneider, Tom. "Information Theory Primer." http://schneider.ncifcrf. gov/paper/primer/ (accessed November 3, 2012).

Internet: Applications

The Internet has many important applications. Of the various services available via the Internet, the three most important are e-mail, Web browsing, and peer-to-peer services*. E-mail, also known as electronic mail, is the most widely used and successful of Internet applications. Web browsing, where Web is short for World Wide Web, is the application that had the greatest influence in dramatic expansion of the Internet and its use during the 1990s. Peer-to-peer networking is the newest of these three Internet applications, and also the most controversial, because its uses have created problems related to the access and use of copyrighted materials.

E-Mail

Whether judged by volume, popularity, or impact, e-mail has been and continues to be the principal Internet application. This is despite the fact that the underlying technologies have not been altered significantly since the early 1980s. In recent years, the continuing rapid growth in the use and volume of e-mail has been fueled by two factors. The first is the increasing numbers of Internet Service Providers (ISPs)* offering this service, and secondly, because the number of physical devices capable of supporting e-mail has grown to include highly portable devices such as personal digital assistants (PDAs)*, smart phones (cellular phones built with a mobile operating system), and cellular (cell) telephones.

The volume of e-mail also continues to increase because there are more users, and because users now have the ability to attach documents of various types to e-mail messages. While this has long been possible, the formulation of Multipurpose Internet Mail Extensions (MIME) and its adoption by software developers has made it much easier to send and receive attachments, including word-processed documents, spreadsheets, and graphics. The result is that the volume of traffic generated by e-mail, as measured in terms of the number of data packets* moving across the network, has increased dramatically in recent years, contributing significantly to network congestion.

E-mail has become an important part of personal communications for hundreds of millions of people, many of whom have replaced it for letters or telephone calls. In business, e-mail has become an important advertising medium, particularly in instances where the demand for products and services is time sensitive. For example, tickets for an upcoming sporting event are marketed by sending fans an e-mail message with information about availability and prices of the tickets. In addition, e-mail serves, less obviously, as the basis for some of the more important collaborative applications that have been developed, most notably International Business Machines Corporation's (IBM's) Lotus Notes.

In the near future, voice-driven applications will play a much larger role on the Internet, and e-mail is sure to be one of the areas in which voice-driven applications will emerge most rapidly. E-mail and voice mail will be integrated, and in the process it seems likely that new models for Internet-based messaging will emerge.

Synchronous communication, in the form of the highly popular instant messaging, may be a precursor of the messaging models of the near future. Currently epitomized by AOL Instant Messenger (AIM) and Microsoft's Live Messenger, instant messaging applications generally allow users to share various types of files (including images, sounds, Uniform Resource Locators (URLs)*), stream content, and use the Internet as a medium for telephony, as well as exchanging messages with other users in real time and participating in online chat rooms.

In the 2010s, Microsoft's Outlook is one of the more popular e-mail programs purchased. Some of the more commonly used free e-mail programs include IncrediMail, Opera, Pegasus Mail, and Windows Live.

Web Browsing

The Web browser is another Internet application of critical importance. Unlike e-mail, which was developed and then standardized in the early, noncommercial days of the Internet, the Web browser was developed in a highly commercialized environment dominated by such corporations as Microsoft and Netscape, and heavily influenced by the World Wide Web Consortium (W3C). While Microsoft and Netscape have played the most obvious parts in the development of the Web browser, particularly from the public perspective, the highly influential role of the W3C may be the most significant in the long term.

Founded in 1994 by British computer scientist and inventor Timothy "Tim" John Berners-Lee (1955–), the original architect of the Web, the goal of the W3C has been to develop interoperable technologies that lead the Web to its full potential as a forum for communication, collaboration, and commerce. As of October 2012, Berners-Lee was the director of

* **packets** collections of digital data elements that are part of a complete message or signal; packets contain their destination addresses to enable reassembly of the message or signal

* **Uniform Resource Locators (URLs)** references to a document or a document container using the Hypertext Transfer Protocol (HTTP); consist of a hostname and path to the document

* **XML** the acronym for eXtensible Markup Language; a method of applying structure to data so that documents can be represented

* **protocol** an agreed understanding for the sub-operations that make up a transaction, usually found in the specification of inter-computer communications

the W3C. What the W3C has been able to do successfully is to develop and promote the adoption of new, open standards for Web-based documents. These standards have been designed to make Web documents more expressive (Cascading Stylesheets), to provide standardized labeling so that users have a more explicit sense of the content of documents (Platform for Internet Content Selection, or PICS), and to create the basis for more interactive designs (the Extensible Markup Language, or XML*). Looking ahead, a principal goal of the W3C is to develop capabilities that are in accordance with Berners-Lee's belief that the Web should be a highly collaborative information space.

However, during the first few years of Web growth, the competition between Microsoft and Netscape for the browser market was fierce, and both companies invested heavily in the development of their respective browsers. Changes in business conditions toward the end of the 1990s and growing interest in new models of networked information exchange caused each company to focus less intensely on the development of Web browsers, resulting in a marked slowing of their development and an increasing disparity between the standards being developed by W3C and the support offered by Internet Explorer or Netscape Navigator.

In the early 2010s, the major Web browsers are Google's Chrome, Mozilla's Firefox, Microsoft's Internet Explorer, Opera Software's Opera, and Apple's Safari. Internet Explorer holds about 50 percent of the desktop browsing market and Safari possesses about 60 percent of the mobile market, as of the end of 2011, both leaders in their respective fields.

Now, the future of the Web browser may be short-lived, as standards developers and programmers elaborate the basis for network-aware applications that eliminate the need for the all-purpose browser. It is expected that as protocols* such as XML and the Simple Object Access Protocol (SOAP) grow more sophisticated in design and functionality, an end user's interactions with the Web will be framed largely by desktop applications called in the services of specific types of documents called from remote sources.

The open source model has important implications for the future development of Web browsers. Because open source versions of Netscape have been developed on a modular basis, and because the source code is available with few constraints on its use, new or improved services can be added quickly and with relative ease. In addition, open source development has accelerated efforts to integrate Web browsers and file managers. These efforts, which are aimed at reducing functional distinctions between local and network-accessible resources, may be viewed as an important element in the development of the seamless information space that Berners-Lee envisions for the future of the Web.

Peer-To-Peer Computing

One of the fastest growing, most controversial, and potentially most important areas of Internet applications is peer-to-peer (P2P) networking. Peer-to-peer networking is based on the sharing of physical resources, such as hard drives, processing cycles, and individual files among computers and other intelligent devices. Unlike client-server networking, where some computers are dedicated to serving other computers, each computer in peer-to-peer networking has equivalent capabilities and responsibilities.

Internet-based peer-to-peer applications position the desktop at the center of a computing matrix, usually on the basis of cross-network protocols such as the Simple Object Access Protocol (SOAP) or XML-RPC (Remote Procedure Calling), thus enabling users to participate in the Internet more interactively.

There are two basic P2P models in use today. The first model is based on a central host computer that coordinates the exchange of files by indexing the files available across a network of peer computers. This model has been highly controversial because it has been employed widely to support the unlicensed exchange of commercial sound recordings, software, and other copyrighted materials. Under the second model, which may prove ultimately to be far more important, peer-to-peer applications aggregate and use otherwise idle resources residing on low-end devices to support high-demand computations. For example, a specially designed screensaver running on a networked computer may be employed to process astronomical or medical data.

The Future

The remarkable developments during the late 1990s and early 2000s suggest that making accurate predictions about the next generation of Internet applications is difficult, if not impossible. Two aspects of the future of the Internet that one can be certain of, however, are that network bandwidth* will be much greater, and that greater and its management will be critical factors in the development and deployment of new applications. What will greater yield? In the long run, it is difficult to know, but in the short term it seems reasonable to expect new communication models, videoconferencing, increasingly powerful tools for collaborative work across local and wide area networks, and the emergence of the network as a computational service of unprecedented power.

 See also **Animation • Film and Video Editing • Graphic Devices • Music Composition**

Resources

Books

Berners-Lee, Tim, and Mark Fischetti. *Weaving the Web: The Original Design and Ultimate Destiny of the World Wide Web.* San Francisco: HarperCollins, 1999.

Freeman, John. *The Tyranny of E-mail: The Four-thousand-year Journey to Your Inbox.* New York: Scribner, 2009.

Browser Litigation

In January of 2002, Netscape Communications, owned by AOL Time Warner, filed suit against Microsoft, which produces Internet Explorer (IE). Netscape alleged that Microsoft engaged in illegal activities (e.g., unfair competition practices) to gain the vast share of the browser market. Once the most-used browser, Netscape Communications Corporation claimed that Microsoft violated anti-trust laws when it made IE an integral part of its Windows operating system. According to *USA Today*, some 92 percent of personal computers run Microsoft's Windows operating system as of 2002. In 2003, Microsoft and Netscape agreed to settle their differences when Microsoft compensated AOL Time Warner, Netscape's parent company, $750 million. Microsoft also gave AOL the ability to use Internet Explorer (IE) royalty-free for seven years and to have a long-term license to use its Windows Media 9 Series technology. When AOL acquired Netscape in 1999, the Mozilla Organization was established. In November 2004, Mozilla released its Firefox Web browser. As of 2012, Firefox is the second or third most used Web browser in the world (depending on the reporting source), with 20 to 24 percent of the browser market. Microsoft's Internet Explorer remains the world's most used browser.

* **bandwidth** a measure of the frequency component of a signal or the capacity of a communication channel to carry signals

* **supercomputers** very high performance computers, usually comprised of many processors and used for modeling and simulation of complex phenomena, like meteorology

* **wide area network (WAN)** an interconnected network of computers that spans upward from several buildings to whole cities or entire countries and across countries

Loshin, Pete, and Paul Hoffman. *Essential E-Mail Standards: RFCs and Protocols Made Practical.* New York: Wiley, 2000.

McHoes, Ann McIver, and Joli Ballew. *Operating Systems Demystified.* New York: McGraw-Hill, 2012.

Vu, Quang Hieu, Mihai Lupu, and Beng Chin Ooi. *Peer-to-Peer Computing: Principles and Applications.* Heidelberg: Springer, 2010.

Zalewski, Michal. *The Tangled Web: A Guide to Securing Modern Web Applications.* San Francisco: No Starch Press, 2012.

Web Sites

ARS Technica, and Peter Bright. "The End of an Era: Internet Explorer Drops Below 50% of Web Usage." http://arstechnica.com/information-technology/2011/11/the-end-of-an-era-internet-explorer-drops-below-50-percent-of-web-usage/ (accessed October 8, 2012).

World Wide Web Consortium. "About W3C." http://www.w3.org/Consortium/ (accessed October 8, 2012).

Internet: Backbone

The first Internet backbone was invented to assist in the attempt to share supercomputers*. The U.S. government realized that supercomputing was crucial to advances in science, defense, and economic competitiveness but the budget for research was insufficient to provide supercomputers for all scientists who needed them. Thus, the first Internet backbone, called the NSFNET because it was funded by the U.S. National Science Foundation (NSF), linked (or networked) to six supercomputing centers (University of California at San Diego, National Center for Atmospheric Research, National Center for Supercomputing Applications at the University of Illinois, Pittsburgh Supercomputing Center, Cornell University, and John von Neumann Supercomputing Center/Princeton University) and their associated regional networks in the United States in order to provide supercomputer access to scientists. Today, a single government-managed Internet backbone has been transformed into a multitude of different backbones, most of which are private commercial enterprises.

Backbone Basics

A backbone is a high-speed wide area network (WAN)* connecting lower speed networks. A country typically has several backbones linking all of its Internet Service Providers (ISPs). In the United States, these backbones are linked in a small number of interconnection points. Finally, national backbones interconnect in a mesh with other countries, usually with international trunk lines via land, undersea, or satellite.

The current Internet is a loose connection of TCP/IP networks* (Transmission Control Protocol/Internet Protocol) networks organized into a multilevel hierarchy using a wide variety of technologies. At the lowest level, computers are connected to each other, and to a router, in a local area network (LAN)*. Routers can be connected together into campus, metropolitan, or regional networks. Non-backbone ISPs exist solely to provide Internet access to consumers. For Internet connectivity, at some point all non-backbone networks must connect to a backbone ISP (the highest level). It is typical for a large corporation to connect with one or more backbone ISPs. Backbone and non-backbone ISPs exchange traffic at what is generally called peering points. Federal agencies have always shared the cost of common infrastructure such as peering points for interagency traffic—the Federal Internet Exchanges (FIX-E and FIX-W) were built for this purpose and have served as models for the Network Access Points (NAPs) and IX* facilities that are prominent features of today's Internet.

Technology

In the NSFNET, each interconnected supercomputing site had an LSI-11 microcomputer called a fuzzball. These fuzzballs were running TCP/IP and were connected with 56 kilobits per second (Kbps, where kilo stands for 1 thousand) leased lines. NSFNET was an immediate success and was overloaded from the day it started. NSFNET version 2 leased 448 Kbps fiber optic channels and IBM RS/4000s were used as routers. In 1990, NSFNET version 3 was upgraded to T1 lines (1.544 megabits per second [Mbps], where mega represents 1 million). Later that same year, NSFNET upgraded to T3 lines (45 Mbps). European backbone networks (e.g., EBONE) had a similar evolution from 2 Mbps to 34 Mbps. Current speeds of Internet backbones are based on SONET* (Synchronous Optical NETwork) framing speeds in the gbps* range.

Because peering points handle large volumes of traffic, they are typically complex high-speed switching networks within themselves although concentrated in a small geographical area (single building). Commonly, peering points use asynchronous transfer mode (ATM) switching technology at the core to provide traffic quality-of-service management, with IP running on top.

Transmission Mechanisms

The Internet can be viewed as a collection of sub-networks or Autonomous Systems (ASes) that are controlled by a single administrative authority. These ASes are interconnected together by routers with high-speed lines. Routing within an AS (interior routing) does not have to be coordinated with other ASes. Two routers that exchange routing information are exterior routers if they belong to two different ASes. For scalability, each AS designates a small number of exterior routers. The protocol that exterior routers use to advertise routing information to other ASes is called the Exterior Gateway Protocol (EGP).

* **TCP/IP networks** interconnected computer networks that use Transmission Control Protocol/ Internet Protocol

* **local area network (LAN)** a high-speed computer network that is designed for users who are located near each other

* **IX** short for Internet Exchange; the asterisk indicates that there are different possible types of Internet Exchanges-the two most common are the Commercial Internet Exchange (CIX) and the Federal Internet Exchange (FIX)

* **SONET** the acronym for Synchronous Optical NETwork, a published standard for networks based on fiber optic communications technology

* **gbps** acronym for gigabits per second; a binary data transfer rate that corresponds to a thousand million (billion, or 10^9) bits per second

From the point of view of an exterior router, the Internet consists of other exterior routers and the lines connecting them; two exterior routers are considered connected if they share a common network, and all networks can be grouped into three categories: (1) stub networks (all traffic goes to end computer systems); (2) transit networks (all traffic goes to other ASes); and (3) multiconnected networks (traffic goes to both end computer systems and selectively to other ASes).

Routers in the NSFNET Internet backbone exchanged routing information periodically—once a single backbone router learned a route, all backbone routers learned about it. When the single Internet backbone became multiple backbones, the Internet transitioned from a core backbone routing architecture to a peer backbone routing architecture with interconnections at several points. While the desired goal is shortest-path routing, peer routing uses route aggregation between exterior routers as opposed to individual routes for individual computers, which may not result in shortest paths. Also, peer backbones must agree to keep routes consistent among all exterior routers or routing loops will develop (circular routes).

History

The U.S. Department of Defense funded research on interconnecting computers in networks using packet switching that eventually culminated in a wide area network called ARPANET. ARPANET was the network (there were no other networks to connect to) that linked Advanced Research Projects Agency (ARPA) researchers working on central Internet ideas like TCP/IP. Although ARPANET was successful, it was restricted to sites that received funding from ARPA. However, many other universities were interested in forming networks using packet switching, even if they did not receive ARPA funding. This led to the construction of a series of backbone networks, some based on protocols other than TCP/IP (e.g., SNA [Systems Network Architecture], DECNET [Digital Equipment Corporation Network), before the NSFNET linked isolated regional TCP/IP networks into an Internet backbone:

- BITNET—academic IBM mainframe computers;
- CSNET—NSF/Computer Science Community;
- EARN—European Academic and Research Network;
- ESNET—U.S. Department of Energy Network;
- FIDONET—dial-in E-mail Network;
- JANET—U.K. Joint Academic Network;
- HEPNET—U.S. Department of Energy (High Energy Physicists);
- MFENET—U.S. Department of Energy (Magnetic Fusion Energy);
- NASA Science Internet—U.S. National Aeronautics and Space Administration;

- SPAN—NASA Space Scientists (DECnet);
- USAN—NSF Satellite Academic Network;
- USENET—based on AT&T's UNIX built-in UUCP communication protocols.

From 1985 to 1988, regional TCP/IP networks were formed around government institutions and universities, most supported with government funding. In 1988, these NSF regional and mid-level TCP/IP networks were interconnected via a backbone funded by NSF (also supported by donations from International Business Machines Corporation [IBM], Microwave Communications Inc. [MCI], and Merit Network, Inc. [MERIT]). Given Internet growth in capacity demand, NSF realized it could not pay for managing a network forever so it did three things.

First, in 1992, it encouraged IBM, MERIT, and MCI to form a nonprofit company, Advanced Networks and Services (ANS), which built the first private Internet backbone called ANSNET.

Second, to ease transition and make sure regional networks could still communicate, NSF funded four different network operators to establish Network Access Points (NAPs): PacBell (San Francisco, California), Ameritech (Chicago, Illinois), MFS (Washington, D.C.), and Sprint (Pennsauken, New Jersey). Every new Internet backbone provider had to connect to all four NAPs if it wanted to receive NSF funding. This arrangement meant that regional networks would have a choice of potential new Internet backbone providers to transmit traffic between NAPs. Other NAPs have also emerged: Metropolitan Area Exchange (MAE)-East, MAE-West, and Commercial Internet Exchange (CIX).

Third, NSF enforced an Acceptable Use Policy on the NSFNET, which prohibited usage "not in support of Research and Education." The predictable (and intended) result was stimulation of other commercial backbone networks in addition to ANSNET such as UUNET and PSINET.

NSF's privatization policy culminated in 1995 with the defunding of the NSFNET backbone. The funds previously earmarked for the NSFNET were competitively redistributed to regional networks to buy Internet backbone connectivity from the numerous new private Internet backbone networks that had emerged.

At about the same time in the mid-1990s, a European Internet backbone formed, EBONE, consisting of twenty-five networks interconnecting regions of Europe. Each country in Europe has one or more national networks, each of which is approximately comparable to an NSF regional network.

Technical Issues

As a result of having multiple backbones for Internet traffic, different agreements have evolved for handling traffic between networks at NAPs. The most common agreements between backbones take two forms: (1) Peering—exchanging traffic at no cost; and (2) Transit—exchanging traffic where one backbone pays another for delivery. As a result of increased congestion at NAPs, most backbones have begun to interconnect directly

Focus on ESNET

Operated by the U.S. Department of Energy, ESNET is short for the Energy Sciences Network. The goal of the high-speed network is to provide a link for collaboration between DOE scientists, researchers, and other staff throughout the country and abroad. Begun in 1976, ESNET was able to connect to more than 100 other networks by 2012.

with one another outside of NAPs in what has come to be known as private peering. At one point, it was estimated that 80 percent of Internet traffic was exchanged via private peering. Many backbones have taken a hybrid approach—peering with some backbones and paying for transit on other backbones. Those few backbones that interconnect solely by peering and do not need to purchase transit from any other backbones are referred to as top-tier backbones. Because of the proprietary and dynamic nature of this information, it is difficult to state with accuracy the exact number of top-tier backbones, but the following have been reported as such: AT&T, Cable & Wireless, Century Link, Sprint, Inteliquent, Level 3 Communications, and Verizon Business. According to the annually produced report *Global Internet Geography Report* by the telecommunications market research and consulting firm, Telegeography, the Verizon global IP network had the largest number of autonomous system connections of any public IP network in the world as of the end of 2010. Verizon has held the number one spot in eleven out of the last twelve years (since the report was first produced in 1999).

Recently, there has been a call for regulation of backbone interconnection agreements since larger backbones have started to refuse to peer with smaller backbones. There is no accepted convention that governs when it is beneficial for two backbones to peer. While intuition would suggest equal size, there are many measures of backbone size—geographic coverage, transmission capacity, traffic volume, and number of customers—it is unlikely that any two backbones would match on many of these metrics. There is a growing consensus that Internet backbone interconnection agreements are complex contracts with private costs and benefits that can only be decided upon by the participating backbones.

 See also **Embedded Technology (Ubiquitous Computing)** • **Internet** • **World Wide Web**

Resources

Books

Comer, Douglas E. *The Internet Book: Everything You Need to Know about Computer Networking and How the Internet Works.* 3rd ed. Upper Saddle River, NJ: Pearson Prentice Hall, 2007.

Web Sites

The Free Library. "Verizon Global IP Network Ranks No. 1 as Most-Connected Internet Network." http://www.thefreelibrary.com/Verizon+Global+IP+Network+Ranks+No.+1+as+Most-Connected+Internet...-a0243757031 (accessed October 8, 2012).

Office of Legislative and Public Affairs, National Science Foundation. "A Brief History of NSF and the Internet." http://www.nsf.gov/od/lpa/news/03/fsnsf_internet.htm (accessed October 8, 2012).

Internet Control and Cyberwarfare

The Internet is a global network connecting, as of 2011, more than one billion computers used by 2.1 billion people. Personal information, medical records, opinions, industrial secrets, military communications, financial transactions, messages between conspirators, orders for goods and services, and many other types of communications travel over the Internet. Because much of this information is valuable, it sometimes is targeted for interception or disruption. Various parties may seek to shut down systems or websites, vandalize website contents, enforce laws or political orthodoxies, spread misinformation, spy, steal, or harass. They may seek monetary gain or a sense of power or to achieve political or military goals.

Any attempt to prevent the Internet from functioning as its users intend is an attack on Internet security. Most businesses and owners of personal computers purchase software designed to counter such Internet threats as viruses, spam, malware, phishing, and government surveillance. Encryption (secret coding of messages) is built into all Web browsers to enable the secure transfer of credit-card numbers over the Internet. Most attacks on Internet security are software-based, but such parts of the Internet as fiber-optic cables serving millions of users are vulnerable to direct physical attack. In general, attacks by individual hackers or criminal groups are treated as matters of Internet security. Actions by political groups, terrorist organizations, or national governments, especially if directed at other governments or military systems, are often termed "cyberwarfare."

Since the late 1980s, computer networks have increased greatly in complexity and the amount of data stored. In all but the least-developed countries, banking, trade, personal communications, government, and military operations depend almost entirely on the smooth transfer of large amounts of data through computer networks, which are vulnerable to penetration—unauthorized access—simply by receiving information from the outside world. Programs that steal information can enter a computer through a network connection, and networks themselves are sometimes objects of hacking attacks.

Hackers continue to use the Internet for criminal gain, including identity theft. In August 2009, U.S. law enforcement agencies charged a U.S. citizen and two unnamed Russian co-conspirators with hacking corporate computer systems used to process consumer payments and with stealing information on approximately 130 million credit and debit cards. The hackers allegedly used Structured Query Language (SQL) injection attacks to lift information from targeted company databases that use the SQL computer language to manage and store corporate and consumer data. These attacks injected malicious computer code into database software that enabled hackers to gain access to such data as usernames, login passwords, and personal and financial account information.

Countries may also be accused of facilitating or encouraging hacking attacks on foreign government and corporate computer systems. In 2007, according to media reports, security experts accused government-backed

Chinese hackers of attempting to penetrate nonclassified U.S. government computers, the German Chancellor's office, and the computer systems of Rolls Royce and Royal Dutch Shell. China subsequently denied the allegations.

The threats posed to national and corporate infrastructure by cyberwarfare and cyberattacks prompted the U.S. Congress to contemplate legislation that would give the U.S. president broad powers to regulate the Internet and related infrastructure on national security grounds. The Protecting Cyberspace Act proposed in June 2010 would allow the president to declare national cyber-emergencies and limit or prohibit Internet access by Internet service providers (ISPs) or other Web-related companies. Critics fear that the legislation could be used by the executive branch to restrict freedom of speech by preventing whistleblowers from posting information on the Internet. Supporters of the legislation counter that the law is needed to protect government and corporate infrastructure from foreign and domestic cyberattacks.

Domain Name System (DNS)

Control of the Internet is also evolving. The system that regulates domain names, the Domain Name System (DNS), confers control over a range of top-level domain functions. In the 1980s, the DNS was run by the U.S. National Science Foundation and a loose affiliation of contractors, university professors, and volunteers. By 1998, the nonprofit Internet Corporation for Assigned Names and Numbers (ICANN), a private corporation, was formed and awarded a U.S. federal contract to arbitrate trademark claims and administer domain names. In response to international criticism that the United States had too much control of the Internet, ICANN was granted autonomy by the United States on October 1, 2009.

Within weeks of gaining autonomy, ICANN granted permission for Internet users to develop and use non-Latin-script web addresses. Experts say that the change will enable greater access for almost one billion current Internet users who speak languages with non-Latin scripts. Internationalized Domain Names (IDNs) are set to become operational in 2010. The change was made possible by technological advances that allow the DNS to recognize and translate non-Latin characters into Internet protocol (IP) addresses. Proponents contended that the change would allow the Internet to become a more global resource, while critics argued that the change could compromise the globally unifying power of the Internet and facilitate the creation of fragmented subnetworks based upon language. Experts anticipate that the majority of non-Latin Internet addresses will contain Chinese, Arabic, and Russian script.

Control of the Internet also includes the ability to exert censorship restrictions. Some of the world's governments seek to censor, intercept, decode, disrupt, guard, or otherwise control Internet traffic. In several countries, Internet control implies the monitoring and control of the Internet behaviors of its citizens. Some countries have periodically blocked access to various Web sites, including Wikipedia, United Nations News, and the human-rights group Amnesty International. The OpenNet Initiative asserts that close to forty-five countries filter or heavily censor the Internet for political content or individual speech. Most countries have such restrictive Internet laws as those that provide for limiting the content available to children in school or ban the illegal transfer of copyrighted materials.

In 2010, computer network experts warned of a looming shortage of unique Internet Protocol (IP) addresses that could strangle Internet traffic in 2011. Addresses on the Internet are designated and processed as IP numbers. DNS servers further convert friendly names such as "Google" into the registered IP address associated with that name. For companies in the United States, IP addresses are parceled out by the American Registry for Internet Numbers (ARIN). Robust Internet growth, especially with the numbers of attached devices (each requiring a unique IP address when online) means that by the end of 2010, less than 1 out 20 IP addresses were available for assignment.

In May 2011, the U.S. Senate Judiciary Committee approved a bill titled "Preventing Real Online Threats to Economic Creativity and Theft of Intellectual Property Act" (also known as the PROTECT IP Act, or PIPA), which allows copyright holders to suppress or disrupt search engine links to sites with a pattern and practice of copyright infringement. The Bill awaits approval by the full Senate and reconciliation with similar House bills before becoming law. The Bill seeks to limit traffic referrals and disrupt payments to sites allegedly engaging in digital piracy or selling counterfeit goods. Critics contended that the bill is flawed because the threshold for action remains unclear and that only large media companies would be able to fight indiscriminate or false claims by alleged copyright holders.

In January 2012, numerous websites launched protests against the Stop Online Piracy Act (SOPA), PIPA's companion bill in the U.S. House of Representatives. Websites participating in the protest encouraged visitors to contact their elected representatives. Other websites, including the English-language version of Wikipedia, blacked out their websites for twenty-four hours. In the wake of the protests, five U.S. senators withdrew their support of PIPA, and U.S. Senate majority leader Harry Reid (1939–) announced a postponement of the vote on PIPA.

Cyberwarfare

Cyberwarfare, or cyberwar, involves using computers to penetrate or impair the computers of an enemy. The term sometimes refers to physical attacks carried out on computer hardware, but it usually means a purely computational conflict. Cyberwarfare can be waged by loose associations of individuals, terrorist and militant groups, or governments, and may be either offensive or defensive. The goals of cyberwarfare typically include theft of information, corruption of information, or the shutdown of computer networks crucial to military, government, or economic activity.

Cyberwarfare is attractive partly because a state can almost always deny responsibility for computer espionage or vandalism. Cyberwarfare is also a useful tactic in uneven conflicts or asymmetric warfare between small countries or terrorist groups and powerful states.

In 2007, Director of U.S. National Intelligence John Michael "Mike" McConnell (1943–) advised President George W. Bush (1946–) that a successful cyberattack on a major U.S. bank could cause economic disruption of the United States greater than that caused by the terrorist attacks of September 11, 2001.

Reacting to what experts characterized as an evolving pattern of cyberattacks that started in 2008, U.S. Defense Department officials in May 2011 warned that cyberattacks could constitute acts of war against the United States that merit military response.

In February 2003, the U.S. government released its *Strategy to Secure Cyberspace*. The document stated that "healthy functioning of cyberspace is essential to our economy and our national security… A spectrum of malicious actors can and do conduct attacks against our critical information infrastructures. Of primary concern is the threat of organized cyber attacks capable of causing debilitating disruption to our Nation's critical infrastructures, economy, or national security." The Strategy outlined a national-level approach to prevent, analyze, and respond to cyberattacks.

Since the late 1990s, the number of attacks on U.S. business and government computer systems has risen steadily. Although many of the early attacks allegedly originated in China and Russia, attacks are now routinely launched from sites around the world. In response, in 2008, the U.S. Congress approved a $17 billion, five-year program to enhance national computer security.

A common cyberwarfare tactic is the distributed denial-of-service attack (DDOS). In a DDOS attack, software running on thousands of desktop computers connected to the Internet causes many demands for service to converge on a target computer or network. If the target is unable to deal with these requests, the attack may deny service to legitimate users, effectively shutting down the target system. A DDOS attack temporarily crippled the government of the eastern European nation of Estonia in 2007 after a political dispute with Russia. The Russian government denied involvement in the attacks.

A DDOS attack usually proceeds by hijacking desktop computers whose users are unaware of the attack. However, the computers may be recruited openly. For example, in the summer of 2009, social networking sites including Twitter began encouraging people to join a DDOS attack against the government of Iran, where election results were the subject of open protest.

Denial-of-service cyberattacks are especially damaging or inconvenient for large numbers of users, sometimes including groups larger than the intended target. In August 2009, for example, hackers hit Facebook and Twitter servers with denial-of-service attacks that slowed traffic and prevented legitimate users from access to these social networking and messaging sites. Cyber experts offered early speculation that the attacks were related to ongoing tensions between Russia and Georgia because the ultimate target of the attacks was a pro-Abkhazia activist. Following a brief war with Georgia in 2008, Russia recognized the breakaway Georgian region of Abkhazia as an independent republic. Georgia continues to claim the region as an autonomous republic. Experts openly speculate that motives for the attacks might range from disrupting sites run by the activist to garnering attention and sympathy for the pro-Abkhazia cause.

In early April 2009, following completion of an initial review of cybersecurity by the Obama Administration, U.S. President Obama pledged to increase the U.S. commitment to cybersecurity and to bolster defense against increasingly common cyberattacks.

In May 2009, during a speech announcing the results of a top-to-bottom review by the National Security Council and Homeland Security Council of the U.S. federal government's cybersecurity measures, President Obama characterized the threat of cyberattacks as a serious economic and national security challenge. In June 2009, the Obama administration released a public strategy announcing that a cybersecurity coordinator, or cyberczar, would be placed in charge of the cyberwarfare efforts of the Pentagon, the National Security Agency, and the Department of Homeland Security. Other countries have adopted similar cybersecurity plans and policies.

The line between terrorist and politically or privately motivated hacking can be difficult to draw. A group of hackers using a few thousand dollars worth of commercially available equipment can, with skill and luck, cause consternation and expensive damage to an organization thousands of times larger and more powerful than itself. For example, in the 1998 Solar Sunrise incident, two high-school students in California mentored by an eighteen-year-old Israeli orchestrated a cyberattack on U.S. Department of Defense networks that penetrated over five hundred computer systems at U.S. military bases and universities around the world.

In August 2010, Pentagon officials revealed a previously classified cyberattack in 2008 that they described as one of the most significant breaches of cybersecurity in U.S. history. Cybersecurity experts claimed that an unidentified foreign intelligence agent infected Department of Defense computers, which compromised the security of computers used by Central Command to oversee operations in Afghanistan and Iraq.

The international community is divided over the best way to address cyberwarfare. The United States and Russia, in particular, remain at odds on the issue. The United States favors an approach that encourages international law enforcement cooperation to catch and criminally prosecute individuals who authorize or engage in cyberwarfare. Russia favors an international treaty on cyberwarfare that would include increased government oversight of the Internet. The United States opposes such a treaty, citing concerns that regulation of the Internet by governments could lead to increased censorship.

In February 2010, member of the online activist group calling itself "Anonymous" allegedly hacked into a security firm investigating recent cyberattacks on U.S. companies freezing business with the Wikileaks organization. FBI agents in the United States and police in other countries executed more than 40 arrest and seizure warrants on suspected members.

Another aspect of cyberwarfare is the ability to attack the computer systems of military targets, including nuclear facilities and aerial vehicles. In December 2011, Iran claimed to use cyberwarfare to down an RQ–170 Sentinel, a U.S. stealth unmanned aerial vehicle, or drone. U.S. officials claimed that the drone strayed into Iranian airspace and crashed. Video of the captured drone released by Iran, however, showed that the aircraft sustained little or no damage.

In 2010, the Stuxnet computer worm damaged as many as 1,000 uranium enrichment centrifuges at Iranian nuclear enrichment facilities. Stuxnet specifically targeted certain types of industrial machinery control systems, including those used on centrifuges, causing the centrifuges to spin uncontrollably until they destroyed themselves. Most computer security analysts and several European intelligence agencies argued that either Israel or the United States—or both countries—were involved in creating Stuxnet. In June 2012, following a *New York Times* report on the incident, U.S. officials revealed that Obama secretly ordered the Stuxnet attack to slow Iran's nuclear weapons program. According to anonymous U.S. officials, the United States and Israel collaborated to create the Stuxnet worm, although Israel has denied participating in its development. Some cybersecurity experts assert that the virus, in part or in whole, has resurfaced outside of Iran, possibly indicating that Iran also has attempted to engage in cyberwarfare.

In May 2012, computer security experts revealed the discovery of "Flame," which many computer security analysts have described as the most sophisticated malware ever created. Like Stuxnet, Flame appears to have targeted Iranian interests, although the malware may have infected as many as 1,000 computer systems throughout the Middle East and North Africa. Analysts from Kaspersky Lab, a computer security company, discovered Flame after the Iranian Oil Ministry reported that malware was stealing and deleting data from its computer systems. Flame captured screenshots, copied files, monitored network activity, recorded keystrokes, and used computer microphones to record audio. On June 19, 2012, an article in the *Washington Post*, citing anonymous sources, indicated that the United States and Israel designed Flame to disrupt Iran's nuclear program. Kaspersky Lab analysts state that it may take ten years of code analysis to understand the extent and nature of Flame.

Resources

Books

Boler, Megan. *Digital Media and Democracy Tactics in Hard Times.* Cambridge, MA: MIT Press, 2008.

Collins, Richard. *Three Myths of Internet Governance: Making Sense of Networks, Governance and Regulation.* Bristol, UK: Intellect, 2009.

Dinniss, Heather Harrison. *Cyberwarfare and the Laws of War.* Cambridge, MA: Cambridge Univ. Press, 2012.

Guadamuz, Andres. *Networks, Complexity and Internet Regulation: Scale-Free Law.* Cheltenham, UK: Edward Elgar, 2011.

Janczewski, Lech, and Andrew M. Colarik. *Cyber Warfare and Cyber Terrorism.* Hershey, PA: Information Science Reference, 2008.

Kutais, B. G. *Internet Policies and Issues.* New York: Nova Science Publishers, n.d.

MacKinnon, Rebecca. *Consent of the Networked: The World-Wide Struggle for Internet Freedom.* New York: Basic Books, 2012.

Marvel, Elisabette M. *China's Cyberwarfare Capability.* New York: Nova Science Publisher's, 2010.

Matheson, Donald, and Stuart Allan. *Digital War Reporting.* Cambridge: Polity, 2009.

Reed, Chris. *Internet Law.* Cambridge: Cambridge University Press, 2004.

Uda, Robert T. *Cybercrime, Cyberterrorism, and Cyberwarfare: Crime, Terror, and War Without Conventional Weapons.* Bloomington, IN: Xlibris Corp, 2009.

United Nations. *Cyberwarfare and Its Impact on International Security.* New York: United Nations, 2009.

Internet: History

The Internet is an example of a type of network called a packet-switched network*. These networks differ from telephone networks in a number of important ways. Technological differences aside, one significant difference between these networks is that packet-switched networks are designed to support a wide variety of applications, whereas the telephone network was designed to support one application (voice communications) optimally, though a few other applications are possible as well.

Intellectually, the origin of the Internet can be traced back to the early to mid–1960s, when Leonard Kleinrock (1934–), Joseph Licklider

* **packet-switched network** a network based on digital communications systems whereby packets of data are dispatched to receivers based on addresses that they contain

Network Control Protocol (NCP) a host-to-host protocol originally developed in the early 1970s to support the Internet, which was then a research project

local area network (LAN) a high-speed computer network that is designed for users who are located near each other

graphical user interface (GUI) an interface that allows computers to be operated through pictures (icons) and mouse-clicks, rather than through text and typing

Transmission Control Protocol (TCP) a stream-orientated protocol that uses Internet Protocol (IP); it is responsible for splitting data into packets, transferring it, and reassembling it at the receiver

(1915–1990), Paul Baran (1926–2011), Lawrence Rogers, and others developed the ideas and theories underpinning these general purpose packet-switched networks. By 1967 some early experiments with using packet-switching technologies were taking place at the National Physical Laboratory in England. In 1969, the U.S. Defense Department's Advanced Research Projects Agency (DARPA) funded a larger scale network project. The initial network interconnected the University of California-Los Angeles, Stanford Research Institute, University of California-Santa Barbara, and the University of Utah. Researchers at these institutions began to develop the software needed to make the network operate, and, by the end of 1969, were able to send some data packets over the network. But the capabilities were very rudimentary, and much work remained to be done.

In the early 1970s, the network software, which caused the computers in the network nodes to perform basic packet-switching functions, was standardized into the Network Control Protocol (NCP)*, and new sites were added. By 1971, there were fifteen locations (nodes) on the network, serving twenty-three host computers. As the basic network software was being developed, so were the (initially rudimentary) applications that would use the network. One of the early applications was electronic mail; the use of the now standard "@" sign for e-mail originated in 1972.

While the primary focus had remained on constructing packet-switched networks, Robert Kahn (1938–) posed the "Internet problem"—namely how to get autonomous networks to exchange information—in 1972. The idea that a network could support (and even encourage) heterogeneity would ultimately be of great importance to the success of the Internet over technologies that were unable to provide this support easily.

The network continued to grow as well. By 1973, the first international site was introduced, which was to the University College in London via Norway; in addition, the ARPANET supported approximately 2,000 users. The genesis of today's computer environment was also being developed at this time, with the basic theory of the *Ethernet* local area network (LAN)*, which is today the dominant local networking system, and the modern computer workstation. The *Alto* workstation was developed at Xerox's Palo Alto Research Center (PARC) and had a graphical user interface (GUI)* with icons and a mouse. While nobody could predict the extent to which these technologies would come to dominate computing, they, together with Kahn's statement of the Internet problem, would combine to form the Internet as it is known today.

By 1974, enough had been learned about techniques for implementing packet-switching technology that a second generation protocol and the associated network software could be proposed. This was called the Transmission Control Protocol (TCP)*. This proposal included what users today understand as TCP and IP. The initial tests of TCP did not take place until 1975. By this time, commercial packet-switching services (though not based on NCP or TCP) had come into being, and the possibilities that these networks afforded began to be imagined. In fact, in 1976 Queen Elizabeth II sent an e-mail.

TCP continued to be developed during this time, and, in 1978, TCP and IP were divided into separate components so that their functions could be improved. Other notable events of the late 1970s included the development of the first Multi-User Domain (MUD), the proliferation of mailing lists, and the emergence of emoticons. By this time the utility of electronic mail was more widely recognized. To extend this capability beyond the domain of the ARPANET, new networks were formed. They included CSNET, BITNET (because it is time network), and FIDONET. Each of these networks used different network protocols, had different organizational forms, and reached different users. CSNET was targeted at university computer science departments and received funding from the National Science Foundation. BITNET was targeted at a more diverse academic audience, and was organized cooperatively so that each member paid for its connection to the nearest node, and agreed to transport others' traffic. FIDONET was built upon message forwarding over dialup telephone lines and was generally used by home computer users and hobbyists.

Though Kahn had articulated the Internet problem in 1972, and work on TCP had begun in 1978, it was not until 1982 that the conversion from NCP to TCP/IP took place (the crossover took place on January 1, 1983), and the notion of the Internet was first defined as a set of interconnected networks. The conversion to TCP/IP was bolstered when the U.S. Department of Defense declared TCP/IP to be the standard for its computer networking applications. Other events of the early and mid 1980s include:

- Increased international expansion.
- The introduction of the Domain Name System (DNS), with the now familiar.com,.org,.edu names.
- Gateways between ARPANET, CSNET, and BITNET.
- The involvement of the National Science Foundation (NSF) in the funding of the Internet backbone segments (NSFNET) reaching between the five university supercomputer centers they funded (Princeton, Pittsburgh, San Diego, Cornell, and Urbana-Champaign). This would be the demise of CSNET and BITNET, because it became easy for networks to be directly connected.
- Network news was developed.

By the late 1980s, commercial interest in computer networking was growing. This was prohibited by the NSF's Acceptable Use Policy, so limited private networks (such as UUNET) began emerging. This was also the time of the first "bug," the Internet worm that disrupted many of the hosts attached to the network. The worm incident prompted the establishment of the Computer Emergency Response Team (CERT) at Carnegie Mellon University. By the end of the decade, there were more than 100,000 computers attached to the network.

It was also during this time that the utility of the Internet as an information resource began to emerge. Many researchers made their reports

*file transfer protocol (FTP) a
communications protocol used
to transfer files

available via anonymous File Transfer Protocol (FTP)*. However, the problem of locating reports of interest brought the techniques of information storage and retrieval from the library and information science community to the Internet. The first tool for locating reports was *Archie*. Released in 1990, Archie was an index and search tool for anonymous FTP sites that researchers could use to locate information more efficiently. The next step was more interactive information content, which was embodied in *Gopher* for textual information, released in 1991; soon thereafter, an index of Gopher sites, called *Veronica*, was released in 1992. Gopher was still limited, however. The hypertext-based World Wide Web (WWW) was released initially in 1991 by Tim Berners-Lee (1955–); the Web provided a framework for integrated information content. Despite this, no compelling interface for the Web existed until Mosaic was released in 1993. Even without the Web, the number of computers connected to the Internet increased by an order of magnitude (to 1 million) in only three years.

The promise of the Internet was not lost on commercial users. In the early 1990s, private network service providers (for example, PSINET) emerged to carry commercial traffic. These service providers created the Commercial Internet Exchange (CIX) to exchange traffic among themselves so that a user of any commercial network could contact a user of any other commercial network. The NSF came under increasing pressure to privatize the NSFNET. This was finally accomplished in 1994. The NSF continued to support next generation Internet research through projects such as the very high-speed Backbone Network Service (vBNS). With the removal of the restrictive Acceptable Use Policy of the NSF, commercial Internet ventures flourished with the introduction of streaming audio in 1995, Internet banking, and the like.

The growth explosion that followed privatization had a large impact on the broader telecommunications sector of the United States and world economies. Many traditional carriers were developing an Internet strategy, and the idea of "convergence" was central to these plans. In short, convergence refers to the notion that, as content (such as text, audio, image, and video) was digitized, any underlying network technology could be used for transport. This meant that IP carriers could easily invade the traditional "turf" of telephone companies, and other communication providers. This idea of convergence was one of the underlying forces behind the passage of the Telecommunications Act of 1996, which redefined the regulatory structure of the telecommunications industry. In essence this legislation attempted to create a policy convergence framework that could mirror the technological convergence that was going on in the industry.

The emergence of the Internet placed substantial pressure on existing legal structures as well. The Electronic Frontier Foundation was founded in 1990 to explore these questions. As commercial interests in digital rights became significant following the Internet's privatization, issues such as trademarks, cryptography, copyright, and privacy became important legal as well as public policy issues.

Additional Information

Although the Internet has changed economic and social patterns in much of the world, access to the Internet remains limited throughout much of the world, especially in developing countries. Meanwhile, in the industrialized world, computer scientists such as Tim Berners-Lee were warning that the nature of the Internet was being threatened by the desire of Internet service providers to begin favoring some types of messages over others, especially those from higher-paying customers. Since its beginnings in the 1970s, the Internet had been characterized by "net neutrality"—that is, all users had equal access to long-distance transmission equipment. Favoring certain corporate or higher-paying customers over others would result in slower access for non-favored clients, eliminating net neutrality, which Berners-Lee and others claim is essential to the Internet's continued growth and vitality. The U.S. Congress has considered laws that would guarantee net neutrality but no such law had been passed of late 2012. The Federal Communications Commission (FCC) regulates service provider actions and Internet openness. In 2011, the FCC published new guidelines that required providers to have transparent network management practices (including pricing and bandwidth restrictions), allow the transmission of lawful content, and not discriminate unreasonably when transmitting lawful network traffic. Critics assert the regulations do not sufficiently preserve open access to the Internet because providers still are permitted to charge variable prices for different Internet speeds and may engage in bandwidth throttling (limiting the amount of bandwidth that a given service may use) as a means of influencing consumer behavior and discouraging streaming media usage over traditional cable or satellite television. The Internet continues to evolve as issues of access and equity are debated intensely.

 See also **Bell Labs • Government Funding: Research • Internet: Backbone • Telecommunications • Telephony**

Resources

Web Sites

Leiner, Barry M., et al. "A Brief History of the Internet." http://www.internetsociety.org/internet/internet-51/history-internet/brief-history-internet (accessed November 1, 2012).

PBS News Hour. "The Internet of Things: IoT." http://video.pbs.org/video/2192094313 (accessed November 1, 2012).

World Wide Web Consortium. "W3C." http://www.w3.org (accessed November 1, 2012).

Expressing Emotion

Emoticons, or "emotion icons," were created to help people express their state of mind in e-mails. On occasion, the tone of an e-mail can be misunderstood because the receiver cannot see the sender's facial expressions. Without such visual cues, a humorous statement can be misconstrued as a serious or sarcastic comment. The smiley face:) and the frowning face:(and the winking face;) are the most popular emoticons. However, e-mail senders continue to devise other creative ways to express emotions, including =8-o for "fright" and:-$ for "put your money where your mouth is" and:*) for being "drunk."

* **paradigm** an example, pattern, or way of thinking

* **firewall** a special purpose network computer or software that is used to ensure that no access is permitted to a sub-network unless authenticated and authorized

Intranet

One of the most desirable features of the Internet is the ability to access information from anywhere, independent of geographical location. However, there are valid reasons why a corporation or other organization may not want to grant worldwide access to its internal business information. This has led to Internet-like services restricted to inside a company that is referred to as an intranet. Intranets have been called a paradigm* shift in internal business operations because of the potential networking efficiencies (dynamic online corporate information instantly accessible) and the standard, universal computer interface for all employees within an organization.

An intranet is an enterprise network (spanning geographical boundaries to connect different types of computers in various parts of an organization) that provides users with Internet application tools (i.e., Web browsers) to access organizational information. Note that an intranet is an internal network to link organizational members to organizational information that is completely controlled by the organization. If any Internet connection does exist (one does not have to exist), a firewall* prevents outside computers anywhere on the Internet from accessing computers on the intranet.

Uses and Applications

Intranets are popular for several reasons: (1) the infrastructure is often already in place in terms of computers, software, and connectivity for any networks with Internet access; (2) they work, allowing all organizational members instant and uniform access to broadcast organizational information, internal databases, and internal collaboration; (3) they scale well because the technology is the same as that used in the Internet; and (4) intranets are secure from the Internet. Due to the popularity of the World Wide Web (commonly called the Web), most intranets are implementations of an enterprise network providing access to Web server(s).

In the Web context, to create an intranet requires the following: (1) establishing a Web server, requiring hardware and software; (2) establishing Web server access by building a TCP/IP (Transmission Control Protocol/Internet Protocol) network—TCP/IP is the protocol suite that provides interoperability on the Internet; (3) loading client Web browsers on each user's computer; and (4) creating a Web homepage document using HTML (hypertext markup language) or an HTML editor. A big advantage of using an intranet is that most employees are already familiar with using the Internet's Web so little extra training is needed.

Security

Protection for an intranet connected to the Internet is provided by a firewall—a computer or group of computer systems that enforces an access control policy by blocking traffic or permitting traffic.

Typically, a firewall is one computer that sits between the intranet and the Internet filtering packets* according to various criteria. Firewalls simplify security management because network security can be consolidated on firewall systems rather than being distributed on systems all over an internal network. Firewalls thus offer a convenient point where logging and auditing functions can provide summaries about traffic flows passing through, traces of inbound and outbound connections, attempts to break through, and alarms for attacks as they occur. Without a firewall, protection defaults to individual computer security mechanisms implemented on each intranet computer device. Before implementing an intranet relying on a firewall, an organization must inventory all its traffic routing since a firewall cannot filter that are not routed through it.

A Web-based intranet allows an organization to control information by tracking aggregate Web traffic and individual user traffic. Emerging intranet products are developing methods to infer user information from Web server request log information in files that can be used with relational databases* for specific queries. Other products track Web page users' access, the paths users follow through Web pages, and the amount of e-mail an individual user sends and receives. It has already become common commercial practice for companies to keep track of search topics requested by an individual user and compile databases that allow tailored information designed for individual users.

Examples

Most companies in the twenty-first century implement some form of intranet for internal operations. For example, KPMG (whose initials are found within the 1987 merger of Peat Marwick International and Klynveld Main Goerdeler), a management consulting firm, moved all of its information assets to an intranet called KWorld. The success of Cisco Systems has been largely attributed to its innovative corporate intranet. Even while selling systems using a non-interoperable proprietary protocol (Systems Network Architecture—SNA), International Business Machines Corporation (IBM) was also widely credited with having the largest TCP/IP corporate intranet. In fact, in 2005, IBM's intranet, known internally as *w3 On Demand Workplace*, was selected as one of The Year's 10 Best Intranets by the Nielsen Norman Group. In 2012, LivePerson, Inc., a provider of real-time chat, voice, and content solutions, was selected by Nielsen Norman as having the best Intranet Design. The People's Republic of China (PRC) is attempting to build a national intranet to take advantage of established Internet connectivity. If implemented successfully it would be the largest intranet in the world.

▶ *See also* **Internet • Network Design • Networks • Telecommunications**

Speedy Alternative

At many large companies, staff announcements made via paper memo are a thing of the past. Instead, organizations post information via their own Intranets on topics ranging from employee activities, cafe lunch menus, services offered by various departments, and benefits information. Such notices can be added or updated quickly and distributed to staff en masse with the push of a button.

* **packets** collections of digital data elements that are part of a complete message or signal; packets contain their destination addresses to enable reassembly of the message or signal

* **relational database** a collection of records that permits logical and business relationships to be developed between themselves and their contents

Resources

Books

Belkhamza, Zakariya, and Syed Azizi Wafa, eds. *Measuring Organizational Information Systems Success: New Technologies and Practices*. Hershey, PA: Business Science Reference, 2012.

Comer, Douglas E. *The Internet Book: Everything You Need to Know about Computer Networking and How the Internet Works*. 3rd ed. Upper Saddle River, NJ: Pearson Prentice Hall, 2007.

White, Martin S. *The Intranet Management Handbook*. Medford, NJ: Information Today, 2011.

Web Sites

International Business Machines Corporation. "IBM Intranet Experience Suite." http://www-01.ibm.com/software/collaboration/products/intranetexperience/features/ (accessed October 8, 2012).

LivePerson. "LivePerson Named One of World's Ten Best Intranets by Nielsen Norman Group." http://pr.liveperson.com/index.php?s=43&item=333 (accessed October 8, 2012).

WebWire. "IBM's Intranet One of the World's Top Ten." http://www.webwire.com/ViewPressRel.asp?aId=8397 (accessed October 8, 2012).

J

Java Applets

An applet is a small program that is embedded inside another application. Applets are not intended to run on their own. A Java applet is an applet written in the Java programming language. They are most commonly embedded in Web pages to run in the environment of a Web browser. Web pages are written in Hypertext Markup Language (HTML)*. The web browser interprets the HTML source in order to render the pages on a display screen. Java applets are one way to add functionality to a basic page written in HTML, particularly with regard to graphical user interfaces (GUIs)* and multimedia. A Java applet is like a window application running within the embedding Web page. It can provide much more sophisticated features in graphical user interfaces for interaction, as well as other functionalities such as animation and special effects.

The Web browser must be equipped with the Java Virtual Machine (JVM) to handle Web pages embedded with Java applets. The JVM is a Java interpreter that makes it possible to run compiled Java code; it enables the browser to run Java applets when rendering the embedding Web page. The HTML source uses the <APPLET> tag to embed a Java applet in the Web page. The parameters of the <APPLET> tag can specify the width and height of the window in the Web page for the applet, and also refer to the file for the compiled code of the Java applet. The file usually would have the ".class" extension in the file name. This extension in the naming convention indicates that it is a file for compiled Java code. The following illustrates a simple HTML source sequence to embed a Java applet in the file myapplet.class.

```
<APPLET height = 100 width = 200 code = "myApplet.class">
    </APPLET>
```

In the preceding <APPLET> tag, the parameters height and width instruct the browser to reserve a window in the web page, 100 pixels* high and 200 pixels wide, as screen real estate for the applet. The compiled code of the Java applet is in the file myApplet.class, specified for the parameter code. To render the Web page, the browser accesses the file for the applet code, and runs the JVM to execute the applet. The </APPLET> tag closes the scope of the <APPLET> tag, as required in the syntax* of HTML.

A Java applet is different from a regular Java application program in that it is not started with its main method. Instead, the first time the browser renders the Web page, the JVM loads the applet code from the

* **Hypertext Markup Language (HTML)** an encoding scheme for text data that uses special tags in the text to signify properties to the viewing program (browser) like links to other documents or document parts

* **graphical user interfaces (GUIs)** interfaces that allow computers to be operated through pictures (icons) and mouse-clicks, rather than through text and typing

* **pixel** a single picture element on a video screen; one of the individual dots making up a picture on a video screen or digital image

* **syntax** a set of rules that a computing language incorporates regarding structure, punctuation, and formatting

* **init method** a special function in an object oriented program that is automatically called to initialize the elements of an object when it is created

file specified. To run the applet, it invokes the init method* first and then the start method. Thereafter, whenever the browser leaves the Web page, the JVM invokes the stop method; and subsequently whenever the browser returns to the page, it invokes the start method again. The start and stop methods are then repeated as many times as the browser would enter and leave the Web page. Before the browser unloads the applet from its cache memory, the JVM then invokes the destroy method. For every instance of a Java applet embedded in a Web page, the is always the first to be invoked, and is invoked only once. Thereafter, the start and stop methods may be invoked as many times as needed. The destroy method is also invoked only once and is always the last method invoked before the applet is unloaded from the cache (such as when the browser terminates).

The init method is designed for the applet to acquire and set up resources for use. For example, if a person would like a Web page to play music whenever the browser opens the page, he or she will use the init method to acquire the audio channels for use, and set up the audio file for playback. The person will then use the start method to begin playback of the audio file. Whenever the browser leaves to go to another page, the stop method will stop playback and mark the position of the music playback. When the browser returns to the Web page, the start method can then resume music playback at the place where it left off at the previous stop method. The destroy method releases the resources acquired, since it is the last method invoked. These four methods are often called the life cycle methods of a Java applet; the method declarations are listed:

```
public void init(void);

public void start(void);

public void stop(void);

public void destroy(void);
```

The parameters height and width in the <APPLET> tag assign an applet screen real estate in the web page for graphical display. Whenever it becomes necessary to refresh or update the display, the JVM of the browser invokes the paint method of the applet: public void paint(Graphics g);

The parameter "g" is the Graphics object for the window in the embedding web page of dimensions specified by the height and width in the <APPLET> tag. The paint method can use it to draw the content for display in the Web page.

A Java applet must support all these methods: init, start, stop, destroy, and paint in order to function properly. The Java class library provides the Applet class with default implementation for all five methods. One can make use of inheritance in object-oriented programming when he or she derives an applet class from Applet; the applet will then inherit these methods from the base class Applet. One has to implement the methods in the applet class only when he or she needs to override the default implementation.

A simple Java applet, myApplet, will illustrate the functionality. The complete HTML source of the web page, embedding the applet using the <APPLET> tag, follows:

```
<HTML>
    <HEAD><TITLE>myApplet</TITLE></HEAD>
    <BODY><H1>My Applet</H1>
    <HR><APPLET CODE="myApplet.class" WIDTH=200
HEIGHT=50></APPLET><HR>
    </BODY>
    </HTML>
```

The web page shows the heading "My Applet" and the window for the applet. The complete source program for the Java applet follows:

```
// myApplet.java - a simple Java applet example.
    import java.applet.*; // to use class Applet
    import java.awt.*; // to use Color and Graphics
    public class myApplet extends Applet
    {
    int count = 0;
    Color spectrum[] = new Color[3];
    // init: to set up resources of 3 colors.
    public void init()
    {
    spectrum[0] = Color.blue;
    spectrum[1] = Color.red;
    spectrum[2] = Color.green;
    }
    // start: to increment count for next color.
    public void start()
    {
    count == count + 1;
    }
    // paint: to update content of display.
    public void paint(Graphics g)
    {
    g.setColor(spectrum[count%3]); // Change color.
    g.drawString("Applet DEMO: "+count,10,20);
    }
    }
```

The applet keeps a count of how many times the start method has been invoked. The applet paints the text string "Applet DEMO: " followed by the count. The color of the text rotates in the sequence of blue, red, and green: every time the browser leaves and then returns to the page, the color changes, because the start method increments the count.

▶ *See also* **Internet • Object-Oriented Languages • Procedural Languages • Programming • World Wide Web**

Help for Beginners

Programs exist to help people without Java or HTML knowledge create applets to spruce up their home pages. Such programs claim that users can create "cool" effects for their Web sites in just a matter of minutes.

* **Hypertext Markup Language (HTML)** an encoding scheme for text data that uses special tags in the text to signify properties to the viewing program (browser) like links to other documents or document parts

* **interface** a boundary or border between two or more objects or systems; also a point of access

* **compiled** a program that is translated from human-readable code to binary code that a central processing unit (CPU) can understand

* **cookie** a small text file that a web site can place on a computer's hard drive to collect information about a user's browsing activities or to activate an online shopping cart to keep track of purchases

* **Uniform Resource Locator (URL)** a reference to a document or a document container using the Hypertext Transfer Protocol (HTTP); consists of a hostname and path to the document

Resources

Books

Coad, Peter, Mark Mayfield, and Jonathan Kern. *Java Design: Building Better Apps and Applets.* 2nd ed. Upper Saddle River, NJ: Yourdon Press, 1999.

Gottleber, Timothy T. *Excellent HTML with an Introduction to Java Applets.* Boston: Irwin/McGraw-Hill, 1998.

Web Sites

Oracle. "The Java Tutorials: Lesson: Java Applets." http://docs.oracle.com/javase/tutorial/deployment/applet/ (accessed October 15, 2012).

JavaScript

JavaScript is a programming language designed specifically for electronic documents on the World Wide Web. Documents on the web are written in Hypertext Markup Language (HTML)*. JavaScript programs are embedded within HTML to add dynamic interactivity to Web documents.

JavaScript may look like the programming language Java, but it is not Java. As a scripting language, JavaScript is intended to take Web page designers a step beyond HTML without the complexity of a full programming language. A simple JavaScript program can add interesting interactive functions to a web page. JavaScript is also suitable for the development of large and elaborate user interfaces* in Web documents. Good programming skills are necessary to master it, and sophisticated tools are becoming available for JavaScript development.

JavaScript is not compiled*. Embedded within HTML, JavaScript is interpreted by the Web browser. A JavaScript program can control document content and its appearance, interacting with the HTML source code and the browser functions. It makes use of the user interface mechanisms already in HTML to interact with users of the web document. It can manipulate embedded images, but cannot produce graphical displays. It should not read or write files, except in using cookies* as permitted by the Web browser. It can access other Web documents using the Uniform Resource Locator (URL)*, but it cannot make network connections on its own.

The following is an example of the JavaScript program embedded in an HTML document. JavaScript program code is embedded between the <SCRIPT> and the</SCRIPT> tags.

```
<HTML><HEAD>
    <TITLE>Java Script Example One</TITLE>
    </HEAD><BODY>
    <HR>
```

```
<H3>JavaScript Example: HELLO</H3>
<HR>
<SCRIPT LANGUAGE=JavaScript>
//
// Ask for the user's name to greet. (Default name is Peter.)
  //
  var name = prompt ("Tell me your name, please.","Peter");
  //
  // Set name to STRANGER if user refuses to enter a name.
  //
  if (name == null) name = "STRANGER";
  //
  // Generate greeting with the name, in different styles.
  //
  var greeting = "Hello" + name + "!";
  document.write (greeting.bold()+"<BR>");
  document.write (greeting.italics()+"<BR>");
  document.write (greeting.toUpperCase()+"<BR>");
</SCRIPT>
</BODY></HTML>
```

The HTML document makes use of the <SCRIPT> tag to include a JavaScript program. When the browser opens up the document, it interprets the JavaScript program. The short program uses the browser's prompt function to prompt the user to enter a name, and then generates the content of the page with the name that is entered.

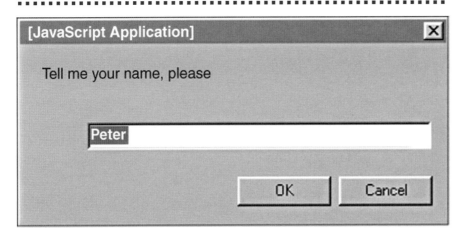

Figure 1. Pop-up dialog box. *Netscape Communicator browser window © 1999 Netscape Communication Organization- -used with permission (Netscape Communications has not authorized, sponsored, endorsed, or approved this publication and is not responsible for its content)*

* **concatenates** the joining together of two elements or objects; for example, words are formed by concatenating letters

In the JavaScript source program, the double slash "//" indicates a program comment until the end of line. The keyword *var* declares variable for use. The variables declared in the program are name and greeting. Any text included within a pair of double quotes (or single quotes) is a text string. Using the plus sign (+) between text strings concatenates* them to form a longer string. The program calls the prompt function provided by the browser to first pop up a dialog box to prompt the user. The first argument of the function call is the text string to describe the information being requested. The second argument is the default text entry initially placed in the pop-up dialog box. Figure 1 illustrates the pop-up dialog box when the browser opens up the HTML document.

The user can then type in an entry and click "OK," or refuse to supply an entry and cancel. The variable name in the JavaScript program will then pick up the entry. If no entry is supplied, the variable name becomes null, having no value. The next line in the program then checks to see if "name" has a value; if it does not have a value it is set to STRANGER. The next line in the program goes on to form the greeting string in the variable greeting. Because addition concatenates the strings, if the name entered is "Quincy," the variable greeting would have the string "Hello Quincy!" The next three lines then generate the document content with the greeting string in different styles. The function document.write() takes the string argument, and generates that as content in the HTML document. Note the different styles generated using the functions on the string—bold, italics, regular type setting to uppercase. Appropriate HTML source code is generated accordingly. The following illustrates the web page generated, with Peter as the name entered.

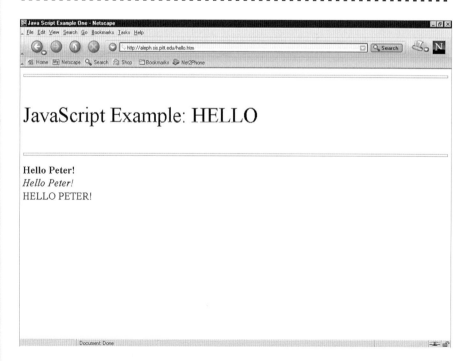

Figure 2. Web page generated using JavaScript. *Netscape Communicator browser window © 1999 Netscape Communication Organization--used with permission (Netscape Communications has not authorized, sponsored, endorsed, or approved this publication and is not responsible for its content)*

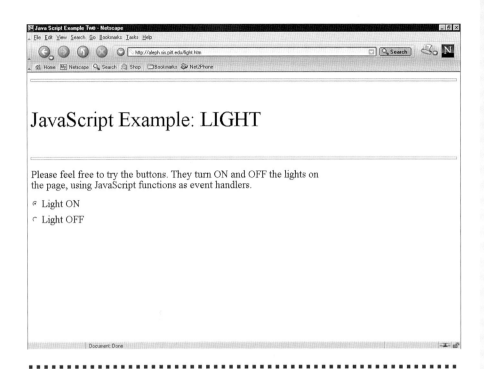

JavaScript Example: LIGHT

Please feel free to try the buttons. They turn ON and OFF the lights on the page, using JavaScript functions as event handlers.

○ Light ON
○ Light OFF

Figure 3. Web page rendered by a browser opening up the HTML document. *Netscape Communicator browser window © 1999 Netscape Communication Organization--used with permission (Netscape Communications has not authorized, sponsored, endorsed, or approved this publication and is not responsible for its content)*

Unlike Java, JavaScript is a loosely typed language. It means that variables used in the program do not have a definite type: a variable can take up any type of content, and they are all declared with the keyword "var." For example, a variable may take a text string as content, but the same variable can also take an integer number and use it in a calculation. Like many other programming languages, JavaScript also has control structures such as functions, conditional (if) statements and loop (while) statements, as well as data structures such as arrays.

JavaScript is an object-based language: A JavaScript program can create and use objects of existing types provided for it, but cannot create new types of objects. Therefore, it is not an object-oriented programming language like Java. A significant design point in JavaScript is its access to the Document Object Model (DOM) used in the web browser. The DOM is the data structure in the web browser used to manage the documents viewed and used on the browser. When the browser is running, it has a window open for viewing of documents. Each document in turn comprises its content, links, anchors, images, and other components. All these are objects available to the JavaScript programs running in the browser. In the earlier program example, document.write() invokes the write() method in the current document object, generating content in the document as HTML source.

Along with the DOM, the web browser in use also generates events. An event occurs when the user interacts with the user interfaces on the web page presented by the web browser. For example, when the user clicks the mouse button with the mouse cursor over a radio button on the web page, it generates the onClick event. The HTML source can specify in the value of the onClick parameter in the <INPUT> tag, to call a JavaScript

Javascript's Founder

JavaScript was invented by Brendan Eich at Netscape Communications, Inc. in 1995. Originally it was called LiveScript. In December 1995, along with the beta release of Netscape Navigator 2.0, the language was renamed JavaScript.

function. The specific event will therefore invoke the JavaScript function as an event handler to perform the necessary processing. The following is an illustrative example.

```
<HTML><HEAD>
    <TITLE>JavaScript Example Two</TITLE>
    <SCRIPT LANGUAGE=JavaScript>
    function onButton()
    {
    <space n="25" axis="horizontal">var thisBox = document.
myForm.radio1;
    <space n="25" axis="horizontal">if (thisBox.checked == true)
    <space n="25" axis="horizontal">{
    <space n="33" axis="horizontal">document.myForm.radio2.
checked = false;
    <space n="33" axis="horizontal">document.bgColor='white';
    <space n="33" axis="horizontal">alert("Thanks!");
    <space n="25" axis="horizontal">}
    }
    function offButton()
    {
    <space n="25" axis="horizontal">var thisBox = document.
myForm.radio2;
    <space n="25" axis="horizontal">if (thisBox.checked == true)
    <space n="25" axis="horizontal">{
    <space n="33" axis="horizontal">document.myForm.radio1.
checked = false;
    <space n="33" axis="horizontal">document.bgClor='black';
    <space n="33" axis="horizontal">alert("Hey! Turn the lights
back ON!");
    <space n="25" axis="horizontal">}
    }
    </SCRIPT>
    </HEAD><BODY>
    <HR>
    <H3>JavaScript Example: LIGHT</H3>
    <HR>
    <P>Please feel free to try the buttons.
    They turn ON and OFF the lights on the page,
    using JavaScript functions as event handlers.<BR>
    <FORM NAME=myForm>
    <INPUT TYPE=radio NAME=radio1 onClick="onButton();"
CHECKED>
    Light ON<BR></line><line><INPUT TYPE=radio
NAME=radio2 onClick="offButton();">
    Light OFF<BR>
    </FORM>
    </BODY></HTML>
```

Note in the preceding HTML source how the event onClick also names a parameter for the <INPUT> tag, and the value of the parameter makes a call to the JavaScript function. The JavaScript functions can also use the name of the components to alter its state. The following shows the web page rendered by a browser opening up the HTML document. The radio buttons provide for user interaction to change the background color of the document, using JavaScript functions as event handlers.

Since its inception, JavaScript has already gone through four releases at the time of this writing, the latest being JavaScript 1.3. JavaScript is still developing. There can be compatibility problems such that the same JavaScript program may behave differently with different web browsers and different browser versions. The European Computer Manufacturers' Association (ECMA) and the International Organization for Standardization (ISO) have adopted ECMAScript, which is based on JavaScript, as a standard. The adopted standard will surely help to resolve the compatibility problems.

See also **Internet • Object-Oriented Languages • Procedural Languages • Programming • World Wide Web**

Resources

Books

Flanagan, David. *JavaScript: The Definitive Guide.* 6th ed. Beijing, China, and Sebastopol, CA: O'Reilly & Associates, 2011.

Goodman, Danny. *JavaScript Bible.* 7th ed. Indianapolis: Wiley, 2010.

Web Sites

Google.com. "HTML, CSS, and JavaScript from the Ground Up" http://code.google.com/edu/submissions/html-css-javascript/#javascript (accessed November 3, 2012).

Journalism

Since the early 1950s, computers have played a major role in journalism and mass communication. As early as 1956, computers were used to analyze political polling data and national election returns.

In the beginning, only the largest media organizations could afford computer-based technology. Today, computers are present in virtually every newsroom in the country. Journalists use computer technology in three major areas: (a) gathering information to be used in news stories; (b) producing newspaper and magazine articles and television or radio newscasts; and (c) distributing news stories and programs to the general public. Prior to the introduction of computers in journalism, news deadlines had to be set early enough for the material to be produced, published

* **mainframe** large computer used by businesses and government agencies to process massive amounts of data; generally faster and more powerful than desktop computers but usually requiring specialized software

or recorded, and disseminated in a timely manner. The use of computers in journalism now allows the very latest news to appear in print or on the air—as well as in online form via the Internet.

Computers Enter the Newsroom

Newspapers began using computers in the early 1970s. These were large mainframe* machines designed specifically to be used for copyediting and typesetting to produce the actual newspaper pages. Initially, computers were not used to gather the news, whether for print or for broadcast use.

Computers first appeared in television newsrooms in the early 1980s. As was the case in print journalism, the first television news computers were proprietary machines that, unlike today's personal computers, were designed to perform a single function. One of the first proprietary television newsroom computers was manufactured by Dynatech Newstar. It allowed broadcast reporters to write scripts and read wire stories. Later versions of the program added the ability for newscast producers to organize newscasts and create detailed rundowns of the news program's content.

In the late 1980s, the computer systems shifted from proprietary hardware and software to personal desktop computers as PCs and Macintosh computers became more powerful. Today, virtually all newspaper, television, and radio news content is produced using computer terminals or notebook computers. These computers connect the newsroom with other parts of the media production process. Page layout software—such as Quark Express, Adobe PageMaker, and InDesign—has streamlined the production of newspapers by making it possible for entire pages to be created easily on the desktop. In television, computers can transmit production information, including on-screen graphics and closed-captioning text, directly to the control room for use on the air.

Members of the international and local South African press prepare at the main media center in Johannesburg, during the World Summit on Sustainable Development. © *YOAV LEMMER/AFP/ Getty Images.*

In the mid-1990s, desktop computers became powerful enough to handle the creation of multimedia products such as pictures, graphics, video, and sounds. Just as desktop publishing changed the way page layouts were created, programs like Adobe Photoshop changed the way in which media companies created graphics and pictures. Prior to the use of computers, newspapers used traditional photographic film and chemicals in "wet" darkrooms to create pictures. By the early 2000s, many newspapers had switched to digital cameras to capture photographs and "digital" darkrooms to process them.

Digital Graphics and Audio

In television, the first computer-based graphics and video editing systems appeared in the early 1990s. Like other computer applications, the first systems were based on propriety hardware and were extremely expensive. It was not uncommon for a television graphics computer hardware and application software to cost more than $250,000. Early computer-based, or non-linear, video editing programs were equally expensive. Now, programs such as Apple Final Cut Pro and Adobe Premiere are affordable for many hobbyists, as well as television stations and video production companies.

Except for some smaller entities, such as local television newsrooms, non-linear video editing has largely replaced traditional tape-to-tape editing in which scenes were physically recorded from one videotape recorder to another. With computer-based editing, the pictures can be assembled electronically on a computer screen. Some television stations, such as the Gannett Corporation's WKYC in Cleveland, Ohio, have instituted an all-digital workflow. Video for news stories is either recorded digitally to begin with, or else is converted to a digital format as soon as the reporter gets back to the station after covering an event. The digital video is then available to everyone in the news production process (reporters, photographers, editors, producers, and promotions department) via networked desktop computers. This speeds up the production process and makes it possible for last minute changes to be made in the news programs.

Computers are also used by radio stations to create digital audio. News reporters can edit interviews with newsmakers and add commentary from reporters without having to splice the audiotape physically or record it from one tape recorder to another.

Computer Assisted Reporting

Journalists also use computers to gather information for stories. The term for this function is "computer assisted reporting." For example, reporters can sift through complicated databases, such as census information supplied by the U.S. government to gather specific information about individual communities. Computer assisted reporting can help journalists to spot trends in a community, such as an increase in cancer rates among a certain segment of the population or a decrease in the number of young people who are planning to attend college. Computer assisted reporting can also be used to examine and investigate police statistics, such as the

A Vital News Tool

According to Bruce Garrison, professor of journalism at the University of Miami in Coral Gables, Florida, journalists' dependence on computers for news gathering and connecting to the World Wide Web is now almost 100 percent. Of course, as with any other general source of news or background data, reporters must be cautious not to use websites that may contain unreliable information.

An increasing number of journalists are using online social media as part of the job as well. According to a 2012 study, 55 percent of journalists around the world use social media sites such as Twitter and Facebook to locate stories, and 43 percent said they used these sites to help verify existing stories.

number of traffic citations that have been issued to public officials for which the fines were never paid.

The Internet provides a major source of information for journalists, particularly when they are working on a breaking story. For example, there are several aviation-related web sites that reporters can turn to for current and background information after a major airplane crash. These websites can help reporters collect technical information about the type of airplane involved and its maintenance history. Many sites are also available to help reporters gather scientific, geographical, historical, and health-related information.

News Online

The latest use of computers in journalism is to disseminate information via sites on the World Wide Web. Most major newspapers, television networks, local television stations, and major radio stations have websites that feature news content. It is possible to "read" almost any newspaper in the world if it is available on the Internet. Newspaper and television companies have tried several business models to make money with their websites. However, journalism websites have struggled to attain a consistent profit. Surveys indicate that most people are, as yet, unwilling to pay for Web-based news content. Many media Web sites rely on on-screen advertising for their revenue. In some cases, however, the advertising revenue does not support the cost of producing the Web material.

Meanwhile, the market share of traditional media sources, such as newspapers and network television, continued a general decline throughout the 2000s. For instance, according to an April 2010 report from the Audit Bureau of Circulations (a non-profit association that includes both publishers and advertisers) U.S. weekday newspaper circulation had fallen nearly 9 percent over the previous six-month period. While some of the lost circulation could be attributed to the economic recession that commenced in 2008, those numbers nonetheless reflected the continuing trend of decreasing circulation that had started years earlier.

And in a 2012 survey of more than 3,000 Americans by the Poynter Institute, 64 percent of respondents said they used the Internet for news, compared to 38 percent who still relied on newspapers. The younger the respondents, the more likely they were to use technology and Internet connectivity for news. Among Millennial respondents, smartphones actually surpassed newspapers as a news source, with 40 percent of Millennials using their smartphones for news, compared to just 22 percent who read newspapers.

The Future

It is difficult to determine what effect computers will ultimately have on journalism. A generation ago, only large newspaper companies had the economic muscle to publish a daily newspaper. In the 2010s, anyone with a page layout program and access to the Internet can reach readers around the world. Likewise, the high cost of video production used to mean that only television stations and networks could afford to produce programs. The development of affordable desktop video has changed that, too. As Internet bandwidth* increases, more and more companies will be able to produce their own video programs and distribute them over the World Wide Web. This is a far cry from those early mainframe computers used on election night in 1956.

▶ *See also* **Architecture** • **Desktop Publishing** • **Document Processing**

* **bandwidth** a measure of the frequency component of a signal or the capacity of a communication channel to carry signals

Resources

Books

Gillmor, Dan. *We the Media: Grassroots Journalism by the People, for the People.* Sebastopol, CA: O'Reilly Media, 2006.

Web Sites

Mediabistro.com. "55 percent of Journalists Worldwide Use Twitter, Facebook to Source News Stories." http://www.mediabistro.com/alltwitter/digital-journalism_b24440 (accessed October 19, 2012).

Poynter.org. "Survey: Americans Turn to Established Media for Breaking News, Mobile." http://www.poynter.org/latest-news/top-stories/190586/new-data-show-shifting-patterns-as-people-seek-news-across-platforms/ (accessed October 23, 2012).

M

Marconi Guglielmo
Italian Physicist
1874–1937

Known as the father of radio, Guglielmo Marconi was born April 25, 1874 in Bologna, Italy. He was the younger son of an Italian landowner, Giuseppe Marconi, and Anne Jameson, whose father was the founder of the Jameson Irish whiskey distillery. As a youngster, Marconi spent the winter months in England or Florence, Italy, with his mother, brother, and English relatives. Schooling for the Marconi brothers was divided between their mother, who taught them English and religion, and a tutor, who provided instruction in Italian and other subjects. Perhaps through teaching her sons, Anne Marconi became aware her son's intellectual abilities and his determination to solve problems on his own. She supported Marconi's efforts throughout her life. He began exploring the properties of electricity at a young age by reading scientific publications and duplicating and modifying experiments. This exploration continued throughout his life resulting in the foundational work he did in the field of wireless technology and telecommunications.

Marconi attended primary and secondary schools. He was not noted for his scholarship. Instead of attending university, arrangements were made for him to study with Vincenzo Rosa, a professor of electrophysics. These sessions introduced Marconi to the work of Heinrich Hertz, James Clerk Maxwell, Oliver Joseph Lodge, and others conducting experiments to explain electromagnetic waves. Marconi approached the field with the idea of using these waves for wireless communication. His greatest contribution was applying theoretical and basic discoveries to develop useful applications. To test his ideas, Marconi built the necessary equipment from materials around the estate. His experiments were conducted in a laboratory at his home. The first hurdle to overcome was increasing the distance that a wireless transmission could travel. Marconi achieved greater distances by increasing the range of the transmitters, by improving the sensitivity of the receivers, and by using antennas. His standard message for testing equipment became the three-dot Morse code for the letter "S."

Once his messages were traveling more than a mile across the family estate, it was time to seek funding from the Italian government. His request was denied. The next logical place to apply was England because wireless telegraphy would benefit the country's naval and maritime

Drive to Succeed

As an inventor and scientist, Marconi worked "around the clock" to find solutions. He would focus completely on the task, shutting himself away from family and all other considerations. This degree of concentration and determination helps explain how Marconi achieved so much at a very young age.

activities. Also, his English relatives could and would help. In 1896, at age twenty-two, Marconi set out for England. He first applied for an English patent, then met with Sir William Peerce, chief engineer of the English Postal and Telegraph Services. Recognizing the value and potential of Marconi's work, Peerce became an advocate and close friend. Ship-to-ship and ship-to-shore wireless telegraphy was operational the following year and Marconi founded his first company, Wireless Telegraph and Signal Company Limited.

The next hurdle to overcome was sending a message across the Atlantic Ocean. The widely held theory was that the curvature of the Earth made the transmission impossible. Marconi enlisted the expertise of John Fleming to solve the technical problems related to his continuing experiments to transmit across the Atlantic. The first transatlantic transmission from Cornwall, England, to Newfoundland, Canada, occurred in 1901 proving that the curvature of the Earth did not limit transmissions. He solved the problem of messages going to multiple receivers by using different transmission frequencies and setting the sender and receiver to the same frequency. Marconi continued exploring the possibilities of radio waves for uses beyond telecommunications and is credited with proposing the use of microwaves as a form of physical therapy.

Marconi's approach to patents and business was very conservative. When applying for patents or support for his work, he would explain the function of his invention or outline the improvements over previous methods but did not include a full disclosure of the design until a patent was granted. He followed the same procedures when demonstrating his equipment. This method protected his work from others and allowed him more fully to realize the monetary value of his systems. Many honors were bestowed on him, including the Nobel Prize for Physics in 1909, which he shared with Karl Ferdinand Braun who modified Marconi's transmitters to increase their range and usefulness. Marconi's business empire stretched across Europe and the United States, and one result of his international reputation was his appointment to represent Italy at the Paris Peace Conference after World War I. (Marconi had served in the Italian Army and Navy during World War I.) He continued being productive until a few years before his death from a heart condition. Marconi died in Rome on July 20, 1937.

 See also **Geographic Information Systems • Telecommunications • Wireless Technology**

Resources

Books

Masini, Giancarlo. *Marconi*. New York: Marsilio Publishers, 1995.

Mobile Computing

As the Internet becomes increasingly popular, a new paradigm* is being developed in networked computing known as *nomadic computing* or more commonly called *mobile computing*. Mobile computing aims to provide a network infrastructure* and corresponding terminal capability to perform all desktop-like computing functions seamlessly at any place or time, even while the terminal is moving. This means that anytime and anywhere, a user would be able to browse the Web, check e-mail, play digital music, and perform all other computing activities without having to be behind a desktop at home or work. At its best, mobile computing would allow a user to have access to a consistent working environment.

Practically, mobile computing is a challenge for several reasons. For anytime, anywhere functionality, the user must be able to carry the mobile computing device. The computing device must be small, light, and at the same time be capable of performing the complex tasks of a desktop computer. Anytime, anywhere access to a network will also require wireless connectivity as the user cannot be tied to a place where a wired connection is available. Both of these requirements are quite challenging to fulfill.

Currently, small lightweight devices operating on battery power are resource constrained. The display cannot be large, bright, or complex as this affects size and power consumption. For the same reason, the processing power, memory, storage space, and communication ports are limited or non-existent. Ideally, mobile computing devices would be dumb terminals* with all the services and computation performed by a powerful server* computer on a network. In such a scenario, the mobile computing

* **paradigm** an example, pattern, or way of thinking

* **infrastructure** the foundation or permanent installation necessary for a structure or system to operate

* **dumb terminal** a keyboard and screen connected to a distant computer without any processing capability

* **server** a computer that does not deal directly with human users, but instead handles requests from other computers for services to be performed

Web-enabled smart phones and the growing range of applications that go with them have the potential to alter the retail landscape in several ways. © *Davie Hinshaw/Charlotte Observer/MCT via Getty Images.*

* **ubiquitous** to be commonly
available everywhere

* **Global Positioning System
(GPS)** a method of locating a
point on earth's surface that uses
received signals transmitted from
satellites to calculate position
accurately

device would simply be a display for the information transferred from the server. However, current wireless connectivity is neither ubiquitous* nor uniform. Data rates on wireless connections can range between 9.6 kbps (kilobits per second, where kilo stands for 1,000) in outdoor areas with wide coverage to 50 mbps (megabits per second, where mega represents 1,000,000) or more in indoor areas with local coverage. This means that a user may not be always connected, and if the user is connected, the connections could be very slow or quite fast.

One solution to the problem of dynamic connection quality and disconnections is for the mobile computing device to download the information when there is good connectivity and then be able to work offline. The mobile computer must be sophisticated enough to store the information and process it offline. However, this approach is contradictory to the requirement that mobile computing devices be simple and dumb. As the flow of information is over wireless connections, security also becomes an issue and is especially challenging due to the size and resources of the device. There is consequently a tradeoff between the form factor of the device and the ability of the device to provide the user with a rich set of services.

Advances in technology have reduced many of these limitations, and mobile computing is becoming more advanced every year. Thus, mobile computing devices are becoming smaller, lighter, and more powerful than were their predecessors. They also come in various types and connectivity options. Several prominent brands of mobile operating systems (OSs) for these mobile computing devices currently in use are Android (from Google), Blackberry (Research In Motion), iOS (Apple), and Windows Phone (Microsoft). Often referred to as palmtop computers or handheld computers just a few years ago, these devices have come to be called smartphones and tablet computers. They are capable of such tasks as word processing, spreadsheet applications, Web browsing, calendar notations, and address management. These devices are becoming extremely thin, have a high-resolution, and include bright color displays.

Because the size of handheld computers is expected to be small, but they are required to perform many tasks, manufacturers have adopted an expansion slot approach. Essentially, a handheld computer is equipped with a slot where a variety of attachments can be connected. Attachments could include memory cards for storage, a Global Positioning System (GPS)* receiver for determining the user's location, a digital camera, an MP3 (short for MPEG-2 Audio Layer III) player for digital music, or modules for network connectivity—wired or wireless. Some of the attachments have their own power supply, increasing the size/weight of the handheld computer, but because they can be used only when needed, it eliminates the necessity of having all capabilities available in the handheld computer at the same time. The expansion slots of one device may not match that of a device from another vendor.

Wireless connectivity for handheld computers also comes in several varieties. Handheld computers come with built-in infrared ports that can be used to exchange information with a network or another computer at short range. They can connect to wireless local area networks (WLANs)* based on the IEEE 802.11 standard, but marketed under the Wi-Fi brand name, which is an abbreviation for Wireless Fidelity. These Wi-Fi connections, often available in retail establishments, are usually free to users. They can also connect to wireless services such as those provided by Verizon Wireless, AT&T Wireless, U.S. Cellular, and Sprint, which provide service over larger areas spanning cities, along highways and even on mountaintops, although only with paid subscriptions. The wireless service providers use such 3G (where 3G stands for third generation) mobile telecommunications network technologies, in association with commercial cell towers, such as CDMA2000 (Code division multiple access 2000), EDGE (Enhanced Data rates for GSM Evolution), and W-CDMA (Wideband Code Division Multiple Access). In 2012, the 4G (fourth generation) mobile network technology is being introduced increasingly throughout the United States, mostly in urban areas. Verizon is the largest 4G provider in the country, offering its 4G LTE (short for long term evolution) network to more than 200 million Americans. Many cellular telephone service providers are also making cell phone modules available for attachment to the expansion slots of handhelds computers. Bluetooth, a wireless standard for personal area networking*, is also available for many handheld computers.

Recently, the free Linux operating system has been modified to run on handheld computers of different types. Some manufacturers are also adopting Linux for their handheld computers. As this operating system carries no licensing fee, it could further reduce the cost of handheld computers. In developing countries like India, voice activated Linux-based simputers* have been developed for mass usage in rural areas where the computing infrastructure is limited. Device integration, such as the integration of cell phones and handheld computers, is also occurring. Location aware mobile computing—in which a person is able to obtain information on local restaurants, theaters, coffee-shops, maps, driving directions, traffic, weather, news, tourist attractions, and the like on a handheld computer—is also becoming prominent.

▶ *See also* **Embedded Technology (Ubiquitous Computing)** • **Geographic Information Systems** • **Wireless Technology**

Resources

Books

Chen, Kevin Y., and H. K. Lee, eds. *Mobile Computing Research and Applications.* New York: Nova Science Publishers, 2009.

Kamal, Raj. *Mobile Computing.* New Delhi: Oxford University Press, 2007.

What is MP3?

MP3 is a compressed audio format that was derived from the MPEG video format in the late 1980s. Files in MP3 format are not exactly small—approximately 1 megabyte per minute of CD-quality sound. However, they are a small fraction of the size of audio files found on commercially available compact discs, yet for most users the sound quality is comparable. Because of the small file size, MP3s are downloaded and managed easily by users with modest computer power and may be loaded into small portable devices that listeners can enjoy anywhere.

* **local area networks (LANs)** high-speed computer networks that are designed for users who are located near each other

* **personal area networking** the interconnectivity of personal productivity devices like computers, mobile telephones, and personal organizers

* **simputers** simple to use computers that take on the functionality of personal computers, but are mobile and act as personal assistants and information organizers

* **silicon chip** a common term for a semiconductor integrated circuit device

Kurkovsky, Stan, ed. *Multimodality in Mobile Computing and Mobile Devices: Methods for Adaptable Usability.* Hershey, PA: Information Science Reference, 2010.

Othman, Mazliza. *Principles of Mobile Computing and Communications.* Boca Raton, FL: Auerbach, 2008.

Web Sites

HowStuffWorks.com, Marshall Brain, and Tracy V. Wilson. "How Wi-Fi Works." http://computer.howstuffworks.com/wireless-network.htm (accessed October 11, 2012).

Verizon Wireless. "4G LTE." http://network4g.verizonwireless.com/ (accessed October 11, 2012).

Molecular Computing

Molecular computing is the science of using individual molecules to build computer programs. Instead of running software on a traditional computer, some scientists are now trying to replace the silicon chip* with test tubes, liquids, and even living cells due to a concern about the limits of miniaturization—a real and pressing problem that threatens the future advancement of computers.

To get an idea of how small computers have already become, think of a standard processor chip and imagine this: if the chip circuit were magnified such that the individual components were the size of office buildings, and the interconnections between them were the size of streets and

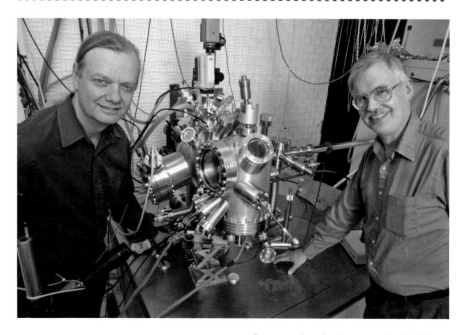

R. Stanley Williams (left) Hewlett Packard's Director of Quantum Science Research, and Philip Kuekes (right) HP Senior Scientist and Computer Architech, standing next to a scanning tunneling microscope that was used as part of HP's molecular electronics research. © *AP Images/PAUL SAKUMA.*

* **silicon** a chemical element with symbol Si; the most abundant element in earth's crust and the most commonly used semiconductor material

* **nanocomputing** the science and engineering of building mechanical machines at the atomic level

avenues, then the entire circuit at this scale would stretch from London, England, to San Francisco, California. Very impressive, but can it continue? The answer is no.

When it comes to creating smaller and smaller computers, existing technology—white-suited technicians in clean-rooms making silicon chips—will eventually hit a very solid wall imposed by the realities of physics. Once circuits are miniaturized down to the atomic level, components begin to interfere with one another, and the whole chip becomes useless. It is for this reason that some people are investigating alternatives to silicon* to build the computers of the future.

Scientists in the field of nanocomputing* are investigating several different possibilities, including the use of biological molecules. It seems that deoxyribonucleic acid (DNA), the very stuff of life, may hold the key. A tiny, almost invisible drop of water can contain trillions of molecules of DNA. Nature has information storage down to a fine art: a human body contains countless copies of the genetic sequence that makes a person who he or she is, and yet one single copy of that sequence would occupy a large encyclopedia if it were printed out.

Moreover, when scientists manipulate solutions of DNA, they operate on trillions of strands simultaneously. This massive parallel processing, combined with the incredible degree of miniaturization offered by DNA, leads scientists to believe it could form one of the main components of twenty-first-century computers.

The personal computer or laptop stores information in the form of bits, each of which may take the value one or zero. A computer software program is nothing more than a string of ones and zeroes, which is interpreted by the computer processor. DNA molecules are similar in that they are simply strings of, not ones and zeroes, but As, Gs, Cs, and Ts (this is how the 1997 film *Gattaca,* starring Ethan Hawke and Jude Law, got its name). The human genetic sequence can be thought of as software, which is then interpreted by human hardware—the various processes that guide development from a single cell to a fully functioning human being.

The key to using DNA to compute is that it can be manufactured in the laboratory. A request for a particular sequence (say, AGTTCA) can be given to a technician, and, after a short wait, a machine produces countless copies of the same short DNA sequence, ready for use. So how can DNA be used to solve a computing problem?

The problem of coloring has a long history. Given a map of the mainland United States, each state can be colored one of four colors such that no two states sharing a border are colored the same. However, what happens if there are only three colors, say, red, green, and blue? Will it still be possible to not color two adjacent states the same? This problem is easy to describe, but fiendishly difficult to solve once the map gets only moderately large.

Computer Sciences, 2ⁿᵈ Edition

"Bunny Suits"

Employees involved in manufacturing microchips don special white suits reminiscent of those worn by crews handling hazardous materials or medical personnel dealing with highly contagious diseases. Sometimes called bunny suits, the protective clothing worn in microchip processing plants is necessary to keep hair, skin, and dust particles from getting into the tiny microchips. One speck of dust could cause the microchip to malfunction, so precautions are taken to keep the environment free of such particles. In addition, employees must remove makeup, wear gloves and cover their shoes with booties, and go through an air shower before entering the work area.

---

* **supercomputers** very high performance computers, usually comprised of many processors and used for modeling and simulation of complex phenomena, like meteorology

The first thing to do is to generate all possible ways to color the map, each way represented by a single long sequence of DNA. This is done by mixing together trillions of copies of smaller sequences each encoding, say, "color Michigan green," "color Wisconsin blue," or "color Michigan red" as a distinct sequence of bases. If the sequence encoding is correct, these sequences stick together to form larger sequences, where each state is represented only once. Of course, most of these longer sequences encode undesirable colorings, for example, where both California and Nevada (which are, of course, neighbors) are colored green.

However, if enough DNA is used, a correct coloring is probably in there somewhere; it is the needle in a very large haystack. The next step is to remove from the test tube all of the undesirable colorings—the equivalent of the hay. For each state border, any sequences that color two neighboring states the same is removed. This is done by adding extra DNA sequences and a dash of chemicals to the tube. This process is repeated for each border until all that is left is the needle—a sequence encoding a correct coloring of the map.

Of course, biological operations work on geological time scales compared to twenty-first-century supercomputers*. The power of the DNA computer lies in its massive parallel processing capability; when a chemical is added to the test tube it acts on every strand simultaneously. Because the average tube holds trillions of strands, that is a lot of computing going on at once.

Some scientists are going one stage further and re-engineering the genetic programs of living cells. The machinery of life that controls the development of cells can now be re-programmed to give the cells simple, human-defined decision-making capabilities. By replacing specific sequences within their genetic code, it may soon be possible to engineer cells to act as microbial robots that seek out disease or deliver drugs at the point of infection. Consequently, many different experiments are being conducted in the area of molecular computing. For instance, Japanese researchers are using slime mold to develop the best route through a maze, which someday could be used to design an efficient transport network. In another experiment, British and Japanese researchers are using the bacterium *Magnetospirilllum magneticum* to develop miniscule hard drives because these microorganisms eat iron and become magnetized, which enables them to swim along earth's magnetic field to locate life-providing oxygen. Although molecular computing is still in its developmental infancy, its potential in the future is great for many medical applications. Of course, these various developments may take decades to bear fruit, and some may never get beyond the concept stage. What is clear, however, is that the fusion of computers and biology will provide some of the most exciting scientific breakthroughs of the twenty-first century.

▶ *See also* **Medical Systems • Molecular Biology • Nanocomputing**

Resources

Books

Agutter, Paul S., and D. N. Wheatley. *About Life: Concepts in Modern Biology*. Dordrecht, Netherlands: Springer, 2007.

Bray, Dennis. *Wetware: A Computer in Every Living Cell*. New Haven, CT: Yale University Press, 2009.

Forbes, Nancy. *Imitation of Life: How Biology Is Inspiring Computing*. Cambridge, MA: MIT Press, 2004.

Helms, Volkhard. *Principles of Computational Cell Biology: From Protein Complexes to Cellular Networks*. Weinheim, Germany: Wiley-VCH, 2008.

Ramachandran, K. I., G. Deepa, and K. Namboori. *Computational Chemistry and Molecular Modeling: Principles and Applications*. Berlin: Springer, 2008.

Web Sites

Discovery News. "Slime Mold Bio-Computer Could Solve Complex Problems." http://news.discovery.com/tech/slime-mold-computer-111229.html (accessed October 12, 2012).

Popular Science, and Clay Dillow. "Using Magnetic Bacteria to Construct the Biocomputer of the Future." http://www.popsci.com/science/article/2012-05/using-magnetic-bacteria-builders-researchers-could-construct-biocomputer-future (accessed October 12, 2012).

NO

Nanocomputing

Nanocomputing, a part of the emerging field of nanotechnology, describes computing that uses extremely small, or nanoscale, devices (one nanometer [nm] is one-billionth of a meter). In 1989, the 486 central processing unit (CPU) was manufactured with individual transistors* and other components roughly one micron (1,000 nanometers) across. In 2001, the state-of-the-art had advanced so that integrated circuits* (ICs) were widely manufactured with features as small as about 100 nm, which is about the same size as a virus. By early 2010, Intel—the world's foremost producer of integrated circuits by market value—had introduced a variety of CPUs, including the Intel Core i3, Core i5, and Core i7 processors, possessing 32 nm features (this is a calculated size; some individual components are a little bigger than 32 nm, while some are slightly smaller). As of 2012, the Core i7, a brand name from Intel, includes numerous families of desktop and laptop 64-bit x86-64 processors using microarchitectures called Ivy Bridge, Nehalem, Sandy Bridge, and Westmere.

Until the mid–1990s, the term nanoscale generally denoted circuit features smaller than 100 nm. After the IC industry started to build commercial devices at such size scales in the early 2000s, the term nanocomputing was then reserved for device features well below 50 nm, to even the dimensions of individual molecules, which range in size from only a few nanometers, to less than a single nanometer, depending upon the type of molecule. Scientists and engineers continue to conceive of new ways to perform computing using extremely small devices and individual molecules; however, no commercially available nanotechnology-scale computers currently exist.

All computers must operate by basic physical processes. Contemporary digital computers use currents and voltages in tens of millions of complementary metal oxide semiconductor (CMOS) transistors covering a few square centimeters of silicon. If device dimensions could be scaled down by a factor of 10 or even 100, then circuit functionality would increase 100 to 10,000 times.

Furthermore, if such a new device or computer architecture were to be developed, this might lead to million-fold increases in computing power. Such circuits would consume far less power per function, increasing battery life and shrinking, or even eliminating altogether, the boxes and fans that are currently necessary to cool circuits. Also, they would be remarkably fast and able to perform calculations that are not yet possible on any computer. Benefits of significantly faster computers include

* **transistor** a contraction of TRANSfer resISTOR; a semiconductor device, invented by John Bardeen (1908–1991), Walter H. Brattain (1902–1987), and William Shockley (1910–1989), which has three terminals; can be used for switching and amplifying electrical signals

* **integrated circuits** circuits with the s, resistors, and other circuit elements etched into the surface of a single chip of semiconducting material, usually silicon

Researchers working at Hewlett-Packard on nano-imprint lithograph (NIL) equipment. © *Ken James/Bloomberg via Getty Images.*

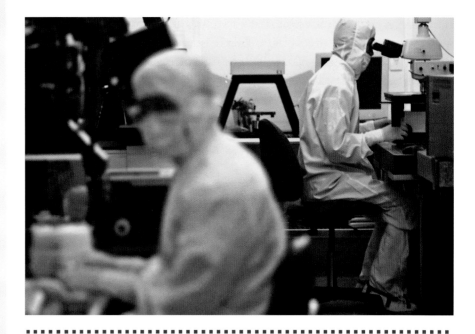

* **artificial intelligence (AI)**
a branch of computer science dealing with creating computer hardware and software to mimic the way people think and perform practical tasks

* **single-chip** a computer system that is constructed so that it contains just one integrated circuit device

* **gigabytes** units of measure equivalent to a thousand million (billion, or 10^9) bytes

* **microampere** a unit of measure of electrical current that is one-millionth (10^{-6}) amperes

* **quantum mechanical** something influenced by the set of rules that govern the energy and wave behavior of subatomic particles on the scale of sizes that are comparable to the particles themselves

more accuracy in predicting weather patterns, recognizing complex figures in images, and developing artificial intelligence (AI)*. Potentially, single-chip* memories containing thousands of gigabytes* of data will be developed, capable of holding entire libraries of books, music, or movies.

Modern transistors are engineering marvels, requiring hundreds of careful processing steps performed in ultraclean environments. Today's transistors operate with microampere* currents and only a few thousand electrons generating the signals, but as they are scaled down, fewer electrons are available to create the large voltage swings required of them. This compels scientists and engineers to seek new physical phenomena that will allow information processing to occur using other mechanisms than those currently employed for transistor action.

Future nanocomputers could be evolutionary, scaled-down versions of today's computers, working in essentially the same ways and with similar (but nanoscale) devices. Or, they may be revolutionary, being based on some new device or molecular structure not yet developed. Research on nano-devices is aimed at learning the physical properties of very small structures and then determining how these can be used to perform some kind of computing functions.

Current nanocomputing research involves the study of very small electronic devices and molecules, their fabrication, and architectures that can benefit from their inherent electrical properties. Nanostructures that have been studied include semiconductor quantum dots, single electron structures, and various molecules. Very small particles of material confine electrons in ways that large ones do not, so that the quantum mechanical* nature of the electrons becomes important.

Quantum dots behave like artificial atoms and molecules in that the electrons inside of them can have only certain values of energy, which can be used to represent logic information robustly. Another area of research is that of single electron devices, which, as the name implies, represent information by the behavior of only one, single electron. The ultimate scaled-down electronic devices are individual molecules on the size scale of a single nanometer.

Chemists can synthesize molecules easily and in large quantities; these can be made to act as switches or charge containers of almost any desirable shape and size. One molecule that has attracted considerable interest is that of the common deoxyribonucleic acid (DNA), best known from biology. Ideas for attaching smaller molecules, called functional groups, to the molecules and creating larger arrays of DNA for computing are under investigation. These are but a few of the many approaches being considered.

In addition to discovering new devices on the nanoscale, it is critically important to devise new ways to interconnect these devices for useful applications. One potential architecture is called cellular neural networks (CNN)* in which devices are connected to neighbors, and as inputs are provided at the edge, the interconnects cause a change in the devices to sweep like a wave across the array, providing an output at the other edge.

An extension of the CNN concept is that of quantum-dot cellular automata (QCA)*. This architecture uses arrangements of single electrons that communicate with each other by Coulomb repulsion over large arrays. The arrangement of electrons at the edges provides the computational output. The electron arrangements of QCA are controlled by an external clock and operate according to the rules of Boolean logic*.

Another potential architecture is that of crossbar switching in which molecules are placed at the intersections of nanometer-scale wires. These molecules provide coupling between the wires and provide computing functionality.

The fabrication of these nanoscale systems is also a critical area of investigation. Current ICs are manufactured in a parallel process in which short wavelength light exposes an entire IC in one flash, taking only a fraction of a second. Serial processes, in which each device is exposed separately, are currently too slow to expose billions of devices in a reasonable amount of time. Serial processes that are capable of attaining nanometer resolution include using beams of electrons or ions to write patterns on an IC. Atomic resolution can be achieved by using currents from very sharp tips, a process called scanning probe lithography, to write on surfaces one atom at a time, but this technique is too slow for manufacturing unless thousands of tips can be used in parallel.

It is reasonable to search for nanoscale particles, such as molecules, that do not require difficult fabrication steps. An alternative to the direct patterning of nanoscale system components is that of self-assembly, a process in which small particles or molecules arrange themselves into desirable patterns. Regardless of the method used to create arrays of nanostructures, organizing the nanodevices into useful architectures, getting

* **cellular neural networks (CNN)** a neural network topology that uses multidimensional array structures comprised of cells that work together in localized groups

* **quantum-dot cellular automata (QCA)** the theory of automata as applied to quantum dot architectures, which are a proposed approach for the development of computers at nanotechnology scales

* **Boolean logic** a system, developed by English mathematician George Boole (1815–1864), which treats abstract objects (such as sets or classes) as algebraic quantities; Boole applied his mathematical system to the study of classical logic

data in and out, and performing computing are problems that have not yet been solved.

In summary, nanocomputing technology has the potential for revolutionizing the way that computers are used. However, in order to achieve this goal, major progress in device technology, computer architectures, and IC processing must first be accomplished. It may take decades before revolutionary nanocomputing technology becomes commercially feasible.

Many organizations are researching ways to develop a nanocomputer. One of these is the NanoComputer Dream Team, a nonprofit organization dedicated to designing and making the world's first nanoscale computer. Originally spearheaded by Bill Spense, then the publisher of *Nanotechnology* magazine, this loosely based group of more than 300 computer programmers, physicists, chemists, engineers, and other scientists continues to work on ways to develop the first nanocomputer. They had hoped to unveil their nanocomputer on November 1, 2011, but as of late 2012 their goal still remained unfulfilled. According to the Whiptech.com article *Nano Computers*, "The Nanocomputer Dream Team wants to use these techniques to build an atomic computer. Such a computer, they say can then be used to control simple molecular construction machines, which can then build more complex molecular devices, ultimately giving complete control of the molecular world."

▶ *See also* **Artificial Life • Central Processing Unit • Generations, Computers • Molecular Computing • Neural Networks**

Resources

Books

Eshaghian-Wilner, Mary Mehrnoosh, ed. *Bio-Inspired and Nanoscale Integrated Computing*. Hoboken, NJ: John Wiley, 2009.

Foster, Lynn E. *Nanotechnology: Science, Innovation and Opportunity*. Upper Saddle River, NJ: Prentice Hall, 2006.

Givant, Steven R., and Paul R. Halmos. *Introduction to Boolean Algebras*. New York: Springer, 2009.

Grassian, Vicki H., ed. *Nanoscience and Nanotechnology: Environmental and Health Impacts*. Hoboken, NJ: Wiley, 2008.

Myhra, Sverre, and John C. Riviere. *Characterization of Nanostructures*. Boca Raton, FL: Taylor & Francis, 2013.

Hsu, James J. Y. *Nanocomputing: Computational Physics for Nanoscience and Nanotechnology*. Singapore: Pan Stanford, 2009.

Schmid, Günter. *Nanotechnology*. Weinheim, Germany: Wiley-VCH, 2008.

Tilstra, Luanne, and Thomas F. George. *The Science of Nanotechnology: An Introductory Text*. New York: Nova Science Publishers, 2008.

Web Sites

Science.gov, U.S. Government. "Nanotechnology." http://www.science. gov/browse/w_113P.htm (accessed October 15, 2012).

Whiptech.com. "Nano Computers." http://www.whiptech.com/ computer.future/nano.html (accessed October 15, 2012).

Newell, Allen

American Scientist and Mathematician
1927–1992

A scientist and mathematician, Allen Newell is best remembered for his work and research on artificial intelligence (AI)*. Some of his most well known initiatives include the Logic Theorem Machine, a mechanical device that would be used to create new theorems, as well as the SOAR project, a research initiative that attempted to implement cognitive or rule-based computer simulations.

Newell was born in San Francisco, California, on March 19, 1927, the son of Dr. Robert R. Newell, a distinguished professor of radiology at Stanford Medical School, and Jeanette Le Valley Newell. He attended Lowell High School—the intellectual high school of San Francisco— where he was inspired academically and fell in love (at age sixteen) with fellow student Noel McKenna. Newell and McKenna married at age twenty and remained married for forty-five years.

* **artificial intelligence (AI)**
a branch of computer science dealing with creating computer hardware and software to mimic the way people think and perform practical tasks

◀

Allen Newell (right) and Herbert A. Simon develop 'thinking machine.' © *AP Images/Courtesy of The Allen Newell and Herbert A. Simon Collections, Carnegie Mellon University Archives.*

* **pattern recognition** a process used by some artificial-intelligence systems to identify a variety of patterns, including visual patterns, information patterns buried in a noisy signal, and word patterns imbedded in text

* **axioms** statements that are taken to be true, the foundation of a theory

Newell had no intention of following a scientific career upon graduation from high school. However, after working a summer in a shipyard, he enlisted in the U.S. Navy, and it was during his tenure in the navy that he became interested in scientific enterprise. He was serving on a ship that carried scientific observers to the Bikini atoll (island) to study the effect of nuclear tests, and Newell was assigned the task of mapping the radiation distribution over the atolls. Newell discovered how exciting science could be, and thereafter, he characterized himself simply as a scientist.

Newell received his bachelor of science degree in physics from Stanford University in 1949, spent a year at Princeton doing graduate work in mathematics, and obtained a Ph.D. from Carnegie Institute of Technology (now Carnegie Mellon University) in industrial administration in 1957.

Newell's primary interest, like that of his colleague Herbert A. Simon (1916–2001), was in understanding human intelligence and cognition. He developed the SOAR project with students and colleagues, including John E. Laird, a professor at the University of Michigan, and Paul S. Rosen-bloom, a professor at the University of Southern California, and others. Essentially, SOAR was a rule-based computer simulation or emulation of a cognitive system that was capable of learning and solving problems. The rules are defined by such structures as "If … then …," similar to structures that are thought by some to govern human behavior.

Like Simon, Newell was primarily interested in organizations and their behavior, but he soon moved toward individual cognition. He and Simon had met while Newell was working for the RAND Corporation in Santa Monica, California. It was Simon who influenced Newell to come to Carnegie Tech to obtain a doctorate. Simon and Newell collaborated, and Newell continued to work for RAND in Pittsburgh, as a one-man "office" until he became part of the Carnegie Institute faculty in 1961.

Newell's interest in human learning and thinking was also spurred by Oliver Selfridge, an artificial intelligence researcher, who created theories on pattern recognition*, that is, the recognition of letters and other patterns. This led Newell to think of computing as a symbolic manipulation, rather than an arithmetic one, and led him to write a chess playing program about 1955, which was then implemented by himself, Simon, and John Clifford Shaw in 1956.

Newell also collaborated with Simon and Shaw on the Logic Theorem Machine, a program to find or develop theorems. The theorems were discovered by working backward from the theorem to the axioms* in an inductive method of discovery, looking for patterns or regularity in the data. This was an interest that would last his entire life. Newell was also a member of the initial Dartmouth conference, considered to be the first conference in artificial intelligence, along with Simon, Marvin Minsky, John McCarthy, and others.

Newell won the A. M. Turing Award with Simon in 1975. He was also the recipient of the first Award for Research Excellence from the International Joint Conference on Artificial Intelligence and was elected the first president of the American Association for Artificial Intelligence.

With Stuart Card and Thomas Moran, Newell also participated in some of the early research in Human Computer Interaction. This involved the GOMS system of Goals, Operators, Methods, and Selection, a structure for studying human behavior with the computer (and other machines, e.g., calculators) as well as the performance of any task. He also developed the mechanism, with Simon, of "talking out loud" to study the way people solve problems, and the pair was instrumental in developing means-end analysis, a way of explaining how people solve problems that is based on the theory that people notice a discrepancy between their current state and some goal state and employ some operator or operation to remove or overcome the difference.

With Shaw and Simon, Newell developed the information processing languages (IPL-I through IPL-V), which, although not as popular as LISP, were early languages for artificial intelligence. He later took a lead in the effort to develop OPS5 (and other OPS languages), a rule-based language for building artificial systems such as expert systems. His final project, ongoing after his death, was, however, the SOAR system. This was a system that purported to give an architecture of cognition, meant to explore the nature of a unified theory of cognition, a "mental" architecture.

 See also **Artificial Intelligence • Decision Support Systems • Simon, Herbert A.**

Resources

Books

Card, Stuart K., Thomas P. Moran, and Allen Newell. *The Psychology of Human-Computer Interaction*. Hillsdale, NJ: Erlbaum, 1983; reprint. Boca Raton, FL: CRC Press, 2008.

Periodicals

Rosenbloom, Paul S., John E. Laird, Allen Newell, and Robert McCarl. "A Preliminary Analysis of the Soar Architecture as a Basis for General Intelligence." *Artificial Intelligence* 47, nos. 1–3 (1991): 289–325.

Web Sites

Simon, Herbert A. *Biographical Memoirs*. Washington, DC: National Academies Press. http://www.nap.edu/readingroom/books/biomems/anewell.html (accessed November 2, 2012).

Newell and Simon

Due to Newell's long association with Herbert A. Simon, it is easy to lose track of Newell as an independent researcher. Yet, although his early career was heavily influenced and entwined with that of Simon, he conducted independent work both during and after his early association with Simon. In fact, after the 1970s and until his death, Newell mostly communicated with Simon via weekly chats, but did little direct collaboration.

* **T1 digital circuitry** a type of digital network technology that can handle separate voice and/or digital communications lines

* **analog** a quantity (often an electrical signal) that is continuous in time and amplitude

Nyquist, Harry

Swedish-born American Electrical Engineer
1889–1976

Harry Nyquist was an electrical engineer who was affiliated with AT&T from 1917 to 1954 as a researcher and inventor. His practical contributions to the computer science industry include improvements to long distance telephone circuits and picture transmission systems. His theoretical accomplishments in telecommunications laid the groundwork for T1 digital circuitry*.

Nyquist was born on February 7, 1889, in Nilsby, Sweden. His family name was originally Jonsson. His parents, Lars and Kataerina Jonsson, had problems receiving their mail in Sweden because other men in the area were also named Lars Jonsson. A common local solution to such problems was for one family to change its name; thus, his family became the Nyquists. Although they were not wealthy and education was not free, the Nyquists managed to send all eight of their children to school for at least six years. Nyquist was a promising student who was encouraged to become a teacher. Since his family could not afford the extensive education necessary for a teaching degree, Nyquist, at age fourteen, decided to emigrate to the United States. For the next four years he worked at the construction site of a chemical factory in Sweden to qualify as an employable emigrant and to earn passage money.

In 1907 Nyquist arrived in the Unites States, and by 1912 he entered the University of North Dakota. He earned a bachelor of science degree in electrical engineering two years later, and his master's in 1915. Nyquist left North Dakota for Yale University to pursue a doctorate in physics, which he completed in 1917.

Upon graduation from Yale, Nyquist went to work for AT&T, where he remained until he retired in 1954. Nyquist started in the research department of AT&T. In the mid–1920s AT&T established Bell Laboratories as a research facility for studying theoretical and practical aspects of communication. Nyquist became a researcher with Bell Labs.

At that time Nyquist worked on telegraphy problems related to linear circuits—circuits that transmit electromagnetic signals in a fashion that allows the sending of multiple messages at different frequencies at the same time and allows two signals to travel in opposite directions at the same time. His observations were that the line speed of transmission was proportional to the width of the frequencies used. Nyquist published this theory in 1924 in the paper "Certain Factors Affecting Telegraph Speed." In his 1928 publication, "Certain Topics in Telegraph Transmission Theory," Nyquist presented the principles for converting analog* signals, (i.e., voice or music) to digital signals, binary 0s and 1s, and back to, without loss of the signal's meaning.

The theorem that he offered was that a sample of twice the highest signal frequency rate captures the signal perfectly thereby making it possible to reconstruct the original signal. This work laid the foundation for many advances in telecommunications. Claude Shannon (1916–2001) incorporated this work in his development of information theory*. It was not until the transistor* was invented in 1947 that sampling, encoding, and transmitting of signals could be done fast enough to develop commercial communications systems that converted analog to digital signals. Today's T1 circuits, which carry digital signals converted from analog voice signals, are designed around the requirements of Nyquist's sampling theorem.

In addition, Nyquist expanded on J. B. Johnson's studies of thermal noise by providing a mathematical explanation which has become critically important for communications systems. His 1934 discovery of how to determine when negative feedback amplifiers are stable helped control artillery using electromechanical feedback systems during World War II.

Nyquist developed a method to transmit pictures—a crude but working facsimile (fax) machine—in which a photographic transparency was scanned, the scanned data was converted to electric signals in proportion to the intensity of shades and tones of the image, and these signals were sent over telephone lines to a photographic negative film. The film was developed using standard darkroom techniques. Today's fax machines work on the same principles.

Nyquist's thirty-seven-year career at Bell Laboratories included contributions to long distance telephone technology as well as the development of communication systems to transmit pictures. His accomplishments ranged from the theoretic to the technical and practical. In 1960 the Institute of Electrical and Electronics Engineers (IEEE) awarded Nyquist its medal of honor for significant contributions to the field of electronic engineering.

After retiring from Bell Laboratories in 1954, Nyquist served as a government consultant on military communications. He died on April 4, 1976, in Harlingen, Texas, at the age of eighty-seven.

 See also **Bandwidth • Shannon, Claude E • Telecommunications**

Resources

Books

Åström, Karl Johann. *Harry Nyquist: A Tribute to the Memory of an Outstanding Scientist.* Stockholm: Royal Swedish Academy of Engineering Sciences, 2003.

Online Privacy

Online privacy, sometimes also called on-line privacy, Internet privacy, or Web privacy, is the right of people to have their personal information safeguarded on the Internet. Such personal privacy includes the right to store information such as pin numbers or passwords on Web sites. Online

Man of Many Inventions

Nyquist was a prolific inventor. Of the 150 patents issued to him, 138 were for inventions related to telecommunications.

* **information theory** a branch of mathematics and engineering that deals with the encoding, transmission, reception, and decoding of information
* **transistor** a contraction of TRANSfer resISTOR; a semiconductor device, invented by John Bardeen, Walter Brattain, and William Shockley, which has three terminals; can be used for switching and amplifying electrical signals

privacy includes the right of people to be able to peruse Web sites without having to disclose personal information such as age, e-mail address, gender, mailing address, marital status, and other such information. It also involves being able to disclose such information to trusted Web sites under the presumption that such information will be protected and used only in appropriate ways. Such personal data can be any bit of information that identifies an individual to another individual or company.

Most professional Web-site owners possess a privacy policy that informs people about the manner in which the owner of that site discloses, gathers, uses, and otherwise manages its relationship with its customers and others accessing its Web site. It also informs people about what information is collected and whether it is kept confidential, shared with business partners, or sold to other organizations. Some important questions to ask, whose answers hopefully are included within the privacy policy, are:

- Is information collected and, if so, how much is collected?
- Is this information revealed to others for any purpose and, if so, to what specific others and for what specific purposes?
- Is this information cross-referenced in any way?
- Are people allowed to review collected information and to make modifications?
- How is this collected information secured?
- How long is this information held, and how it is deleted?

Online seal (certification) programs are used on the Web as a way to regulate privacy policies on Web sites voluntarily. These programs were created by an industry wishing to provide a safe and secure experience while being online. As part of this security program, many Web sites display privacy seals. One of the major seals is the VeriSign Secured Seal, which is provided by the VeriSign SSL Service. When accessing a Web site, the VeriSign Secured Seal may appear. To verify Web site information, visitors to a particular Web site can verify whether or not it is a VeriSign Secure Site Seal member. Other privacy seal verification organizations are GeoTrust, Trust Guard, eTrust, Webtrust, TRUSTe, and GlobalSign.

Because of the importance of online privacy, many organizations have been formed to protect personal rights on the Internet's Web. One of these organizations is The Online Privacy Alliance (OPA), whose mission is to promote self-regulatory initiatives to create an "environment of trust" to "foster the protection of individuals' privacy online and in electronic commerce." The OPA recommends several ways to maintain one's privacy on the Web:

- "Don't talk to strangers": Chat rooms and news groups generally are not secure so e-mailing people from such sites provides many people with one's e-mail address. Programs provided by such groups as ZeroKnowledge (http://www.zeroknowledge.com/) allow one to e-mail anonymously. OPA warns, "Beware of any stranger appealing to your sympathy, fear, sense of duty, vanity, laziness, lust, guilt or greed."

- ■ "Don't accept food from strangers": Cookies are small pieces of data sent from a Web site and stored in a user's Web browser so that information is available readily when browsing that site. However, cookies can be dangerous to unsuspecting users when used for deceitful purposes. Users can block cookies manually by selecting appropriate setting within a Web browser or block them automatically with such plug-ins as Taco (for Web browsers Firefox and Internet Explorer), Better Privacy (Firefox), Ghostery (Chrome, Firefox, and Internet Explorer), and CCleaner (all major browsers).

- ■ "Don't allow eavesdroppers": Use Secure Sockets Layer browsers (SSL browsers) because they scramble messages for more secure surfing of the Web. The major Web browsers support SSL, including Apple's Safari, Google's Chrome, Microsoft's Internet Explorer, and Mozilla's Firefox. They provide easy, quick ways to delete privacy concerns such as cookies, Web cache, and browsing history. In addition, a Web site that uses SSL technology will have https on its Web address rather than http, such as the Web address for the privacy seal verification organization GlobalSign: https://www.globalsign.com/.

Online privacy statements on Web sites have been often criticized for being too difficult and too lengthy to read. Although research into this subject is limited, some researchers have looked into this problem. In 2008, American researchers Aleecia McDonald and Lorrie Faith Cranor, both of Carnegie Mellon University, looked at online privacy policies. After examining many privacy statements on Web sites, they found that

FTC chairman Joe Leibowitz, with FTC commissioner, Maureen Ohlhausen, testifies on Capitol Hill before the Senate Commerce, Science and Transportation Committee hearing about protecting the privacy of online consumers. © AP Images/J. Scott Applewhite.

the shortest one was only 144 words, whereas the longest one ran about fifteen pages, or more than 7,500 words. The average size of a privacy statement, from seventy-five of the most popular Web sites in the United States, was 2,500 words. Such a statement would take an average person about ten minutes to read in its entirety. However, McDonald and Cranor found that most people ignore privacy policies. They state, "Studies show privacy policies are hard to read, read infrequently, and do not support rational decision making."

As of November 2012, the U.S. government does not regulate online privacy, including privacy statements on Web sites. The U.S. Federal Trade Commission is looking into this matter but has yet to act in any way.

Books

Currie, Stephen. *Online Privacy*. San Diego, CA: ReferencePoint Press, 2012.

Gellman, Robert, and Pam Dixon. *Online Privacy: A Reference Handbook*. Santa Barbara, CA: ABC-CLIO, 2011.

Web Sites

Masons, Pinsent. "Average Privacy Policy Takes 10 Minutes to Read, Research Finds." Out-Law.com. http://www.out-law.com/page-9490 (accessed November 7, 2012).

The New York Times. "How Privacy Vanishes Online." http://www. nytimes.com/2010/03/17/technology/17privacy.html (accessed November 7, 2012).

The New York Times. "Resisting the Online Tracking Programs." http:// www.nytimes.com/2010/11/11/technology/personaltech/11basics. html?_r=1& (accessed November 7, 2012).

P

Patents

Patents have become an important form of intellectual property* protection for computer software and informational media, supplementing and sometimes replacing copyright protection. Patents are exclusive rights granted by the federal government to the inventors of new and useful machines, articles, substances, or processes. The patent right is offered in return for full disclosure by inventors as to how to make and use their patented invention.

The holder of a patent has the right to prevent others from making, using, selling, offering to sell, or importing the invention, and he or she can sue for damages if any of these exclusive rights is violated. However, because the patent right is extensive and nearly absolute, patents are granted only for very significant advances in technology: the invention cannot have been obvious to those of skill in that technology.

As a consequence, unlike other forms of intellectual property protection, such as copyrights* and trademark rights*, patent rights do not arise spontaneously. In the United States, patents are only issued after an administrative application procedure in the United States Patent and Trademark Office (USPTO). The inventor must submit an application that fully describes and explains the invention as well as sets out the limits of technology being claimed. This description will form the basis for the published patent once the application is approved. If the patent is granted, a full description of the invention and its use is published by the government in the patent. These published patent disclosures form a fund of knowledge for the public.

In the United States, the term of the exclusive right lasts for twenty years from the earliest claimed filing date, and at the end of the patent term, the invention passes into the public domain; that is, anyone may freely use it. Should the USPTO grant a patent improperly, the patent may be invalidated by a challenge in court.

As in the case of most intellectual property, including copyright and trademarks, there is no such thing as a worldwide patent. Successful applications to the USPTO will result in a patent that is good only in the United States. If inventors desire patent protection in other countries, then in general they must apply for a patent in the patent office of each country where a patent is wanted. However, there are certain exceptions to the general rule of having to apply for a patent in each individual nation. For instance, the European Patent Convention (EPC) is a treaty among many European nations that allows a patent applicant to file and

* **intellectual property** the acknowledgement that an individual's creativity and innovation can be owned in the same way as physical property

* **copyrights** the legal rules and regulations concerning the copying and redistribution of documents

* **trademark rights** a trademark is a name, symbol, or phrase that identifies a trading organization and is owned by that organization

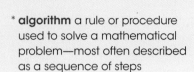

* **algorithm** a rule or procedure used to solve a mathematical problem—most often described as a sequence of steps

prosecute (i.e., pursue) his patent in just one national patent office and in one language (such as English, French, or German); and even though a patent will eventually have to be translated into various European languages, EPC rules allow deferral of the cost of those translations until the time that the patent is actually granted (which could be several years). The patent applicant may also choose to file the patent claim in the European Patent Office (EPO).

The expense of having to file many patent applications in many different countries may be prohibitive, so inventors must frequently be selective as to the countries in which they wish to apply. The countries in which an inventor chooses to apply will be determined by long-range business plans; usually, inventors will choose to apply for patents in the countries where they are most likely to license their inventions.

Because patent law covers processes, and computer software constitutes a type of process, patent law might seem a natural form of intellectual property protection for software inventions. However, software and related inventions were nearly excluded from patent protection altogether. Patent protection does not extend to natural "discoveries," as it does to manufactured inventions. Thus, laws of nature and mathematical formulae are typically not considered patentable.

During the early 1980s, the U.S. Supreme Court issued two opinions denying patent protection to computer programs on the grounds that a software algorithm* is like a mathematical formula, and therefore unpatentable. The court soon modified this position to hold that computer programs are not patentable by themselves, but only in association with a tangible machine or tangible output. During the next twenty years, this position gradually evolved in lower courts to a position that software would be patentable if it produced a "useful result."

The United States Patent Office began routinely accepting patent applications claiming software inventions first as new and useful processes, or as articles of manufacture when associated with some hardware or tangible media. This acceptance of software as patentable subject matter resulted in the explosive proliferation of software patents during the 1990s and 2000s, both in the United States and abroad.

The acceptance of software patents by U.S. courts opened the door to widespread patenting of other types of processes or methods related to digital media. Because the standard for patentability is a "useful result," many processes involving computers now come under patent protection. Such processes need not be internal to the computer's operation, but may involve activity and interface with the user. Such patentable processes might include Web-based methods for instruction, electronic commerce, and informational display. Some of these method patents have been controversial because critics view them as being too obvious to deserve patent protection.

In an effort to coordinate disparate, national intellectual property laws, the World Trade Organization (WTO) administers the Agreement on Trade Related Aspects of Intellectual Property Rights (TRIPS). The WTO is an international organization that regulates trade among member states. TRIPS went into effect in 1996. All WTO members must agree to adopt and enforce TRIPS as a condition of WTO membership. As of late 2012, the WTO had 157 member states.

Under TRIPS, nations must issue patents to inventions that meet certain requirements for patentability, and governments must issue patents for a term of at least twenty years. TRIPS also forbids favoring local citizens and showing unreasonable prejudice to computer software or patent rights holders. TRIPS requires that protections for computer programs fall under the copyright protections provided to literary works, including rights arising upon creation and terms of at least the life of the author plus fifty years.

In 2011, the USPTO issued a total of 247,713 patents. In 2011, the USPTO granted the greatest number of patents to IBM (6,148 U.S. patents), Samsung (4,868), and Canon (2,818). 2011 was the nineteenth year in a row that IBM held the number one spot for U.S. patents issued by the USPTO. Software patents have become and increasingly large percentage of the patents issued by the USPTO, even though U.S. patent laws do not specifically address software patents. Since 2000, software patents litigation has greatly increased largely because of patent trolls—individuals or companies that buy, often vague or overly general, patents for the purpose of suing alleged infringers. Consequently, many technology innovators and analysts claim that the software patent system in the United States is broken and stifles creativity and product development.

▶ See also **Copyright**

Resources

Books

Mueller, Janice M. *Patent Law*. 3rd ed. New York: Wolters Kluwer Law, 2009.

Feldman, Robin. *Rethinking Patent Law*. Cambridge, MA: Harvard University Press, 2012.

Photography

The digital imaging technologies commonly used today evolved from technologies created by the National Aeronautics and Space Administration (NASA) and the Jet Propulsion Laboratory (JPL) in the early 1960s. Government scientists were looking for a way to transmit imaging data more accurately from outer space to Earth. The analog

Trade Secrets vs. Patent Protection

An alternative to patent protection is trade secrecy protection. Trade secrets can include software, databases, or any type of valuable information that is not generally known but which gives the owner a business advantage. The owner of a trade secret must take reasonable steps to keep the information confidential, such as locking away important documents, or passwords protecting computer files. The law prevents competitors from obtaining trade secrets through theft, bribery, espionage, or hiring away a business' employees. Competitors are permitted to discover independently a trade secret through their own efforts, or to reverse engineer a trade secret by examining a product in order to learn how it works. Employees of technology firms are frequently required to sign confidentiality agreements promising to keep their employers' valuable information secret.

* **degradation** the reduction in quality or performance of a system

* **topographic** pertaining to the features of a terrain or surface

* **silver halide** a photosensitive product that has been used in traditional cameras to record an image

* **pixel** a single picture element on a video screen; one of the individual dots making up a picture on a video screen or digital image

(wave) technologies used at the time were prone to degradation* during transmission. The scientists devised a way to digitize the images taken by satellites and rocket mounted cameras. By turning the analog transmission into a digital code, the scientists solved the problems of image degradation. The imaging data could be sent long distances without a loss of quality, thus rendering a more accurate view of distant galactic sights.

The newly invented digital technologies were too expensive for the general public, but they were commonly used by governments, scientists, and corporations for topographic*, atmospheric, military, medical, and astronomic purposes. The invention of the microchip, a small yet powerful processor, in the early 1980s enabled the creation of smaller, more affordable digital imaging equipment and the personal computer for the home and small business. The first commercial digital camera appeared in 1981 with the release of the Sony Mavica.

Most digital cameras look similar to and share many common functions of 35 millimeter (mm) cameras. Digital cameras have lenses, bodies, and flashes along with controls for focus and zoom like traditional cameras. Several manufacturers created a digital back that integrated existing analog cameras with the new digital technologies. Digital backs are mounted onto the back of analog cameras. The sensory mechanism of the digital back takes the place of the film and fits into position on the same plane as the film.

Unlike their film-based predecessors, digital cameras use disks instead of film for storage, and they often have controls for image playback, in-camera special effects, and image editing. These special digital controls enable the photographer to access the picture instantly and decide upon the quality of the image. Then, the image can be saved or deleted. These editing functions are enabled by the digital camera's memory (or random-access memory, shortened to RAM).

The most fundamental difference between digital and analog photography is the way an image is captured. Film-based photographic systems use light sensitive materials, usually a silver halide*, to record physically the impression of light bouncing off a subject. A digital camera converts the light bouncing off the subject into a mathematical model that can be read and reconstructed to approximate the original scene.

An image is transformed from analog to digital in the camera using an electronic grid of chips that sense, map, and quantify light. The information from the grid is then sent and converted to digital code by processors. The digital camera's lens projects an analog image onto the grid, and each small square of the grid records the intensity, color, and location of the light. The unit of measure for digital pieces of information is a pixel*. The color information is established using three filters: red, green, and blue. The camera does not sense color; it measures the gradations of intensity between the three filters. The processor then converts the information into a code. The light striking each is given a numeric value: 0 for true black through 255 for true white. The numeric value then becomes part of the binary number system* (bit code), a code of 0s and 1s eight bits long. This code is what a computer reads, processes, and reconstructs as a photographic image.

The large file size of digital images often makes them hard to process and transmit. To reduce the file size, digital camera images are often converted and stored as JPEG (Joint Photographic Experts Group)* files. JPEGs are a standardized, compressed file type. Through compression and standardization, file sizes are reduced and made more convenient to store and transmit. They are also formatted in a uniform way that makes digital imaging with personal computers more feasible.

Digital cameras for personal use are made with a wide range of features, prices, and sizes. For all of them, the term resolution is often used to indicate the quality of produced images. The image sensor, what is usually a charge-coupled device (CCD) or complementary metal–oxide–semiconductor (CMOS) sensor chip, helps to provide the amount of resolution in such cameras. These chips contain pixels (short for picture elements; or the smallest physical points that control an image produced by cameras and other such devices) that sense photons (elementary light particles) when they hit the sensor. Thus, the more pixels a camera contains (for the most part), the better the resolution that will result for the images taken. However, resolution is also determined by lens quality, sensor size, and other important considerations. Pixel count often is used to indicate the number of pixels used to create an image. For instance, a 640x480 image would have 307,200 pixels (just multiply the two numbers), or about 307 kilopixels (KP, where kilo stands for one thousands pixels). Digital cameras used by amateur photographers, as of 2012, go up to about 17.8 megapixels (MP, where mega represents one million pixels), whereas professional photographers may use digital cameras that go up to 80.1 MP. For instance, the Nikon COOLPIX L810 digital camera is classed at 16.1 MP.

The proliferation of digital photography is tied to advances in personal computers and business applications. Many people have taken up digital photography because of the expansion of affordable personal computers into the home. A computer set up for digital imaging often includes a color monitor, a color printer, a disk drive (compatible with the camera's), a program for image editing, a negative scanner, and a flatbed scanner.

Flatbed scanners have a flat glass bed where an image can be placed, scanned, digitized, and opened in a computer program. The scanner contains a laser-equipped carriage; the laser goes over the length of the bed, scanning the image line by line. The laser beam then reflects information back to the sensors, which convert the information much like a digital camera. A negative scanner works similarly but comes with a guide for the insertion of negatives and transparencies. A drum scanner is used for high quality, professional scanning. With drum scanners the image is placed

* **binary number system** a number system in which each place represents a power of 2 larger than the place on its right (base-2)

* **JPEG (Joint Photographic Experts Group)** organization that developed a standard for encoding image data in a compressed format to save space

Getting Started

In addition to advertising its products on the Internet, Shutterfly, once a product called Kodak Gallery by the Eastman Kodak Company, also offers instructional guides to beginning digital photographers. Topics include "Tips from Our Expert" and "Secrets to Enduring Travel Photos."

---

* **interpolation** estimating data values between known points but the values in between are not and are therefore estimated

inside a cylinder that rotates at high speeds while the laser tracks across the image.

Scanners come with software for limited editing in the scanning phase. The image scanned can commonly be adjusted for scale, media, contrast, and color balance. The scanned image is then usually opened in a more sophisticated program. The measure of scanner quality is the bit depth. Digital imaging software uses interpolation* to scale images. Interpolation is a method for resampling images to adjust scale. The intensity and value of a group of pixels is established, then that group of pixels is transformed into one pixel with an average value. Extreme shifts in the scale of digital images can result in the loss of image quality; over-can create blurry, jagged, or pixilated images.

Once loaded on the computer's storage drive, and opened in an image editing program, digital photographs become easily manageable. Images can be edited, montaged, distorted, or completely fabricated while retaining the believability of traditional photographs. Many image-editing programs enable the user to adjust the scale, color balance, contrast, and levels of an image. More complicated programs allow the user to manipulate the image further by adding special effects, filters, and text, copying and pasting other images, painting and drawing, and converting file types. The most common editing program is Adobe PhotoShop, which has become the standard in publishing, design, and academia. Once digital images are edited with the computer, they can be printed, sent via e-mail attachment, opened in other programs, or used to create Web pages.

 See also **Art • Desktop Publishing • Fashion Design • Journalism • World Wide Web**

Resources

Books

Bucher, Chris. *Teach Yourself Visually Digital Photography.* 4th ed. Indianapolis: Wiley, 2010.

Simon, Steve. *The Passionate Photographer: Ten Steps toward Becoming Great.* Berkeley, CA: New Riders, 2012.

Wignall, Jeff. *Focus on Digital Photography Basics.* New York: Lark Books, 2010.

Web Sites

Photography.com. "Digital Photography: History and Tips." http://www.photography.com/articles/digital-photography/digital-photography/ (accessed October 17, 2012).

Shutterfly.com. "Who We Are." http://www.shutterfly.com/learn/index.jsp (accessed October 17, 2012).

Political Applications

Computers have revolutionized the manner in which the political process is conducted in at least four areas: (1) computerization of political information; (2) international communication and communication between politicians and their constituencies; (3) political data processing; and (4) political events simulation.

Computerization of Political Information

The computerization of political information is linked to the computerization of libraries, as well as various private and public archives; and to the dissemination via the Internet of documents published by governments, non-profit organizations, and special interest "think tanks." Computers enable users to seek books and articles in periodicals, newspapers, and websites on any given political subject. Through these resources, the general public can stay informed about local, regional, state, national, and global political issues.

The Internet has had a significant impact on the degree of political information available to the general public. Prior to the advent of the Internet, political document archives were not easily accessible to ordinary citizens. Now, many websites allow people to peruse documents acquired via the Freedom of Information Act (FOIA)*. Current documents are often available through the Internet immediately after they have been issued. In addition, most politically oriented non-profit organizations and think tanks have websites featuring their reports on a wide variety of political. These Internet resources enhance the democratic process because they offer all citizens the opportunity to become much more knowledgeable about a wide range of political issues.

* **Freedom of Information Act (FOIA)** permits individuals to gain access to records and documents that are in the possession of the government

◀

Chinese delegates use a touchscreen computer to surf the National People's Congress (NPC) Web site in Beijing. © *AP Images/NG HAN GUAN.*

Politics and Computerized Communication

Widespread computer use affects the direct communication of political messages as well. Political campaigns now rely on computerized mailing lists, campaign Web sites, blogs, social media, and Internet media exposure to disseminate information on issues, organize volunteers, and many other uses. Education of voters and the promotion of ideas and mutual understanding take place through e-mail, text messaging, and social media sites such as Facebook and Twitter. Computerization even is responsible for improving the quality of presentation at public political discussions through the use of computer-generated slides, charts, graphs, maps, and other print and video materials.

Direct Mail Political campaigns have long used direct mail to communicate with potential voters. The purpose of direct mailing is to influence opinion or solicit donations. Computers allow for the use of mailing lists and the production of letters that are targeted to specific constituent interests. This is accomplished by creating databases based on personal characteristics such as the recipients' place of residence, financial status, religion, political affiliation, race, gender, educational background, ethnicity, and sexual orientation.

The Internet The Internet has become one of the primary tools for political campaigns to promote their message. Almost all elected officials have official government and campaign websites. Computers have made politicians more accessible by allowing their constituents to communicate with their elected officials via e-mail or social media. Even the informal structures of the Internet, including social media and message boards, have become part of the political process of promoting ideas and encouraging mutual understanding. For example, people from different countries that engage in discussions about mutually important issues, such as war or trade issues, may be more likely to understand opposing viewpoints on important geopolitical issues.

In this age of nearly instant communication, politicians have to be wary that every public comment or quip they utter can be recorded on audio or video, and then almost instantly uploaded to a website, from whence people around the country and the world can view the clip. For instance, in the 2006 U.S. senatorial campaign, Republican incumbent George Allen (1952–) was recorded on video uttering the term "macaca"—which some people consider to be a pejorative term—towards a person of Indian descent. The person at whom the remark was aimed worked for Allen's rival, Jim Webb (1946–). The video of the incident was available not only on television, but could be viewed online as well at Web sites such as YouTube. Many political analysts believe that the negative publicity associated with Allen's remarks played a decisive role in his defeat to Webb in the fall 2006 general election.

During the 2008 presidential campaign, candidate Barack Obama received negative publicity over his comments that many small-town people in the Midwest "cling to guns, or religion, or antipathy towards people who aren't like them; or anti-immigrant sentiment, or anti-trade sentiment …." The comments were recorded at a fundraiser and disseminated through the Internet and mainstream media. During the 2012 presidential election campaign, candidate Mitt Romney stated that 47 percent of the American electorate "are dependent upon government, who believe that they are victims, who believe that government has a responsibility to care for them, who believe that they are entitled to health care, to food, to housing, to you-name-it." Romney continued to say that 47 percent of Americans do not pay income tax. Romney's comments were surreptitiously recorded at a fundraiser and widely circulated over social media and the Internet.

Finally, British Prime Minister Gordon Brown, while campaigning in the 2010 election cycle, was caught on audio (while in his car) stating that a woman he had just encountered was a "bigoted woman." At the time, Mr. Brown was unaware that his comments were being recorded. The ensuing flap caused by his remarks later led to an apology on his part to the woman he had denigrated; Gordon Brown ultimately resigned as prime minister of Great Britain after the May 2010 parliamentary elections. All of these controversial recordings are currently available on the Internet for public review, and probably always will be. These examples show how careful politicians must now be in the Internet age, because even off-the-cuff or "private" comments can potentially be recorded and make their way online; and sometimes such controversial remarks can cause great harm to their careers.

Political Materials Political presentation materials, whether print or electronic, have been influenced by computerization as well. Television and Internet coverage of political discussions—debates between candidates, for example—require sleek visual presentations. Software tools, including desktop publishing and video presentation programs, help politicians present their views in attractive formats.

Political Data Processing

Political data processing includes the outlining of voting districts; the statistical analysis of polling results, voting results, and census results; voting and vote counting; and campaign-related data processing.

District Boundaries Non-partisan computer models are available to help with the logistical outlining of voting districts. Some computer models attempt to create an equally proportioned electorate in each district. Other models use the organization of districts on existing legislative boundaries and then connect them to other districts to achieve population parity. Although different software models take political logistics into consideration at varying degrees, all of them must recognize political boundaries such as towns and counties and geographical boundaries such as mountains and bodies of water.

* **punched card** a paper card with punched holes which give instructions to a computer in order to encode program instructions and data

Polling and Statistical Analysis Many companies conduct polls on various political topics and analyze their results. In most cases their predictions are quite accurate. The results of public opinion polls and questionnaires help politicians determine how to react to the information learned through polls. Candidates may change aspects of their campaigns depending upon perceived strengths and weaknesses that may be defined geographically or demographically. Using computerized statistical models, strategists also can identify issues that may influence voters with particular political allegiances or those who are considered "independent" or "undecided."

The Internet provides an ideal medium for polling, especially from the perspective of access to potential respondents. It is inexpensive when compared with other methods, so more and more polls are conducted online. Their results are widely used in numerous political campaigns, although methodology and accuracy rates vary widely.

Since the 1952 presidential elections, computers have been used to perform a statistical analysis that uses a small sampling to predict the outcome of an election. Television networks and the Internet have increasingly used computers to project election outcomes, although inaccurate early predictions following the presidential election of 2000 caused elected officials and media representatives to consider whether or not the desire to publicize early outcome predictions can skew the election process itself.

The computerized statistical analysis of census results started with punched cards* more than a hundred years ago and has moved on to using modern computer technology. Census analysis is important for politicians because it can show demographic trends.

Voting and Vote Counting Computerized vote counting is common throughout the United States. Computerized votes are often tallied from cards on which voters fill in an oval or a square with a pen or pencil to represent their vote. Computerized voting machines are also available.

Internet technologies have become sophisticated enough that they can be used in the voting process, allowing people to vote online rather than in polling booths. During the 2012 U.S. election, at least 32 states and the District of Columbia allowed military or overseas voters to submit ballots via email, secure Internet portals, or fax machines. Before online voting will become widespread in the United States, however, certain technological precautions will be needed to establish a voter's identity and prevent election fraud.

Campaign Administration Computer programs are also useful to politicians from an administrative perspective. They are useful in campaign scheduling and in calculating the distribution and allocation of funds.

Political Event Simulation

The simulation of political events is being done using both deterministic models and artificial intelligence (AI)*. A deterministic model usually consists of a set of differential equations. The solutions of these equations supposedly mimic the development of real-life political events. AI is a branch of programming that attempts to emulate reasoning and perception exercised by human beings. Many mathematical methods are used to produce this emulation.

An example of using AI to model political events is an expert system*. At the creation of such a system, political experts are interviewed. Based on the results of these interviews, a set of rules is established. This set constitutes a computerized model. The model can be applied to the evaluation of a new political situation. Whether deterministic models or artificial intelligence are used, simulation results should be interpreted with caution. However, it is a nice tool to have to analyze some of the possible outcomes of a political event.

 See also **Babbage, Charles • Government Funding, Research • Internet • National Aeronautics and Space Administration (NASA)**

Resources

Books

Herrnson, Paul S., et al. *Voting Technology: The Not-So-Simple Act of Casting a Ballot.* Washington, D.C.: Brookings Institution Press, 2008.

The Hanging Chad

Punched cards and the ability of tabulating machines to record accurate voting results came into question during the 2000 U.S. presidential election, which ultimately saw Vice President Al Gore lose to Texas Governor George W. Bush. The race came down to which candidate would secure the electoral votes in Florida. The race was so close that people's attention turned to those stacks of ballots that were not counted because the voter failed to punch through the holes on the card cleanly. Such failed punches were called a "hanging chad" or a "pregnant chad." Efforts were made to review punched cards manually and see if a determination could be made regarding the voters' intent. Ultimately, the problems associated with hanging chads led some election officials to consider alternative voting methods, including computer touch-screen ballots.

* **artificial intelligence (AI)** a branch of computer science dealing with creating computer hardware and software to mimic the way people think and perform practical tasks

* **expert system** a computer system that uses a collection of rules to exhibit behavior which mimics the behavior of a human expert in some area

RS

Routing

Computer networks allow messages to be exchanged between computers in different parts of the world. These messages may contain e-mails, requests for web pages, or the contents of a Web page. When traveling from the source computer to the destination computer, messages typically pass through a number of other computers on the network. Routing is the function of choosing which computers a message should pass through on its way from source to destination. Some computers in the network, called routers, exist only to route messages onward in the network. Routing must be performed in large networks such as the Internet as well as in smaller networks such as within a university.

When a message is received from the network, the computer that receives the message—unless it is the intended recipient—must perform a routing action. Routing the message means choosing which of the connected computers should receive the forwarded message.

Each message includes the address of its intended destination, and this address is used to choose the route of the message. To route a message, the computer does not need to know anything about where the destination computer is. It merely needs to know in which direction to send the message. This is similar to the way addresses are used on normal letters. If U.S. Postal Service workers receive a letter for someone in France, they will probably not know anything about the exact location of the person that is to receive the letter. Despite this, the U.S. Postal Service can still route the letter by simply forwarding the letter to France. Then the French postal network takes care of routing the letter to its final destination.

In a global network such as the Internet, there are many possible routes for a message to take between a source and destination computer. The overwhelming number of possibilities makes routing messages very complicated. Also, the structure of the network is not fixed; computers or connections may be temporarily unavailable, in which case a route must be chosen to bypass the unavailable part of the network.

It is best to route the messages as directly as possible. One option is to choose the route so that the message passes through the minimum number of computers on its way from its source to destination. It is also possible to take into account other factors, such as the speed of the connections between computers on the route. By choosing a route with faster connections, the message will reach its destination faster, even though it may pass through more computers on its way. Another factor to consider

Routing before Y2k. © *AP Images/ALAN KLEIN.*

* **algorithm** a rule or procedure used to solve a mathematical problem—most often described as a sequence of steps

when routing is the current state of the network. If parts of the network become overloaded, then messages routed through these parts of the network will suffer delays. Routing messages around the overloaded parts of the network will speed up the delivery of the messages and avoid adding to an already overloaded network.

Static Routing

The simplest approach to routing is static routing. In this case each computer on the network has a fixed routing table. When a message is received, the computer checks the address of the message against the routing table and then forwards the message to whichever computer is indicated by the routing table. The routing table may include alternative entries to deal with the case where part of the network is currently unavailable.

Static routing requires very little processing power, which is considered an advantage. However, this simple solution has the disadvantage that it cannot adapt to current situations in the network. For example, parts of the network may become overloaded if too many messages are being transmitted. With static routing, no change will be made to the routing algorithm* to take into account the overloading. It is possible to adapt to such an overload situation and route messages away from the overloaded part of the network with what is known as dynamic routing.

Dynamic Routing

In the simplest form of dynamic routing, each computer can adapt its routing based on its current situation. Thus, none of the computers knows about the overall state of the network; each computer adapts its routing

* **queue** the ordering of elements or objects such that they are processed in turn; first-in, first-out

based solely on its own situation. Messages are put in a queue* before being transmitted. If the for a connection grows too big, this indicates that the connection is becoming overloaded. The computer can adapt its routing to avoid, where possible, the connections with large queues. This approach allows the computer to balance the load on its connections but the computer has no knowledge of the state of the rest of the network. Therefore, although the computer can prevent its own outgoing connections from becoming overloaded, it may still be sending messages to overloaded parts of the network.

A second form of dynamic routing is where computers share information about their current state with each other. This gives each computer a better understanding of the overall situation in the network so it can route messages away from overloaded parts of the network. One approach is for each computer to send information about the state of its connections to all directly-connected computers. Each computer combines the incoming status information with its own current state to generate status messages, which are then sent to connected computers. This allows each computer to build up a picture of which parts of the network are overloaded, allowing it to route messages away from the overloaded parts of the network. With this solution, it is critical to find a balance between sending too many status messages, which themselves may cause overloading, and too few status messages, in which case the network may adapt too slowly to an overload situation.

The choice of routing strategy will depend on the network. Static routing may be suitable for small local networks, but for a large global network, such as the Internet, dynamic routing is necessary to avoid overloading parts of the network.

▶ *See also* **Asynchronous Transfer Mode (ATM)** • **Bandwidth** • **Network Design** • **Networks**

Resources

Books

Chao, H. Jonathan, and Bin Liu. *High Performance Switches and Routers.* Hoboken, NJ: Wiley-Interscience, 2007.

Perlman, Radia. *Interconnections: Bridges, Routers, Switches, and Internetworking Protocols.* Reading, MA: Addison Wesley, 2000.

Comer, Douglas E. *Computer Networks and Internets.* 5th ed. Upper Saddle River, NJ: Prentice Hall, 2008.

Medhi, Deepankar, and Karthikeyan Ramasamy. *Network Routing: Algorithms, Protocols, and Architectures.* The Morgan Kaufmann series in networking. Amsterdam: Elsevier/Morgan Kaufmann Publishers, 2007.

* **spider** a computer program that travels the Internet to locate Web documents and FTP resources, then indexes the documents in a database, which are then searched using software that the search engine provides

* **hyperlinks** connections between electronic documents that permit automatic browsing transfer at the point of the link

Google is the the world's most popular search engine. © *David Paul Morris/ Bloomberg via Getty Images.*

▼

Search Engines

A search engine is an information retrieval system that allows someone to search the vast collection of resources on the Internet and the World Wide Web. All major search engines are similar: the users enters keywords, phrases, or (in some instances) questions in a search form. After clicking on the search command button, the database returns a collection of links (hyperlinks) to resources that contain the search terms. These hyperlinks are listed in some sort of order, usually from most relevant to least relevant, or by how important the Web pages are, depending on the search engine used. Search engines are composed of computer programs that create databases automatically. They should not be confused with human-built directories, such as Yahoo!, which depend on people for development and maintenance.

Search Engine Basics

Search engines have three components. The first part is a computer program called a *spider* or *robot,* which gathers information on the Internet. The spider* retrieves hyperlinks attached to documents. It starts with an existing database and follows the existing hyperlinks* to gather new

and updated resources to add to the list. If a Web page does not contain hyperlinks to other Web pages, the search engine can look for meta tags, or pieces of coded added to Web sites that help search engines find and categorize them. Other types of resources that ordinary spiders are unable to locate include files that are not written in Hypertext Markup Language (HTML)*, and from specialized databases that require the user to fill out a search form. Spiders automatically do this gathering of documents at intervals that differ from service to service.

Second, resources collected by the spider are loaded into a database that indexes them using a formula that is unique to each. The index contains a copy of every Web page the spider finds. People can also submit Web pages to this database in case the spider either fails to access it quickly enough, or if there are no links on the pages. While most search engines claim to index the entire World Wide Web, none actually do. Although spiders have many different ways of collecting information from Web pages, the major search engines claim to index the entire text of each Web document in their databases. This is called full-text indexing*. Some search engines may not index common words such as: and, a, I, to. These are called *stop words.*

The third part of the search engine is software that allows users to enter keywords in search forms using some type of *search expression,* with syntax* that is supported by the search engine. The search results are then listed in order according to a ranking algorithm*. Some search engines list results by *relevancy,* while others list them by how many Web pages link to them, thereby showing the most important, or popular, Web pages first, and others group results together by subject. Many search engines employ a combination of these.

Search engine optimization (SEO), the optimizing of Web sites to be found and highly ranked by search engines so that a link to the site will appear in the at the top of search engine results, has become an important business advertising strategy. Companies and individuals can manipulate keywords, meta tagging, and hyperlinks within a site to cause it rise in search engine rankings. Similarly, some search engines now allow for paid advertising by way of highlighting links or making them feature prominently in searches. On Google, such sponsored links appear at the top or to the side of the search results page with a different colored background to differentiate them from natural search results.

Search Features

It is important to understand the different search features available before beginning to use a search engine as each engine has its own way of interpreting and manipulating search expressions. Because a search can retrieve many documents, it is common to have a number of hits, but only a few that are relevant to the query submitted. This is called low precision/ high recall*. On the other hand, a searcher may be satisfied with having very precise search results, even if a very small set of hits is returned.

* **Hypertext Markup Language (HTML)** an encoding scheme for text data that uses special tags in the text to signify properties to the viewing program (browser) like links to other documents or document parts

* **full-text indexing** a search engine feature in which every word in a document, significant or insignificant, is indexed and retrievable through a search

* **syntax** a set of rules that a computing language incorporates regarding structure, punctuation, and formatting

* **algorithm** a rule or procedure used to solve a mathematical problem—most often described as a sequence of steps

* **low precision/high recall** a phenomenon that occurs during a search when a large set of results are retrieved, including many relevant and irrelevant documents

* **high precision/low recall** a phenomenon that occurs when a search yields a small set of hits; although each one may be highly relevant to the search topic, some relevant documents are missed

* **high precision/high recall** a phenomenon that occurs during a search when all the relevant documents are retrieved with no unwanted ones

* **field searching** a strategy in which a search is limited to a particular field; in a search engine, a search may be limited to a particular domain name or date, narrowing the scope of searchable items and helping to eliminate the chance of retrieving irrelevant data

This is defined as high precision/low recall*. Ideally, the search engine would retrieve all of the relevant documents that are needed. This would be described as high precision/high recall*. Search engines support many search features, though not all engines support each one. If they do support certain features, they may use different syntax in expressing them. Before using a search feature, the user should always check the search engine's help pages to understand how the feature is expressed, if it is supported at all. Some examples of search syntax and features used by search engines are: Boolean operators (and, or, not), implied Boolean operators (+ and −), phrase searching, natural language searching, proximity searching, truncation, and field searching*.

Types of Search Engines

Search engines can be divided into three basic types: general or major search engines, meta-search engines, and specialty search engines. Each of the major search engines attempts to do the same thing—index as much of the Web as possible—so they handle a huge amount of data. Due to this tremendous amount of information, documents of little useful content may be picked up, making the use of ranking schemes important. In most first-generation search engines, such as AltaVista and HotBot, results were ranked by *relevancy*. Relevancy is determined by algorithms that usually count how many times the keywords typed in the search form appear in the documents that exist in the database. Second-generation tools such as Google use ranking algorithms that employ techniques such as grouping and sorting results, importance or popularity of Web sites, and human judgment from prior searches. *Meta-search engines* are tools that search more than one search engine or directory at once, compiling the results and consolidating them into an overall list.

Examples of meta-search engines are Metacrawler, Dogpile, and Search.com. One drawback of meta-search engines is that they do not include all of the search engines possible, and they are unpredictable in how they handle complex searches. They can be useful for obscure searches.

Specialty search engines, or specialized databases, are search tools that focus on particular subjects, or types of file format (e.g. images or music files). These databases can be time savers because their databases are much smaller and focused on a particular subject area, or type of resource. For example, if a certain legal opinion is needed, a searcher may achieve greater success with FindLaw (http://www.findlaw.com) rather than spending the time in a major search engine looking through perhaps hundreds of results.

Difficulties and Benefits of Major Search Engines

Search engines send their spiders to crawl the Web periodically, so without additional features, searches may variably return recently-added and current material. For example, Google compiles recent additions to news

Web sites and media outlets under its Google News search. Google's specialty searches enable users to search for images or items from online stores as well as filter search results based on language or within a local area. Google also has integrated its search engine, mail, maps, and social media services into a unified online user interface.

Some content cannot be gathered by ordinary search engine spiders. Content such as some types of dynamically generated Web pages, pages that contain no hyperlinks, pages not cataloged in any directory, and certain file types can remain part of the Web that is hidden from the major search engines. This is referred to as the *invisible Web.*

Another difficulty is that information found in major search engines is that the ultimate responsibility is placed upon the individual to evaluate what is found. Many general or major search engines, realizing the added benefit of human-managed information, include *directories* such as the Open Directory Project, in conjunction with the computerized indexes. The usefulness of being able to search for obscure topics, multi-faceted subjects, specific Web pages and sites, in addition to information from specific dates, languages, news stories, images, and more, makes search engines necessary tools for the searcher to learn and use.

Popular English and Multi-Language Search Engines

Some of the most popular search engines include:

- Bing. http://bing.com
- Google. http://www.google.com
- MetaCrawler. http://www.metacrawler.com
- Search.com. http://www.search.com
- Yahoo! http://yahoo.com

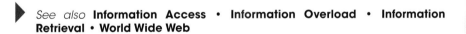

See also **Information Access** • **Information Overload** • **Information Retrieval** • **World Wide Web**

Resources

Books

Levy, Steven. *In The Plex: How Google Thinks, Works, and Shapes Our Lives.* New York: Simon & Schuster, 2011.

Web Sites

How Stuff Works. "How Internet Search Engines Work." http://computer.howstuffworks.com/internet/basics/search-engine.htm (accessed November 1, 2012).

Search Engine Watch. http://searchenginewatch.com (accessed November 1, 2012).

Boolean Operators

Boolean operators help expand or narrow the scope of a search. A search for rivers OR lakes returns documents with either word in them. A search for rivers AND lakes returns documents with both words in them. A search for rivers AND lakes NOT swamps returns documents that mention both rivers and lakes but omits those that also mention swamps. Implied Boolean Operators are characters such as + and −, which can be used to require or prohibit a word or phrase as part of a search expression. The + acts somewhat like AND, and the − acts as NOT would in a Boolean expression. For example, the Boolean expression rivers AND lakes NOT swamps may be expressed as +rivers +lakes −swamps.

Directories

A directory is a topical list of Internet resources, arranged hierarchically. Directories differ from search engines in one major way—the human element is involved in collecting and updating the information included.

* **telegraph** a communication channel that uses cables to convey encoded low bandwidth electrical signals

* **deregulation** the lowering of restrictions, rules, or regulations pertaining to an activity or operation (often commercial)

Service Providers

Communications service providers provide people with the means to communicate with one another by telephone, mobile phone, and Internet. Telecommunications service providers also make available cable or satellite access for television, computer, and wi-fi connectivity. Service providers are constantly trying to locate and build solutions that will tie organizations and individuals together no matter what their locations.

Early Telecommunications Service Providers

The first identifiable telecommunications service provider was the telegraph* office of the late 1800s. Telegraph offices typically were owned or operated by the U.S. federal government in conjunction with local and state authorities. They provided the first end-to-end connectivity of wiring to enable instantaneous communication between two distant points. These simple offices created the foundation for modern day commercial telecommunication organizations.

One of the most notable service providers, Bell Telephone Company, dominated American communications for decades. This organization became the leader in wiring the country with telephone service and providing dial tone, call connectivity, phone services (e.g., call accounting and consolidated billing), telephone equipment, and simple yet expensive connectivity for a large number of private corporations that were starving for connectivity to tie their slowly evolving information technology infrastructures together. Bell Telephone remained dominant until its final breakup in 1980. The U.S. government had determined that the company maintained a monopoly on the telecommunications industry, obstructing competition and innovation.

Deregulation of Telecommunications

The breakup of Bell Telephone was a first step in opening the industry to competition for all telecommunications systems of the United States, but there was still work to be done. By 1995, despite government intervention, there were still a finite number of service providers trying to compete in a heavily regulated industry. However, the type and number of innovations needed to propel the world into the twenty-first century were emerging far too slowly to handle the needs of the customers and the organizations they operated. At that time, the Internet was ready to explode in popularity, and the speed of connectivity was an issue and concern that slowed its deployment. Without further deregulation*, the telecommunications infrastructure did not respond quickly enough to the demands for change.

The U.S. Telecommunications Acts of 1995 and 1996 were designed to address this concern. These acts have set the stage for the continuing technology revolution still being experienced today. The acts opened up new avenues of competition and innovation within traditionally regulated telecommunication markets. It quickly became possible to purchase bandwidth*, or the speed of connectivity, from the lowest-cost provider despite customer location. The only limitation was that remote or rural areas of the country did not have the cabling infrastructure* to tie it all together, but that changed as the cost of running cable drastically dropped. The wide adoption of fiber optics* as a medium to transfer data is making it possible for even the most remote schools and communities to become connected to the global digital world. Advances in satellite communication have provided more options for telecommunications connectivity in remote areas. Furthermore, emerging technologies such as 4G LTE cellular data networks and WiMax wireless networks enable mobile connectivity and reduce the reliance on traditional infrastructure.

Types of Service Providers

There are many service providers of varying types. There are the traditional Internet Service Providers (ISPs)* that provide basic access to the Internet and traditional telecommunication providers fighting with large multinational companies for access to local telephone customers in order to provide them with their needed long distance and local telephone service. Tier 1 service providers provide uplinks* for smaller ISPs, providing local high speed digital subscriber line (DSL)* service or cable modem service to residential and small business customers.

There are Application Service Providers (ASPs) that are connected to the T1/E1 telecommunications carriers. The ASPs provide colocation* services for Web sites, Web-enabled application servers, and managed private networking for telecommuters who need to be connected to their corporate employers' networks. There are storage service providers, also known as cloud providers, who provide online-accessible e-storage to corporations and individuals. This list grows almost as fast as the imaginations of the entrepreneurs behind this revolution.

Economic Realities

As a result of deregulation, companies that thought they could provide these types of complex services, and perhaps had an ingenious twist on how to provide it, could enter the market; these efforts met with varying degrees of success. In the stock rush of 1999 and 2000, even technology-driven dreamers with only a mediocre idea could obtain funding. Often it was a requirement to take more money than was needed. The monies were handed out by profit-driven venture capitalists who rushed into a strong stock market hoping to create mind-boggling degrees of wealth overnight.

Many of the venture capitalists and their well-funded entrepreneurs succeeded; however, many core business principles that helped to build traditional, solid companies of the 1980s and 1990s were overlooked in the effort to join the technology bandwagon quickly. In the stock market struggles that began at the end of 2000, most of the poor financial performance was linked with failures of the dot.coms*, but the telecommunications industry was partially to blame. This period of poor market

* **bandwidth** a measure of the frequency component of a signal or the capacity of a communication channel to carry signals

* **infrastructure** the foundation or permanent installation necessary for a structure or system to operate

* **fiber optics** transmission technology using long, thin strands of glass fiber; internal reflections in the fiber assure that light entering one end is transmitted to the other end with only small losses in intensity; used widely in transmitting digital information

* **Internet Service Providers (ISPs)** commercial enterprises which offer paying subscribers access to the Internet for a fee

* **uplinks** connections from a client machine to a large network; frequently used when information is being sent to a communications satellite

* **digital subscriber line (DSL)** a technology that permits high-speed voice and data communications over public telephone networks; it requires the use of a DSL modem

* **colocation** the placement of multiple computer servers and networking equipment in a central location, typically for lease

* **dot.com** a common term used to describe an Internet-based commercial company or organization

performance and business failures in the tech industry became known as the "dot-com bubble" or "dot.bomb."

Casualties included several DSL providers that offered connectivity to hundreds of thousands of customers and businesses. The customers, once connected, were dependent on the DSL provider and susceptible to connection interruptions or infrastructure collapses. Unfortunately, several large DSL providers in the market failed. The companies providing service often carried tremendous debt and needed to experience continued growth in order to cover payments and expenses. Some of these companies disappeared virtually overnight, leaving their customers scrambling to find ways to reconnect their business-essential and home-use communication lines. Technological advances also undermined DSL providers, as faster and easier connections became available through coaxial cable providers (many of whom also deliver cable television services).

As the telecommunications industry moves forward, new options are becoming available that will change the way people do business and interact with their environments. Fiber-optic, cable, and wireless has expanded to cover almost all areas. Many individuals have come to rely on more than one service provider and technology for daily communications and access to the Internet. For example, a person may use one service provider for home telephone service, another for home wi-fi, and yet another for a mobile smartphone. More home residences are moving from traditional landline telephones to mobile devices: In 2011, more than one in four U.S. households relied only on mobile phones. Other households have replaced traditional phone lines with voice over Internet Protocol (VoIP) communications. Many VoIP providers, such ISPs and Skype, allow individuals to use either traditional-looking phones, Internet-enabled smartphones, tablets, or computers for communication.

Service Providers in the Future

Visionary entrepreneurs will develop ways to increase speed and push the costs of connectivity lower than they are now. These new service providers will make every effort to combine the best of all of the previous providers, providing unparalleled layers and levels of connectivity. Telecommunications service providers, having evolved from telegraph systems to wireless systems throughout the years, continue to be the core of the telecommunications revolution.

▶ *See also* **Internet** • **Internet: Backbone** • **Telecommunications** • **World Wide Web**

Resources

Books

Anderson, Michael R. *Deploying Wireless Internet Service Providers (WISPs)*. Oxford: Newnes, 2008.

Grant, August E. and Jennifer H. Meadows, eds. *Communication Technology Update and Fundamentals*, 12th ed. Amsterdam and Boston: Focal Press/Elsevier, 2010.

Rainer, R. Kelly. *Introduction to Information Systems*. 4th ed. Hoboken, NJ: Wiley, 2012.

Vanberg, Margit. *Competition and Cooperation among Internet Service Providers: A Network Economic Analysis*. Baden-Baden, Germany: Nomos, 2009.

* **information theory** a branch of mathematics and engineering that deals with the encoding, transmission, reception, and decoding of information

Shannon, Claude E.
American Mathematician and Electrical Engineer
1916–2001

An American mathematician and electrical engineer, Claude E. Shannon has been called the father of information theory*. His early work had a significant impact on the early development of digital computer technology, and later in the twentieth century, his theories about communication contributed to the rapid evolution of telecommunications capabilities.

Shannon was born in Gaylord, Michigan, on April 30, 1916. As a child, he became interested in engineering and problem solving. These

Dr. Claude E. Shannon and his electronic "mouse," 1952. © *Keystone/ Getty Images*.

* **Boolean algebra** a system developed by George Boole that deals with the theorems of undefined symbols and axioms concerning those symbols

* **vacuum tube** an electronic device constructed of a sealed glass tube containing metal elements in a vacuum; used to control electrical signals

characteristics were revealed in such pastimes as the creation of a fully functioning telegraph system between his home and that of a friend who lived a half-mile away. In the fall of 1932, Shannon entered the University of Michigan, intending to major in electrical engineering. During his undergraduate years, he developed a keen interest in mathematics as well. In 1936 he completed his bachelor's degree with majors in both subjects.

Shortly after graduation, Shannon accepted a job at the Massachusetts Institute of Technology (MIT), where he earned two master's degrees, one in mathematics and one in electrical engineering, as well as a doctorate in mathematics. In this first job, Shannon worked with an early analog computer built by Vannevar Bush, who was also the vice president of MIT. The machine, called a differential analyzer, was a mechanical system based on electrical relay circuits. Shannon applied the principles of Boolean algebra* and symbolic logic, which he studied as an undergraduate, to the problem of describing the way the differential analyzer's relay circuits worked.

In 1937 Shannon submitted a master's thesis on the subject. Titled "A Symbolic Analysis of Relay and Switching Circuits," the paper has been called "one of the most influential master's theses ever written," because in it, Shannon laid the logical foundation for building digital circuitry. All contemporary computer systems are based on Shannon's symbolic explanation of the behavior of relay circuits.

By 1940 Shannon had completed his graduate studies at MIT and joined Bell Laboratories as a researcher studying the electronic transmission of information. During World War II, Shannon's energies were directed toward the interception and transmission of codes and other military applications of electronic technologies that were being developed to assist in the war effort. He became acquainted with Alan Turing, a British pioneer of computer technology, and others whose work would contribute to the mid-twentieth century evolution of the computer as a business tool.

Shannon's interest in understanding the electronic communication of information led him to focus on this subject in his research. In 1949 he issued *The Mathematical Theory of Communication,* a work that formed the foundation for the field of inquiry known as information theory. Shannon proposed that data could be broken into small components called "bits" to be transmitted electronically. The ideas Shannon proposed found their application during the last quarter of the twentieth century when telecommunications technology had advanced enough to demonstrate aspects of Shannon's theory that could not be supported by the technology of vacuum tubes*. Shannon's information theory continues to shape the development of electronic communications media, from consumer products such as compact disks and home computers to business and scientific endeavors including the exploration of outer space with unmanned vehicles.

In the 1950s Shannon explored the frontiers of artificial intelligence (AI)*, building chess-playing computers and a maze-running mechanical mouse. He was convinced that computers could be designed and programmed to function in ways similar to the human brain. By the late 1950s Shannon was teaching at MIT in addition to conducting research at the Bell Labs. From 1958 to 1978, he served full-time as MIT's Donner Professor of Science. He won many awards during his career as an academic, and he directly influenced a generation of electrical engineers involved in the cutting edge of computer development.

After his retirement in 1978, Shannon continued to invent gadgets and explore emerging applications of electronic technology. In addition to lecturing and publishing occasionally, he enjoyed mastering early computer games like Pac-Man, and indulged his interest in inventing by creating such contraptions as a two-seated unicycle. In fact, he was known to have mastered the skill of riding a unicycle, which was a gift from his wife, while juggling multiple objects.

Shannon married Mary Elizabeth Moore, a Bell Labs co-worker, in 1949. Together they eventually raised three children. Shannon died on February 24, 2001, following a long struggle with Alzheimer's disease.

Although Claude Shannon is not a household name, his life's work influences people worldwide daily through technology that is commonplace today, including fax machines, Internet instant messaging, and satellite, radio or television transmissions. Although his original ideas predated the technical ability to implement them, the mathematical theories he used to describe the hypothetical dissemination of information through digital electronic means are at the foundation of virtually every form of modern digital communications technology.

 See also **Bandwidth • Bell Labs • Internet • Telecommunications**

Resources

Periodicals

"Computing before Silicon." *Technology Review* 103, no. 3 (May/June 2000): 120.

Web Sites

"Biography of Claude Elwood Shannon." AT&T Research. http://www.research.att.com/~njas/doc/shannonbio.html (accessed November 2, 2012).

Calderbank, Robert, and Neil J. A. Stone. "Claude Shannon 1916–2001." AT&T Shannon Research and Technology Center. http://www.research.att.com/~njas/doc/ces5.html (accessed November 2, 2012).

* **artificial intelligence (AI)** a branch of computer science dealing with creating computer hardware and software to mimic the way people think and perform practical tasks

* **artificial intelligence (AI)** a branch of computer science dealing with creating computer hardware and software to mimic the way people think and perform practical tasks

Simon, Herbert A.
American Professor of Computer Science and Psychology
1916–2001

Herbert A. Simon combined the study of social and behavioral science with the disciplines of mathematics, physics, and economics in a career that included a longtime focus on the science of decision-making in organizations. Of particular note is his analysis of decision-making and problem-solving, but he was also interested in artificial intelligence (AI)* and the use of the computer to study intelligence and cognition, both in problem-solving, such as the discovery of theorems, and in game playing, such as chess.

Simon was born in Milwaukee, Wisconsin, on June 15, 1916. His father was an electrical engineer and his mother an accomplished pianist. He enrolled at the University of Chicago in 1933 and graduated in 1936 with a degree in political science. He received his doctorate through the University of Chicago in 1943 while heading a research group at the University of California, Berkeley, between 1939 and 1942. He taught at the Illinois Institute of Technology from 1942 to 1949, and he engaged in research with colleagues at the University of Chicago and the Cowles Commission for Research in Economics. His next professional post was at the Carnegie Institute of Technology (now Carnegie Mellon University), where he helped build the Graduate School of Industrial Administration.

Simon's career in Pittsburgh as an academic, researcher, and author spanned more than fifty years. He was well respected by colleagues and students. He believed that the approach of the "hard" sciences, such as physics and mathematics, could be applied to the behavioral sciences, both in economics and political science, his first field of study, and the behavioral sciences, primarily psychology and cognitive science.

Drs. Herbert Simon (left) and Allen Newell, pioneers in artificial intelligence. © *Time & Life Pictures/Getty Images.*

One of Simon's earliest books, published in 1947, was *Administrative Behavior*. The book was an expansion of his doctoral dissertation, which began his studies of rationality. Later publications include *Models of Man* (1957), *The Sciences of the Artificial* (1969), *Human Problem Solving*, with Allen Newell (1972), and *Models of Discovery* (1977), among others. In 1991 he published an autobiography, *Models of My Life*.

Simon firmly believed that the computer could and should aid in the study of human cognition and, ultimately, that what the computer could do in terms of cognition was "think." He considered the computer to be a laboratory for epistemology, the study of knowledge or truth, as well as a tool for investigating the human mind. In 1954 Simon began using computers to model problem-solving.

Simon developed what he termed the theory of "satisficing," that is, the making of decisions on the basis of a satisfactory rather than optimal (absolute best) solution. This is a technique familiar to anyone who has done even such a routine task as develop a schedule of college courses for a term. One must make choices that meet certain requirements for one's degree, balancing other factors such as personal preferences for times of classes, subjects one is interested in, distance to and from classes, and cost to create a satisfactory, albeit possibly imperfect, schedule.

Simon studied "bounded rationality," the theory of making rational decisions under constraints such as a lack of knowledge, computational difficulty, and personal and social circumstances. The decisions are rational, but not in the sense of an all-knowing, infallible optimizer. This leads to finding acceptable, but not necessarily optimal, solutions to problems.

From 1966 until his death on February 9, 2001, Simon was Richard King Mellon University Professor of Computer Science and Psychology. He won the Nobel Prize in Economics in 1978 for "pioneering research into the decision-making process within economic organizations." He was awarded the National Medal of Science in 1986 and the A.M. Turing Award by the Association of Computing Machinery (ACM) in 1975, with Allen Newell (1927–1992). He collaborated with Newell and Clifford Shaw to write a computer program, the Logic Theorist, or the Logic Theorem Machine, designed to find logical proofs. Together, the three also collaborated on a software program designed to play chess as a human, not an expert. He was involved in several computer projects to study human cognition and form models of human learning, problem solving, and "thinking" using computer programs.

▶ *See also* **Artificial Intelligence • Chess Playing • Decision Support Systems • Newell, Allen**

Resources

Books

Newell, Allen, and Herbert A. Simon. *Human Problem Solving*. Englewood Cliffs, NJ: Prentice-Hall, 1972.

A Prediction Ahead of Its Time

In 1957 Herbert Simon predicted that a computer would beat a grand master in chess in ten years. Although, as he noted, he was off by a factor of 4 (40 years), he did correctly anticipate this potential complexity of computing technology, if not the timeframe within which it would be achieved.

* **Supercomputers** very high performance computers, usually comprised of many processors and used for modeling and simulation of complex phenomena, like meteorology

Simon, Herbert A. *Models of My Life*. New York: Basic Books, 1991; reprint. Cambridge, MA: MIT Press, 1996.

Web Sites

Simon, Herbert A. *Autobiography*. Nobelprize.org. http://www.nobelprize.org/nobel_prizes/economics/laureates/1978/simon-autobio.html (accessed November 2, 2012).

Social Impact

Computing technologies, like most other forms of technology, are not socially neutral. They affect, and are themselves affected, by society. Computers have changed the way people relate to one another and their living environment, as well as how humans organize their work, their communities, and their time. Society, in turn, has influenced the development of computers through the needs people have for processing information. The study of these relationships has come to be known as "social informatics."

Computing technology has evolved as a means of solving specific problems in human society. The earliest kinds of computational devices were the mechanical calculators developed by Blaise Pascal (1623–1662) in 1645 and Gottfried Leibniz (1646–1716) in 1694 for solving the navigational and scientific problems that began to arise as Europe entered a new and heightened period of scientific development and international commerce. In 1801 Joseph-Marie Jacquard (1752–1834) invented perhaps the first type of programmed machine, called Jacquard's Loom, in order to automate the weaving of cloth with patterns. Jacquard was motivated by the desire of capitalists in the early Industrial Age who wanted to reduce the cost of producing their goods through mass production in factories.

The twentieth century saw the development of scientific research and engineering applications that required increasingly complex computations. Urgent military needs created by World War II spurred the development of the first electronic computers; the devices in use today are the descendants of these room-sized early efforts to streamline military planning and calculation. The needs and desires of society have subsequently influenced the development of a vast array of computing technologies, including supercomputers*, graphics processors, games, digital video and audio, mobile computing devices, and telephones.

In the twenty-first century, computers are used in almost every facet of society, including (but not limited to) agriculture, architecture, art, commerce and global trade, communication, education, governance, law, music, politics, science, transportation, and writing. In general, computing technologies have been applied to almost every situation falling into one of two categories. The first category covers applications that require the organization, storage, and retrieval of large amounts of information such as library catalogs or bank records. The second category includes applications that require the coordination of complex processes, such as the control of machinery involved in the manufacture of cars or the printing of books and newspapers.

Impact of Computers on Work

One of the ways that computers have made an impact on society is in how people have organized themselves in workplace groups in relationship to computers. The earliest computers were developed to perform specific tasks in science, engineering, or warfare that had previously been done by hand. Soon general-purpose computers could automate almost any information processing task required to manage an organization, such as payroll processing and record management. However, since early-generation computers were relatively expensive, all of an organization's information processing tasks were typically centralized around the one large computer it could afford. Departments and people in such organizations would likewise be organized in a centralized fashion to facilitate their access to the computer. Companies with centralized information processing, for example, usually had most of their administrative offices in the same geographic location as their computer resources.

Subsequent developments in computing technology changed the way companies organized people who perform similar tasks. The advent of computer networking and lower cost minicomputers* enabled entire organizations that were once centralized around a single computer to rearrange themselves into geographically dispersed divisions. The integration of telecommunications with computing allowed people in remote places such as branch offices to use computers located in distant parts of their organization. This decentralization continued with the advent of the personal computer. PCs provided a low-cost way for large organizations to transform themselves further by redistributing information processing responsibilities to small departments and individuals in many locations.

Not only have computers changed the way in which workplaces structure their tasks and workers, they have also dramatically changed the work itself. Computer-aided manufacturing (CAM) was first introduced in the 1950s with numerically controlled machines. These and other forms of computer-based automation have been associated with the loss of jobs and certain skills, and the need to master new skills. Since the middle of the twentieth century, computer-controlled devices have gradually eliminated certain types of jobs and the need for people to perform particular skills. As a consequence, workers have had to learn new skills in order to continue working in environments that increasingly depend on computers.

One major result has been the shift of some economies, such as that of the United States, from manufacturing to service jobs. Entirely new categories of jobs have been created to support and implement computer technology. In addition, the ease of networking computers has led

* **minicomputers** computers midway in size between a desktop computer and a mainframe computer; most modern desktops are much more powerful than the older minicomputers

businesses to relocate jobs to remote locations. For example, a number of companies now hire computer programmers who are located in other countries, such as India, in order to save on labor costs. Within the United States, increasing numbers of companies allow employees to work from their homes or work centers away from the corporate headquarters. These so-called telecommuters are able to communicate with their employers and deliver their work using the Internet.

The advent of e-mail, the World Wide Web, and other Internet technologies has perhaps made the most significant impact on the social fabric of American society. People can now communicate with others in remote places, and can do so easily, affordably, and often anonymously. They can search for, share, and transfer more information, and more quickly, than ever before. People separated by long distances can nevertheless organize themselves into "virtual communities" based on shared interests, regardless of their geographic locations. The Internet has also changed the way both education and entertainment can be delivered into private homes and public spaces.

Effects of the Computer Age

Psychologists have long been interested in observing and analyzing the way humans interact with computers. Research in human-computer interaction has studied how people read and process information presented to them on computer screens, the types of input errors people are most likely to make when using different computer systems, and the effectiveness of various kinds of input devices such as keyboards, mice, trackpads, and light pens. Psychological issues have also been identified in how people behave toward other people when they use computing technologies such as e-mail and how they behave toward computers. Studies have shown, for example, that people use the anonymity that e-mail and other Internet technologies afford to construct alternate identities for themselves. Other studies indicate that people often apply the same rules of social behavior, such as politeness, toward computers as they would to other people.

The impact of computers on lifestyles has largely paralleled the impact of computing on social organization, work, and personal communication. The effect has become more pronounced as personal computing devices become increasingly more commonplace in American society. In particular, computers coupled with telecommunications technologies enable many people to live and work more independently and remotely than ever before. Individuals using personal computers can publish books, make airline reservations, and hold meetings to share information with any number of people across the globe. Some observers view these developments positively, while others are concerned that the widespread use of computers has led to lifestyles that contain increasing amounts of work.

Social Networking Web Sites

Social networking Web sites have become a very popular means of social interaction. People using such Web sites typically create a profile of themselves, which includes personal information that they wish to share.

The user also usually lists various social links, such as friends, clubs, and other social groups to which they belong, lists of their favorite music or Web sites, and so forth. Users can interact with one another in a variety of ways. Besides using the social networking Web site to post messages, pictures, and thoughts, they can also use e-mail, Web-based instant messaging, cell phone talk and text messaging, and real-time video through use of a webcam. Participation in such social networking services can bring personal rewards, including greater social interactions, new romantic opportunities, and career and educational benefits. There can of course be negative effects as well, such as those involving user privacy, online intimidation (or cyberbullying), and excessive time devoted to online interactions to the detriment of other activities.

As of November 2012, Facebook, with more than one billion registered users, reigned as the most popular social media site—and second most popular Web site overall in the world. Micro-blogging site Twitter and the Chinese social media Web site Qzone are the next most popular social media sites with more than 500 million users each. Most social media sites have applications that run on smartphones and tablet computers, which have become an increasingly popular method for users to connect to social media sites.

 See also **E-Commerce • Embedded Technology (Ubiquitous Computing) • Ethics • Human Factors: User Interfaces • Internet • Jacquard's Loom | Privacy**

Resources

Books

Kizza, Joseph Migga. *Ethical and Social Issues in the Information Age.* 4th ed. London: Springer-Verlag, 2010.

Qualman, Erik. *Socialnomics: How Social Media Transforms the Way We Live and Work*, revised ed. Hoboken, NJ: Wiley, 2011.

Social Informatics

Social informatics is a multidisciplinary field of study that examines the social and organizational roles and impacts of information and communication technologies. It examines many issues, including: impacts of computerization on work, the usefulness and usability of computer hardware and software, security and privacy, law, information needs and uses, and technological risks.

TUV

TCP/IP

How do computer networks operate and why has the Internet been successful? A large part of the answer to both of these questions is what is known as the Transmission Control Protocol/Internet Protocol (TCP/IP) suite of computer communication protocols*, usually referred to by their acronym TCP/IP. As late as the mid–1980s, there were many islands of computer networks that could not communicate with each other. These networks were limited in size and speed, and the technologies on which they were based used closed proprietary standards, meaning that they could not communicate with each other. TCP/IP has changed everything; what exists now is a fast, worldwide, and single network based on open standards: the Internet.

TCP/IP is the defining interoperability protocol for connecting computers to one another upon which the Internet is built. The creators of the TCP/IP protocol suite recognized that the task of communications is too complex and too diverse to be accomplished by a single layer. Thus, the functionality required for network interoperability is divided into separate layers that depend on each other.

The Transmission Control Protocol (TCP) and the Internet Protocol (IP) are the two primary protocols of this layered suite, at the transport and network layers respectively. The TCP protocol is implemented in end computer systems at the edge of the network while the IP protocol is implemented in intermediate network devices within the core of the network. Together, TCP/IP provides an end-to-end architecture for the Internet based on the principle that intelligence should be placed in end computer system applications, while the network should remain as simple as possible given the broad range of possible applications that the network might support. Many have credited the TCP/IP end-to-end architecture with subsequent Internet innovations, including the World Wide Web (commonly shortened to simply the Web), because new applications can be easily implemented in an end computer system without the need to change the network infrastructure.

* **protocol** an agreed understanding for the sub-operations that make up a transaction, usually found in the specification of inter-computer communications

Protocols

A communications protocol is an agreement that specifies a common set of language (semantics), grammar (syntax), and timing (synchronization) for the exchange of information between computers. TCP is a communications protocol, not a piece of software; there are many different software

packet-switching an operation used in digital communications systems whereby packets (collections) of data are dispatched to receivers based on addresses contained in the packets

algorithm a rule or procedure used to solve a mathematical problem—most often described as a sequence of steps

implementations of the TCP protocol but only one TCP protocol itself, which has endured despite many challenges. TCP is a connection-oriented protocol that specifies the format of the data and reciprocal acknowledgments that any two computers must exchange to achieve a reliable transfer. TCP identifies a connection by a pair of endpoints. Each endpoint consists of an identifier in the format *IP number, TCP port number*. Thus, a given TCP port number can be shared by multiple connections. TCP assumes little about its underlying communication system, so it can be used with a large variety of packet-switching* systems including the Internet Protocol.

Within the Internet, the basic unit of data is an IP packet and the basic mechanism of transfer is packet-switching. Routing refers to the algorithm* for choosing a path over which to send packets. A computer with multiple network connections (a router) examines the IP address field within the packet header and matches it to a table (IP routing table). Conceptually, three possible things could happen: (1) a match is made in the routing table and the packet is sent out to the specified router interface where it may be delayed behind other packets; (2) no match is made in the routing table so the packet is sent out via the default router interface where it may be delayed behind other packets; or (3) the router is so loaded down that packets have nowhere to go (match or no match) and thus the packet is lost (bit bucket).

IP routing is referred to as an unreliable (packets may be lost, duplicated, delayed, or delivered out-of-sequence), best-effort (not guaranteed due to varying levels of Internet traffic), or connectionless (each packet is handled independently) packet-delivery system. However, TCP matched with IP makes the Internet reliable. All computers that connect to the Internet run IP software and most of them also run TCP software. TCP handles the problems IP does not handle without duplicating the work IP does well. In fact, it is because TCP and IP work together so well that the entire set of protocols that the Internet uses is known as the TCP/IP protocol suite. That they work together is not a coincidence. In 1974, American computer scientists Vinton Cerf (1943–) and Robert Kahn (1938–) designed TCP and IP to work together simultaneously and to complement each other. The original TCP/IP protocol suite was based on successful software implementations in the Advanced Research Projects Agency Network (ARPANET), Packet Radio, and Packet Satellite networks so there was never any question of it not working as intended.

TCP/IP as a Standard

Open system standards like TCP/IP provide the agreed upon rules for communication between computers, independent of any vendor's proprietary product. TCP/IP was adopted as a U.S. Department of Defense (DoD) standard in 1980. The interoperability of the TCP/IP standard has allowed applications to be built at higher layers of abstraction without being burdened by the details of individual, lower-layer implementations.

ARPA Roots of TCP/IP and the Internet

TCP/IP is the direct result of protocol research and development conducted on experimental packet-switched networks. In the 1970s the U.S. Department of Defense (DoD) Advanced Research Projects Agency (ARPA) funded three separate grants to implement TCP/IP, which led to three independent implementations within a short time. This is important because independent implementations are a basic requirement for an Internet standard. At the same time, ARPA funded a project to develop a portable operating system, which eventually converged with UNIX. The University of California-Berkeley released an especially popular version of this ARPA-funded UNIX (Berkeley Software Distribution; sometimes alternately known as BSD UNIX, or as Berkeley UNIX) which also incorporated TCP/IP. Because its development was publicly funded, it was freely available. As universities found that they had TCP/IP functionality at their disposal via BSD UNIX, many began to form regional networks that eventually converged into the one large network that is now known as the Internet.

 See also **Babbage, Charles • Government Funding: Research • Internet • National Aeronautics and Space Administration (NASA)**

Resources

Books

Casad, Joe. *Sams Teach Yourself TCP/IP in 24 Hours.* Sams Publishing, 2012.

Comer, Douglas E. *The Internet Book: Everything You Need to Know about Computer Networking and How the Internet Works.* 4th ed. Upper Saddle River, NJ: Prentice Hall, 2007.

Loshin, Peter. *TCP/IP Clearly Explained.* 4th ed. Amsterdam and Boston: Morgan Kaufmann Publishers, 2003.

Seth, Sameer, and M. Ajakumar Venkatesulu. *TCP/IP Architecture, Design and Implementation in Linux.* Hoboken, NJ: Wiley, 2008.

Stevens, W. Richard, and Kevin R. Fall. *TCP/IP Illustrated.* 2nd ed. Upper Saddle River, NJ: Addison-Wesley, 2012.

Periodical

Cerf, Vinton G., and Robert E. Kahn. "A Protocol for Packet Network Interconnection." *IEEE Transactions on Communication Technology* COM-22 (1974): 627–641.

TCP/IP and the Internet

The glue that holds the Internet together is TCP/IP. Once the U.S. Department of Defense mandated the use of TCP/IP, vendors began to incorporate it into their products. With the release of the World Wide Web application in the 1990s, TCP/IP connectivity brought graphical Web pages into the homes and businesses of millions worldwide. TCP/IP connectivity has now become a commodity service offered by internet service providers (ISPs).

* **interface** a boundary or border
between two or more objects or
systems; also a point of access

* **bandwidth** a measure of the
frequency component of a
signal or the capacity of a
communication channel to carry
signals

* **broadband access** a term
given to denote high bandwidth
services

* **translational bridges** special
network devices that convert
low-level protocols from one type
to another

* **graphical user interface
(GUI)** an interface that allows
computers to be operated
through pictures (icons) and
mouse-clicks, rather than
through text and typing

Web Sites

Department of Computer Science, University of Texas. "A Technical History of TCP/IP." http://www.cs.utexas.edu/users/chris/think/ Early_Days_Of_TCP/index.shtml (accessed October 24, 2012).

President George W. Bush, the White House. "Dr. Vinton Cerf and Dr. Robert Kahn: Medal of Freedom Recipients." http:// georgewbush-whitehouse.archives.gov/government/cerf-kahn-bio.html (accessed October 24, 2012).

Telnet

Telnet was officially adopted as a widely accepted computer communications protocol in May 1983. It was created and implemented to allow servers and PCs to communicate through the creation of a widely deployed communication interface* where commands that were issued by the host computer were sent across a link as simple, clear text. Communication links of the time were typically very slow. The servers receiving the telnet transmission would execute the commands, summarize the results, and transmit them back across the same slow link to the host.

In the early days of computer networking, bandwidth* was afforded only at a premium. Its deployment was difficult, which required specialized skills. Telnet was able to minimize the impact and cost associated with this problem. Telnet allowed network managers to control devices remotely, and to run some simple applications across what could be hundreds or even thousands of miles without consuming all on the network, or access points.

Even today, with the advent of broadband access*, telnet has its place as a tool to be exploited in controlling one's digital assets. At the heart of all major and medium sized networks, one will likely find a router designed to join different networks together. These devices are provided an address so that all devices in the network for communication between the network and or the Internet can reach them. This address can also be reached via telnet. This simple fact makes telnet a very powerful protocol that can be used to troubleshoot, configure, and deploy new equipment on a network. In fact, telnet remains a useful tool for the managing of equipment on many networks. However, by the beginning of the 2010s telnet had largely been superseded by other network protocols for the purpose of remote login.

Telnet Concerns

All switches, routers, and translational bridges* built by such companies as Cisco, Ericsson, Extreme Networks, and so on, come with a Command Line Interface (CLI). The CLI is a text-driven interface that is very obscure; it can be quite intimidating for first time users as they attempt to manage and configure a device. This is in stark contrast to a graphical user interface (GUI)* that is intuitive and simple to use. The downside of a GUI is that it can often saturate a wide area link, and consume all available bandwidth, thus causing bottlenecks for users that can cost a great deal of money. The CLI is still widely used, however, and it is the perfect fit for managing a device or series of devices. Unfortunately, this method does not scale well for management because telnet can access only one device at a time. Thus, in a network of several hundred devices, the CLI with telnet access would not be a manageable condition, and would require a more robust management application to handle such a sizeable network.

There are other concerns about using the telnet protocol; for one, it is not secure. Text transferred to and from server devices and hosts is typically clear text. Even passwords for configuration of major devices are submitted across the wire unencrypted. This creates a serious management problem. When deploying the telnet protocol, a company's network manager must take care to secure unencrypted data from users outside the company network, as well as from internal employees, with whom the majority of all security violations originate. Typically, the best line of defense is to not allow the protocol to traverse the networks, thus making it impossible to breach the system with telnet. However, this results in the inability to utilize telnet for network configuration and management, which forces the purchase of expensive management applications. The decision to deploy or not to deploy telnet is a complicated management choice.

FTP

The File Transfer Protocol (FTP) was developed around the same time as telnet, and allowed for succinct transfer of files between servers and hosts and for the deployment of early remote storage solutions. This was particularly welcome in the early days of the Internet because bandwidth was at a premium. FTP would address this limitation and allow data to be transferred more efficiently.

Early implementers were also delighted with the option for remote storage of data because personal computer (PC) storage capabilities remained limited while user needs were growing. FTP and its usage are based on a simple command line utility. In addition, because FTP was a standard, it guaranteed that dissimilar systems and networks could interact with reasonable robustness and little variance in configuration.

FTP is continues to be used widely in the early twenty-first century. Any user who gets an account with an Internet service provider (ISP) will likely be supplied space for a personal Web site. To access this secured space, the user typically will utilize an FTP program for the downloading and uploading of HyperText Markup Language (HTML) pages and graphical content for the Web site. An example of an a GUI-based FTP application called CuteFTP. CuteFTP is a free shareware* application that can be downloaded from many sites on the Internet. Developed by Globalscape, the free software is supplemented, as of 2012, with products that users can purchase, such as CuteFTP Pro and CuteFTP Home for PCs, and CuteFTP Mac Pro for Apple computers.

* **shareware** a software distribution technique, whereby the author shares copies of his programs at no cost, in the expectation that users will later pay a fee of some sort

Net Congestion

FTP is also used in most of the world's major Web sites and it can cause system usage congestion. The once-unregulated Napster music service, which facilitated free downloads of copyrighted music, provides an example of this. (Napster was forced to shut down its Web site in 2001 after being ordered by a court injunction to stop trading copyrighted music. After going through bankruptcy, it merged with online music store Rhapsody in 2011.) The massive downloads of music files, such as by Napster, were done typically via FTP. This created a problem for many organizations. FTP is meant to alleviate bandwidth usage limitations, but left unto itself it will consume whatever bandwidth is available. When employees of corporations spent hours downloading music from Napster, they were taxing corporate networks that were already carrying heavy data traffic. FTPs continue to be popular because they are simple and easily deployed. It will continue to pose a bandwidth concern when it is used under certain conditions.

* **hoaxes** false claims or assertions, sometimes made unlawfully in order to extort money

FTP and telnet can be powerful tools for manipulating the Web, in part because they require little networking knowledge to use them effectively and efficiently. From a technical perspective, telnet and FTP utilize a series of handshakes and negotiation parameters. The handshake is like the drone of a modem or fax machine as it attempts to connect with a compatible device somewhere in cyberspace. These handshakes and negotiation parameters are specified in Requests for Comments number 854 for telnet, and number 354 for FTP, respectively. The technical details of their implementation are extensive and beyond the scope of this article. Fortunately, understanding the technical aspects is not a prerequisite to using telnet or FTP because anyone who accesses the Internet will likely, at some time, make use of these protocols.

▶ *See also* **E-Commerce • FTP • Internet • TCP/IP**

Resources

Books

Comer, Douglas E. *The Internet Book: Everything You Need to Know about Computer Networking and How the Internet Works.* 4th ed. Upper Saddle River, NJ: Prentice Hall, 2006.

Suzuki, Kenji. *Formal Techniques for Networked and Distributed Systems—FORTE 2008: 28th IFIP WG 6.1 International Conference, Tokyo, Japan, June 10–13, 2008: Proceedings.* Lecture notes in computer science, 5048. Berlin: Springer, 2008.

Web Sites

Department of Computer Science, University of Texas. "The Design of the Telnet Protocol." http://www.cs.utexas.edu/users/chris/think/ARPANET/Telnet/Telnet.shtml (accessed October 25, 2012).

Globalscape. "CuteFTP Client Software." http://www.globalscape.co.uk/cuteftp (accessed October 25, 2012).

TCPIP Guide.com, and Charles M. Kozierok. "Telnet Overview, History and Standards." http://www.tcpipguide.com/free/t_TelnetOverviewHistoryandStandards.htm (accessed October 25, 2012).

Urban Myths

An urban myth, also known as an urban legend, is a fictional tale that circulates widely, is told and retold with differing details, and is supposedly true. Urban myths are present in all media, including oral, print, and electronic. There is no single source from which these stories are derived or one method by which they are generated. For instance, some are deliberately manufactured hoaxes* created to cause alarm and concern, whereas others are created by people who have encountered a humorous or remarkable story and wish to retell it in a personalized way. Urban myths can be created for entertainment and illustration of a point or are created by people who do not remember the exact details of a story that they have heard or read.

History of Urban Myths

It is not known who coined the phrase urban myth, but the phenomenon has been studied as a serious form of folklore since the 1930s. Seminal studies of urban myths include American writer Alexander Woollcott's (1887–1943) monograph *While Rome Burns* (1934) and French author Marie Bonaparte's (1882–1962) study of "The Corpse in the Car" legend that appeared in the psychiatric journal *American Imago* (1941).

American folklorists began to collect "urban belief tales," as they were then termed, in the 1940s and 1950s. Notable works from this period include Richard K. Beardsley and Rosalie Hankey's studies on "The Vanishing Hitchhiker" (1942–43); Ernest Baughman's article on "The Fatal Initiation" (1945); J. Russell Reaver's article on "The Poison Dress" (1952); American folklorist B. A. Botkin's (1901–1975) book *Sidewalks of America* (1954); and American folklorist Richard M. Dorson's (1916–1981) textbook *American Folklore* (1959).

In 1968, a groundbreaking urban myth publication appeared: the journal *Indiana Folklore*, produced by Indiana University's Folklore Institute, which is now part of the university's Department of Folklore and Ethnomusicology. For a number of years thereafter, folklorists turned their focus to analyzing the history, variety, persistence, and widespread acceptance as literal truth of urban myths.

To this day, studies of urban myths continue to flourish. There are international conferences on modern legends such as those held at the Centre for English Cultural Tradition and Language at the University of Sheffield. The International Society for Folk Narrative Research holds annual meetings and publishes a newsletter, *FOAFtale* (Friend of a Friend Tale) *News*, and an annual journal, *Contemporary Legend*. An indication of the popularity of urban myth studies is that 1,116 items were listed in Gillian Bennett and Paul Smith's compilation *Contemporary Legend: A Folklore Bibliography* (1993).

Computer-Related Urban Myths

The following are just a few examples of urban myths that have a computer connection.

- Early attempts at computer translation of text from one human language to another produced hilarious results. For instance, American writer John Steinbeck's (1902–1968) novel *Grapes of Wrath* became *Angry Raisins*. The adage "Out of sight, out of mind" became "Blind and insane" and "The spirit was willing, but the flesh is weak" became "The vodka was good, but the meat was rotten."

Computer Sciences, 2nd Edition

Urban Myths Today

Computers have become the primary means by which urban myths and other pieces of misinformation are disseminated, including everything from "stupid computer user" stories to virus warning hoaxes. The dehumanized nature of communication over the Internet, as well as the relative ease of forwarding information compared to recounting stories in person, have contributed to more urban myths and hoaxes circulating today than in previous times.

■ A photo e-mail claiming to be the last picture taken from the top of the World Trade Center in New York City just seconds before a hijacked airplane (seen in the background) slammed into the building on September 11, 2001.

■ Internet Service Providers will donate one cent toward "Brian's" (or any child who is currently hospitalized) operation for every person who forwards this e-mail.

■ National Aeronautics and Space Administration (NASA) scientists discovered a missing day in time that corresponds to Biblical accounts of the Sun's standstill in the sky (i.e., Joshua 10:12–13, and 2 Kings 20:8–11).

None of these myths are true, but all of them have been shared among friends and strangers, often via the Internet, as if they were fact.

Urban myths have been around since the beginning of humankind's history, for they almost certainly developed out of every culture's oral traditions. The Internet is merely another medium by which these myths are transmitted to people who have not yet been exposed to such tales. At best, urban myths disseminated via the Internet can be considered as junk e-mail. At worst, they can be libelous (e.g., Marlboro/Snapple/Troop clothing is owned by the Ku Klux Klan) and a danger to people's lives (e.g., taking twenty aspirin tablets after unprotected sex will halt pregnancies). Unfortunately, there is no technical solution to this problem. Spam filters designed to limit the delivery of spam, or junk, e-mail are unable to combat the problem because e-mails containing urban myths often come from known associates and are technically indistinguishable from other e-mail. The only difference is the semantic meaning of the content. Like gossip and rumors, urban myths are a part of life and have to be tolerated. To combat urban legends, various web sites have been established to help people determine fact from fiction. These include: <http://www.snopes.com> and <http://www.truthorfiction.com/>.

 See also **Hacker** • **Hacking**

Resources

Books

Bennett, Gillian, and Paul Smith, eds. *Urban Legends: A Collection of International Tall Tales and Terrors.* Westport, CT: Greenwood Press, 2007.

Brunvand, Jan Harold. *Encyclopedia of Urban Legends*, updated and expanded ed. Santa Barbara, CA: ABC-CLIO, 2012.

Heath, Chip, and Dan Heath. *Made to Stick: Why Some Ideas Survive and Others Die.* New York: Random House, 2007.

Lance, Charles E., and Robert J. Vandenberg, eds. *Statistical and Methodological Myths and Urban Legends: Doctrine, Verity and*

Fable in the Organizational and Social Sciences. New York: Routledge, 2009.

Roeper, Richard. *Debunked!: Conspiracy Theories, Urban Legends, and Evil Plots of the 21st Century.* Chicago: Chicago Review Press, 2008.

Turner, Harry. *Urban Legends.* London: Janus, 2005.

Zimmerman, Keith, and Kent Zimmerman. *Mythbusters: The Explosive Truth behind 30 of the Most Perplexing Urban Legends of All Time.* New York: Simon Spotlight Entertainment, 2005.

* **graphical user interfaces (GUIs)** interfaces that allow computers to be operated through pictures (icons) and mouse-clicks, rather than through text and typing

* **syntax** a set of rules that a computing language incorporates regarding structure, punctuation, and formatting

Visual Basic

Visual Basic is one of the most widely used programming languages in the world. The major reason for its popularity is that it allows programmers to create Windows applications quickly and easily.

The origins of Visual Basic are found in a programming language created in 1964 by Hungarian-American mathematician John George Kemeny (1926–1992) and American computer scientist Thomas Eugene Kurtz (1928–). BASIC (Beginners All-purpose Symbolic Instruction Code) was originally an interpreted language that was designed to simplify the programming process and make programming more accessible to the world at large. Using that philosophy, Microsoft integrated a BASIC interpreter into its operating system MS-DOS (Microsoft Disk Operating System). Despite its wide distribution and relative simplicity, BASIC was not able to compete with faster, compiled languages such as C or C++. Thus, BASIC was commonly used for trivial or educational purposes, whereas other applications were usually developed in other languages.

In the late 1980s, Microsoft Windows and other graphical user interfaces (GUIs)* were still in their infancy. Most personal computers (PCs) were still using text-based operating systems. As people began to realize the benefits of graphical operating systems, Microsoft Windows gained popularity. Unfortunately, creating Windows-based programs was exceedingly difficult. Extensive code had to be written to define precisely what the interface would look like as well as how a user would interact with it.

To overcome this problem, Microsoft revived BASIC in 1991 by introducing Visual Basic 1.0. Using BASIC's heritage of simplicity and its general syntax*, this new development tool gave programmers an easy way to create Windows applications. In the years since, Microsoft has continued to improve Visual Basic by releasing newer versions. These improvements include not only enhancements to the development environment but also modernization of the core BASIC language as well. These renovations include making BASIC object oriented and fully event driven, and overcoming the limitations of being interpreted, allowing programmers

* **compiled executable code** the binary code that a central processing unit (CPU) can understand; the product of the compilation process

to generate a compiled executable code*. Version 6 of Visual Basic, in 1998, was designated by Microsoft to be the final release of the product. However, its successor, Visual Basic.NET, which runs on Microsoft's .NET software framework, has come to be known as Visual Basic. The latest version of Visual Basic.NET is 4.5, which Microsoft released in August 2012.

Using Visual Basic

The process of creating a program in Visual Basic can be clearly described in three stages: (1) Draw the interface on the screen by adding controls. (2) Define important characteristics of the controls. (3) Write code to determine how a control will react to user actions.

In the first step, the programmer creates the interface using an on-screen drawing tool. Windows controls, such as buttons and input boxes, are added to a workspace using an application similar to Paint (the standard Windows drawing utility). Almost all of the standard Windows interface components are available by default. More advanced controls, such as status bars, can also be added.

Every control has a set of characteristics that make it unique. For example, buttons have properties such as name (how the program will refer to it) and caption (the text that will be used to label it). In the second step, the programmer sets the initial values for the control in order to customize the appearance and behavior of the controls.

In addition to the properties, every type of control has different ways that the user can interact with it. For example, buttons are clicked, or text is entered into an input box. These are known as events. Whenever an event occurs, the program must respond appropriately. The programmer is responsible for empowering the controls by providing a specific set of instructions regarding how the system should respond to the events. This usually comes in the form of doing some calculation and then updating the properties of other controls on the screen to reflect the current state of the system.

At this stage, the program must be run to evaluate that it is working properly. While testing the program, the programmer has the ability to examine the inner workings of the program and even change the program while it is running. After the programmer is certain that the application functions properly, Visual Basic compiles the code into a working executable program that can be distributed to other users.

In addition to creating new programs and applications, Microsoft has also extended portions of Visual Basic to existing applications. Large-scale, popular applications like Microsoft Word, Excel, and Access contain a limited subset of Visual Basic capabilities known as Visual Basic for Applications (VBA). Often used as a macro-language, VBA can be used to control parts of existing applications. This is a very useful feature for automating repetitive tasks or for customizing existing applications to meet a user's personal needs.

Another variation of Visual Basic offers an alternative to JavaScript. Visual Basic Scripting Edition, or VBScript, can be embedded into HTML (hypertext markup language) pages and distributed over the Internet. VBScript can be very useful for making dynamic web pages or for validating user input before it is submitted.

Both of these dialects of Visual Basic follow essentially the same syntax rules as the full-programming edition. Although some variation exists, this allows programmers to extend their existing skills without needing to learn something completely new.

Like its text ancestor, Visual Basic has greatly simplified the task of programming and enjoys widespread distribution. Unfortunately, to some degree, it has also inherited the stigma of being a second-rate programming language. This conception actually arises from the trade-off between ease-of-use and control. Visual Basic attempts to shield programmers from some of the details associated with what occurs at lower levels of the computer. This restricts the programmer to generalized, high-level functions. Alternative languages, such as C++ grants programmers more control over how processing occurs, and thus they can optimize the code to the specific task at hand. If sub-second optimizations are critical to the success of the program, Visual Basic may not be adequate. However, most applications to be run by businesses will not benefit from such minute speed-ups and programmers will find that the simplified development makes Visual Basic very appealing.

 See also **Java Applets • Javascript • Procedural Languages • Programming**

Resources

Books

Deitel, Paul, Harvey Deital, and Abbey Deitel. *Simply Visual Basic 2010*. Boston: Pearson, 2013.

Mansfield, Richard. *Mastering VBA for Microsoft Office 2010*. Indianapolis: Wiley, 2010.

Overland, Brian R. *Visual Basic 6 in Plain English*. Foster City, CA: IDG Books World-Wide, 1999.

Shelly, Gary B., and Corinne Hoisington. *Microsoft Visual Basic 2008 for Windows, Mobile, Web, and Office Applications: Complete*. Boston: Course Technology, 2009.

Web Sites

Microsoft. "Visual Basic Resources." http://www.cs.gmu.edu/cne/itcore/virtualmemory/vmhistory.html (accessed October 29, 2012).

VBtutor.net. "Visual Basic Tutorial." http://www.vbtutor.net/ (accessed October 29, 2012).

Glossary

. . . .

3D printing   a manufacturing process in which machines lay down successive layers of materials to create three-dimensional products from digital information. Also known as additive manufacturing.

4G   shorthand for fourth generation mobile communication and mobile Internet standards, including LTE and Mobile WiMAX networks.

abacus   an ancient counting device that probably originated in Babylon around 2400 BCE.

acuity   sharpness or keenness, especially when used to describe vision.

additive manufacturing   an additive manufacturing process in which machines lay down successive layers of materials to create three-dimensional products from digital information. Also known as 3D printing.

address bus   a collection of electrical signals used to transmit the address of a memory location or input/output port in a computer.

aerodynamics   the science and engineering of systems that are capable of flight.

agents   systems (software programs and/or computing machines) that can act on behalf of another, or on behalf of a human.

aggregate   a numerical summation of multiple individual scores.

ailerons   control surfaces on the trailing edges of the wings of an aircraft—used to manage roll control.

ALGOL   a language developed by the ALGOL committee for scientific applications—acronym for ALGOrithmic Language.

algorithm   a rule or procedure used to solve a mathematical problem—most often described as a sequence of steps.

all-points-addressable mode   a technique for organizing graphics devices where all points (pixels) on the screen are individually accessible to a running program.

alpha beta pruning   a technique that under certain conditions offers an optimal way to search through data structures called "trees."

alphanumeric   a character set which is the union of the set of alphabetic characters and the set of single digit numbers.

ambient   pertaining to the surrounding atmosphere or environment.

ambiguity   the quality of doubtfulness or uncertainty; often subject to multiple interpretations.

amortized   phasing out something in until it is gradually extinguished, like a mortgage loan.

amplitude   the size or magnitude of an electrical signal.

analog   a quantity (often an electrical signal) that is continuous in time and amplitude.

analogous   a relationship of logical similarity between two or more objects.

analytic simulation   modeling of systems by using mathematical equations (often differential equations) and programming a computer with them to simulate the behavior of the real system.

Analytical Engine   Charles Babbage's vision of a programmable mechanical computer.

animatronics the animation (movement) of something by the use of electronic motors, drives, and controls.

anthropomorphic having human form, or generally resembling human appearance.

anti-aliasing introducing shades of gray or other intermediate shades around an image to make the edge appear to be smoother.

app short for application or application software, apps are software features designed to perform specific tasks or improve the user interface with Internet-based resources in a mobile operating system. Apps are common to smartphones, tablets, and other Internet-enabled portable devices.

applet a program component that requires extra support at run time from a browser or run-time environment in order to execute.

approximation an estimate.

arc tangent the circular trigonometric function that is the inverse of the tangent function; values range from $-\prod/2$ to $\prod/2$.

artificial intelligence (AI) a branch of computer science dealing with creating computer hardware and software to mimic the way people think and perform practical tasks.

ASCII an acronym that stands for American Standard Code for Information Interchange; assigns a unique 8-bit binary number to every letter of the alphabet, the digits (0 to 9), and most keyboard symbols.

assembler a program that translates human readable assembly language programs to machine readable instructions.

assembly language the natural language of a central processing unit (CPU); often classed as a low level language.

asynchronous events that have no systematic relationship to one another in time.

attenuation the reduction in magnitude (size or amplitude) of a signal that makes a signal weaker.

authentication the act of ensuring that an object or entity is what it is intended to be.

automata theory the analytical (mathematical) treatment and study of automated systems.

automaton an object or being that has a behavior that can be modeled or explained completely by using automata theory.

autonomous self-governing, or being able to exist independently.

autonomy the capability of acting in a self-governing manner; being able to exist independently or with some degree of independence.

axioms statements that are taken to be true, the foundation of a theory.

Bakelite an insulating material used in synthetic goods, including plastics and resins.

ballistics the science and engineering of the motion of projectiles of various types, including bullets, bombs, and rockets.

bandwidth a measure of the frequency component of a signal or the capacity of a communication channel to carry signals.

bar code a graphical number representation system where alphanumeric characters are represented by vertical black and white lines of varying width.

base-2 a number system in which each place represents a power of 2 larger than the place to its right (binary).

base-8 a number system in which each place represents a power of 8 larger than the place to its right (octal).

base-10 a number system in which each place represents a power of 10 larger than the place to its right (decimal).

base-16 a number system in which each place represents a power of 16 larger than the place to its right (hexadecimal).

batch processing an approach to computer utilization that queues non-interactive programs and runs them one after another.

Bayesian networks structures that describe systems in which there is a degree of uncertainty; used in automated decision making.

Bernoulli numbers the sums of powers of consecutive integers; named after Swiss mathematician Jacques Bernoulli (1654–1705).

binary existing in only two states, such as "on" or "off," "one" or "zero."

binary code a representation of information that permits only two states, such as "on" or "off," "one" or "zero."

binary coded decimal (BCD) an ANSI/ISO standard encoding of the digits 0 to 9 using 4 binary bits; the encoding only uses 10 of the available 16 4-bit combinations.

binary digit a single bit, 1 or 0.

binary number system a number system in which each place represents a power of 2 larger than the place on its right (base-2).

binary system a machine or abstraction that uses binary codes.

binomial theorem a theorem giving the procedure by which a binomial expression may be raised to any power without using successive multiplications.

bit a single binary digit, 1 or 0—a contraction of Binary digIT; the smallest unit for storing data in a computer.

bit mapped display a computer display that uses a table of binary bits in memory to represent the image that is projected onto the screen.

bit maps images comprised of bit descriptions of the image, in black and white or color, such that the colors can be represented by the two values of a binary bit.

bit rate the rate at which binary bits can be processed or transferred per unit time, in a system (often a computer communications system).

bit serial mode a method of transferring binary bits one after another in a sequence or serial stream.

bitstream a serialized collection of bits; usually used in transfer of bits from one system to another.

Boolean algebra a system developed by George Boole that deals with the theorems of undefined symbols and axioms concerning those symbols.

Boolean logic a system, developed by George Boole, which treats abstract objects (such as sets or classes) as algebraic quantities; Boole applied his mathematical system to the study of classical logic.

Boolean operators fundamental logical operations (for example "and" and "or") expressed in a mathematical form.

broadband access a term given to denote high bandwidth services.

browsers programs that permit a user to view and navigate through documents, most often hypertext documents.

bugs errors in program source code.

bus a group of related signals that form an interconnecting pathway between two or more electronic devices.

bus topology a particular arrangement of buses that constitutes a designed set of pathways for information transfer within a computer.

byte a group of eight binary digits; represents a single character of text.

C a programming language developed for the UNIX operating system; it is designed to run on most machines and with most operating systems.

cache a small sample of a larger set of objects, stored in a way that makes them accessible.

calculus a method of dealing mathematically with variables that may be changing continuously with respect to each other.

Callback modems security techniques that collect telephone numbers from authorized users on calls and then dial the users to establish the connections.

capacitates fundamental electrical components used for storing electrical charges.

capacitive touch one of the two primary types of touch screen technology, it detects touches utilizing the conductive electrical properties of human skin. This systems, common on many popular smartphones, allows for user control of the device with very light touches.

capacitor a fundamental electrical component used for storing electrical charge.

carpal tunnel syndrome a repetitive stress injury that can lead to pain, numbness, tingling, and loss of muscle control in the hands and wrists.

cartography map-making.

cathode ray tube (CRT) a glass enclosure that projects images by directing a beam of electrons onto the back of a screen.

cellular automata a collection or array of objects that are programmed identically to interact with one another.

cellular neural networks (CNN) a neural network topology that uses multidimensional array structures comprised of cells that work together in localized groups.

central processing unit (CPU) the part of a computer that performs computations and controls and coordinates other parts of the computer.

certificate a unique electronic document that is used to assist authentication.

chaos theory a branch of mathematics dealing with differential equations having solutions which are very sensitive to initial conditions.

checksum a number that is derived from adding together parts of an electronic message before it is dispatched; it can be used at the receiver to check against message corruption.

chromatic dispersion the natural distortion of pulses of light as they move through an optical network; it results in data corruption.

cipher a code or encryption method.

client a program or computer often managed by a human user, that makes requests to another computer for information.

client/server technology computer systems that are structured using clients (usually human-driven computers) to access information stored (often remotely) on other computers known as servers.

cloud computing the use over a network of remote hardware and software computing resources.

cloud storage a remote network of computing resources accessible over the Internet that hosts user files. Also called a cyberlocker or file hosting service and popular as a location for remote computer back-ups or storing media, cloud storage allows users to access files stored "in the cloud" from other computers, tablets, or smartphones.

coaxial cable a cable with an inner conducting core, a dielectric material and an outer sheath that is designed for high frequency signal transmission.

cognitive pertaining to the concepts of knowing or perceiving.

collocation the act of placing elements or objects in a specific order.

commodity raw material or service marketed prior to being used.

compiled a program that is translated from human-readable code to binary code that a central processing unit (CPU) can understand.

compiled executable code the binary code that a central processing unit (CPU) can understand; the product of the compilation process.

compilers programs that translate human-readable high-level computer languages to machine-readable code.

computer-aided design (CAD) the use of computers to replace traditional drawing instruments and tools for engineering or architectural design.

computer-assisted tomography the use of computers in assisting with the management of X-ray images.

computer peripheral a device that is connected to a computer to support its operation; for example, a keyboard or a disk drive unit.

concatenates the joining together of two elements or objects; for example, words are formed by concatenating letters.

concentric circles circles that have coincident centers.

conceptualization a creative process that is directed at envisaging a structure or collection of relationships within components of a complex system.

concurrency control the management and coordination of several actions that occur simultaneously; for example, several computer programs running at once.

concurrent pertaining to simultaneous activities, for example simultaneous execution of many computer programs.

configuration files special disk files containing information that can be used to tell running programs about system settings.

cookie a small text file that a Web site can place on a computer's hard drive to collect information about a user's browsing activities or to activate an online shopping cart to keep track of purchases.

copyrights the legal rules and regulations concerning the copying and redistribution of documents.

cord cutting a term that refers to forging traditional cable and satellite-based television subscription services in favor of online streaming media.

cosine a trigonometric function of an angle, defined as the ratio of the length of the adjacent side of a right-angled triangle divided by the length of its hypotenuse.

counterfeiting the act of knowingly producing non-genuine objects, especially in relation to currency.

crawls severe weather warnings that are broadcast on the bottom of TV screens.

creative commons licensing a free, easy-to-understand, rights management scheme that allows creators to reserve or waive some of their intellectual property rights in the interest of sharing and using works in public forums such as the Internet.

cross-platform pertaining to a program that can run on many different computer types (often called hardware platforms).

CRT the acronym for cathode ray tube, which is a glass enclosure that projects images by directing a beam of electrons onto the back of a screen.

cryptanalysis the act of attempting to discover the algorithm used to encrypt a message.

cryptanalyst a person or agent who attempts to discover the algorithm used to encrypt a message.

cryptography the science of understanding codes and ciphers and their application.

cryptosystem a system or mechanism that is used to automate the processes of encryption and decryption.

cuneiform in the shape of a wedge.

cybercafe a shop, cafe, or meeting place where users can rent a computer for a short time to access the Internet.

cybernetics a unified approach to understanding the behavior of machines and animals developed by Norbert Wiener (1894–1964).

cycloids pertaining to circles, in either a static way or in a way that involves movement.

dark fiber a fiber optic network that exists but is not actively in service, hence the darkness.

data mining a technique of automatically obtaining information from databases that is normally hidden or not obvious.

data partitioning a technique applied to databases (but not restricted to them) which organizes data objects into related groups.

data reduction technique an approach to simplifying data, e.g. summarization.

data warehousing to implement an informational database used to store shared data.

de facto as is.

de jure strictly according to the law.

debug the act of trying to trace, identify, and then remove errors in program source code.

decimal system a number system in which each place represents a power of 10 larger than the place to its right (base-10).

decision trees classifiers in which a sequence of tests are made to decide the class label to assign to an unknown data item; the sequence of.

deformations mechanical systems where a structure is physically misshapen, e.g., dented.

degrade to reduce quality or performance of a system.

delimiters special symbols that mark the beginnings and/or endings of other groups of symbols (for example to mark out comments in program source code).

demographics the study of the statistical data pertaining to a population.

densities measures of the density of a material; defined as the mass of a sample of material, divided by its volume.

deregulation the lowering of restrictions, rules, or regulations pertaining to an activity or operation (often commercial).

die the silicon chip that is the heart of integrated circuit fabrication; the die is encased in a ceramic or plastic package to make the completed integrated circuit (IC).

dielectric a material that exhibits insulating properties, as opposed to conducting properties.

Difference Engine a mechanical calculator designed by Charles Babbage that automated the production of mathematical tables by using the method of differences.

differential analyzer a computer constructed in the early 1930s by Vannevar Bush at Massachusetts Institute of Technology (MIT); it solved differential equations by mechanical integration.

digital a quantity that can exist only at distinct levels, not having values in between these levels (for example, binary).

digital certificates certificates used in authentication that contain encrypted digital identification information.

digital divide imaginary line separating those who can access digital information from those who cannot.

digital library distributed access to collections of digital information.

digital media receiver any device that connects to a network to locate, download, or stream digital media files from a server so that users can broadcast them to their television. They are also known as media streaming devices or digital media hubs.

digital signature identifier used to authenticate the sender of an electronic message or the signer of an electronic document.

digital subscriber line (DSL) a technology that permits high speed voice and data communications over public telephone networks; it requires the use of a DSL modem.

digital subscriber loop (DSL) the enabling of high-speed digital data transfer over standard telephone cables and systems in conjunction with normal telephone speech data.

digital watermarks special data structures permanently embedded into a program or other file type, which contain information about the author and the program.

digitizes converts analog information into a digital form for processing by a computer.

diode a semiconductor device that forces current flow in a conductor to be in one direction only, also known as a rectifier.

diode tube an obsolete form of diode that was made of metal elements in a sealed and evacuated glass tube.

direction buttons buttons on a program with a graphical user interface that provide

a way of navigating through information or documents.

discrete composed of distinct elements.

disintermediation a change in business practice whereby consumers elect to cut out intermediary agencies and deal directly with a provider or vendor.

distance learning the form of education where the instructor and students are separated by either location or time (or both), usually mediated by some electronic communication mechanism.

distributed denial of service (DDoS) an attack in which large numbers of messages are directed to send network traffic to a target computer, overloading it or its network connection; typically, the attacking computers have been subverted.

distributed systems computer systems comprising many individual computers that are interconnected and act in concert to complete operations.

documentation literature in a human readable form that is referred to in support of using a computer or computer system.

domain a region in which a particular element or object exists or has influence; (math) the inputs to a function or relation.

doping a step used in the production of semiconductor materials where charged particles are embedded into the device so as to tailor its operational characteristics.

dot.com a common term used to describe an Internet-based commercial company or organization.

dragged to have been moved by the application of an external pulling force; quite often occurring in graphical user interfaces when objects are moved with a mouse.

DRAM the acronym for Dynamic Random Access Memory; high density, low cost and low speed memory devices used in most computer systems.

driver a special program that manages the sequential execution of several other programs; a part of an operating system that handles input/output devices.

drop-down menu a menu on a program with a graphical user interface that produces a vertical list of items when activated.

dumb terminal a keyboard and screen connected to a distant computer without any processing capability.

duplex simultaneous two-directional communication over a single communication channel.

dynamic changing; possessing volatility.

dynamic links logical connections between two objects that can be modified if the objects themselves move or change state.

EBCDIC the acronym for Extended Binary Coded Decimal Interchange Code, which assigns a unique 8-bit binary number to every letter of the alphabet, the digits (0-9), and most keyboard symbols.

e-books short for electronic books; books available for downloading onto an e-book reader.

e-reader an electronic device that displays and stores books and other texts.

egress to move out of an object, system, or environment.

electromagnetic a piece of metal that becomes magnetic only when electricity is applied to it; in general, the more electricity applied to metal, the stronger its magnetism.

electromagnetic relays switches that have a high current carrying capacity, which are opened and closed by an electromagnet.

electromagnetic spectrum a range of frequencies over which electromagnetic radiation can be generated, transmitted, and received.

embedded computers computers that do not have human user orientated I/O devices; they are directly contained within other machines.

embedded systems another term for "embedded computers"; computers that do not have human user orientated input/output devices; they are directly contained within other machines.

emoticons symbols or key combinations used in electronic correspondence to convey emotions.

enciphered encrypted or encoded; a mathematical process that disguises the content of messages transmitted.

encryption also known as encoding; a mathematical process that disguises the content of messages transmitted.

end-effector the end piece of a robotic arm that can receive various types of grippers and tools.

end users computer users.

enterprise information system a system of client and server computers that can be used to manage all of the tasks required to manage and run a large organization.

entropy a measure of the state of disorder or randomness in a system.

ephemeris a record showing positions of astronomical objects and artificial satellites in a time-ordered sequence.

ergonomic being of suitable geometry and structure to permit effective or optimal human user interaction with machines.

esoteric relating to a specialized field of endeavor that is characterized by its restricted size.

ether a highly volatile liquid solvent; also, the far regions of outer space.

ethernets a networking technology for mini and microcomputer systems consisting of network interface cards and interconnecting coaxial cables; invented in the 1970s by Xerox corporation.

Euclidean geometry the study of points, lines, angles, polygons, and curves confined to a plane.

expert system a computer system that uses a collection of rules to exhibit behavior which mimics the behavior of a human expert in some area.

fiber optics transmission technology using long, thin strands of glass fiber; internal reflections in the fiber assure that light entering one end is transmitted to the other end with only small losses in intensity; used widely in transmitting digital information.

field searching a strategy in which a search is limited to a particular field; in a search engine, a search may be limited to a particular domain name or date, narrowing the scope of searchable items and helping to eliminate the chance of retrieving irrelevant data.

file transfer protocol (FTP) a communications protocol used to transfer files.

filter queries queries used to select subsets from a data collection, e.g., all documents with a creation date later than 01/01/2013.

firewall a special purpose network computer or software that is used to ensure that no access is permitted to a sub-network unless authenticated and authorized.

firing tables precalculated tables that can give an artillery gunner the correct allowances for wind conditions and distance by dictating the elevation and deflection of a gun.

flashdrive a small, typically portable, solid state drive (SSD) utilizing flash memory for storing or transferring computer data.

floating point operations numerical operations involving real numbers where in achieving a result, the number of digits to the left or right of the decimal point can change.

flowcharts techniques for graphically describing the sequencing and structure of program source code.

fluid dynamics the science and engineering of the motion of gases and liquids.

Freedom of Information Act (FOIA) permits individuals to gain access to records and documents that are in the possession of the government.

freon hydrocarbon based gases used as refrigerants and as pressurants in aerosols.

frequency bands ranges of signal frequencies that are of particular interest in a given application.

frequency modulation a technique whereby a signal is transformed so that it is represented by another signal with a frequency that varies in a way related to the original signal.

full-text indexing a search engine feature in which every word in a document, significant or insignificant, is indexed and retrievable through a search.

fuzzy logic models human reasoning by permitting elements to have partial membership to a set; derived from fuzzy set theory.

gallium arsenide a chemical used in the production of semiconductor devices; chemical symbol GaAs.

gates fundamental building blocks of digital and computer based electric circuits that perform logical operations; for example logical AND, logical OR.

Gaussian classifiers classifiers constructed on the assumption that the feature values of data will follow a Gaussian distribution.

gbps   acronym for gigabits per second; a binary data transfer rate that corresponds to a thousand million (billion, or 109) bits per second.

Geographic Information Systems (GIS)   computing systems that capture, compare, create, analyze, organize, and display geographical data in a searchable and visually useful ways.

geometric   relating to the principles of geometry, a branch of mathematics related to the properties and relationships of points, lines, angles, surfaces, planes, and solids.

germanium   a chemical often used as a high performance semiconductor material; chemical symbol Ge.

gestural interface   technologies designed to use mathematical algorithms to interpret or respond to human gestures.

GIF animation   a technique using Graphic Interchange Format where many images are overlaid on one another and cycled through a sequence to produce an animation.

GIF image   the acronym for Graphic Interchange Format where a static image is represented by binary bits in a data file.

gigabit networking   the construction and use of a computer network that is capable of transferring information at rates in the gigahertz range.

gigabytes   units of measure equivalent to a thousand million (billion, or 109) bytes.

gigahertz (GHz)   a unit or measure of frequency, equivalent to a thousand million (billion, or 109) hertz, or cycles per second.

Global Positioning System (GPS)   a method of locating a point on the Earth's surface that uses received signals transmitted from satellites to accurately calculate position.

granularity   a description of the level of precision that can be achieved in making measurements of a quantity; for example coarse granularity means inexpensive but imprecise measurements.

graphical user interface (GUI)   an interface that allows computers to be operated through pictures (icons) and mouse-clicks, rather than through text and typing.

groupware   a software technology common in client/server systems whereby many users can access and process data at the same time.

gyros   a contraction of gyroscopes; a mechanical device that uses one or more spinning discs which resist changes to their position in space.

half tones   black and white dots of certain sizes, which provide a perception of shades of gray.

ham radio   a legal (or licensed) amateur radio.

haptic   pertaining to the sense of touch.

Harvard Cyclotron   a specialized machine (cyclotron) developed in 1948 at Harvard University; it is used to carry out experiments in sub-atomic physics and medicine.

head-mounted displays (HMD)   helmets worn by a virtual reality (VR) participant that include speakers and screens for each eye, which display three-dimensional images.

hertz (Hz)   a unit of measurement of frequency, equal to one cycle per second; named in honor of German physicist Heinrich Hertz.

heuristic   a procedure that serves to guide investigation but that has not been proven.

hexadecimal   a number system in which each place represents a power of 16 larger than the place to its right (base-16).

high-bandwidth   a communication channel that permits many signals of differing frequencies to be transmitted simultaneously.

high precision/high recall   a phenomenon that occurs during a search when all the relevant documents are retrieved with no unwanted ones.

high precision/low recall a phenomenon that occurs when a search yields a small set of hits; although each one may be highly relevant to the search topic, some relevant documents are missed.

high-speed data links digital communications systems that permit digital data to be reliably transferred at high speed.

hoaxes false claims or assertions, sometimes made unlawfully in order to extort money.

holistic looking at the entire system, rather than just its parts.

hydraulic motion being powered by a pressurized liquid (such as water or oil), supplied through tubes or pipes.

hydrologic relating to water.

hyperlinks connections between electronic documents that permit automatic browsing transfer at the point of the link.

Hypertext Markup Language (HTML) an encoding scheme for text data that uses special tags in the text to signify properties to the viewing program (browser) like links to other documents or document parts.

Hypertext Transfer Protocol (HTTP) a simple connectionless communications protocol developed for the electronic transfer (serving) of HTML documents.

I/O the acronym for input/output; used to describe devices that can accept input data to a computer and to other devices that can produce output.

I/O devices devices that can accept "input" data to a computer and to other devices that can produce "output."

icon a small image that is used to signify a program or operation to a user.

illiquid lacking in liquid assets; or something that is not easily transferable into currency.

ImmersaDesks large 4 x 5 foot screens that allow for stereoscopic visualization; the 3-D computer graphics create the illusion of a virtual environment.

ImmersaWalls large-scale, flat screen visualization environments that include passive and active multi-projector displays of 3-D images.

immersive involved in something totally.

in-band pertaining to elements or objects that are within the limits of a certain Local Area Network (LAN).

inference a suggestion or implication of something based on other known related facts and conclusions.

information theory a branch of mathematics and engineering that deals with the encoding, transmission, reception, and decoding of information.

infrared (IR) waves radiation in a band of the electromagnetic spectrum within the infrared range.

infrastructure the foundation or permanent installation necessary for a structure or system to operate.

ingot a formed block of metal (often cast) used to facilitate bulk handling and transportation.

ingress the act of entering a system or object.

init method a special function in an object oriented program that is automatically called to initialize the elements of an object when it is created.

input/output (I/O) used to describe devices that can accept input data to a computer and to other devices that can produce output.

Inquisition the establishment of a religious court (1478–1834) where Christians as well as non-Christians were prosecuted for heresy.

intangible a concept to which it is difficult to apply any form of analysis; something which is not perceived by the sense of touch.

integrated circuit a circuit with the transistors, resistors, and other circuit elements etched into the surface of a single chip of semiconducting material, usually silicon.

integrated modem a modem device that is built into a computer, rather than being attached as a separate peripheral.

intellectual property the acknowledgement that an individual's creativity and innovation can be owned in the same way as physical property.

interconnectivity the ability of more than one physical computer to operate with one or more other physical computers; interconnectivity is usually accomplished by means of network wiring, cable, or telephone lines.

interface a boundary or border between two or more objects or systems; also a point of access.

Internet Protocol (IP) a method of organizing information transfer between computers; the IP was specifically designed to offer low-level support to Transmission Control Protocol (TCP).

Internet Service Provider (ISP) a commercial enterprise which offers paying subscribers access to the Internet (usually via modem) for a fee.

interpolation estimating data values between known points but the values in between are not and are therefore estimated.

intranet an interconnected network of computers that operates like the Internet, but is restricted in size to a company or organization.

ionosphere a region of the upper atmosphere (above about 60,000 meters or 196,850 feet) where the air molecules are affected by the sun's radiation and influence electromagnetic wave propagation.

isosceles triangle a triangle that has two sides of equivalent length (and therefore two angles of the same size).

iterative a procedure that involves repetitive operations before being completed.

Jacquard's Loom a weaving loom, developed by Joseph-Marie Jacquard ((1752–1834), controlled by punched cards; identified as one of the earliest examples of programming automation.

Java applets applets written in the Java programming language and executed with the support of a Java Virtual Machine (JVM) or a Java enabled browser.

joysticks the main controlling levers of small aircraft; models of these can be connected to computers to facilitate playing interactive games.

JPEG (Joint Photographic Experts Group) organization that developed a standard for encoding image data in a compressed format to save space.

k-nearest neighbors a classifier that assigns a class label for an unknown data item by looking at the class labels of the nearest items in the training data.

Kbps a measure of digital data transfer per unit time—one thousand (kilo, K) bits per second.

keywords words that are significant in some context or topic (often used in searching).

kilohertz (kHz) a unit or measure of frequency, equivalent to a thousand (or 103) hertz, or cycles per second.

kinematics a branch of physics and mechanical engineering that involves the study of moving bodies and particles.

kinetics a branch of physics or chemistry concerned with the rate of change in chemical or physical systems.

labeled data a data item whose class assignment is known independent of the classifier being constructed.

lambda calculus important in the development of programming languages, a specialized logic using substitutions that was developed by Alonzo Church (1903–1995).

LEDs the acronym for Light Emitting Diode; a diode that emits light when passing a current and used as an indicating lamp.

lexical analyzer a portion of a compiler that is responsible for checking the program source code produced by a programmer for proper words and symbols.

Library of Congress Classification the scheme by which the Library of Congress organizes classes of books and documents.

light-emitting diode (LED) a discrete electronic component that emits visible light when permitting current to flow in a certain direction; often used as an indicating lamp.

linear pertaining to a type of system that has a relationship between its outputs and its inputs that can be graphed as a straight line.

Linux operating system an open source UNIX operating system that was originally created by Linus Torvalds in the early 1990s.

liquid crystal display (LCD) a type of crystal that changes its level of transparency when subjected to an electric current; used as an output device on a computer.

local area network (LAN) a high-speed computer network that is designed for users who are located near each other.

logarithm the power to which a certain number called the base is to be raised to produce a particular number.

logic a branch of philosophy and mathematics that uses provable rules to apply deductive reasoning.

lossy a nonreversible way of compressing digital images; making images take up less space

by permanently removing parts that cannot be easily seen anyway.

low precision/high recall a phenomenon that occurs during a search when a large set of results are retrieved, including many relevant and irrelevant documents.

lumens a unit of measure of light intensity.

magnetic tape a way of storing programs and data from computers; tapes are generally slow and prone to deterioration over time but are inexpensive.

mainframe large computer used by businesses and government agencies to process massive amounts of data; generally faster and more powerful than desktop computers but usually requiring specialized software.

malicious code program instructions that are intended to carry out malicious or hostile actions; e.g., deleting a user's files.

mammogram an X-ray image of the breast, used to detect signs of possible cancer.

Manhattan Project the U.S. project designed to create the world's first atomic bomb.

mass spectrometers instruments that can identify elemental particles in a sample by examining the frequencies of the particles that comprise the sample.

mass spectrometry the process of identifying the compounds or elemental particles within a substance.

media streaming device a device that enables users to connect to a network or server and view digital media files on their television; also known as a digital media receiver or digital media hub.

megahertz (MHz) a unit or measure of frequency, equivalent to a million (or 106) hertz, or cycles per second.

memex   a device that can be used to store personal information, notes, and records that permits managed access at high speed; a hypothetical creation of Vannevar Bush.

menu label   the text or icon on a menu item in a program with a graphical user interface.

metadata   data about data, such as the date and time created.

meteorologists   people who have studied the science of weather and weather forecasting.

metropolitan area network (MAN)   a high-speed interconnected network of computers spanning entire cities.

microampere   a unit of measure of electrical current that is one-millionth (10^{-6}) amperes.

microchip   a common term for a semiconductor integrated circuit device.

microcomputer   a computer that is small enough to be used and managed by one person alone; often called a personal computer.

microprocessor   the principle element in a computer; the component that understands how to carry out operations under the direction of the running program (CPU).

millisecond   a time measurement indicating one-thousandth (or 10^{-3}) of a second.

milliwatt   a power measurement indicating one-thousandth (or 10^{-3}) of a watt.

minicomputers   computers midway in size between a desktop computer and a mainframe computer; most modern desktops are much more powerful than the older minicomputers.

minimax algorithm   an approach to developing an optimal solution to a game or contest where two opposing systems are aiming at mutually exclusive goals.

Minitel   network used in France that preceded the Internet, connecting most French homes, businesses, cultural organizations, and government offices.

mnemonic   a device or process that aids one's memory.

Mobile device management (MDM)   software that aids in standardizing settings, managing programs, protecting confidential information, and securing mobile devices.

mobile operating system (MOS)   the software that allows smartphones, tablets, other portable devices to run programs and apps.

modalities   classifications of the truth of a logical proposition or statement, or characteristics of an object or entity.

modem   the contraction of MOdulator DEModulator; a device which converts digital signals into signals suitable for transmission over analog channels, like telephone lines.

modulation   a technique whereby signals are translated to analog so that the resultant signal can be more easily transmitted and received by other elements in a communication system.

modules   a generic term that is applied to small elements or components that can be used in combination to build an operational system.

molecular modeling   a technique that uses high performance computer graphics to represent the structure of chemical compounds.

motherboard   the part of the computer that holds vital hardware, such as the processors, memory, expansion slots, and circuitry.

MPEG (Motion Picture Coding Experts Group)   an encoding scheme for data files that contain motion pictures—it is lossy in the same way as JPEG (Joint Photographic Experts Group) encoding.

multiplexes operations in ATM communications whereby data cells are blended into one continuous stream at the transmitter and then separated again at the receiver.

multiplexor a complex device that acts as a multi-way switch for analog or digital signals.

multitasking the ability of a computer system to execute more than one program at the same time; also known as multiprogramming.

mylar a synthetic film, invented by the DuPont corporation, used in photographic printing and production processes, as well as disks and tapes.

nanocomputing the science and engineering of building mechanical machines at the atomic level.

nanometers one-thousand-millionth (one billionth, or 10^{-9}) of a meter.

nanosecond one-thousand-millionth (one billionth, or 10^{-9}) of a second.

nanotechnology the design and construction of machines at the atomic or molecular level.

narrowband a general term in communication systems pertaining to a signal that has a small collection of differing frequency components (as opposed to broadband which has many frequency components).

National Computer Security Center (NCSC) a branch of the National Security Agency responsible for evaluating secure computing systems; the Trusted Computer Systems Evaluation Criteria (TCSEC) were developed by the NCSC.

Network Control Protocol (NCP) a host-to-host protocol originally developed in the early 1970s to support the Internet, which was then a research project.

network packet switching the act of routing and transferring packets (or small sections) of a carrier signal that conveys digital information.

neural modeling the mathematical study and the construction of elements that mimic the behavior of the brain cell (neuron).

neural networks pattern recognition systems whose structure and operation are loosely inspired by analogy to neurons in the human brain.

Newtonian view an approach to the study of mechanics that obeys the rules of Newtonian physics, as opposed to relativistic mechanics; named after Sir Isaac Newton (1643–1727).

nonlinear a system that has relationships between outputs and inputs which cannot be expressed in the form of a straight line.

O-rings 37-foot (11-meter) rubber circles (rings) that seal the joints between the space shuttle's rocket booster segments.

OEM the acronym for Original Equipment Manufacturer; a manufacturer of computer components.

offline the mode of operation of a computer that applies when it is completely disconnected from other computers and peripherals (like printers).

Open Systems Interconnections (OSI) a communications standard developed by the International Organization for Standardization (ISO) to facilitate compatible network systems.

operands when a computer is executing instructions in a program, the elements on which it performs the instructions are known as the.

operating system a set of programs which control all the hardware of a computer and provide user and device input/output functions.

optical character recognition the science and engineering of creating programs that can recognize and interpret printed characters.

optical computing a proposed computing technology which would operate on particles of light, rather than electric currents.

optophone a system that uses artificial intelligence techniques to convert images of text into audible sound.

orthogonal elements or objects that are perpendicular to one another; in a logical sense this means that changes in one have no effect on the other.

oscillator an electronic component that produces a precise waveform of a fixed known frequency; this can be used as a time base (clock) signal to other devices.

oscilloscopes measuring instruments for electrical circuitry; connected to circuits under test using probes on leads and having small screens that display the signal waveforms.

out-of-band pertaining to elements or objects that are external to the limits of a certain local area network (LAN).

overhead the expense or cost involved in carrying out a particular operation.

packet-switched network a network based on digital communications systems whereby packets of data are dispatched to receivers based on addresses that they contain.

packet-switching an operation used in digital communications systems whereby packets (collections) of data are dispatched to receivers based on addresses contained in the packets.

packets collections of digital data elements that are part of a complete message or signal; packets contain their destination addresses to enable reassembly of the message or signal.

paradigm an example, pattern, or way of thinking.

parallel debugging specialized approaches to locating and correcting errors in computer programs that are to be executed on parallel computing machine architectures.

parallel processing the presence of more than one central processing unit (CPU) in a computer, which enables the true execution of more than one program.

parametric modeling a system using variables or parameters that can be observed to change as the system operates.

parity a method of introducing error checking on binary data by adding a redundant bit and using that to enable consistency checks.

pattern recognition a process used by some artificial-intelligence systems to identify a variety of patterns, including visual patterns, information patterns buried in a noisy signal, and word patterns imbedded in text.

PDF the acronym for Portable Document Format, developed by Adobe Corporation to facilitate the storage and transfer of electronic documents.

peer-to-peer services the ways in which computers on the same logical level can interoperate in a structured network hierarchy.

permutations significant changes or rearrangement.

personal area networking the interconnectivity of personal productivity devices such as computers, mobile telephones, and personal organizers.

personal digital assistants (PDA) small-scale hand-held computers that can be used in place of diaries and appointment books.

phosphor a coating applied to the back of a glass screen on a cathode ray tube (CRT) that emits light when a beam of electrons strikes its surface.

photolithography the process of transferring an image from a film to a metal surface for etching, often used in the production of printed circuit boards.

photonic switching the technology that is centered on routing and managing optical packets of digital data.

photons the smallest fundamental units of electromagnetic radiation in the visible spectrum—light.

photosensitive describes any material that will change its properties in some way if subjected to visible light, such as photographic film.

picoseconds one-millionth of a millionth of a second (one-trillionth, or 10^{12}).

piezoelectric crystal an electronic component that when subjected to a current will produce a waveform signal at a precise rate, which can then be used as a clock signal in a computer.

PIN (personal identification number) a password, usually numeric, used in conjunction with a cryptographic token, smart card, or bank card, to ensure that only an authorized user can activate an account governed by the token or card.

ping sweeps technique that identifies properties belonging to a server computer, by sending it collections of "ping" packets and examining the responses from the server.

piracy the unlawful copying and redistribution of computer software, ignoring the copyright and ownership rights of the publisher.

pixel a single picture element on a video screen; one of the individual dots making up a picture on a video screen or digital image.

pixilation the process of generating animation, frame by frame.

plug-in a term used to describe the way that hardware and software modules can be added to a computer system, if they possess interfaces that have been built to a documented standard.

pneumatic powered by pressurized air, supplied through tubes or pipes.

polarity the positive (+) or negative (–) state of an object, which dictates how it will react to forces such as magnetism or electricity.

polarizer a translucent sheet that permits only plane-polarized light to pass through, blocking all other light.

polygon a many-sided, closed, geometrical figure.

polynomial an expression with more than one term.

polypeptide the product of many amino acid molecules bonded together.

population inversion used in quantum mechanics to describe when the number of atoms at higher energy levels is greater than the number at lower energy levels—a condition needed for photons (light) to be emitted.

port logical input/output points on computers that exist in a network.

port scans operations whereby ports are probed so that information about their status can be collected.

potentiometer an element in an electrical circuit that resists current flow (a resistor) but the value of the resistance can be mechanically adjusted (a variable resistor).

predicate calculus a branch of logic that uses individuals and predicates, or elements and classes, and the existential and universal quantifiers, all and some, to represent statements.

privatized to convert a service traditionally offered by a government or public agency into a service provided by a private corporation or other private entity.

progenitor the direct parent of something or someone.

propositional calculus a branch of logic that uses expressions such as "If … then …" to make statements and deductions.

proprietary a process or technology developed and owned by an individual or company, and not published openly.

proprietary software software created by an individual or company that is sold under a license that dictates use and distribution.

protocol an agreed understanding for the sub-operations that make up a transaction, usually found in the specification of inter-computer communications.

prototype a working model or experimental investigation of proposed systems under development.

proxy server a server, system, or application in a computer network that acts as an intermediary for clients needing to mask a computer's location or identity on the network, get around network access restrictions, or that otherwise cannot access information on other servers directly.

pseudocode a language-neutral, structural description of the algorithms that are to be used in a program.

public key information certain status and identification information that pertains to a particular public key (i.e., a key available for public use in encryption).

public key infrastructure (PKI) the supporting programs and protocols that act together to enable public key encryption/decryption.

punched card a paper card with punched holes which give instructions to a computer in order to encode program instructions and data.

quadtrees data structures resembling trees, which have four branches at every node (rather than two as with a binary tree); used in the construction of complex databases.

quality-of-service (QoS) a set of performance criteria that a system is designed to guarantee and support as a minimum.

quantification to quantify (or measure) something.

quantum-dot cellular automata (QCA) the theory of automata as applied to quantum dot architectures, which are a proposed approach for the development of computers at nano-technology scales.

quantum mechanical something influenced by the set of rules that govern the energy and wave behavior of subatomic particles on the scale of sizes that are comparable to the particles themselves.

queue the ordering of elements or objects such that they are processed in turn; first-in, first-out.

radar the acronym for RAdio Direction And Ranging; a technique developed in the 1930s that uses frequency shifts in reflected radio waves to measure distance and speed of a target.

radio telescopes telescopes used for astronomical observation that operate on collecting electromagnetic radiation in frequency bands above the visible spectrum.

random access memory (RAM) a type of memory device that supports the nonpermanent storage of programs and data; so called because various locations can be accessed in any order (as if at random), rather than in a sequence (like a tape memory device).

raster a line traced out by a beam of electrons as they strike a cathode ray tube (CRT).

raster scan pattern a sequence of raster lines drawn on a cathode ray tube such that an image or text can be made to appear.

read-only memory (ROM) a type of memory device that supports permanent storage of programs.

real-time a system, often computer based, that ensures the rates at which it inputs, processes, and outputs information meet the timing requirements of another system.

recursive operations expressed and implemented in a way that requires them to invoke themselves.

recursive functions functions expressed and implemented in a way that requires them to call themselves.

relational database a collection of records that permits logical and business relationships to be developed between themselves and their contents.

relay contact systems systems constructed to carry out logic functions, implemented in relays (electromechanical switches) rather than semiconductor devices.

resistive touch one of the two primary types of touch screen technology, it detects variously applied pressure as device-controlling touches.

resistors electrical components that slow the flow of current.

retinal scan a scan of the retina of the eye, which contains a unique pattern for each individual, in order to identify (or authenticate) someone.

robotics the science and engineering of building electromechanical machines that aim to serve as replacements for human laborers.

routers network devices that direct packets to the next network device or to the final destination.

routing the operation that involves collecting and forwarding packets of information by way of address.

satellite an object that orbits a planet.

scalar a quantity that has magnitude (size) only; there is no associated direction or bearing.

scalar processor a processor designed for high-speed computation of scalar values.

schematic a diagrammatic representation of a system, showing logical structure without regard to physical constraints.

scripting languages modern high level programming languages that are interpreted rather than compiled; they are usually cross-platform and support rapid application development.

search engine optimization (SEO) takes advantage of the way search engines crawl and index the Internet to increase visibility and prominence of a Web site among search engine results.

Secure Sockets Layer (SSL) a technology that supports encryption, authentication, and other facilities and is built into standard UNIX communication protocols (sockets over TCP/IP).

semantics the study of how words acquire meaning and how those meanings change over time.

semiconductor solid material that possesses electrical conductivity characteristics that are similar to those of metals under certain conditions, but can also exhibit insulating qualities under other conditions.

semiconductor diode laser a diode that emits electromagnetic radiation at wavelengths above about 630 nanometers, creating a laser beam for industrial applications.

sensors devices that can record and transmit data regarding the altitude, flight path, attitude, etc., so that they can enter into the system's calculations.

sequentially operations occurring in order, one after another.

server a computer that does not deal directly with human users, but instead handles requests from other computers for services to be performed.

SGML the acronym for Standard Generalized Markup Language, an international standard for structuring electronic documents.

shadow mask a metal sheet behind the glass screen of a cathode ray tube (CRT) that ensures the correct color phosphor elements are struck by the electron beams.

shareware a software distribution technique, whereby the author shares copies of his programs at no cost, in the expectation that users will later pay a fee of some sort.

Sherman Antitrust Act the act of the U.S. Congress in 1890 that is the foundation for all American anti-monopoly laws.

signaling protocols protocols used in the management of integrated data networks that convey a mix of audio, video, and data packets.

SIGs short for "Special Interest Group," SIGs concentrate their energies on specific categories of computer science, such as programming languages or computer architecture.

silica silicon oxide; found in sand and some forms of rock.

silicon a chemical element with symbol Si; the most abundant element in the Earth's crust and the most commonly used semiconductor material.

silicon chip a common term for a semiconductor integrated circuit device.

Silicon Valley an area in California near San Francisco, which has been the home location of many of the most significant information technology-related companies and universities.

silver halide a photosensitive product that has been used in traditional cameras to record an image.

simplex uni-directional communication over a single communication channel.

simputers simple to use computers that take on the functionality of personal computers, but are mobile and act as personal assistants and information organizers.

sine wave a wave traced by a point on the circumference of a circle when the point starts at height zero (amplitude zero) and goes through one full revolution.

single-chip a computer system that is constructed so that it contains just one integrated circuit device.

slide rule invented by Scotsman John Napier (1550–1617), it permits the mechanical automation of calculations using logarithms.

smart card a credit-card style card that has a microcomputer embedded within it; it carries more information to assist the owner or user.

smart devices devices and appliances that host an embedded computer system that offers greater control and flexibility.

smart matter materials, machines, and systems whose physical properties depend on the computing that is embedded within them.

smartphone an Internet-enabled cellular phone with computing ability that utilizes a mobile operating system and apps.

social informatics a field of study that centers on the social aspects of computing technology.

social media online sites or communities—such as Facebook or Twitter—where users share information, photos, video, music, and other media with other users.

softlifting the act of stealing software, usually for personal use (piracy).

software-defined networks (SDNs) the same as virtual private networks (VPNs), where the subscriber can set up and maintain a communications system using management software, on a public network.

solid-state drive (SSD) a data storage device without moving mechanical parts that utilizes an array of circuit assemblies as memory.

sonar the science and engineering of sound propagation in water.

SONET the acronym for Synchronous Optical NETwork, a published standard for networks based on fiber optic communications technology.

sound card a plug-in card for a computer that contains hardware devices for sound processing, conversion, and generation.

source code the human-readable programs that are compiled or interpreted so that they can be executed by a computing machine.

speech recognition the science and engineering of decoding and interpreting audible speech, usually using a computer system.

spider a computer program that travels the Internet to locate Web documents and FTP resources, then indexes the documents in a database, which are then searched using software the search engine provides.

spreadsheet an accounting or business tool that details numerical data in columns for tabulation purposes.

static without movement; stationary.

stellar pertaining to the stars.

streaming media audio or video that are viewable without delay or completely downloading because they are received over the Internet or other computer network by the user as a constant stream of data packets.

streaming media media such a music, videos, movies, and television shows available over the Internet.

subnet a logical section of a large network that simplifies the management of machine addresses.

supercomputer a very high performance computer, usually comprised of many processors and used for modeling and simulation of complex phenomena, like meteorology.

superconductivity the property of a material to pass an electric current with almost no losses; most metals are superconductive only at temperatures near absolute zero.

swap files files used by an operating system to support a virtual memory system, in which the user appears to have access to more memory than is physically available.

syllogistic statements the essential tenets of western philosophical thought, based on hypotheses and categories.

synchronization the time domain ordering of events; often applied when events repeatedly occur simultaneously.

synchronized events occurring at specific points in time with respect to one another.

synchronous synchronized behavior.

synergistic relating to synergism, which is the phenomenon whereby the action of a group of elements is greater than their individual actions.

syntactic analyzer a part of a compiler that scans program source code ensuring that the code meets essential language rules with regard to structure or organization.

syntax a set of rules that a computing language incorporates regarding structure, punctuation, and formatting.

T1 digital circuitry a type of digital network technology that can handle separate voice and/ or digital communications lines.

tablet (or tablet computer) is an Internet-enabled portable computing device with a touch screen user interface.

tangible of a nature that is real, as opposed to something that is imaginary or abstract.

task partitioning the act of dividing up work to be done so that it can be separated into distinct tasks, processes, or phases.

taxonomy the classification of elements or objects based on their characteristics.

TCP the acronym for Transmission Control Protocol; a fundamental protocol used in the networks that support the Internet (ARPANET).

TCP/IP networks interconnected computer networks that use Transmission Control Protocol/Internet Protocol.

TCP/IP protocol suite Transmission Control Protocol/Internet Protocol; a range of functions that can be used to facilitate applications working on the Internet.

telegraph a communication channel that uses cables to convey encoded low bandwidth electrical signals.

telemedicine the technology that permits remote diagnosis and treatment of patients by a medical practitioner; usually interactive bi-directional audio and video signals.

telemetry the science of taking measurements of something and transmitting the data to a distant receiver.

teleoperation any operation that can be carried out remotely by a communications system that enables interactive audio and video signals.

teletype a machine that sends and receives telephonic signals.

terabyte one million million (one trillion, or 1012) bytes.

thermal ignition the combustion of a substance caused by heating it to the point that its particles have enough energy to commence burning without an externally applied flame.

thermodynamic relating to heat energy.

three-body problem an intractable problem in mechanics that involves the attempts to predict the behavior of three bodies under gravitational effects.

thumbnail an image which is a scaled down copy of a much larger image; used to assist in the management of a large catalog of images.

time lapse mode to show a sequence of events occurring at a higher than natural speed so it looks like it is happening rapidly rather than in real time.

title bar the top horizontal border of a rectangular region owned by a program running in a graphical user interface (GUI); it usually contains the program name and can be used to move the region around.

tomography the process of capturing and analyzing X-ray images.

topographic pertaining to the features of a terrain or surface.

topology a method of describing the structure of a system that emphasizes its logical nature rather than its physical characteristics.

touch screen an interface that allows users to control the computing device by touching its screen.

trademark rights a trademark is a name, symbol, or phrase that identifies a trading organization and is owned by that organization.

trafficking transporting and selling; especially with regard to illegal merchandise.

training data data used in the creation of a classifier.

transaction processing operations between client and server computers that are made up of many small exchanges that must all be completed for the transaction to proceed.

transducers devices that sense a physical quantity, such as temperature or pressure, and convert that measurement into an electrical signal.

transistor a contraction of TRANSfer resISTOR; a semiconductor device, invented by John Bardeen, Walter Brattain, and William

Shockley, which has three terminals; can be used for switching and amplifying electrical signals.

translational bridges   special network devices that convert low-level protocols from one type to another.

Transmission Control Protocol (TCP)   a stream-orientated protocol that uses Internet Protocol (IP); it is responsible for splitting data into packets, transferring it, and reassembling it at the receiver.

transmutation   the act of converting one thing into another.

trigonometry   a branch of mathematics founded upon the geometry of triangles.

triodes   nearly obsolete electronic devices constructed of sealed glass tubes containing metal elements in a vacuum; triodes were used to control electrical signals.

Trojan horse   potentially destructive computer program that masquerades as something benign; named after the wooden horse employed by the Acheans to conquer Troy.

tunneling   a way of handling different communication protocols, by taking packets of a foreign protocol and changing them so that they.

Turing machine   a proposed type of computing machine that takes inputs off paper tape and then moves through a sequence of states under the control of an algorithm; identified by Alan Turing (1912–1954).

twisted pair   an inexpensive, medium bandwidth communication channel commonly used in local area networks.

ubiquitous   to be commonly available everywhere.

ultrasonic   the transmission and reception of sound waves that are at frequencies higher than those audible to humans.

Uniform Resource Locator (URL)   a reference to a document or a document container using the Hypertext Transfer Protocol (HTTP); consists of a hostname and path to the document.

Universal Product Code (UPC)   the first barcode standard developed in 1973 and adopted widely since.

UNIX   operating system that was originally developed at Bell Laboratories in the early 1970s.

uplinks   connections from a client machine to a large network; frequently when information is being sent to a communications satellite.

vacuum tube   an electronic device constructed of a sealed glass tube containing metal elements in a vacuum; used to control electrical signals.

valence   a measure of the reactive nature of a chemical element or compound in relation to hydrogen.

variable   a symbol, such as a string of letters, which may assume any one of a set of values known as the domain.

vector graphics   graphics output systems whereby pairs of coordinates are passed to the graphics controller, which are interpreted as end points of vectors to be drawn on the screen.

vector processing   an approach to computing machine architecture that involves the manipulation of vectors (sequences of numbers) in single steps, rather than one number at a time.

vector supercomputer   a highly optimized computing machine that provides high performance using a vector processing architecture.

velocities   vector quantities that have a magnitude or speed and a direction.

Venn diagrams   diagrams used to demonstrate the relationships between sets of objects, named after John Venn, a British logician.

venture capitalists persons or agencies that speculate by providing financial resources to enable product development, in the expectation of larger returns with product maturity.

video capture cards plug-in cards for a computer that accepts video input from devices like televisions and video cameras, allowing the user to record video data onto the computer.

video compression algorithms special algorithms applied to remove certain unnecessary parts of video images in an attempt to reduce their storage size.

virtual channel connection an abstraction of a physical connection between two or more elements (or computers); the complex details of the physical connection are hidden.

virtual circuit like a virtual channel connection, a virtual circuit appears to be a direct path between two elements, but is actually a managed collection of physical connections.

Virtual Private Networks (VPNs) a commercial approach to network management where privately owned voice and data networks are set up on public network infrastructure.

virtual reality (VR) the use of elaborate input/output devices to create the illusion that the user is in a different environment.

virtualization as if it were real; making something seem real, e.g., a virtual environment.

visible speech a set of symbols, comprising an alphabet, that "spell" sounds instead of words.

visualization a technique whereby complex systems are portrayed in a meaningful way using sophisticated computer graphics systems; e.g., chemical molecules.

voice over Internet protocol (VoIP) communication technology that delivers telephone calls, video calls, and voice communications via Internet Protocol.

volatile subject to rapid change; describes the character of data when current no longer flows to a device (that is, electrical power is switched off).

waveform an abstraction used in the physical sciences to model energy transmission in the form of longitudinal or transverse waves.

Web surfers people who "surf" (search) the Internet frequently.

wide area network (WAN) an interconnected network of computers that spans upward from several buildings to whole cities or entire countries and across countries.

wireless lavaliere microphones small microphones worn around the speakers' necks, which attach to their shirts.

wireless local area network (WLAN) an interconnected network of computers that uses radio and/or infrared communication channels, rather than cables.

workstations computers (usually within a network) that interact directly with human users (much the same as "client computers").

xerography a printing process that uses electrostatic elements derived from a photographic image to deposit the ink.

XML the acronym for eXtensible Markup Language; a method of applying structure to data so that documents can be represented.

Directory of Computer Sciences Organizations

A

Apple, Inc.
1 Infinite Loop
Cupertino, CA, 95014
USA
Telephone: (408) 996-1010
Email: media.help@apple.com
Web site: www.apple.com

Argonne National Laboratory: Mathematics and Computer Science Division
9700 South Cass Avenue, Building 240
Argonne, IL, 60439-4844
USA
Telephone: (630) 252-8808
Web site: http://www.mcs.anl.gov

Association for the Advancement of Artificial Intelligence
2275 East Bayshore Road, Suite 160
Palo Alto, CA, 94303
USA
Telephone: (650) 328-3123
Fax: (650) 321-4457
Web site: http://www.aaai.org

Association for Computer Machinery
2 Penn Plaza, Suite 701
New York, NY, 10121-0701
USA
Telephone: (800) 342-6626
Email: acmhelp@acm.org
Web site: http://www.acm.org

Association for Information Systems
PO Box 2712
Atlanta, GA, 30301-2712
USA
Telephone: (404) 413-7445
Email: onestop@aisnet.org
Web site: https://ais.site-ym.com

B

Bell Laboratories
600-700 Mountain Avenue
Murray Hill, NJ, 07974
USA
Telephone: (908) 508-8080
Email: execoffice@alcatel-lucent.com
Web site: http://www.alcatel-lucent.com/belllabs

Bletchley Park
The Mansion, Bletchley Park
Milton Keynes, MK3 6EB
UK
Telephone: +44 (0) 1908 640404
Fax: +44 (0) 1908 274381
Email: info@bletchleypark.org.uk
Web site: http://www.bletchleypark.org.uk

C

Cisco Systems, Inc.
170 West Tasman Drive
San Jose, CA, 95134
USA
Telephone: (408) 526 4000
Web site: www.cisco.com

Computer History Museum
1401 North Shoreline Boulevard
Mountain View, CA, 94043
USA
Telephone: (650) 810-1010
Fax: (650) 810-1055
Web site: http://www.computerhistory.org

Computing and Information Technology Interactive Digital Educational Library (CITADEL)
Web site: http://citidel.villanova.edu

Cray, Inc.
901 Fifth Avenue, Suite 1000
Seattle, WA, 98164
USA
Telephone: (206) 701-2000
Fax: (206) 701-2500
Email: crayinfo@cray.com
Web site: www.cray.com

D

Defense Advanced Research Projects Agency
675 North Randolph Street
Arlington, VA, 22203-2114
USA
Telephone: (703) 526-6630
Email: outreach@darpa.mil
Web site: http://www.darpa.mil

E

Electronic Frontier Foundation
454 Shotwell Street
San Francisco, CA, 9411-1914
USA
Telephone: (415) 436-9333
Fax: (415) 436-9993
Email: info@eff.org
Web site: https://www.eff.org

G

GE Global Research
1 Research Circle
Niskayuna, NY, 12309
USA
Telephone: (518) 387-7914
Web site: http://ge.geglobalresearch.com

Google Developers Academy
Web site: https://developers.google.com/academy/

Google, Inc.
1600 Amphitheatre Parkway
Mountain View, CA, 94043
USA

Telephone: (650) 253-0000
Fax: (650) 253-0001
Web site: www.google.com/about/
company

H

Hewlett-Packard Co.
3000 Hanover St.
Palo Alto, CA, 94304
USA
Telephone: (650) 857-1501
Fax: (650) 857-5518
Web site: www.hp.com

Hon Hai Precision Industry Co., Ltd. (Foxconn)
105 S. Puente Street
Brea, CA, 92821
USA
Telephone: (714) 626-6900
Fax: (714) 626-6901
Email: foxconn-service@foxconn.
com
Web site: www.foxconnchannel.com

I

Institute of Electrical and Electronics Engineers (IEEE) Computer Society
2001 L Street NW, Suite 700
Washington, DC, 20036-4928
USA
Telephone: (202) 371-0101
Fax: (202) 728-9614
Email: help@computer.org
Web site: http://www.computer.org

Intel Corp.
2200 Mission College Boulevard
Santa Clara, CA, 95952
USA
Telephone: (408) 765-8080
Web site: www.intel.com

International Business Machines Corp.
1 New Orchard Road
Armonk, NY, 10504
USA
Telephone: (800) 426-4968
Web site: www.ibm.com

International Standards Organization
1, ch. de la Voie-Creuse, CP 56
Geneva, CH-1211 Geneva 20
Switzerland
Telephone: +41 22 749 01 11
Email: central@iso.org
Web site: http://www.iso.org

Internet Society
1775 Wiehle Avenue, Suite 201
Reston, VA, 20190-5108
USA
Telephone: (703) 439-2120
Fax: (703) 326-9881
Email: isoc@isoc.org
Web site: https://www.internetsociety.
org

L

Los Alamos National Laboratory
PO Box 1663
Los Alamos, NM, 87545
USA
Telephone: (505) 667-7000
Email: community@lanl.gov
Web site: http://www.lanl.gov

M

Massachusetts Institute of Technology (MIT) Computer Science and Artificial Intelligence Laboratory (CSAIL)
The Strata Center, Building 32,
32 Vassar Street
Cambridge, MA, 02139
USA
Telephone: (617) 253-5851
Fax: (617) 258-8682
Web site: http://www.csail.mit.edu

Microsoft Corp.
1 Microsoft Way
Redmond, WA, 98052
USA
Telephone: (425) 882-8080
Web site: www.microsoft.com

Microsoft Research (MSR)
1 Microsoft Way
Redmond, WA, 98052
USA

Telephone: (800) 642-7676
Web site: http://research.microsoft.
com

N

NASA Advanced Supercomputing (NAS) Division
Ames Research Center
Moffett Field, CA, 94035
USA
Telephone: (650) 604-4377
Email: contact-nas@nas.nasa.gov
Web site: http://www.nas.nasa.gov

National Center for Supercomputing Applications
1205 West Clark Street, Room 1008
Urbana, IL, 61801
USA
Telephone: (217) 244-0710
Email: help@ncsa.illinois.edu
Web site: http://ncsa.illinois.edu

The National Museum of Computing
Block H, Bletchley Park
Milton Keynes, MK3 6EB
UK
Telephone: +44 (0)1908 374708
Email: lin.jones@tnmoc.org
Web site: http://www.tnmoc.org

O

Oak Ridge Leadership Computing Facility
PO Box 2008
Oak Ridge, TN, 37831-6161
USA
Telephone: (865) 241-6536
Fax: (865) 241-2850
Email: help@olcf.ornl.gov
Web site: http://www.olcf.ornl.gov

Oracle Corp.
500 Oracle Parkway
Redwood Shores, CA, 94065
USA
Telephone: (650) 506-7000
Web site: www.oracle.com

P

Palo Alto Research Center (PARC)
3333 Coyote Hill Road
Palo Alto, CA, 94304
USA
Telephone: (650) 812-4000
Web site: www.parc.com

S

Samsung Electronics Co., Ltd.
85 Challenger Road
Ridgefield Park, NJ, 07660
USA
Telephone: (800) 726-7864
Fax: (864) 752-1632
Web site: www.samsung.com

SAP
3999 West Chester Pike
Newton Square, PA, 19073
USA
Telephone: (610) 661-1000
Web site: www.sap.com

SRI International
333 Ravenswood Ave.
Menlo Park, CA, 94025
USA
Telephone: (650) 859-2000
Web site: www.sri.com

T

Texas Instruments, Inc.
12500 TI Boulevard
Dallas, TX, 75243
USA
Telephone: (972) 995-2011
Web site: www.ti.com

Thomas J. Watson Research Center
1101 Kitchawan Road
Yorktown Heights, NY, 10598
USA
Telephone: (914) 945-3000
Web site: http://www.research.ibm.com/labs/watson

W

World Wide Web Consortium (W3C)
32 Vassar Street, Room 32-G515
Cambridge, MA, 02139
USA
Telephone: (617) 253-2613
Web site: http://www.w3.org

Cumulative Index

Page numbers referring to illustrations are in *italic* type. Volume numbers are included.
Bold page numbers refer to the main entry on the subject.

A

A. M. Turing Award, 1:24, 25, 248, 251

AALs (ATM adaptation layers), 2:14–15, 4:20, 22–23

Abacuses, 1:**1–2**, *2*, 49–50

ABR (available bit rate) service, 2:14

Abu Ghraib prison, 4:86

Acceptor impurities, 1:243, 244

Access motion time, 2:242

Accessibility technology. *See* Assistive computer technology for persons with disabilities

Accounting software, 3:**1–4**, *2*, 5

Accounts payable software, 3:1

Accounts receivable software, 3:1–2

ACM. *See* Association for Computing Machinery (ACM)

Acrobat Reader, 3:130

Activation of software, 3:225

Active matrix liquid crystal displays, 2:82–84

ADA (Americans with Disabilities Act), 4:13–14, 18

Ada computer language, 1:153, 2:198–199

Adams, Michael, 3:45

Adaptive technology. *See* Assistive computer technology for persons with disabilities

Adding machines, 1:2, 3

Additive sound synthesis, 3:171

Address buses, 2:10

Addressing protocols, 2:47, 150

See also Internet Protocol (IP); TCP/IP (Transmission Control Protocol/Internet Protocol)

Adleman, Leonard, 1:221, 4:58

Administrative factors, scaling, 2:215

Adobe Systems

Flash plug-in, 1:15, 2:237

founding, 3:244

PDF file format, 2:135, 3:130, 4:102

PhotoShop software, 3:22, 4:232

Postscript page description language, 3:82, 85, 243, 244

ADS-B (automatic dependent surveillance-broadcast), 3:11

ADSLs (asymmetric digital subscriber lines), 2:59, 4:29

Advance phase, hacking, 3:122

Advanced Encryption Standard algorithms, 4:57

Advanced mobile phone system (AMPS), 2:39–40

Advanced Networks and Services (ANS), 4:175

Advanced Research Projects Agency Network. *See* ARPANET

Advanced Video Coding (AVC), 2:121

Adventure video games, 1:15

Advertising

cookies and, 4:46

data mining and, 4:65–66

e-commerce, 1:70, 71

fast-forwarding through commercials, 2:262

free e-mail providers, 1:73, 74–75

journalism Web sites, 4:202

search engines, 4:243

AEA (Aerial Experiment Association), 2:24

AECL (Atomic Energy of Canada Limited), 4:119

Aerial Experiment Association (AEA), 2:24

AFCS (Automated Facer Cancelor System), 1:*197*

AFNOR (Association Francais de Normalization), 1:120

Africa

abacuses, 1:1

digital divide, 4:162

Agents, 1:136–137, 4:**1–3**, 12, 156

Agents on the Web (online column), 4:3

Agreement on Trade Related Aspects of Intellectual Property Rights (TRIPS), 4:228–229

Agriculture, 3:*4*, **4–8**

AI. *See* Artificial intelligence (AI)

AIEE (American Institute of Electrical Engineers), 1:122

Aiken, Howard, 1:54, 62, 66, 268, 2:283, 3:253

AIM (AOL Instant Messenger), 4:169

Aircrack network security program, 3:214

Aircraft flight control, 3:*8*, **8–12**

Aircraft navigation systems, 3:173–175, 176–177

Aircraft traffic management, 3:*12*, **12–15**

Airline reservation systems (ARSs), 1:33, 3:*16*, **16–19**

AirPlay mirroring, 1:19

AirPort technology, 1:144

AITP (Association for Information Technology Professionals), 4:118, 119

Akers, John, 1:110

Al Jazeera network, 3:221

al-Khowarizmi, Mohammed, 2:4

Alcatel-Lucent, 1:34

Alcatel-Lucent Bell Labs, 1:*32*, 2:*226*

Alcom, Al, 1:79

Aldus Publishing, 3:82, 85, 242

Algol-60 Report, 2:**1–3**

Algol programming language, 2:1–3, 194–195, 3:187, 188

Algorithms, 2:*4*, **4–6**

Algol programming language, 2:1–2

encryption, 4:55–56, 57

music composition, 3:170

parallel processing, 2:173–174, 175

programming, 2:201, 202

Turing Machine, 1:251

Alife. *See* Artificial life

Allen, George, 4:234

Allen, Paul, 1:84, 169, 172, 4:112

Alliance for Telecommunications Industry Solutions (ATIS), 1:120

Alpha beta pruning, 3:44

Altair computers, 1:84, 169, 4:112

Asynchronous transfer mode (ATM), 4:**19–23**, *20*, 22*t*
    See also ATM transmission
Atanasoff-Berry Computer (ABC), 1:55–56, 63, 66
Atanasoff, John V., 1:50, 55–56, 62–63, 66, 2:90–91
Atari, Inc.
    early video games, 1:82, 2:95–96
    founding, 1:79, 4:154
    Jobs, Steve employment, 1:142
    video game development, 1:15
ATIS (Alliance for Telecommunications Industry Solutions), 1:120
Atlantis (space shuttle), 3:229
ATM adaptation layers (AALs), 2:14–15, 4:20, 22–23
ATM Forum, 2:14
ATM layers, 4:20, 22
ATM machines (automated teller machines), 2:253, 3:*29*, **29–32**
ATM transmission, 1:194–195, 2:12, **13–15**, 4:173
Atomic bomb development. *See* Manhattan Project
Atomic Energy of Canada Limited (AECL), 4:119
AT&T
    Bell Labs, 1:31–32, 33–34
    frequency division multiplexing, 3:41
    software-defined networks, 2:270
    as top-tier backbone, 4:176
AT&T Labs, 1:33–34
Attenuation, fiber optics, 2:93
Auction sites, 4:108
    See also eBay
AUDEO voice synthesizer, 3:*234*
Audio books, 4:97
Audio files, 2:121, 3:113–114
Audio oscillators, 3:126
Audio synthesis. *See* Music, computer
Audiometer invention, 2:24
Augment interactive multimedia system, 1:105
Authentication, 4:**24–26**
    digital signatures, 4:86–89, *87, 88*
    distributed, 1:222
    e-banking, 4:93
    e-commerce, 4:99
    e-journals, 4:101, 102
    FTP, 4:133
    with HTTPS, 1:67

    password protection, 1:220
    security software processes, 1:219, 2:221
    tokens, 2:217–218, 4:25, 107
Authorization, 1:219, 2:221
Auto-pilots, 3:9–11
Auto-Tune audio processor, 2:144
AutoCAD, 3:22
AutoDesk 3D Studio Viz, 3:22
AutoDesk Inc., 3:22
AutoDesSys Inc., 3:22
Automata (short story), 4:126–127
Automata theory, 1:32
Automated Facer Cancelor System (AFCS), 1:*197*
Automated teller machines (ATMs), 2:253, 3:*29*, 29–32
Automatic data processing, 2:85
    See also Data processing; Document processing
Automatic dependent surveillance-broadcast (ADS-B), 3:11
Automation, 3:*194,* 194–197
Automatons, 1:212–213, 4:126–127, 143, 144
    See also Robotics
Automobile industry
    driverless vehicles projects, 4:44
    onboard navigation systems, 3:176
    robotics use, 1:213, 214, 3:62–63
Autonomous Systems (ASs), 4:173–174
Autonomous vehicles, 4:44
Available bit rate (ABR) service, 2:14
Avatar (film), 4:8
AVC (Advanced Video Coding), 2:121
Aviation simulation. *See* Flight simulation
Aztec abacuses, 1:1

B

Babbage, Charles, 1:*29,* **29–31**
    analytical engines, 1:6–7, 20, 29–30, 50, 181, 182, 184, 3:191
    funding sources, 1:95–96
    King, Ada Byron collaboration, 1:30, 96, 151
    music applications, 1:184, 2:143
    printer concept, 2:191
    Royal Astronomical Society medal, 3:26–27
    Zuse, Konrad connection, 2:283
Baby Bells, 1:33

Backbone, Internet, 4:172–176, 186
Backgrounds, animation, 1:9, 10
Backlighting, LCDs, 2:83–84
Backpropagation, 3:180–181
BackTrack network security program, 3:214
Backup devices
    cloud storage, 2:113, 244
    magnetic disks, 2:241–243
    tape drives, 1:158, 2:113, 241
Backus, John, 2:2, 157, 193–194, 195
Backus-Naur form (BNF), 2:2
Bacteria research, 3:34–35
Bacteriorhodopsin, 3:166
Baer, Ralph, 1:79
Ballard, Robert, 3:136
Ballistics charts. *See* Artillery firing charts
Ballmer, Steve, 1:85, 170, 172, 2:*238*
Bandwidth, 1:155, 156, 2:92, 93–94, 4:**27–30**, *28*
    See also Data rates
Bandwidth regulation and restriction, 2:**17–20**
Banking, online. *See* E-banking
Bar codes, 2:167, 203–204, 207, 3:206
Baran, Paul, 4:184
Barbera, Joseph, 1:13
Bardeen, John, 2:**20–22**
    Bell Labs involvement, 1:34, 2:20
    superconductivity research, 1:128
    transistor invention, 1:66, 88, 125, 126, 241, 2:20
Barnes & Noble Nook e-reader, 4:95–96
Bartik, Jean Jennings, 1:66
Base-2 number system, 1:34
    See also Binary number system
Base-8 number system, 1:50, 91
Base-10 number system, 1:34, 35, 36, 50
Base-16 number system, 1:35, 36
Base stations, cellular networks, 3:40–41
Base terminals, transistors, 1:126, 245
Base+offset addressing, 2:*263,* 264, 265, *265,* 266
Basic Input Output System (BIOS), 1:161
BASIC programming language
    Algol origins, 2:2
    Gates, Bill contributions, 1:84, 169, 4:112

Compact disk-recordable (CD-R) technology, 2:244

Compact disk-ReWritable (CDRW) technology, 2:244

Companding, of sound signals, 2:234

Compass global positioning system, 4:138

Compatibility (open systems design), 2:*60*, **60–62**

Compatibility standards, 1:118

Compiler-compilers, 2:2

Compilers, 2:**63–65**
    grammar developments, 2:2
    high-level languages, 1:93
    Hopper, Grace contributions, 1:102
    minicomputers, 1:175, 176
    procedural languages, 2:192–193

Complement method, 1:208

Complementary Metal Oxide Semiconductor (CMOS) technology
    chip manufacturing, 3:47–48
    image sensors, 4:231
    mainframes, 1:156
    NASA applications, 1:191, 3:231
    overview, 1:161

Compound statements, 2:2

Compression. *See* File compression

CompuServe, 3:216

Computation. *See* Calculating machines

Computational chemistry, 4:39

Computational steering, 3:210

Computed tomography (CT), 3:65–67, 134

Computer-aided architectural design (CAAD), 3:21–22

Computer-aided design (CAD)
    architecture applications, 3:21–22
    CAM integration, 3:38–39
    computerized manufacturing and, 3:60–61
    fashion, 3:107, 108, 109
    overview, 3:37–38
    Sutherland, Ivan contributions, 3:20–21, 37

Computer-aided engineering (CAE), 3:39, 61

Computer-aided manufacturing (CAM), 3:38–39, 60–65, 4:255

Computer-aided process planning (CAPP), 3:63–64

Computer animation. *See* Animation

Computer assisted instruction (CAI), 3:**50–53**

Computer assisted reporting, 4:201–202

Computer Associates, 4:115

Computer bugs. *See* Debugging

Computer Emergency Response Team (CERT), 4:87–88, 185

Computer Fraud and Abuse Act of 1986, 1:**42–46**

Computer games. *See* Games

Computer integrated manufacturing (CIM), 3:64

Computer languages. *See* Programming languages

Computer music. *See* Music, computer

Computer Oracle and Password System (CRACK), 3:214, 215

Computer output microfilm (COM), 2:191

Computer professionals, 3:**54–57**

Computer Professionals for Social Responsibility, 4:37

Computer programming. *See* Programming

Computer Science: A First Course (Organick, et al.), 3:188

Computer scientists, 1:25, *46*, **46–48**

Computer security. *See* Security

"Computer Space" (video game), 1:79

Computer Supported Cooperative Work (CSCW), 3:57–**60**

Computer system interfaces, 2:**65–68**
    See also Input/output (I/O) devices; User interfaces

Computer vision, 4:**41–45**, 77–78

Computerized manufacturing, 3:**60–65**

Computing Scale Company, 1:107

Computing-Tabulating-Recording Company (C-T-R), 1:101, 107, 268

Conceptualization, for system analysis, 2:247–248

Concurrency control, 2:238, 239

Concurrent client server model, 2:48
    See also Client/server technology

Condensers, for memory, 1:56

Conditional statements, 2:2

Cones (speakers), 2:233

Cones (vision), 4:41–42

Conforming sessions, video editing, 3:113

Connect America project, 4:160

Connection management, 2:150

Connectivity kits, 4:*28*

Connectivity rates. *See* Data rates

Connectors, data transmission, 2:224

Conrail (Consolidated Rail Corporation), 3:207

Constant bit rate (CBR) service, 2:14

Consumer information
    privacy concerns, 1:209–211
    social media access, 3:218–219

Contemporary Legend: A Folklore Bibliography (Bennett and Smith), 4:265

Control Data Corporation (CDC), 1:175, 3:68

Control net layer (process control), 3:*194*, 196

Control units, of CPUs, 2:8, 43–44

Control Video Corp., 1:82

Controller area networks (CANs), 3:6

Convention on Cybercrime (Budapest, Hungary), 1:224

Convergence, in telecommunications, 1:239–240

Convergence Sublayer (CS), 4:22, 23

Conway, John Horton, 4:11, 12

Cook, Timothy D., 1:19, 146

Cookies, 1:210, 4:**45–47**, 225

Copernican revolution, 1:21

Copper cabling, 1:194

Cops Security Checker System (COPS), 3:214

Copy/cut and paste functionality, 3:138

Copy machines, 1:276–277

Copyright, 4:**47–52**, *48*, 161
    See also Intellectual property

Corbis, 4:146

Core memory, 3:253–254

Core, of optical fibers, 2:91

Core series microprocessor, 1:130, 4:215

Corel WordPerfect, 3:128, 262

Cormack, Allan, 3:**65–67**

Cornell University, 2:109, 4:172, 185

The Corpse in the Car (article), 4:265

Corpuses (computer programs), 1:45

Correlation analysis, data mining, 4:67

Cosmological modeling, 3:28

Cost concerns
    data mining, 4:69
    e-commerce transaction costs, 4:97–98
    e-readers, 4:95–96
    fashion design, 3:107

Counterfeiting, 3:224

Covering tracks phase, hacking, 3:122

Cowcatcher invention, 1:31

CPUs. *See* Central processing units (CPUs)

CRACK (Computer Oracle and Password System), 3:214, 215

Crackers (hackers), 4:149

Cracking, 3:225

Cranor, Lorrie Faith, 4:225–226

Crawlers, 1:116

Cray Computer Corporation, 3:69

Cray Research, 1:233, 3:68–69

Cray, Seymour, 1:175, 3:**68–70**

Cray supercomputers, 1:233, 235, 254, 3:68, 69

CRC (cyclical redundancy check) coders, 2:151

Creative Commons (CC) licensing, 3:184, 4:51–52

Creative Technology, 2:236

Credit cards

  ATMs *vs.,* 3:31

  for e-commerce payments, 1:69

  fraud, 1:70

  identity theft, 4:177

  online applications, 4:54

  online fraud, 4:54

Credit online, 4:**52–55**

Credit reports, 4:54

Crick, Francis, 4:39

Crookes, Sir William, 1:253

Crossbar switching, 4:217

Crowd Sourced Art, 4:8

CRT. *See* Cathode ray tube (CRT) displays

Cryptanalysts, 4:56

Cryptographic hash, 1:67

Cryptographic keys, 2:218–219

Cryptography, 4:*55,* **55–59**

  authentication and, 4:24, 25

  defined, 1:67

  digital signatures, 4:87

  e-commerce use, 1:67–68, 4:93

  early computers, 1:56–57, 61

  hardware, 2:218–219

  introduction, 4:185

  Kerberos authentication scheme, 4:101

  mathematical foundations, 3:158

  RSA public-key cryptosystem, 1:221, 4:58

Turing, Alan work, 1:56, 61

VPNs, 2:270

CSCW (Computer Supported Cooperative Work), 3:57–60

CSIRAC, 2:144

CSNET, 4:174, 185

CT (computed tomography), 3:65–67, 134

Cuba, hacking into US systems, 4:150

Cuban Missile Crisis (1962), 4:142

The Cuckoo's Egg: Tracking a Spy through the Maze of Computer Espionage (Stoll), 1:223

Curiosity rover, 2:209

Cursors, 2:182–183

Curved interpolation, 1:11

Customer Information Control System (CICS), 1:157

Cut and paste functionality, 3:138

Cut prints, 1:9

CuteFTP application, 4:263

Cutout animation, 1:9, 10

Cybercafes, 4:**59–62,** *60*

Cybercrime, international treaties, 1:223–224

Cybernetics, 4:**62–64,** 142–144

Cyberpunk fiction, 4:128

Cybersecurity. *See* Security

Cybersecurity Research and Development Act (2002), 1:224

Cybertherapy, 3:161

Cyberwarfare. *See* Internet control and cyberwarfare

Cyclical redundancy check (CRC) coders, 2:151

Cylinders, on magnetic disks, 2:242

Cylindrical slide rules, 1:230, *231*

D

da Vinci Surgical System, 2:210

Daisywheel printers, 2:191

D'Albe, E. E. Fournier, 2:166

Dallas Semiconductor, 2:218–219

Dangling string network monitors, 3:100

Dark fiber networks, 2:94

DARPA (Defense Advanced Research Projects Agency), 1:97, 138, 4:44, 184

See also ARPANET

DARPA Grand Challenge, 4:44

DARPA Robotics Challenge, 4:44

Dartmouth University, 3:141, 142

Data caches, 2:36–37

Data Definition Language (DDL), 2:238

Data Encryption Standard (DES), 4:57

Data entry, interactive systems, 1:133

Data Extraction System (Census Bureau), 1:41

Data flow diagrams (DFDs), 2:251

Data gloves, 2:67, 105, 273

Data Manipulation Language (DML), 2:238

Data mining, 4:**65–70**

  e-commerce, 4:98

  social media users, 3:218

  supercomputer applications, 1:234

Data piracy. *See* Piracy

Data processing, 1:39–42, 3:**71–72,** 4:235–236

Data rates

  ATM transmission, 2:13–14

  broadband communications, 4:29

  cable, 2:58

  fiber optics, 2:59, 93

  mobile computing, 4:208

  MPEG standards, 2:15

  network design considerations, 2:147–148, 257

  telephone lines, 2:58

  USB connections, 2:12, 67, 224

  wireless communications, 2:59, 4:208

  See also Bandwidth

Data sampling. *See* Sampling

Data structures, 2:158

Data visualization, 3:**73–75,** *74,* 209–212, *210,* 238

Data warehousing, 4:**70–73**

Database management software, 3:**75–78**

  agents, 4:1–2

  art applications, 4:9

  automatic data processing, 2:85

  chemistry applications, 4:39, 40

  data warehousing systems, 4:72

  early developments, 1:33

  geographic information systems and, 3:115, 117

  medical applications, 3:161–162

  overview, 3:71–72

  in productivity software, 3:199

  railroad use, 3:206–207

  SQL, 1:94, 2:238–240, *239,* 3:76–77

Laser technology, 3:**145–148,** *146*

Laserwriter printers, 3:82, 85, 243

Lasseter, John, 1:14

LastPass, 4:114

Lathrop, George Parsons, 4:126

Latitude lines, 3:173

Lawrence Livermore National Laboratory, 4:149

LCD. *See* Liquid crystal display (LCD)

LDP (Linux Documentation Project), 3:186

Learning Company, 3:97

Learning disabilities, assistive technology, 4:17

Learning, machine, 3:180–181

Learning Management Systems (LMSs), 3:51–52, 53, 95–97

Least significant numbers, 1:3

Lebanon, cybersecurity attacks, 4:150

Lederberg, Joshua, 3:144

LEDs. *See* Light emitting diodes (LEDs)

Legal cases
  malicious software, 2:118
    software patent protection, 4:228, 229
    Sperry-Rand lawsuit, 2:90–91
  See also Antitrust litigation

Legal systems, 3:**148–151**

Legislation
  computer fraud, 1:42–46
  disabilities, 4:13–14, 18
  driverless cars, 4:44
  hacking, 3:124
  Internet regulation, 3:222, 4:178, 179
  piracy, 3:225, 226
  privacy concerns, 1:210, 211
  telecommunications, 4:186, 246

LEGO-Logo, 2:128

Lego Mindstorms system, 2:128

Leibniz, Gottfried Wilhem von, 1:20, 4:62, 254

Leibowitz, Joe, 4:*225*

Leica (dog), 2:214

Lenses, video cameras, 4:74, 75

LEO (low earth orbit), 2:211, 258–259, 4:139–140

Level 3 Communications, 4:176

Levin, Ira, 4:126

Lex (lexical analyzer), 2:2

Lexical analyzers, 2:2, 63

LEXIS-NEXIS information service, 1:114, 3:149

Libraries, digital, 4:*79,* 79–83

Library applications, 3:**151–153,** 4:233–234

Library of Congress, 4:81

Libya, Arab Spring effects, 3:221

Licensing agreements, software, 3:223–224

Licklider, Joseph, 4:183–184

LIDAR (LIght Detection And Ranging), 4:44

Life cycle methods (Java applets), 4:192

Light emitting diodes (LEDs)
  fiber optics development, 1:202, 2:91
  infrared radiation communications, 2:259
  joysticks, 2:97
  optical mice, 1:182, 2:184

Light pens, 2:113, 186

"Like" feature, 3:264

Line printers, mainframes, 1:158

Linear encoding, 2:234

Linear integrated circuits, 1:126

Linear interpolation, 1:11

Linear Pulse Coding Modulation (LPCM), 2:234

Linear regression, data mining, 4:67

Link, Edwin, 1:226–227

Link layer, OSI Reference Model, 2:151

Linking, objects, 3:138–139

Links, hypertext, 1:105

Links, in networks, 1:193–194, 2:154

Linux Documentation Project (LDP), 3:186

Linux operating system
  development, 2:164–165
  documentation project, 3:186
  mobile applications, 4:209
  open source concept and, 3:185
  scalability, 2:216, 4:145

Lipstick Enigma (artwork), 4:8

Liquid crystal display (LCD)
  CRTs *vs.,* 1:255, 2:84
  overview, 2:81–82
  projection technology, 4:104
  touch screens, 2:254–255

LISP (LISt Processing), 2:**123–125**

List servers, 2:227
  See also Servers

Live Free or Die Hard (film), 4:128

Live Messenger, 4:169

Live streaming technology, 2:237

LivePerson, Inc., 4:189

LiveScript. *See* JavaScript

LMDS (local multipoint distribution service), 2:281

LMSs (Learning Management Systems), 3:51–52, 53, 95–97

Local area networks (LANs)
  bandwidth measurement, 2:17
  bridging devices, 2:*31,* 31–34
  computer supported cooperative work and, 3:57–60
  Internet backbone connections, 4:173
  mainframe connection, 1:158
  network design considerations, 2:147–149
  in office automation systems, 1:197
  origins, 1:239, 4:184
  overview, 1:195
  peer to peer networking and, 1:138–139
  twisted pairs, 1:194, 2:257
  wireless, 2:281

Local/asynchronous distance learning, 3:90

Local direct connection, mainframes, 1:158

Local loops, 4:28

Local multipoint distribution service (LMDS), 2:281

Local/synchronous distance learning, 3:89

Location aware mobile computing, 4:209

LOCI (calculator), 3:254

LOCK (Logical Coprocessing Kernel), 2:217

Locking, for concurrency control, 2:239

Lodge, Oliver Joseph, 4:205

Logarithms
  analog computer calculations, 1:4
  defined, 1:3
  Napier, John development, 1:230, 231
  slide rule calculations, 1:3, 230, 231

Logic
  artificial intelligence development, 1:21
  Boolean, 1:114–115, 116, 2:25–30, 4:245
  digital computing use of, 1:49
  query languages, 1:94
  Turing, Alan work, 1:251

HMMs (Hidden Markov Models), 3:233–234

Hodges, Larry, 2:274–275

Hoff, Marcian ("Ted"), 1:129

Hoffman, E. T. A., 4:126

Holberton, Frances Snyder, 1:66

Holey Optochip, 1:165–166

Holler, F. James, 4:40

Hollerith codes, 2:114

Hollerith, Herman, 1:39, 96, *99*, **99–101**, 107, 2:114

Hollerith tabulating machines, 1:99–101, *100*, 3:71

Holograms, 3:147

HOLWG (High Order Language Working Group), 2:199

Home entertainment, 4:*152*, **152–155**

Home location registers, 3:246–247

Home servers, 2:227
See also Servers

Home system software, 3:**128–132**, 137

Home theater systems, 4:*152*

HomePlug Powerline Alliance, 2:147–148

Honeywell, 2:90–91

Hopfield, John J., 3:180

Hopkins Beast, 1:213

Hopper, Grace, 1:60, **101–103**, *102*

Horty, John, 3:149

Host-based databases, 2:238

Host-based intrusion detection systems, 3:213–214

Host blocking, 4:36

Hounsfield, Godfrey Newbold, 3:*65*, **65–67**

HPCC (High Performance Computing and Communications) program, 2:171

HTC smartphones, 1:240, 2:181

HTML editors, 3:129

HTML (Hypertext Markup Language)
Berners-Lee, Tim contributions, 4:111, 145
browser use, 1:274, 4:31, 32
defined, 1:73
e-banking applications, 4:92
e-journal format, 4:102
e-mail use, 1:72
Java applets and, 4:191–192
JavaScript embedded programs, 4:194–199
overview, 2:*133*, 133–134

source code documentation, 2:160
XHTML development, 2:134–135

HTTP (Hypertext Transport Protocol)
Berners-Lee, Tim contributions, 4:32–33, 111, 145
browser use, 4:30–32
cookies, 4:45–47
defined, 1:67

HTTPS (Hypertext Transport Protocol with Security extension)
defined, 1:67
e-banking use, 4:93
e-commerce use, 1:67–68

Hughes, Chris, 4:117

Human brain research, 4:63

Human-computer interaction. *See* User interfaces

Human factors, user interfaces, 4:**155–157**, 256

Human Rights Watch, 4:36

Human *vs.* computer strengths, 1:76–77

Hurst, George Samuel, 2:254

Hybrid digital-analog music production, 2:142

Hydra chess computer, 3:45

HyperCard, 1:105

Hyperlinks
dynamic links, 4:100
hypertext and, 4:34
integrated software, 3:139
search engine results, 4:242, 243
sponsored links, 4:243

Hypermedia and multimedia, 1:*104*, 2:**103–107**, *104*
documents, 2:86
encyclopedias, 3:130–131
history, 1:104–105, 2:105
indexing speech recognition applications, 3:235, 236
office automation systems, 1:199
realism, 4:157
user interfaces, 3:250–251

Hypertext, 1:**103–105**, 4:32–33, 34, 111

Hypertext Markup Language. *See* HTML (Hypertext Markup Language)

Hypertext Transport Protocol. *See* HTTP (Hypertext Transport Protocol)

Hypertext Transport Protocol with Security extension (HTTPS). *See* HTTPS (Hypertext Transport Protocol with Security extension)

I

I Have No Mouth, and I Must Scream (Ellison), 4:127

I Love You virus (2000), 1:223

i-Minitel, 1:179

I/O controllers, 2:66

I/O (input/output) devices. *See* Input/output (I/O) devices

I, Robot (Asimov), 1:216, 4:127

I, Robot (film), 4:127

I, Robot (game), 1:15

IBM Corporation, 1:**107–112**, *108*
701 computer, 1:88, 108, 4:4
704 computer, 4:4
7090 computer, 1:33, 88
Amdahl, Gene Myron involvement, 4:4
Blue Gene P supercomputer, 3:46
C-T-R origins, 1:101, 107, 268
carbon nanotube development, 3:49
character code developments, 2:52
CHRISTMAS.EXE worm, 1:263
collaboration in industry, 1:170, 171, 2:62, 4:113
computer assisted instruction development, 3:50
Deep Blue chess competition, 1:83, 111, 3:44–45
flash drives, 2:243
FORTRAN association, 2:193, 194
Harvard Mark I involvement, 1:54–55, 108
Internet backbone connections, 4:175
intranet, 4:189
Lotus acquisition, 3:240
Magnetic Tape Selectric Typewriter, 3:259, 262
microcomputer development, 1:168
optical microchip development, 1:165–166
patents, 4:229
PDA introduction, 2:180
RAMAC 305 computer, 1:108
RS/4000 computer, 4:173
SGML development, 2:132
space program computers, 3:227–228
supercomputer development, 1:235, 2:175

MARC (Machine Readable Cataloging), 3:152

Marchand hand calculators, 4:123

Marconi, Guglielmo, 2:257, 279, 4:153, **205–206**

Marconi Memorial Gold Medal, 3:119

Marino, Roland, 2:205

Mark I computers. *See* Harvard Mark I/II/III/IV computers; Manchester Mark I

Mark sense (optical mark recognition), 2:114, 167, 205

Markers (computers), 1:33

Marketing
e-commerce, 1:69
privacy concerns, 1:210

Markup languages, 2:86, **131–136,** *132, 133*
See also HTML (Hypertext Markup Language)

Mars exploration, 3:229, 230–231, 232–233

Mars Pathfinder Mission, 2:209, 3:232

Maser (Microwave Amplification by Stimulated Emission of Radiation), 3:145

Mass spectrometry, 4:40

Massively Multiplayer Online Games (MMOGs), 1:16

Massively parallel architecture, 1:203

Mathematical Markup Language (MathML), 2:135

Mathematics, 3:**157–160**

Mathews, Max, 1:185, 2:144

MathML (Mathematical Markup Language), 2:135

MathWorks, 3:181

The Matrix (film series), 4:128

Matrix technology, printers, 3:242–243

Mauchly, John, 2:**89–91,** *90*
Association for Computing Machinery founding, 1:24
EDVAC development, 2:90, 91
ENIAC development, 1:39–40, 50, 57–58, 63–64, 66, 87, 2:89–90, 3:72
UNIVAC development, 1:88

Max Headroom (film/television series), 4:128

Maxim (hacker), 3:123

Maxis, Inc., 1:83

Maxwell, James Clerk, 4:205

Maze video games, 1:15

MB (megabyte), defined, 1:162

Mbps (megabits per second), 2:17

McAfee, Inc., 1:131

McCain, John, 1:224

McCarthy, John, 1:25, 2:123–125, 4:220

McConnell, John Michael ("Mike"), 4:180

McCormick, Ernest J., 1:76–77

McDonald, Aleecia, 4:225–226

Measurement standards, 1:118

Mechanical calculators, 1:61

Mechanical computers, 1:4

Mechanicals (paste-up boards), 3:84

Medical systems, 3:**160–163**
biology research, 3:33–35
cell phone concerns, 2:40–41, 3:42
computed tomography, 3:65–67, 134
data mining applications, 4:66
decision support systems, 3:80, 81
expert systems, 3:103
image analysis, 3:133–136, *134*
molecular biology research, 3:165–166
molecular computing applications, 4:212
pager use, 3:118–119
pattern recognition applications, 2:177
personal digital assistants, 2:181
robotics use, 1:214, 2:210
virtual reality-based therapies, 2:274–275

Medium earth orbit (MEO), 4:139

Medium-scale integrated (MSI) circuits, 1:175, 2:77–78

MEDLINE system, 1:114

Meeting rooms, electronic, 3:59–60

Megabits per second (Mbps), 2:17, 4:28

Megabyte (MB), defined, 1:162

Megaflops (millions of floating-point operations per second), 1:233

Meissner, L. P., 3:187

Meitner, Lise, 3:66

Melissa virus, 1:260, 261

Meltzer, Marlyn Wescoff, 1:66

Memex devices, 1:61, 104

Memory, 1:**159–163,** *160*
Atanasoff-Berry Computer, 1:56
cache memory, 2:35–37, *36*
early computers, 1:53–60

mainframe capabilities, 1:155, 156

Read Only Memory, 1:160–161, 2:138

video editing needs, 3:114

Whirlwind, 1:60

See also Random access memory (RAM); Virtual memory

Memory devices, 2:**136–140**

Memory management models, 2:*263,* 263–268, *264, 265, 268*

Memory managers, in operating systems, 2:138–139, 162, 163

Memory protection hardware, 1:220

Memory registers. *See* Registers

Menabrea, Luigi Federico, 1:152

Menu bars, 1:271

Menu-based systems, 1:132, 4:156

Menu labels, 1:271

MEO (medium earth orbit), 4:139

Mercury-Atlas (rocket), 3:227

Mercury barometers, 1:208

Merit Network, Inc., 4:175

Mesh topology networks, 1:193, 2:154, 156

Messaging, 4:17, 169

Meta-search engines, 1:275, 4:244

MetaCrawler, 4:245

The Metal Giants (Hamilton), 4:126

Metasploit network security program, 3:214

Metastable state, 3:145–146

Metric system prefixes, 2:95, 4:28

MetroPCS Communications, 1:240, 2:59

Metropolitan Area Exchange (MAE), 4:175

Metropolitan area networks (MANs), 1:195, 2:147–149

Mexico, cybercafes, 4:61

MFENET, 4:174

MFS network, 4:175

MGM (Metro-Goldwyn-Mayer), 1:13

Michelangelo (artist), 4:10

Michie, Donald, 1:249

Michigan Algorithm Decoder (MAD), 3:188

MICR (magnetic ink character recognition), 2:114, 167–168

Micro-communities, social media and, 3:218

Micro Instrumentation and Telemetry Systems (MITS), 1:169, 4:112

Puppet animation, 1:10
Purdue University, 3:214
Purple cryptosystem (Japan), 4:57
PUT command, 4:134
Putin, Vladimir, 3:*12*
Puzzle video games, 1:15
PVCs (permanent virtual channels), 2:13
Pyrolysis mass spectrometry, 4:40

Q

QCA (quantum-dot cellular automata), 4:217
QoS. *See* Quality-of-service (QoS)
Quadtrees, 3:117
Quality-of-service (QoS), 2:271
Quantization, 1:184
Quantization, of sound signals, 2:234
Quantum Computer Services, 1:82
Quantum-dot cellular automata (QCA), 4:217
Quantum dots, 4:216–217
Queries
    Boolean logic, 2:26–27, 29–30
    information retrieval, 1:113, 114–116
Query languages, 1:94, 2:238–240, *239*, 3:76–77
Quick Time media player, 2:237
Quicktime VR, 1:11
QWERTY keyboard layout, 1:148–149
Qzone (social media site), 4:257

R

Racetrack memory, 1:162, 2:139
Racing video games, 1:15
Rack units, 2:228
Radar
    aircraft traffic management, 3:13–14
    Doppler, 3:257
    driverless cars, 4:44
Radio
    cryptography development, 4:56
    home entertainment use, 4:153
    Marconi, Guglielmo contributions, 2:257, 279, 4:153, 205, 206
    newsroom computer use, 4:201
    walkie-talkies, 3:117, 118
Radio-Frequency Identification (RFID), 2:206–207

Radio navigation, 3:9, 12–13, 175
Radio networks, 1:238–239, 2:37–38
Radiofrequency (RF) signals, 2:257, 279
RAID (redundant array of inexpensive disks) technology, 1:158
Raikes, Jeff, 4:113
Railroad applications, 1:31, 3:**205–208**, *206*
RAM. *See* Random access memory (RAM)
Ramade, Camille, 2:206
Random access memory (RAM)
    chips, 1:89, 160
    mainframes, 1:157
    memory management, 2:138–139, 162, 163
    overview, 1:160, 2:137–138
    virtual memory *vs.,* 1:161
Range images, 4:76
Ranger lunar probe series, 3:227
Ranked output, information retrieval, 1:115, 116
Rapid prototyping, 3:62
Raster data, 1:255, 3:38, 244
RAW image format, 4:85
RDBMSs (relational database management systems), 3:72, 76
RDF (Resource Description Framework), 4:34
Read Only Memory (ROM), 1:160–161, 2:138
Reading tools, 2:**203–207**, *204*
Reagan, Ronald, 3:119, 127, 4:120
Real time systems
    military applications, 2:198–199
    NASA computing, 1:189
RealNetworks, 2:237
RealPlayer streaming technology, 2:237
Reaver, J. Russell, 4:265
Recall, in information retrieval, 1:115, 116, 4:164, 243–244
Recommended Standard 232C (RS-232C) protocol, 2:11–12
Recording of music, 1:184
Rectification, 1:253
Recursive functions, 3:189–190
Recursive procedures, 2:127–128, *129*
RED Digital Cinema, 4:75
RED ONE (video camera), 4:75
Reddy, Dabbala Rajagopal ("Raj"), 1:25

Redundancy
    NASA applications, 1:190
    networks, 2:32–33
Redundant array of inexpensive disks (RAID) technology, 1:158
Reel-to-reel tape drives, 2:113, 241
    See also Tape drives
Reference language concept, 2:1
Reflective liquid crystal displays, 2:83
Registers
    CPUs, 2:7–8, 43, 44, 64
    minicomputers, 1:176
Regression analysis, economic data, 3:93–94
Regulation, 2:17–20
    See also Internet control and cyberwarfare; Legislation; U.S. Federal Communications Commission (FCC)
Reid, Harry, 4:179
Relational database management systems (RDBMSs), 3:72, 76
Relays, 1:54, 65, 4:250
Relevance feedback, information retrieval, 1:115, 116, 4:243, 244
Remington-Rand Corporation, 1:40, 2:283
Remote (app), 1:19
Remote Method Invocation (RMI) protocol, 2:49
Remote Procedure Call (RPC) protocol, 2:49
Remote surgery, 2:210, 3:162–163
Renting, unauthorized, 3:224
Renugopalakrishnan, Venkatesan, 3:166
Repeaters, 2:31–32, 257, 258
Repetitive stress injuries, 1:66, 77–78
Replicating rapid prototyper (RepRap) project, 3:62
Reporters without Borders, 4:36, 37
RepRap (replicating rapid prototyper) project, 3:62
Reproduction of documents, 2:85–86
Reputation, online, 4:53
Request for Comments (RFC), 2:15, 4:264
Research
    agriculture, 3:7
    art, 4:9
    astronomy, 3:27–28
    bandwidth, 4:30
    biology, 3:33–36
    chemistry, 4:37–41, *38*

SATAN (Security Administrator Tool for Analyzing Networks), 3:214
Satellite technology, 2:**211–215**
    data links, 2:258–259
    European Space Agency programs, 3:229
    flight management systems, 3:11, 15
    global surveillance, 4:139–142
    railroad use, 3:207
    See also Global Positioning Systems (GPSs)
Satellite-to-satellite communications, 2:212
Satisficing concept, 4:253
Saudi Arabia, cybersecurity attacks, 4:150
Saverin, Eduardo, 4:117
Sayre, David, 2:193
Scaling, 2:**215–217**
Scanners
    digital photography and, 4:231–232
    as input device, 2:114
    optical character recognition, 2:168
Scanning codes, keyboards, 1:148
Scanning phase, hacking, 3:122
Scheduling, decision support systems, 3:80
Schlumberger Excellence in Educational Development (SEED), 4:40
Scholarly Publishing and Academic Resources Coalition (SPARC), 4:101, 102
Schreyer, Helmut, 2:282
Scientific Computing and Imaging Institute (University of Utah), 3:211
Scientific visualization, 3:**209–212**, *210*
SCORM (Sharable Content Object Reference Model), 3:52, 98
Screen readers, 4:15
Script Kiddies (hackers), 4:148
SCRIPT tags, 4:194–195
Script viruses, 1:263
    See also Viruses
Scripting
    JavaScript, 4:194–199
    Visual Basic Scripting Edition, 4:269
Scriptoria (copying rooms), 3:86
Scroll bars, in windows interfaces, 1:271
SCSI (small computer systems interface) standard, 2:66

Sculley, John, 1:144
Scullin, Frederick J., Jr., 1:45
SDNs (software-defined networks), 2:270
SEACOM undersea cable, 4:162
Seals, privacy, 4:224
Search concept, in problem-solving, 1:21–22
Search engine optimization (SEO), 4:243
Search engines, 4:*242*, **242–245**
    Boolean algebra in, 2:29–30
    digital libraries, 4:80–81
    information overload concerns, 4:163–164
    information retrieval, 1:113–116
    overview, 1:275
    Web-based, 1:116
    See also specific sites
Search expressions, 4:243
Search for ExtraTerrestial Intelligence (SETI@home) project, 3:27
Search spaces, 1:21–22
Search strategies, 1:113
Search.com, 4:245
Seaton, Charles W., 1:39
Second generation computers, 1:88
Second generation programming languages, 1:91–92
Secondary Action (animation), 1:14
Secondary storage. *See* Storage devices
Sectors, of floppy disks, 2:242
Secure Computing Corporation, 2:217
Secure Electronic Transactions (SET) protocol, 1:68
Secure Sockets Layer (SSL) protocol, 1:67–68, 4:54, 93, 225
Security, 1:**219–226**, *220*
    applications, 3:213–215
    Certificate Authority, 1:67–68, 2:270, 4:25, 99
    cookies, 4:45–47
    credit online, 4:52–55
    data mining concerns, 4:69
    database management systems, 3:77–78
    digital signatures, 1:221, 4:58, 86–89, *87, 88*
    e-banking, 4:92–93
    e-commerce, 1:67–68, 4:98–99
    e-mail, 1:75
    hardware, 2:217–219

    intranets, 4:188–189
    legislation, 1:42–46
    software, 2:219–222, *220*
    Telnet concerns, 4:263
    See also Hackers; Hacking; Internet control and cyberwarfare
Security Administrator Tool for Analyzing Networks (SATAN), 3:214
Security applications, 3:**213–215**
Security hardware, 2:**217–219**
Security software, 2:**219–222**, *220*
SEED (Schlumberger Excellence in Educational Development), 4:40
Sega video games, 1:82, 4:154
Segmentation and Reassembly (SAR) sublayer, 4:22
Segmentation, image, 4:43
Selectric typewriter, 3:259, 262
Selegue, John P., 4:40
Self-replicating systems, 2:276–277
Selfridge, Oliver, 4:220
Semi-Automated Business Research Environment (Sabre) System, 3:16–17, 18
Semiconductor lasers, 3:147
Semiconductors, 1:125–126, 128, 164–165, 242–243
Semtech, 1:165
Sendmail, 3:186
Senses, virtual reality and, 2:273
SEO (search engine optimization), 4:243
September 11, 2001 terrorist attacks, 3:18, 4:157, 266
Sequencing, in programming, 2:201
Sequoia supercomputer, 1:235, 2:175
Serial and parallel transmission, 2:**222–225**
Serial communications, 2:150–153
Series circuits, 2:29, *30*
Server file systems, 2:228
Servers, 2:**225–228**, *226*
    mainframes, 1:155–156, 158
    minicomputers, 1:173–174
    proxy, 2:227, 4:101–102
    Web servers, 2:225, 227, 4:30–31, 188
    See also Client/server technology
Service providers, 4:**246–249**
    See also Internet service providers (ISPs)

Turing, Alan M., 1:*247*, **247–250**
  ACM involvement, 1:24–25
  algorithm development, 2:5–6
  artificial intelligence test, 1:22–23
  chess programming, 3:45
  cryptography work, 1:56
  cybernetic tortoise, 4:*10*
  cybernetics groundwork, 4:62
  funding sources, 1:96
  as pioneer, 1:61
  Shannon, Claude collaboration, 4:250
Turing Award, 1:24, 25, 248, 251
Turing Machine, 1:248, **250–252,** 2:6, 4:11, 62
Turing test, 1:22–23, 249
Turtle graphics, 2:126, 127
Twisted pairs, 1:194, 2:257
Twitter
  Arab Spring role, 3:219
  DDoS attacks, 4:180, 181
  hacking incident, 4:147
  journalism use, 4:202
  launch, 3:217
  popularity, 4:257
  scaling factors, 2:216
Two-factor authentication, 4:24
2G cellular technology, 1:240
2001: A Space Odyssey (film), 4:127
Tymnet, 3:153
Typewriters, 1:149
Typographics, 2:85–86

U

UARTs (universal asynchronous receiver transmitters), 2:223
Ubiquitous computing (embedded technology), 1:136–137, 3:98–102, 160–161
UBR (unspecified bit rate) service, 2:14
UCSD Pascal, 2:197
UGPIC (Universal Grocery Products Identification Code), 2:203
UIA (User Interface Automation), 4:18
Ultra-large-scale integration, 1:127
Ultrasound imaging, 3:133
Unauthorized renting, 3:224
Uniacke, Mark, 3:46
Unicode Consortium, 2:53
Unicode standard, 1:121, 2:53, 4:94
Uniform resource locators (URLs), 4:30, 111, 145

Unimation Corporation, 1:213
United Airlines, 3:17
United Kingdom
  cybercafes, 4:59, 61, 62
  data.gov.uk project, 4:111
  JANET, 4:174
  molecular computing research, 4:212
United States Patent and Trademark Office (USPTO), 4:227, 228, 229
Units, prefixes, 2:95, 4:28
UNIVAC I (Universal Automatic Computer I), 1:39–40, 87–88, 96, 102, 219, 3:68, 71
Universal asynchronous receiver transmitters (UARTs), 2:223
Universal Grocery Products Identification Code (UGPIC), 2:203
Universal Product Codes (UPCs), 2:167, 203
Universal Resource Identifiers (URIs), 4:33
Universal Serial Bus (USB) protocol, 2:12, 66–67, 224
Universal Turing machines, 4:11
Universities. *See* Colleges and universities
University of Alberta, 3:50
University of Bielefeld, 4:44
University of California system, 4:81, 106, 172, 184, 185, 261
University College, London, 4:184
University of Illinois, 1:258, 3:212, 4:33, 172, 185
University of Kansas, 4:33
University of Michigan, 3:187, 188
University of Minnesota, 3:137
University of North Carolina, 3:216
University of Pennsylvania, 3:191
University of Phoenix, 3:51
University of Pittsburgh, 4:105
University of Utah, 3:211, 4:184
University of Wisconsin, 4:4
Unix operating system
  Bell Labs research, 1:33, 34
  Berkeley version, 4:261
  as command line system, 1:132
  event-driven functionality, 1:134
  Mac OS X based on, 1:19
  TCP/IP incorporation, 4:261
  Viola-WWW browser, 4:33
  windows interfaces, 1:272

See also Linux operating system
Unix-Unix System Mail (UUCP), 1:221
Unshielded copper cabling, 1:194
Unspecified bit rate (UBR) service, 2:14
UPCs (Universal Product Codes), 2:167, 203
Upload *vs.* download bandwidth, 2:258–259, 4:29–30
Ur (King), 4:96
Urban myths, 4:**264–267**
URIs (Universal Resource Identifiers), 4:33
URLs (uniform resource locators), 4:30, 111, 145
U.S. Census Bureau. *See* Census Bureau
U.S. Centers for Disease Control and Prevention (CDC), 3:33–34, 36
U.S. Department of Defense Advanced Research Projects Agency (DARPA), 1:97, 138, 2:274
U.S. Department of Defense (DoD), 1:97, 2:198–199, 4:181, 260, 261
U.S. Department of Energy, 4:176
U.S. Department of Transportation, 3:208
U.S. Federal Communications Commission (FCC)
  bandwidth oversight, 2:17
  Carterfone case, 2:39
  digital television mandate, 4:153
  frequency band regulation, 2:280
  Internet openness regulation, 4:187
  National Broadband Plan, 4:160
U.S. Fish and Wildlife Service, 3:35
U.S. Geological Survey (USGS), 2:213
U.S. Government Printing Office (GPO), 4:89
U.S. Library of Congress, 3:152
U.S. National Library of Medicine, 3:210
U.S. National Science Foundation. *See* National Science Foundation (NSF)
U.S. Navy, 3:20
U.S. Postal Service, 4:78
U.S. State Department, 2:271
USAN (Satellite Academic Network), 4:175
USB flash drives, 2:243
USB (Universal Serial Bus) protocol, 2:12, 66–67, 2:**65–68,** 224
USENET, 3:216, 4:175
User Interface Automation (UIA), 4:18

Voice-driven applications, 4:169

Voice mail, 1:74, 198

Voice-over-Internet-protocol (VoIP), 3:247, 4:248

Voice recognition. *See* Speech recognition

Volatility of RAM, 1:160

Volume software licenses, 3:223–224

von Neumann, John, 2:**275–277,** *276*
   artificial life model, 4:11
   EDVAC development, 1:58–59, 66, 2:90, 91
   Kemeny, John G. collaboration, 3:141
   stored-program concept development, 1:87
   Turing, Alan collaboration, 1:248

von Neumann machines, 1:58–59, 87

Voting, data processing, 4:236, 237

Voting districts, data processing, 4:235

Voyager (space probe), 3:231, 232

VPCs (virtual path connections), 4:21

VPI (Virtual Path Identifier), 4:20–21, 22, 23

VPNs (virtual private networks), 2:268–271

VR. *See* Virtual reality (VR)

VRML (Virtual Reality Modeling Language), 1:10, 11

Vulnerabilities, security software and, 2:220, 3:124

W

W3C. *See* World Wide Web Consortium (W3C)

WAAS (Wide Area Augmentation System), 4:137–138

Wafer-scale integration (WSI), 1:128

Wafers, 3:48

Wal-Mart, 4:69

Walkie-talkies, 3:117, 118

WALL-E (film), 4:128

Wallace and Gromit (animated characters), 1:10

Walt Disney Studios, 1:12–13, 14, 3:126

Walters, Grey, 1:213

Wang, An, 3:**253–255,** 262

Wang, Charles, 4:115

Wang Computer System, 3:262

Wang Laboratories, 3:253, 254

Wang Word Processing System, 3:254, 259, 262

Wannabes (hackers), 4:148

WANs. *See* Wide area networks (WANs)

"Warcraft" (simulation game), 1:83

Warez Dudez (hackers), 4:149

WarGames (film), 4:128

Warnock, John, 3:243–244

Waterfall paradigm, 2:249, 251

Watson (IBM computer), 1:23

Watson, James, 4:39

Watson, Thomas A., 1:240, 2:23

Watson, Thomas J., Jr., 1:108, 109–110, 268

Watson, Thomas J., Sr., 1:107–108, *267,* **267–269**

Wave interruption touch screens, 2:255

Wave table synthesis, 2:235

Wavelength division multiplexing (WDM), 1:202, 2:93

Wearable computing, 2:101, 3:100, 101

Weather forecasting, 3:210, *255,* **255–259**

Weather monitoring, 2:212, 3:119

Web. *See* World Wide Web

Web animation, 1:14–15

Web browsers. *See* Browsers

Web servers, 2:225, 227, 4:30–31, 188

Webb, Jim, 4:234

Webphone, 1:179

Web sites
   as art, 4:8
   intranets, 1:67, 195, 4:188–190
   journalism, 4:202
   political applications, 4:233, 234, 235

WebStar server program, 2:225

Wei, Pei, 4:33

Weighted information retrieval, 1:115, 116

Weiser, Mark, 3:101

Wells, H.G., 3:24, 25

Werbos, Paul J., 3:180

Wergo Records, 1:185

West Publishing Company, 3:149

Western Electric Company (WECo), 1:31–32, 33

Western Music Notation, 3:168

Westlaw, 3:149

Westworld (film), 4:128

What-if analysis, 3:201, 238

Wheatstone, Charles, 1:152, 2:113, 114

While Rome Burns (Woollcott), 4:265

Whirlpool project, 3:20

Whirlwind computer, 1:60

White Hat hackers, 4:148

Whiteboards, interactive, 4:104, 105

Wi-Fi (Wireless Fidelity), 4:209

Wide Area Augmentation System (WAAS), 4:137–138

Wide area networks (WANs)
   Internet backbone connections, 4:172–173
   mainframe connection, 1:158
   network design considerations, 2:147–149
   origins, 1:239
   overview, 1:195
   VPNs *vs.,* 2:268

Wiener, Norbert, 4:62–63

Wii, 1:*80,* 2:*96,* 98

Wilkes, Maurice V., 1:50, 59, 64, 65, 87, 249

Williams, Evan, 3:217

Williams, John, 4:69

Williams, R. Stanley, 4:*210*

Williams, Sir Frederic, 1:59, 64–65

Wily Hacker attack (1986), 1:223

WIMP (windows, icon, menu, and pointer) systems, 1:133, 3:241
   See also Graphical user interfaces (GUIs)

Window interfaces, 1:*269,* **269–273,** 2:86

Window manager functionality, 1:134

Windows Media Player, 2:237

Windows operating system
   accessibility utilities, 4:18
   creation, 1:84
   encryption abilities, 4:58
   GUIs, 2:163–164
   Internet Explorer bundle, 1:85, 274, 4:172
   introduction, 1:171
   Microsoft Excel performance, 3:240
   multitasking capabilities, 1:171
   Visual Basic programming, 4:268
   windows interfaces, 1:272

Windows Phone mobile operating system, 4:208

Windows technology, 1:95

Winklevoss, Cameron, 3:263

Winklevoss, Tyler, 3:263

WIPO (World Intellectual Property Organization) Copyright Treaty, 3:225

Cumulative Index

Y

Y2K scare, 3:124, 4:5

Yacc (Yet another compiler-compiler), 2:2

Yahoo! portal, 1:274, 275, 4:117, 245

Yamaha, 3:171

Yang, Jerry, 1:274, 275, 4:116–117

Yield, LCD manufacturing, 2:83

Yin/yang concept, 1:37

York, Jillian, 3:221

YouTube, 3:217

Z

Z Machine, 3:28

Z1 (early computer), 1:55, 65, 2:282, 282

Z2 (early computer), 1:65, 2:282

Z3 (early computer), 1:65, 2:282

Z4 (early computer), 1:65, 2:282–283

Zero meridian, 3:173, 174

Zeus (Trojan horse), 2:118

Ziller, Irving, 2:193

Zip disks, 2:242–243

Zip drives, 2:242–243

.zip files, 3:130

Zombie Trojan horses, 2:118

ZTE, 2:181

Zuckerberg, Mark, 3:216, **262–265,** *263,* 4:117

Zuse, Konrad, 1:55, 65, 2:**281–283,** *282*

Zweig, Janet, 4:7–8

Computer Sciences, 2nd Edition

345